RELIGION IN ESSENCE
AND MANIFESTATION

G. VAN DER LEEUW

RELIGION
IN ESSENCE AND
MANIFESTATION

VOLUME ONE

Translated by J. E. Turner with Appendices to the
Torchbook edition incorporating the additions
of the second German edition by Hans H. Penner

GLOUCESTER, MASS.

PETER SMITH

1967

"All things with God a changeless
aspect wear"

GOETHE, *West-Eastern Divan*
(*Dowden*)

AUTHOR'S PREFACE TO THE GERMAN EDITION

WHEN I published, in 1925, a short *Introduction to the Phenomenology of Religion*, I felt it necessary to indicate that this was actually only an *Outline* of a larger book, the construction of which lay still in the future. And now that the more substantial work has appeared I must admit that I have made little, if indeed any, advance. For in many respects, to say the least, the present Volume is of the nature of a sketch or summary; so extensive is the domain of the Phenomenology of Religion that even a detailed presentation, such as the generous consideration of the Publisher has enabled me to undertake, must often give the impression that the utmost depths of its content, and the farthest limits of its manifestations, could be adequately dealt with only in a Monograph.

In the meantime I trust that I have now given to all, whose studies include some familiarity with the History of Religion, a useful Introduction to the comprehension of the historical material; and some knowledge of this material is presupposed. As regards Phenomenology itself, Chantepie's volume should be consulted, and especially also the two compilations by Bertholet and Lehmann-Haas. In the Text of the present book, whenever it has been possible, reference has almost invariably been made to these Works in order to illuminate specific instances.

I have assigned great value throughout to the presentation of the manifestations of Religion from the most varied viewpoints possible; and for this purpose I have appealed to writers of extremely diversified opinions—and nationalities also! Whenever it seemed to me that some phenomenon had been described by anyone in a typical form I made no attempt to improve this, but utilized his own terms literally; and I hope that this method has given the book, to some extent, the character of a cooperative effort towards the accurate apprehension of the phenomena.

I need scarcely add that I am profoundly indebted to many others. But a special expression of my gratitude must be accorded to my friend and colleague, Rudolf Bultmann. He has not merely, in the most self-sacrificing and conscientious way, taken part in dealing with the Proofs, but has shown a deep interest in the Contents that has often disconcerted me by its generosity, while it has invariably and materially assisted me. To the Publisher likewise I must offer sincere thanks for the generous manner in which he has facilitated the production of this book.

In accordance with the views of Jaspers, I have tried to avoid, above all else, any imperiously dominating theory, and in this Volume there will be found neither evolutionary, nor so-called anti-evolutionary, nor indeed any other theories. More specifically, those which attempt to reveal the "'primary origin" of Religion have from the outset been excluded, whether they aim at finding this in a primal Dynamism, Animism or Monotheism. What I myself consider may be opposed to theories, as the phenomenological comprehension of History, should be clear from the *Epilegomena*.

It is only too obvious to myself that this Work, in its present form, exhibits many defects, and accords too much attention to certain aspects of the History of Religion with which my own research has familiarized me, as compared with those I have studied in other authors' volumes. In spite of all this I trust that my book will contribute somewhat towards the comprehension of Religion, equally as regards its incalculable cultural wealth and the appeal to faith which it addresses to mankind.

GRONINGEN,
 January 1933

AUTHOR'S NOTE TO THE ENGLISH EDITION

THE present Volume is an integral Translation of the German Edition, of which, however, I have not found it possible to undertake any revision. During the interval since its publication, research of the first order of importance and value has been pursued by many eminent investigators, of whom I may mention Herr Martin Buber, Professor Bronislaw Malinowski and Dr. R. R. Marett; and I very greatly regret that I have been unable, as yet, to give their outstanding conclusions the careful attention they call for.

My discussions of the methodological and historical aspects of the subject appear as *Epilegomena*.

1937

TRANSLATOR'S NOTE

IN translating a work which appears to me, in its wide range of comprehensiveness and its marked originality, to deserve comparison with William James's *Varieties of Religious Experience*, my obligations have been extensive and diversified: in the first place, to the author for the keen interest he has shown throughout the task, which has ensured the authoritative presentation of his own standpoint; and in this respect, it scarcely needs saying that vitally important additions to our knowledge of facts, and equally significant changes in their interpretation, have occurred since James's famous classic was first published. I am similarly indebted to Mr. W. H. Johnston, B.A., and to Mr. Norman Wells, B.A., for their very valuable assistance, and to my friends, Rev. T. Holme and Mr. H. Goodenough, for placing at my disposal the resources of the Liverpool Diocesan Library at Church House; in the same way the volumes supplied by Dr. Williams's Library, London, were most helpful, and I am glad to have this opportunity of offering my thanks to all concerned, as well as to all the authors and publishers who have kindly permitted quotations to be made, and, as on previous occasions, to Messrs. George Allen & Unwin, Ltd., for their skilled advice with regard to all the technical aspects of production, and to my wife for dealing with the proofs and various other important points. Of course I remain fully responsible for any defects that may have escaped detection.

I am equally grateful for the very generous contribution made by the Sir Halley Stewart Trust towards the expenses of translation.

A few Translator's additional Notes appear, as usual, within square brackets.

J. E. TURNER

CONTENTS: *Volume I*

Volume II

PART THREE: *OBJECT AND SUBJECT*
IN THEIR RECIPROCAL OPERATION   339

A. OUTWARD ACTION

B. Founders

EPILEGOMENA

GENERAL LITERATURE CITED

Bibliography

C. CLEMEN, *Religionsgeschichtliche Bibliographie*, 1914–1923.

K. D. SCHMIDT, *Bibliographisches Beiblatt der Theologischen Literaturzeitung*, from 1922.

O. WEINREICH, *Berichte über Allg. Religionswiss. in AR.*, from 1926.

Encyclopaedias and Lexicons

ERE. (*Encyclopaedia of Religion and Ethics*), 1908 *ff.*

H. TH. OBBINK, *Godsdienstwetenschap*, 1920.

RGG. (*Die Religion in Geschichte und Gegenwart²*), 1927–32.

Sources

A. BERTHOLET, *Religionsgeschichtliches Lesebuch²*, 1926 *ff.*

C. CLEMEN, *Fontes historiae religionum*, from 1920.

H. HAAS, *Bilderatlas zur Religionsgeschichte*, from 1924.

E. LEHMANN and H. HAAS, *Textbuch zur Religionsgeschichte²*, 1922.

W. OTTO, *Religiöse Stimmen der Völker*.

R. PETTAZONI, *Mite e Leggende*, from 1948.

Quellen der Religionsgeschichte, published by Gesellschaft der Wiss., Göttingen.

General History of Religion

A. BERTHOLET and E. LEHMANN, *Lehrbuch der Religionsgeschichte*, 1925 (4th Edition, P. D. Chantepie de la Saussaye, *Lehrbuch der Religionsgeschichte*, *cf. infra.*).

A. C. BOUQUET, *Comparative Religion, A Short Outline* (Pelican Books), 1950.

C. CLEMEN, etc. *Religions of the World*, 1931.

J. G. FRAZER, *The Golden Bough³*, 1911–15 (Abridged Edition, 1923; revised ed. by Th. Gaster, 1959).

M. GORCE and R. MORTIER, *Histoire Générale des Religions*, 1944 *ff.*

R. E. HUME, *The World's Living Religions, An Historical Sketch*, 1944.

Illustreret Religionshistorie, edited by J. Pedersen, 1948.

A. JEREMIAS, *Allgemeine Religionsgeschichte³*, 1923.

G. VAN DER LEEUW, etc., *De Godsdiensten der Wereld*, 1948.

MANA, *Introduction à L'histoire des Religions*, since 1944.

G. MENSCHING, *Allgemeine Religionsgeschichte*, 1949.

F. G. MOORE, *History of Religions I²*, 1920, II, 1919.

S. REINACH, *Orpheus*, 1909. Eng. Trans. 1931.

TIELE-SÖDERBLOM, *Kompendium der Religionsgeschichte⁶*, 1931.

Introductions to the History and Phenomenology of Religion

TH. ACHELIS, *Abriss der vergleichenden Religionswissenschaft*, 1904.

TOR ANDRAE, *Die Letzten Dinge*, 1940.

K. L. BELLON, *Inleiding Tot De Natuurlijke Godsdienstwetenschap*, 1948.

K. BETH, *Einführung in die vergleichende Religionsgeschichte*, 1920.

C. J. BLEEKER, *Inleiding Tot Een Phaenomenologie Van Den Godsdienst*, 1934; also, *Grondlijnen Eener Phaenomenologie Van Den Godsdienst*, 1943.

P. D. CHANTEPIE DE LA SAUSSAYE, *Lehrbuch der Religionsgeschichte*[1] I, 1887.

R. DUSSAUD, *Introduction à l'Histoire des Religions*, 1914.

MIRCEA ELIADE, *Traité d'Histoire des Religions*, 1949, Engl. tr., *Patterns In Comparative Religions*, 1958.

H. FRICK, *Vergleichende Religionswissenschaft*, 1928.

J. W. HAUER, *Die Religionen*, I, 1923.

E. O. JAMES, *Comparative Religion, An Introductory and Historical Study*, 1938.

F. B. JEVONS, *An Introduction to the History of Religions*, 1896.

G. VAN DER LEEUW, *Einführung in die Phänomenologie der Religion*, 1925.

E. LEHMANN, in: CHANT. I, 1925.

G. MENSCHING, *Vergleichende Religionswissenschaft*, 1949.

H. TH. OBBINK, *De Godsdienst in zyn verschyningsvormen*, 1933.

A. SETH PRINGLE-PATTISON, *Studies in the Philosophy of Religion*, 1930.

N. SOEDERBLOM, *The Living God, Basal Forms of Personal Religion*, 1933.

C. P. TIELE, *Elements of the Science of Religion*, 1897.

G. WIDENGREN, *Religionens Värld, Religionsfenomenologiska Studier och Over-sikter*, 1945.

W. WUNDT, *Völkerpsychologie IV—VI* [2-3], 1914–20.

Journals

L'Année Sociologique, from 1898.

Anthropos, Edited by W. Schmidt, from 1906.

AR. (*Archiv für Religionswissenschaft*), from 1898.

RHR. (*Revue de l'Histoire des Religions*), from 1880.

SM. (*Studi e Materiali di Storia delle Religioni*), from 1925.

Zalmoxis, Revue des Études Religieuses, edited by M. Eliade, since 1938.

Zeitschrift für Religionspsychologie, Edited by K. Beth, from 1926.

More specific Bibliographies are appended to the relevant chapters, together with special Articles, especially in *RGG*.

PART ONE

THE OBJECT OF RELIGION

CHAPTER I

POWER

1. THAT which those sciences concerned with Religion regard as the *Object* of Religion is, for Religion itself, the active and primary Agent in the situation or, in this sense of the term, the *Subject*. In other words, the religious man perceives that with which his religion deals as primal, as originative or causal; and only to reflective thought does this become the Object of the experience that is contemplated. For Religion, then, God is the active Agent in relation to man, while the sciences in question can concern themselves only with the activity of man in his relation to God; of the acts of God Himself they can give no account whatever.

2. But when we say that *God* is the Object of religious experience, we must realize that "God" is frequently an extremely indefinite concept which does not completely coincide with what we ourselves usually understand by it. Religious experience, in other terms, is concerned with a "Somewhat". But this assertion often means no more than that this "Somewhat" is merely a vague "something"; and in order that man may be able to make more significant statements about this "Somewhat", it must force itself upon him, must oppose itself to him as being Something *Other*. Thus the first affirmation we can make about the Object of Religion is that it is a *highly exceptional* and *extremely impressive* "*Other*". Subjectively, again, the initial state of man's mind is amazement; and as Söderblom has remarked, this is true not only for philosophy but equally for religion. As yet, it must further be observed, we are in no way concerned with the supernatural or the transcendent: we can speak of "God" in a merely figurative sense; but there arises and persists an experience which connects or unites itself to the "Other" that thus obtrudes. Theory, and even the slightest degree of generalization, are still far remote; man remains quite content with the purely practical recognition that this Object is a departure from all that is usual and familiar; and this again is the consequence of the *Power* it generates. The most primitive belief, then, is absolutely empirical; as regards primitive religious experience, therefore, and even a large proportion of that of antiquity, we must in this respect accustom ourselves to interpret the supernatural element in the conception of God by the simple notion of an "Other", of something foreign and highly unusual, and at the same time the consciousness of absolute dependence, so well known to ourselves, by an indefinite and generalized feeling of remoteness.

3. In a letter written by the missionary R. H. Codrington, and published by Max Müller in 1878, the idea of *mana* was referred to for the first time, and naturally in the style of those days, as a "Melanesian name for the Infinite", this description of course being due to Müller;[1] while Codrington himself gave, both in his letter and his own book of 1891, a much more characteristic definition: "It is a power or influence, not physical, and in a way supernatural; but it shows itself in physical force, or in any kind of power or excellence which a man possesses. This Mana is not fixed in anything, and can be conveyed in almost anything; but spirits . . . have it and can impart it. . . . All Melanesian religion consists, in fact, in getting this Mana for one's self, or getting it used for one's benefit."[2] Taken generally, this description has completely justified itself. In the South Sea Islands *mana* always means a Power; but the islanders include in this term, together with its derivatives and compounds, such various substantival, adjectival and verbal ideas as Influence, Strength, Fame, Majesty, Intelligence, Authority, Deity, Capability, extraordinary Power: whatever is successful, strong, plenteous: to reverence, be capable, to adore and to prophesy. It is quite obvious, however, that the supernatural, in our sense of this term, cannot here be intended; Lehmann even reproached Codrington for referring to the supernatural at all, and proposed to retain the simple meaning of "successful, capable". Now *mana* actually has this significance; the warrior's *mana*, for instance, is demonstrated by his continuous success in combat, while repeated defeat shows that his *mana* has deserted him. But Lehmann, on his part, sets up a false antithesis between the ideas of "the supernormal" and "the amazing" on the one hand, and on the other the primitive ideas of "the powerful" and "the mighty" in general. It is precisely a characteristic of the earliest thinking that it does not exactly distinguish the magical, and all that borders on the supernatural, from the powerful;[3] to the primitive mind, in fact, all marked "efficiency" is *per se* magical, and "sorcery" *eo ipso* mighty; and Codrington's own phrase, "in a way

---

[1] *The Origin and Growth of Religion*, 53.   [2] *The Melanesians*, 118, Note 1.
[3] *cf.* here Rudolf Otto, *Das Gefühl des Überweltlichen* (*Sensus numinus*), 1932, 55: "What is comprehended as 'Power' is also comprehended as *tremendum*. It renders its objects *tabu*"; *cf.* E. Arbmann, *Seele und Mana, AR.* 29, 1931, 332.

supernatural", appears to have expressed the accurate implication. Here we must certainly clearly distinguish such ideas from what we ourselves regard as supernatural. Power is authenticated (or verified) empirically: in all cases whenever anything unusual or great, effective or successful is manifested, people speak of *mana*. There is, at the same time, a complete absence of theoretical interest. What is "natural" in the sense of what may ordinarily be expected never arouses the recognition of *mana*; "a thing is *mana* when it is strikingly effective; it is not *mana* unless it is so", asserts a Hocart Islander. It is just as unmistakably authenticated by a dexterous plunge into the sea as by the conduct of the tribal chieftain. It indicates equally good luck (*veine*) as potency, and there is no antithesis whatever between secular acts and sacred; every extraordinary action generates the experience of Power, and the belief in Power is in the fullest sense practical; "originally therefore the conception of magical power and that of capacity in general are most probably identical".[1] Power may be employed in magic, while the magical character pertains to every unusual action; yet it would be quite erroneous to designate potency in general as magical power, and Dynamism as the theory of magic. Magic is certainly manifested by power; to employ power, however, is not in itself to act magically, although every extraordinary action of primitive man possesses a tinge of the magical.[2] The creation of the earth is the effect of the divine *mana*, but so is all capacity; the chief's power, the happiness of the country, depend on *mana*: similarly the beam of the latrine has its own mode, probably because excreta, like all parts of the body, function as receptacles of power. That any reference to magic in the technical sense is superfluous is clear from the statement that "the foreigners were after all victorious, and now the Maori are completely subjected to the *mana* of the English".[3] Yet to the primitive mind the alien authority is no such perfectly reasonable a power as it is to ourselves; again Codrington has described the situation correctly by his "in a way supernatural". Characteristic also is the manner in which the indigenes explain the power of the Christian mass:[4] "If you go to the priest and ask him to pray so that I may die, and he consents, then

---

[1] Preuss, *AR*. IX, 1906.

[2] "To seek to derive numinous power from magical is altogether to invert the situation, since long before the magician could appropriate and manipulate it, it had been 'apperceived as numinous' in plant and animal, in natural processes and objects, in the horror of the skeleton, and also independently of all these." Otto, *Gefühl des Überweltlichen*, 56.

[3] Lehmann, *Mana*, 24.   [4] *ibid.*, 58 (Wallis Island).

he celebrates mass, so that I shall die. I die suddenly, and the people say that the priest's mass is *mana*, because a youth has perished."

It is inevitable, still further, that since Power is in no degree systematically understood, it is never homogeneous nor uniform. One may possess either great or limited *mana*; two magicians may attack each other by employing two sorts of *mana*. Power enjoys no moral value whatever. *Mana* resides alike in the poisoned arrow and in European remedies, while with the Iroquois *orenda*[1] one both blesses and curses. It is simply a matter of Power, alike for good or evil.

4. Codrington's discovery was followed by others in the most diverse parts of the world. The *orenda* of the Iroquois has just been referred to; "it appears that they interpreted the activities of Nature as the ceaseless strife between one *orenda* and another".[2] The Sioux Indians, again, believe in *wakanda*, at one time a god of the type of an originator,[3] at another an impersonal Power which acquires empirical verification whenever something extraordinary is manifested. Sun and moon, a horse (a *wakanda*-dog!), cult implements, places with striking features: all alike are regarded as *wakan* or *wakanda*, and once again its significance must be expressed by widely different terms:—powerful, holy, ancient, great, *etc.* In this instance also the theoretical problem of the universality of *wakanda* is not raised; the mind still remains at the standpoint of empirically substantiating the manifestation of Power.

In contrast with *mana*, however, and together with some other ideas of Power, *wakanda* represents one specific type, since it is capable of transformation into the conception of a more or less personal god. This is also the case with the *manitu* of the Algonquins of North-West America, which is a power that confers their capacity on either harmful or beneficent objects, and gives to European missionaries their superiority over native medicine-men. Animals are *manido* whenever they possess supernatural power;[4] but *manitu* is also employed in a personal sense for spirit, and *kitshi manitu* is the Great Spirit, the Originator. The Dyaks of Borneo, similarly, recognize the power of *petara*, which is something, but also someone, while in Madagascar

---

[1] *cf.* below.

[2] Hewitt, "Orenda and a Definition of Religion", *Amer. Anthropologist*, N.S. IV, 1902.   [3] *cf.* Chap. 18.

[4] *cf.* an animal fairy tale of the Algonquins: "The elks, which were *manido*, knew in advance what the hunter would do"; and they were able, "since they were *manido*, at any time to return to life". W. Krickeberg, *Indianermärchen aus Nord-Amerika*, 1924, 69.

the *hasina*-power confers upon the king, on foreigners and whites their striking and supernormal qualities.

Among the ancient Germans, too, the idea of Power was dominant. The power of life, luck (*hamingja*), was a quantitative potency. Men fought by inciting their luck against somebody (Old Nordic: *etia hamingju*), and were defeated because they possessed too little "luck".[1] The Swedish peasant senses "power" in bread, in the horse, *etc.*, while in Nordic folklore the woman whose child has been stolen by a troll is unable to pursue her because she "has been robbed of her power".

Finally, Power may be assigned to some definite bearer or possessor from whom it emanates. Such a power is the Arabian *baraka*,[2] which is regarded as an emanation from holy men and closely connected with their graves; it is acquired by pilgrimage, and to be cured of some disease a king's wife seeks the *baraka* of a saint. This beneficent power also is confined to specific localities; thus the place in which to study is not indifferent so far as its results are concerned, and in Mecca "the attainment of knowledge is facilitated by the *baraka* of the spot".[3]

5. But even when Power is not expressly assigned a name the idea of Power often forms the basis of religion, as we shall be able to observe almost continually in the sequel. Among extensive divisions of primitive peoples, as also those of antiquity, the Power in the Universe was almost invariably an impersonal Power. Thus we may speak of Dynamism—of the interpretation of the Universe in terms of Power; I prefer this expression to both Animatism and Pre-Animism:—to the former because "Universal Animation" smacks too much of theory. The primitive mind never halts before the distinction between inorganic, and organic, Nature; what it is always concerned with is not Life, which appears to explain itself, but Power, authenticated purely empirically by one occurrence after another; thus the Winnebago (Sioux) offers tobacco to any unusual object because it is *wakan*. From the term "Pre-Animism", however, it would be inferred that, chronologically, priority is due to the idea of Power as contrasted with other conceptions such as the animistic.[4] But here there can be no question

---

[1] V. Grönbech, *Vor Folkeaet i Oldtiden*, I, 1909, 189 f.

[2] Derived from the root *brk*, to bless.

[3] O. Rescher, *Studien über den Inhalt von 1001 Nacht, Islam* 9, 1918, 24 f.

[4] Lehmann (*Mana*, 83) criticizes Marett for abandoning his conception of Pre-Animism as a stage "logically but also in some sense chronologically prior to animism" (*The Threshold of Religion*, 11), because "only the genetic method of approach can lead to the solution of our problem". But this method can in no case attain *our* goal, which is the comprehension of the phenomena in accord with their spiritual content.

whatever as to earlier or later stages in development, but quite simply of the texture or constitution of the religious spirit, as this predominated in other and earlier cultures than our own, but also as it lives and flourishes even in our own day.

6. To recapitulate: I have dealt with the idea of Power which empirically, and within some form of experience, becomes authenticated in things and persons, and by virtue of which these are influential and effective. This potency is of different types: it is attributed to what we regard as sublime, such as Creation, exactly as it is to pure capacity or "luck". It remains merely dynamic, and not in the slightest degree ethical or "spiritual". Nor can we speak of any "primitive Monism", since to do so presupposes theory that does not as yet exist. Power is thought of only when it manifests itself in some very striking way; with what confers efficiency on objects and persons in ordinary circumstances, on the other hand, man does not concern himself. At the same time it is quite true that the idea of Power, as soon as it becomes incorporated within other cultural conditions, expands and deepens into the concept of a Universal Power.

To this Power, in conclusion, man's reaction is amazement (*Scheu*), and in extreme cases fear. Marett employs the fine term "awe"; and this attitude is characterized by Power being regarded, not indeed as supernatural, but as extraordinary, of some markedly unusual type, while objects and persons endowed with this potency have that essential nature of their own which we call "sacred".

K. BETH, *Religion und Magie*[2], 1927.

R. H. CODRINGTON, *The Melanesians*, 1891.

J. N. B. HEWITT, "Orenda and a Definition of Religion", *Amer. Anthropol.* N.S. IV, 1902.

R. LEHMANN, *Mana*, 1922.

R. R. MARETT, *The Threshold of Religion.*

P. SAINTYVES, *La Force Magique*, 1914.

N. SÖDERBLOM, *Das Werden des Gottesglaubens*[2], 1926.

H. WAGENVOORT, *Roman Dynamism*, 1947.

CHAPTER 2

THEORIZING ABOUT POWER

1. AN Esthonian peasant remains poor, while his neighbour grows
steadily richer. One night he meets this neighbour's "luck" engaged in
sowing rye in the fields. Thereupon he wakes his own "luck", who is
sleeping beside a large stone; but it refuses to sow for him, because it
is not a farmer's "luck" at all, but a merchant's; so he himself becomes
a merchant and gains wealth.[1]

In this story Power has become a specific power; and this transition
occurs very early. The power, the effects of which can be quite readily
substantiated, becomes power in particular instances—royal authority,
that of some craft, *etc.* In India this led to the stratification into ruling
castes each of which possesses an appropriate power:—*Brahman*
pertaining to brahmins, *kshatra* to kshatriyas.[2] In this way, too, a special
magical power occasionally becomes differentiated from others, as in
the case of the Egyptian *sa*, a kind of fluid transmitted by the laying
on of hands and other manipulations;[3] while the advance from empirically authenticated and undefined power to theoretically specified
potency is also noteworthy in the idea of Hindu *tapas*. Similarly in
Australia, as elsewhere, "replete with power", "warm" and "hot" are
closely related conceptions. Power develops heat, the primitive mind
believes, with an almost modern scientific accuracy of observation; in
Ceram a house afflicted with smallpox (in which power consequently
appears) is regarded as a "warm house".[4] Similarly *tapas* is heat, that
is the heat of the specific energy of chastening, its power.[5]

But there is another aspect of this systematic differentiation of
potency; for the problem of the universality of Power becomes expressly
postulated and affirmed. A certain Monism already constantly present,
but concealed by practically oriented primitive thought, now rises

---

[1] A. von Löwis of Menar, *Finnische und Esthnische Volksmärchen*, 1922, No. 56. In
the same way, in the *Odyssey*, Eumaeus is divine not "because he was actually Sirius
and his swine the Pleiades, but because special capacities, and indeed partially magical
abilities, pertained to the *major porcarius*, the swine-major, -mayor or -master, as these
excellent functionaries were formerly called". Otto, *Gefühl des Überweltlichen*, 96 f.

[2] H. Oldenberg, *Die Lehre der Upanishaden*, 1915, 48.

[3] G. Maspero, *Études égypt.* i, 308.

[4] F. D. E. van Ossenbruggen, *Bydr. Taal-Land-en Volkenk.*, 70, 1915; 71, 1916.

[5] Oldenberg, *Lehre*, 49; *cf.* Söderblom, *Das Werden des Gottesglaubens*, 83.

unmistakably into view; and what has hitherto been erroneously maintained about the actual idea of Power becomes quite correct— namely that "this interesting sketch of a unified apprehension of Nature and of the Universe reminds us, in virtue of its principle of unity, of Monotheism, and in the light of its realism, of dynamic Monism"[1]:—more indubitably, it is true, of the latter than of the former. For Power is never personal. It becomes a universal Energy, whether in the psychological sense and in direct application to humanity, or on the other hand as cosmological. In the first instance Power becomes Soul, but a superpersonal Soul closely akin to Power; in the second it assumes the form of a divine agency immanently activating the Universe. "Pantheists and monists are the heirs of a very ancient tradition; they sustain among ourselves a conception whose original founders, primitive or savage peoples, deserve more respect and sympathy than they usually receive."[2]

2. Such theoretical considerations, generally foreign to the primitive world, attain steadily increasing influence under the conditions of so-called intermediate or partially developed culture. The changes and processes of the Universe are then no longer accidental and arbitrary effects of distinct powers that emerge at each event and disappear again; they are rather the manifestations of a unitary World-order, appearing in conformity to rules, and indeed to laws. Many ancient peoples were familiar with the idea of a World-course, which however is not passively followed but rather itself moves spontaneously, and is no mere abstract conformity to Law such as are our Laws of Nature, but on the contrary a living Power operating within the Universe. *Tao* in China, *Ṛta* in India, *Asha* in Iran, *Ma'at* among the ancient Egyptians, *Dike* in Greece:—these are such ordered systems which theoretically, indeed, constitute the all-inclusive calculus of the Universe, but which nevertheless, as living and impersonal powers, possess *mana*-like character.

Tao, then, is the path which the Universe follows, and in a narrower sense the regularly recurring revolutions of the seasons. The "two shores" of warmth and heat which define this cycle together constitute *Tao*; there is no place for a God "applying outward force" (to quote Goethe).[3] Creation is the annual renewal of Nature. This regulated cycle, still further, is completely impartial and just; and man should

---

[1] R. Ganschinietz, *Religion und Geisteskultur*, 8, 1914, 316 f.
[2] Saintyves, *La Force Magique*, 46.   [3] cf. p. 185.

strive to conform to *Tao*. But in so doing he need not excite himself:
Tao demands a calm, indeed an almost quietist mood. To good deeds
it is hostile: "Great *Tao* was deserted; then 'humanity' and 'justice'
came into existence, cleverness and sagacity arose, and hypocrisy
flourished." Man should do right in conformity to *Tao*, which is
"eternal without acting (*wu wei*), and yet there is nothing that it does
not effect". Thus from this belief in a primal Power there arises a type
of quietist mysticism. In itself it is self-sufficient, needing neither gods
nor men: "the Norm of men is the earth, that of the earth is heaven,
of heaven *Tao*, but the Norm of *Tao* is . . . its very self".[1] Again,
"*Tao* generates and nourishes all beings, completes and ripens them,
cares for and protects them". But just as little as *mana* is it exhaustively
manifested in the empirical: the essential nature of *Tao* is inscrutable.
"In so far as it is nameless it is the primal ground of heaven and earth;
when it has a name it is the mother of a myriad beings. For lack of a
better term, call it 'the Great'." Here the old *mana* significance returns
once more; but its content has now been "transposed", and is no
longer empirical but speculatively mystical.[2]

The Vedic *Rta*, again, is the Law of the Universe, identical with
moral law; it is regarded as the Law of certain gods, Varuna and Mitra,
and the World-Process is merely the apparent form behind which the
actual *Rta* is concealed: "The gods are thus addressed: Your *Rta*
(Law), which is hidden behind the *Rta* (the course of the Universe),
stands eternally constant, there, where the sun's chargers are un-
harnessed." Thus it becomes the ultimate court of appeal, the ground
of the Universe, its concealed and motivating Power. Just as with
Asha in the religion of Zarathustra, *Rta* is good disposition, correct
belief, the Law of the gods and World-Power simultaneously. The
dominating faith is that the ground of the world may be trusted, and
thus the chaotic empiricism of primitive conditions has been superseded
by a firm conviction of Order.

3. When gods exist they become either elevated above the World-
Order, or subjected thereto. Both the Israelites and the Greeks were
conscious of the flaming power of divine energy, of the *orge* which
strikes with demonic force—for there can be no question of punish-

---

[1] *cf.* p. 127.
[2] *cf.* J. J. M. de Groot, *Universismus*, 1918. [The term "transposed" indicates the
variation of the significance of a phenomenon while at the same time its form remains
unchanged; *cf.* more fully p. 610.]

ment here; but in contrast to the Israelites, the Greeks were unable to bring this demonic power into relation with the gods.[1] They were intensely aware of the antithesis between the arbitrary rule of potencies in this world and the idea of a just order of the Universe: *Moira* or *Aisa*, originally the lot apportioned to each man by the gods—it is διόθεν, "sent from Zeus"—becomes in the brooding mind of an Aeschylus a Power more than divine which, if so it must be, against even the gods guarantees a morally satisfactory control of the world. From the incalculable dominance of gods, whom the poets had transformed into persons, man sought escape in Destiny, as a universal ground and territory over which the gods enjoyed only limited freedom of action.

In the course of natural processes, then, man discovered a secure and, if not sympathetic, at least an impartial foundation even for human life. If for many peoples, even the most primitive, the course of the sun served as the rule of their own lives, still religious theory perceived no inexorable Fate in this necessity of Nature, but rather a guarantee of World-Order. This attitude therefore is not fatalism because the living Power, despite all theorizing, perpetually maintains its central position. Conformity to Law implies no blind Necessity, but a vital Energy realizing a purpose. It was called *Dike*, as in India *Rta*; but its path is the cycle of natural process: "the sun will not exceed his measures", said Heracleitus; "if he does, the Erinyes, the avenging handmaids of Justice, will find him out".[2] To Law, similarly, Sophocles dedicates pious resignation:

> My lot be still to lead
> The life of innocence and fly
> Irreverence in word or deed,
> To follow still those laws ordained on high
> Whose birthplace is the bright ethereal sky.
> No mortal birth they own,
> Olympus their progenitor alone:
> Ne'er shall they slumber in oblivion cold,
> The god in them is strong and grows not old.[3]

And the late-born of the tragedians, Euripides, the advocate of every doubt and the friend of all unrest, places in the mouth of his Hecuba this marvellously calm and heartfelt prayer:

---

[1] The Persians succeeded in this, but only by appealing to a bold Dualism and ascribing all that was demonic to the evil Spirit.

[2] Diels, *Fr.* 94 (Burnet).   [3] *Oedipus Rex*, 863 *ff.* (Storr).

Thou deep Base of the World, and thou high Throne
Above the World, whoe'er thou art, unknown
And hard of surmise, Chain of Things that be,
Or Reason of our Reason; God, to thee
I lift my praise, seeing the silent road
That bringeth justice ere the end be trod
To all that breathes and dies.[1]

Thus early Greek speculation, which set out to discover an *arche*, a primal unity and primal Power in one, ultimately discerned an impersonal, divinely living, cosmic Law; the divine, τὸ Θεῖον, more and more superseded the gods. The Stoics then drew the final conclusion: *Heimarmene*, that is what is allotted, or Destiny, is the *Logos*, the Reason of the cosmos, in accord with which all proceeds; Cleanthes prays to *Pepromene*, the predestined. But even this view of the idea of Fate was just as little an abstraction as was the Necessity of the tragedians and the pre-Socratics. Still the essence of the Universe is always Power, but now an immanent Power, a World-Soul: or better, a "Fluid" dwelling within the Universe, "the personality and the nature of the divinities pervading the substance of the several elements".[2] To the contemporary of Julian the Apostate, finally, divine Power and the creative Necessity of Nature were absolutely one: "To say that God turns away from the evil is like saying that the sun hides himself from the blind."[3]

4. The theoretic treatment of Power thus far presented bears a prominently cosmological character; but it may also possess psychological significance. The power that operates within man then becomes regarded not as his "soul", in the sense familiar to ourselves, but as a particular power subsisting in a peculiar relation to its possessor. It is his own power, though nevertheless it is superior to him.

Before *Moira* became the Power of Destiny it was already the personal lot of man, and this it still remains even to-day among modern Greeks as *Mira*. The Germanic *hamingja*, again, was not the soul, but the power ruling in and over a man. Soul is in no way a primitive concept, and even when primitive mentality began to theorize it had generally not grasped the idea of Soul. We ourselves speak of our psychical qualities, and can "verify" these whenever we wish to do so.

[1] *The Trojan Women*, 884 *ff*. (Murray).
[2] Cicero, *De Deorum Natura*, II, 71. (Rackham).
[3] Sallustius, in Murray, *Five Stages of Greek Religion*, 260

But to the primitive mind, on the other hand, what we regard as purely personal and pertaining to the "soul" appears as actually inherent in man but still superior to him, and in any case as distinguished from him. The Red Indian, according to his own and our ideas, may be very brave; but that avails him nought if he has no war-medicine, that is, no accumulated power for the purpose of war. Power can be bound up with all sorts of material or corporeal objects; it is this state of affairs that has led to the designation of "soul-stuff".[1] From the soul as such, however, all these ideas were distinguished by the power being impersonal, while one might have a greater or smaller quantity of it, and could either lose it or acquire it; in other terms, it was independent of man and superior to him.

In the Greek-Christian world we find the ideas of Power transformed, theoretically, into that of the single Power by means of the concept of *pneuma*. The Stoics had already placed the individual soul, the *hegemonikon*, which from the heart as centre governs the whole body, in the same category as the World-Soul, the *pneuma*, which, as Power, overflows into all things: the human *pneuma* is of the same type as the *pneuma* of the Universe. Thus the primitive idea of Power, together with the equally primitive concept of soul-breath, or rather of the breath-stuff of the soul,[2] were united in a single theory.

In Gnosticism, and also for St. Paul, the *pneuma* is the life principle of man together with the *psyche* and divine Power, which penetrates man from without and transforms him into a "pneumatized" or "spiritual" man. By St. Paul himself, however, the idea of the impersonal divine "fluid" becomes slightly changed and circumscribed through the union with Christ: "the Lord is that Spirit".[3] On the other hand, for Philo the *pneuma* emanating from the Godhead remains impersonal, though for him as for the late Stoics the *pneuma*, when contrasted with the *psyche* and the flesh, is a power superior to man.

But in spite of the identification of the spiritual and the immaterial, originating in Plato's philosophy, in the eyes of the heathen the *pneuma* was just as little purely spiritual—in our own sense—as in those of Christians. Its designation as soul-stuff was always much more than a mere name. In the New Testament, for example, the *pneuma* becomes transmitted like some sort of fluid, as are the other psychological powers *charis*, *dynamis* and *doxa*.[4] They flow from God to man, and the divine *charis* is imparted by formulas of benediction. We

---

[1] *cf.* Chap. 39.   [2] *ibid.*   [3] 2 *Cor.* iii. 17.
[4] *cf.* G. P. son Wetter, *Charis*, 1913. Joh. Schneider, *Doxa*, 1932.

translate this as the Grace of God, although it should not be understood as friendly disposition or mercy, but as Power that is poured out and absorbed. It enables man to perform miracles: Stephen, full of *charis* and *dynamis*, "of faith and power, did great wonders among the people".[1] *Charis* effects *charismata*, Gifts of Grace; these however are no gifts of divine generosity, as we might rationalistically interpret them, but the consequences of divine Power. Ancient Christian terminology perpetuates these ideas: in the Eucharist Christ appears with His powers, His *pneuma*, His *doxa* or *dynamis*.[2] The "glorification" in St. John's *Gospel* again, is a transformation of man which takes place through the infusion of divine Power; and as Wetter affirms quite correctly: "when classical writers refer *e.g.* to religious *gnosis*, *charis* or *doxa*, who does not feel that these primitive tones (of the idea of Power) frequently re-echo from them?"[3]

Not merely the "psychic" powers but also the deeds, thoughts and principles of men frequently become represented as a store of power, largely independent of the bearer. I refer here to the idea of *thesaurus*, in consequence of which cumulative deeds constitute a potency that is effective in favour of the doer, but eventually of another person also; thus the treasury of grace, accumulated through the merit of Christ and the saints, is a living power "operating" in favour of the church. Certainly the connection between Power and the historic Christ has long become illusory here; it has been forgotten that the Lord is the Spirit, and the Power of Christ dispensed among believers.

In India the *thesaurus* concept is absolutely impersonal; *karma* is Power, Law and *thesaurus* simultaneously: "not in the heavens nor in the midst of the sea, not if he hides in the clefts of the mountains, will man escape the power of karma". Thus action has become an impersonal mechanism; and human worth is then appraised as a sum of favourable or unfavourable *karma*, a sort of financial value, that can be transferred to others.[4]

5. In India, then, there has been completed the great equalization

---

[1] *Acts* vi. 8.

[2] *cf.* G. P. son Wetter, *Altchristliche Liturgien, Das Christliche Mysterium*, 1921.

[3] G. P. son Wetter, *Die "Verherrlichung" im Johannesevangelium: Beitr. zur Rel. wiss.* 2, 1914–1915, 72 *f.* (Published by *Rel. wiss. Ges.*, Stockholm.) Dr. Rudolf Bultmann kindly informs me that he also believes that the conception of δοξασθῆναι, as a transformation effected by the infusion of divine power, underlies St. John's terminology, but not that the evangelist himself still retained this idea.

[4] *cf.* H. Oldenberg, *Die Lehre der Upanishaden*, 1915, 113 *f.*

that is the final word in the theory of Power, the unification of human
and cosmic Power, the identification of psychology and cosmology.
The substance of the self and the substance of the All are one and the
same, their separation being merely provisional and, ultimately, no
more than misunderstanding. The *ātman*, originally as soul-breath
the most primitive soul-stuff, became in the theory of the *Upanishads* a
silently operating and immanent Power conforming to Law: "If the
slayer thinks he slays and the slain that he is slain, they both fail to
understand; the one slays not and the other is not slain. The *ātman*
reposes, subtler than the subtle and greater than the great, in the
hearts of creatures. He who is free from desires and without care
sees the greatness of the *ātman* by the grace of the creator. Seated, he
wanders far away; reclining, he travels everywhere; apart from me,
who can recognize this god who is in a state of changing ecstasy?"[1]
On the other hand *Brahman*, originally the power of the word, as it
reveals itself to the brahmins in the sacrificial utterances and their
reciters, became the designation of cosmic Power. *Ātman* and *Brahman*,
however, in the last resort are one: here is there, there is here; he who
understands *tat tvam asi*, "that art thou", knows of only *one* all com-
prehending Power. And thus the primitive and intensely empirical
idea of Power developed into religious Monism.

[1] *Kathaka Upanishad.*

CHAPTER 3

THINGS AND POWER

1. WE moderns have accustomed ourselves to regard things as mere
dead objects with which we deal exactly as we please. Only a poet
could vindicate things:

> Gladly do I hearken to the Things singing.
> Touch them—How stiff and mute they are!
> You kill all my Things.[1]

Here once again a philosopher is sensitive to the potency of things,
which possess a life of their own despite that "loss of power that has
befallen them since the days of the Greeks";[2] for the prevailing emphasis
on the spiritual and internal, as contrasted with the merely institutional
—*Spiritualismus*—the cult of personality, and finally modern machinery,
have transformed the living, "self-activated" things into merely dead
material.

To the primitive mind, on the contrary, the thing is the bearer of a
power; it can effect something, it has its own life which reveals itself,
and once again wholly practically. During an important expedition,
for example, an African negro steps on a stone and cries out: "Ha! are
you there?" and takes it with him to bring him luck. The stone, as it
were, gives a hint that it is powerful. Again: an Ewe tribesman in West
Africa enters the bush and finds a lump of iron there; returning home,
he falls ill, and the priests explain that a *tro* (a divine being) is manifesting its potency in the iron, which in future should be worshipped.[3] Thus
every thing may be a power bearer, and even if it itself provides no
evidence of its influence, it suffices if someone tells it that it is powerful.
What Rilke, in one of his *Stories of God*, makes the children do—they
agree among themselves that the thimble shall be God: "anything may
be God. You have only to tell it to be"—this is the frame of mind
behind so-called Fetishism.

2. Every thing then, to repeat, can be a power bearer. Objects existing
in intimate relation to soul-stuff possess indisputable potency; it is

[1] Rilke.
[2] *cf.* P. Tillich, *Die Überwindung des Persönlichkeitsideals, Logos*, XVI, 1927.
[3] J. Spieth, *Die Religion der Eweer in Süd-Togo*, 1911, 110 *ff.*

for this reason that the Maori, as has already been remarked, regard the latrine as replete with *mana*: the sick bite its beams in order to be cured.[1] This systematic reckoning with the power subsisting in things we call Fetishism, a term coined in the scientific sense by de Brosses in 1760, and originally used by the Portuguese with reference to Negro beliefs and customs.[2] But it was applied only to potent things made by man himself, and therefore not to natural objects. Gradually, however, it attained a more comprehensive meaning, sometimes so extensive that even the worship of Nature could be included, so that the concept then became formless. But if it is really desired to indicate the structure of a spiritual viewpoint by the term usually employed, then it would be advisable to apply it only to those objects that we call "things", but with no distinction between natural and artificial, because primitive man venerates what he has himself made,[3] provided this is "effective", just as much as what Nature gives him when this manifests power. In this latter respect, any peculiarity that differentiates the object from environing Nature is essentially significant: the striking shape of a crooked branch, of a round stone, *etc.*, becomes the "pointer" to the existence of power. It is necessary, further, that the object be not too large, so that one may take it away, or as it were pocket it. Although mountains and trees are regarded as sacred, like the fetish, because of their potency, still they should not be called fetishes; it is just this feeling of being able to carry the sacred power with one that is characteristic of fetishism. "Let us fetch the ark of the covenant of the Lord out of Shiloh unto us, that, when it cometh among us, it may save us out of the hand of our enemies",[4] said the Israelites when the Philistines beset them.

A good example of a fetish is the Australian *churinga*, a peculiarly shaped piece of wood on which an outline sketch of a totem emblem is scratched. The word itself means the "private secret", and the object must be kept secret from the women and children. It is the bearer of a power connected on the one hand with the individual, and on the other with his totem;[5] here again subsists the power superior to, yet nevertheless overflowing into, humanity. The *churinga* are most carefully concealed in a kind of place of refuge.[6]

---

[1] Lehmann, *Mana*, 50.

[2] The Portuguese *feitiço* means artificial, *factitius*, and subsequently magic.

[3] "Veneration", moreover, is to be understood here only in its most general sense. A. C. Kruyt speaks, more accurately, of "feeding" the fetish so that it may retain its power: *Het Animisme in den Indischen Archipel*, 1906, 200.

[4] 1 *Samuel* iv. 3.   [5] *cf*. Chap. 8.   [6] Chap. 57.

Earlier research assumed that the potency of a fetish is a spirit permanently residing within it, but to-day the contrasted hypothesis is in favour. At the same time it is probable that the way in which this power is represented is of secondary significance for the constitution of Fetishism as such. Thus the power of the ark of the covenant sprang from Jahveh, a god, that of the *churinga* from a totem; and the potent influence of the fetish, naturally, is very often simply presupposed quite apart from any kind of attitude to spirits or gods being implied— purely dynamically therefore. Actually, Fetishism is always dynamic; and regarded as an ideal type, it was so originally also, because its essence lies in the idea that power resides within a thing and emanates from it. Whence the power arises is, however, a question in itself.

In view of these considerations we can understand the transition from fetish to idol. In many parts of the world piles of stones were erected, each traveller adding his stone to those already thrown there; such stone heaps being found in South Africa just as in ancient Israel. In later times these cairns were looked upon as monuments or burial mounds; originally, however, it was the potency of the accumulated stones that men thus assured for themselves. In Greece these stone heaps were called *hermae* and were the origin of a divinity—"he of the stone heaps": *Hermes.* But before Hermes received his marvellous human form from the hands of Praxiteles he had to stand by the way-side, as the phallic stone or *herm*, for many years.[1] The august form of Pallas, again, was evolved from the fetish of the double thunder-shield or *palladion.* Of her, just as of Demeter, there were effigies which were half stone fetish and half woman, exactly as Aphrodite was origin-ally a cone. The power of things, in fact, faded only very gradually before that of gods and even of animals. In ancient Egypt fetishes persisted together with animal and human forms of power, and in Greece people loved the *xoana*, the rough wooden blocks, more than Pheidias' marvellous statues; his "Attic Pallas and Rharian Ceres, which stand unsculptured in the shape of a rude and unformed log" (Tertullian), were dearer to him than the Lemnian Athene or the Cnidian Demeter. Forms contrasted with the human actually indicate a diviner remoteness, and yet at the same time a more intimate contact, than does anthropomorphic Power. And this extremely primitive association between transcendence and immanence is essentially characteristic of Fetishism. The time-honoured, time-blackened, blocks of wood, which pious faith takes to have descended from heaven, were

[1] *cf.* M. P. Nilsson, *Griechische Feste*, 1906, 388.

precious to the people's hearts; they remain so to-day in Catholic regions. For it is not before great art creations, nor forms that arouse his sympathy, that man prays most spontaneously and fervently and to which he makes pilgrimages, but the "black Madonnas".[1] It is these that work miracles; and before the fetish numinous awe unites with the intimacy and the consciousness of dominance aroused by things.[2]

The intensity of the attractive power enjoyed, even to-day, by Fetishism, is plainly evident from the use of so-called mascots in modern sport: dolls and animal figures still display themselves as potent, and this not as incarnations of gods in whom trust is no longer placed, but purely and simply as "things". At the missionary exhibition in Nice in 1925, for example, many fetishes were to be seen, and countless visitors wished to buy these at high prices. As this was naturally declined, the directors of the exhibition found themselves compelled to have these objects carefully guarded because attempts were made to steal them.[3]

3. Among potent things *tools* assume a prominent place. To primitive man, indeed, work is the very antithesis of technical occupation—it is creative. The primitive craftsman experiences the power, in virtue of which he completes his task, not as his own; capacity, moreover, is here something far more than modern efficiency. The early hand-worker therefore, particularly the smith, wields a power which he certainly understands how to employ, but of which nevertheless he is not the master; and thus we can realize why smith's work is regarded as sacred in many parts of Africa and Indonesia. In Loango, again, who-ever has cohabited the previous night may not watch the labour lest his impurity should ruin the work; for whatever comes into existence under human hands owes its being to a power superior to man. In the grips and blows of the tools, then, there dwells not only the strength of arms or legs, but also a specific power residing within the implements themselves; and this explains why tools are always made after the same model, since the slightest deviation would injure the potency. Moreover, not only are the working parts of the implements essential, but their ornamentation also.[4] The Toba-Batak of Sumatra sacrifices to his forge, hammer and anvil, to his canoe, rifle and furniture; the West African

[1] cf. Th. Trede, *Das Heidentum in der römischen Kirche*, II, 1890, 90 ff.
[2] Chap. 65.
[3] R. Allier, *Le non-civilisé et nous*, 1927, 181.
[4] Lévy-Bruhl, *How Natives Think*, 40 f.; cf. further on blacksmiths, M. Merker, *Die Masai*, 1910, 111 ff.

Ewe to his bush knife, axe, saw, *etc.*; and the gipsy, though decried as irreligious, swears his oath on the anvil.

Among implements, again, it is *weapons* that are especially potent; indeed, many weapons are nothing more than tools—the axe and hammer. The veneration of the Cretan double axe is universally familiar. The staff also was originally a weapon, which subsequently became the receptacle of royal power. In Egypt, not only was the staff worshipped, but the word denoting it, *shm*, also became an expression for "power" in general, for "to be potent", and at a later stage for a divine force which, together with other *mana*-like influences, rendered the dead king a ruler in the hereafter.[1] Thus we find here three stages: the sceptre—its power—and finally power in general. When king Tuthmosis III sent his general against Joppa he gave him his sceptre which, like the staffs of even private individuals in Egypt, bore a special name—"adorned with beauty".[2] At Chaeronea, again, the Greeks worshipped Agamemnon's sceptre with sacrifices,[3] while the Romans regarded the spear as the fetish of the god Mars. Whoever undertook a war invoked the sacred lance: *Mars vigila:*—"Mars, Awake!" And like the *hasta*, the *ancile* or shield also, which was believed to have fallen from heaven in the days of Numa, was held to be holy.

4. The last instance leads from the mere brute potency of the thing to its significance as the hoard of a communal essence. For the presence of the *ancile* guaranteed that of the supreme government. Similarly, the *palladium*, originally a stone or double shield, and subsequently the *xoanon* or wooden image of the goddess Athene, was the hoard, the power-object of Troy. Were this lost, the town would perish. In ancient Israel the same rôle was filled by the ark of the covenant. The Fox Indians too possessed a "sacred bundle", consisting of an owl, a tobacco pipe, two turtles, a firestone and a flute, which assured the tribal power.[4] The Amandebele of South Africa had their *mamchali*, a small basket without an opening containing "holy" things, a genuine palladium; if it fell into hostile hands it proved itself invulnerable.[5] On Taliabo (Sula Island) there is a sacred spot where a number of

[1] *cf.* W. Spiegelberg, *Der Stabkultus bei den Ägyptern, Rec. de Trav.* 25, 1903, 184; *cf.* 28, 1906, 163 *f.*

[2] S. G. Maspero, *Popular Stories of Ancient Egypt,* 109 *f.* G. Röder, *Altägyptische Erzählungen und Märchen,* 1927, 67.

[3] Pausanias, IX, 40, 11.

[4] K. Th. Preuss, *Glauben und Mystik im Schatten des höchsten Wesens,* 1926, 32.

[5] H. C. M. Fourie, *Amandebele van Fene Mahlangu,* 1921.

dishes, shells, *etc.*, are preserved in the soil; only one man knows where this is, and in case of plague he brings water to the *kampong* or native village in one of the shells. The Indonesians, still further, provide very many instructive examples of this belief in a tribal or communal hoard. The Macassars and Bugis ascribe special significance to the state insignia; whoever possesses these has the country also in his power, for in them the "rulership of the land is as it were concentrated";[1] during a riot in Luwu the Dutch commanding officer required only to seize the insignia of state to break down opposition immediately. Such objects are of different kinds: old spears, daggers, a Koran, stones, *etc.*—but these must usually have been handed down from the tribal ancestors. The imperial insignia of the Holy Roman Empire possessed a similarly concentrated potency even in the Middle Ages. They were regarded as sacred objects, to be approached in procession, and days when they were exhibited to the people were treated as great festival occasions. To a newly elected emperor, therefore, the possession of the insignia was extremely important;[2] like the weapons of Mars in Rome, they were *pignora imperii*:—Pledges of the realm.[3]

Not the power of the tribe or realm only, but similarly that of the family was associated with venerable objects. In Indonesia each family has its so-called *pusaka*, objects frequently of very slight value, which are, however, regarded as sacred and bequeathed from father to son. The ancient Germans too looked upon clothes, weapons and jewels as luck-bearers, the family welfare being often intimately connected with so potent an object. The power of the hero's sword, again, which rendered its wielder invincible, became the permanent *motif* of saga, myth and fairy tale.

5. From fetishes amulets are distinguished; these also are certainly containers of power, only as it were in pocket size. Representations of sacred objects, crosses, suns, *etc.*, but also knots intended to hold power together, stones and almost every imaginable thing were carried on the body as amulets to ward off danger and attract blessings. Like fetishes, these too can acquire their influence from some holy person or situation; but then they are preferably called relics.[4]

[1] C. Spat, *De Rykssieraden van Loewoe, Ned. Indie oud en nieuw*, 3, 1918.
[2] *cf.* L. von Ranke, *Weltgeschichte*, VIII⁴, 1921, 44.
[3] Escutcheons, banners and flags, which even to-day have not lost their religious significance, fall within this category.   [4] *cf.* Chap. 30.

CHAPTER 4

POTENCY. AWE. *TABU*

1. THE experience of the potency of things or persons may occur at any time; it is by no means confined to specific seasons and occasions. Powerfulness always reveals itself in some wholly unexpected manner; and life is therefore a dangerous affair, full of critical moments. If then one examines them more closely, even the most ordinary events, the customary associations with one's neighbours, or similarly one's long familiar tasks, prove to be replete with "mystic" interconnections. We may say indeed (as *e.g.* Marett maintains) that the explanation of any fact, however natural it may appear, is ultimately always "mystic". But we should probably express ourselves in more primitive fashion if we completely ignored our own scheme of explanation in terms of single causes, and in place of this interpreted life as a broad current of mighty powers whose existence we do not specifically observe, but which occasionally makes itself conspicuous by either the damming or the flooding of its waters. If, for instance, one of the Toradja tribes in Celebes is preparing for an expedition and an earthen pot is broken, then they remain at home, saying that it is *measa*.[1] This may be translated as "a sign": only not in any rationalistic sense as indicating some future misfortune, but that the current of life has been interrupted: If then one thing has been broken, why not more? Similarly, when an Ewe tribesman finds refuge from his enemies on a white ant hill he ascribes his escape to the power residing there.[2] Thus the place, the action, the person in which the power reveals itself receive a specific character. Bearers of *mana*, for example, are sharply distinguished from the rest of the world: they are self-sufficient. By the Greeks, similarly, a body struck by lightning was regarded as holy, ἱερός, because powerfulness was manifested in it.[3]

Objects, persons, times, places or actions charged with Power are called *tabu* (*tapu*), a word from the same cultural domain as *mana*. It indicates "what is expressly named", "exceptional", while the verb

---

[1] A. C. Kruyt, "Measa", *Bydr. Taal-, Land- en Volkenkunde Ned. Indie*, 74–76, 1918–1920.

[2] K. Th. Preuss, *Glauben und Mystik im Schatten des höchsten Wesens*, 1926, 25.

[3] *cf.* Euripides, *The Suppliant Women*, 934 ff.

tapui means "to make holy".[1] *Tabu* is thus a sort of warning: "Danger! High voltage!" Power has been stored up, and we must be on our guard. The *tabu* is the expressly authenticated condition of being replete with power, and man's reaction to it should rest on a clear recognition of this potent fullness, should maintain the proper distance and secure protection.

The *tabu* is observed in different ways and with regard to highly contrasted objects. To the Greek the *king* and the *foreigner* or *stranger* appeared as objects of *aidos*, of awe, to be duly respected by keeping one's distance.[2] Almost everywhere the king is looked upon as powerful, so that he should be approached only with the greatest caution, while the foreigner, bearer of a power unknown and therefore to be doubly feared, stands on an equal footing with an enemy; *hostis* is both stranger or foreigner, and enemy. One may either kill the alien, if one is in a position so to do, or bid him welcome; but in no case are his coming and going to be regarded with indifference. *Greeting* is therefore a religious act, intended to intercept the first onset of the power, and into which the name of God is introduced or to which an appeasing influence is attached (*e.g.* the Semitic peace greeting: *adieu*: *Grüssgott*). *Hospitality*, therefore, as well as *war*, is a religious act, intended either to repel the alien power or to neutralize it. *Sex life* is also full of potency, *woman* being distinguished from man by mysterious peculiarities; thus the *veil* served as a defence even before it became a symbol of bashfulness.[3] Everything concerned with the sexual is "exceptional": when one is sexually impure one must be careful, and not *e.g.* undertake any important matter such as war. Nor should one approach a menstruating woman, who is often excluded from a cult for this very reason:—her potent influence would antagonize the power to be acquired by means of the cult; hence the formula: *hostis vinctus mulier virgo exesto*—"Let every stranger, bound person, woman or virgin stand aside"—associated with certain Roman sacrifices. Similarly as regards Cato's warning in connection with the "vow for the cattle: a woman may not take part in this offering nor see how it is performed".[4] Some one day, again, or series of days, is regarded as being more potent than others. Sabbath, Sunday, Christmas Day and their primitive and heathen equivalents are sacred: no work is done, or at least no important affairs undertaken.

---

[1] Söderblom, *Das Werden des Gottesglaubens*, 31 *f.*
[2] *cf. Theol. Wörterbuch zum N.T.*, Αἰδώς.   [3] *cf.* 1 *Cor.* xi. 5 *ff.*
[4] *De Agri Cultura*, 83; *votum pro bubus: mulier ad eam rem divinam ne adsit neve videat quo modo fiat.*

Thus the battle of Thermopylae was lost because the "holy days" (ἱερομηνία) imposed on the Spartans a cessation of hostilities; and for the same reason they arrived at Marathon too late. On very sacred days even the slightest labour was forbidden; for critical times must never be allowed to pass unnoticed but must be met by some relevant exceptional behaviour on man's own part, such as fasting. *Tabu*, then, is the avoidance of deed and of word, springing from awe in the presence of Power. Words concerning critical affairs like hunting, war, sex intercourse, should not be uttered, but rather be replaced by a specially elaborated *tabu* language, remnants of which we still retain in our sportsmen's slang and thieves' jargon. Even a peculiar women's terminology occurs side by side with the men's.

But the mere avoidance, as such, of potency cannot suffice. Among the Kaian of Central Borneo, for example, neither man nor woman may touch slaughtered fowl during the woman's pregnancy, nor may the man pound the soil, *etc.*;[1] to our minds the connection and the purpose here are obscure. The *tabu*, however, is anything but a measure of utility: Power has revealed itself, either as cessation or as super-fluity. It is therefore not only a question of avoiding it, but also of thinking of some defence against it. Sometimes the mode of protection is intelligible to us, as with the veil or some sort of ritual or discipline such as fasting; often, however, we cannot fathom it at all. Associations then appear which we moderns quite fail to understand, and feelings to which we are wholly insusceptible. But even when we do succeed, what we regard as a causative connection does not emerge, just as little as there arises an emotional reaction in the sense of our reverence or devotion, though both these may be incorporated in the primitive ᶜ attitude. The *tabu*, further, may be decreed; some power bearer, a king or priest, can endow an object with his own power and proclaim a season of potency; in Polynesia the king's messenger thus announces the *tabu*:

> *Tabu*—no one may leave his house!
> *Tabu*—no dog may bark!
> *Tabu*—no cock may crow!
> *Tabu*—no pig may grunt!
> Sleep—sleep, till the *tabu* is past![2]

---

[1] A. W. Nieuwenhuis, *Quer durch Borneo*, II, 1907, 101.

[2] P. Hambruch, *Südseemärchen*, 1921, No. 66; *cf.* also Frazer, *The Belief in Immortality*, II, 389; no fire may be kept alight, no canoe launched, no swimming enjoyed. The dogs' and pigs' mouths are tied up so that they cannot bark nor grunt.

In Manipur, in Assam, the village priest ordains a similar communal
tabu called *genna*; the gates of the village are closed; the friend outside
must stay there, and the stranger who may chance to be within remains;
the men cook their own food and eat it without the women. All the
food *tabus* are carefully observed; trading and catching fish, hunting,
mowing grass and felling trees are forbidden. Thus an intentionally
evoked interruption of life occurs: the moment is critical, one holds
one's breath! At particularly sacred times, in fact, holiday-making still
retains a ritual air even in some European rural districts. In Dutch
Gelderland on Christmas Eve fifty years ago, for example, everything
indoors was carefully arranged; neither plough nor harrow might be
left outside, all implements being brought into the barns and the gates
leading to the fields closed. Everything must be locked up and under
cover in its right place, "otherwise '*Derk met den beer*' (the wild hunts-
men) would take it with them".[1]

Violation of the *tabu* brought in its train not punishment, but an
automatic reaction of Power; it was quite unnecessary to inflict any
penalties when Power assailed one spontaneously. With the best
intentions, for instance, Uzzah wished to support the ark of the covenant; the touch of the sacred object, however, entailed death.[2] But it
was no divine arbitrariness, and still less divine justice, that struck
him down: it was the purely dynamic anger of the Lord, אַף יהוה.[3]
Even a comic sidelight is instructive here:—In Thuringia every form
of work was most strictly prohibited on "Golden (Trinity) Sunday";
and a lad who, in spite of this, had sewn a button on his trousers on
the holy day could only with the utmost difficulty save himself from
death by a lightning stroke the next day, by sacrificing the garment
concerned and allowing it to slip into the water, when it was promptly
carried off by Nemesis.[4] From our viewpoint, of course, only the lad
was guilty and not his trousers! But Power questions not as to guilt or
innocence; it reacts, exactly as the electric current shocks anyone who
carelessly touches the wire. In Central Celebes death is the penalty
for incest, not, however, as a punishment, but merely as a means of
limiting the evil results of the outrage to the delinquents; that the
latter should die was regarded as a matter of course.[5] Death by being
cast from the *Saxum Tarpeium*, which the Romans inflicted upon

---

[1] H. W. Heuvel, *Oud-achterhoeksch boerenleven*, 1927, 471.   [2] 2 *Sam.* vi.
[3] Actually, not the wrath of Jahveh, but simply "wrath"; "it was not difficult for
'primitive man' to speak of wrath that was not the wrath of *anyone* whatever". Otto,
Gef. des Überwelt. 55.
[4] O. von Reinsberg-Düringsfeld, *Das festliche Jahr*[2], 1898, 204.   [5] Kruyt, *op. cit.*

traitors, was likewise not punishment but a reaction of the Power; the *tribuni plebis*, who were sacrosanct, that is, the bearers of a most formidable potency, appear as the executioners, while whoever fell, without dying as the result, saved his life; "it is a matter less of an execution than of an intentional accident".[1]

Naturally the effectiveness of the *tabu* was believed in without any reservations whatever. A Maori would die of hunger rather than light a fire with the lighting utensils of a chief,[2] and Howitt heard of a Kurnai boy who had stolen some opossum meat and eaten this before the food *tabus* permitted. The tribal elders persuaded him that he would never be a man; he lay down, and in three weeks was dead.[3] Similar examples might be multiplied indefinitely.

2. We characterize the distance between the potent and the relatively powerless as the relationship between *sacred* and *profane*, or secular. The "sacred" is what has been placed within boundaries, the exceptional (Latin *sanctus*); its powerfulness creates for it a place of its own. "Sacred" therefore means neither completely moral nor, without further qualification, even desirable or praiseworthy. On the contrary, sacredness and even impurity may be identical: in any event the potent is dangerous. The Roman *tribunus plebis*, just referred to, was so sacred, *sacrosanctus*, that merely to meet him on the street made one impure.[4] Among the Maori also *tapu* means "polluted" just as much as "holy"; but in any case it carries a prohibition with it, and therefore prescribes keeping one's proper distance. It is, then, scarcely correct to regard the contrast between sacred and secular as developing out of the distinction between threatening danger and what is not perilous.[5] Power has its own specific quality which forcibly impresses men as dangerous. Yet the perilous is not sacred, but rather the sacred dangerous. In a quite classical way Söderblom has presented the contrast between holy and profane as the primal and governing antithesis in all religion, and has shown how the old viewpoint, that Wonder, Θαυμάζειν, is the beginning of Philosophy, can be applied with yet greater justice to Religion. For whoever is confronted with potency clearly realizes that he is in the presence of some quality with which in

---

[1] A. Piganiol, *Essai sur les Origines de Rome*, 1917, 149.   [2] Frazer, *op. cit.*, 44.

[3] Elsie C. Parsons, "Links between Morality and Religion in Early Culture," *Amer. Anthrop.*, 17, 1915, 46.

[4] Plutarch, *Quaestiones romanae*, 81. This passage seems not quite clear, but in any case impurity, involved by the sacredness of the tribune, is implied.

[5] As B. Ankermann does in Chantepie, 152; *cf.* GENERAL LITERATURE, p. 19 *ante*.

his previous experience he was never familiar, and which cannot be evoked from something else but which, *sui generis* and *sui juris*, can be designated only by religious terms such as "sacred" and "numinous". All these terms have a common relationship in that they indicate a firm conviction, but at the same time no definite conception, of the completely different, the absolutely distinct. The first impulse aroused by all this is avoidance, but also seeking: man should avoid Power, but he should also seek it. No longer can there be a "why" or "wherefore" here; and Söderblom is undeniably correct when, in this connection, he defines the essence of all religion by saying that it is mystery.[1] Of that aspect there was already a deep subjective assurance even when no god was invoked. For to religion "god" is a late comer.

3. In the human soul, then, Power awakens a profound feeling of awe which manifests itself both as fear and as being attracted. There is no religion whatever without terror, but equally none without love, or that *nuance* of being attracted which corresponds to the prevailing ethical level. For the simplest form of religious feeling Marett has suggested the fine word *Awe*, and Otto the term *Scheu*, which is somewhat less comprehensive; the Greek *aidos* too is most pertinent.[2] The expression adopted must be a very general one, since it is a question of establishing an attitude which includes the whole personality at all its levels and in countless *nuances*. Physical shuddering, ghostly horror, fear, sudden terror, reverence, humility, adoration, profound apprehension, enthusiasm—all these lie *in nuce* within the awe experienced in the presence of Power. And because these attitudes show two main tendencies, one away from Power and the other towards it, we speak of the *ambivalent* nature of awe.

Of course *tabu* means a prohibition, and Power reveals itself first of all always as something to be avoided. Everywhere, too, the prohibition announces itself earlier than the command; but Freud has very ably shown how the former always implies the latter.[3] Man is fully conscious only of the prohibition, while the command usually remains unrecognized. What we hate we love, and what we truly love we could at the same time hate. "For each man kills the thing he loves", said Oscar Wilde, and this is far more than a brilliant phrase. In the

---

[1] Very well expressed in the Essay: "Points of Contact for Missionary Work", *Int. Review of Missions*, 1919.

[2] *cf.* Murray, *The Rise of the Greek Epic.*   [3] *Totem and Taboo*, 31 *f.*, 41 *f.*

presence of the something different which we recognize as "Wholly Other", our conduct is always ambivalent. Love may be described as an attempt to force oneself into the place of the other; hate, as the fear of love.

But whether the sacred releases feelings of hate and fear, or those of love and reverence, it always confronts man with some absolute task. The *tabu* has therefore, and not without justification, been described as the oldest form of the categorical imperative.[1] Of course we must not think of Kant's argument in this connection. Nevertheless *tabu* and categorical imperative have in common the character of complete irrationality as well as absoluteness. "Thou shalt"—what one should do is a secondary issue; why one should do it is not a question at all. Confronted with Power, which he experiences as being of completely contrasted nature, man apprehends its absolute demand. An irruption occurs in his life, and he is drawn in two directions: he is seized with dread, and yet he loves his dread.

4. Having once established itself, awe develops into *observance*; and we can trace this advance in the Roman concept *religio*, which originally signified nothing more than *tabu*. In the description of an eerie place, in *Virgil*, the primal awe still glimmers: the sacred grove of the Capitol has a "dread awe" (*religio dira*).[2] But the ancient shudder lives also in custom: a sudden death is a *portentum*—a sign of potency that enters *in religionem populo*,[3] or as we should say, "renders the people impure". It was, then, preferable to put up with a ceremonial repetition of the consular election, rather than permit a *tabu* to remain in force over the people.[4] Again, an illness is thus exorcised: *hanc religionem evoco educo excanto de istis membris . . .*[5] "I call out, I draw out, I sing out, this pollution from these limbs". Thus we can comprehend the definition given by Masurius Sabinus: "*religiosum* is that which because of some sacred quality is removed and withdrawn from us".[6] This is, precisely, the sacred; and constant regard to it is the chief element in

---

[1] Freud, *ibid.* Preface, rather than 114 *f.*, on the equivalence with conscience. So far as I am aware, the first writer to whom the resemblance suggested itself was J. E. Harrison, *Epilegomena to the Study of Greek Religion*, 11.

[2] *Aeneid*, VIII, 347.

[3] Cicero, *De Deorum Natura*, II, 4, 10.

[4] *ibid.* 11; *quam haerere in re publica religionem.*

[5] G. Appel, *De Romanorum precationibus*, 1909, 43.

[6] Gellius, IV, ix, 8; *religiosum est, quod propter sanctitatem aliquam remotum ac sepositum a nobis est.*

the relationship between man and all that is extraordinary. The most probable derivation of the word is from *relegere*—to observe or pay attention; *homo religiosus*, therefore, is the antithesis to *homo negligens*.[1]

We can now understand, still further, how it is that awe, in the long run, must become pure observance, and intense dread mere formalism. In this respect Freud's conclusions are wholly justified: primeval prohibitions "descend, like a hereditary disease".[2] Nevertheless Freud has forgotten that no matter how much man's practical religious conduct may thus be governed by transmissible *tabus*, still profound awe and "aweful" potency must have subsisted to begin with. Observance, then, is just benumbed awe which, at any moment, can be revived. Even in our own country people's "ancient custom", in Indonesian *adat* and in court and university ceremonial, there still lives something of the awe of contact with Power. At the court of Philip IV of Spain, who died in 1665, an officer who freed the queen from the stirrup of her runaway horse had to go into exile; an incident in which it is obvious how the touch *tabu* had developed into court etiquette.

Even when vivid awe has been lost, observance continues to serve highly practical purposes. In Indonesia and Polynesia, for instance, the *tabu* is a means of asserting unquestionable right of possession to a piece of ground; some sign indicates the prohibition of stealing it or trespassing on it.[3] We should none the less be quite mistaken in concluding that the *tabu* came into being by virtue of these purely utilitarian considerations, or even that it was invented by the great ones of the earth for their own profit and benefit. Frequently it may certainly be mere routine practice, but it always has intense awe as its presupposition. The "sign", again, resembles our warning notices so closely that it may readily be confused with them; but the punishment threatened by the police is omitted, although it will doubtless appear of its own accord: on Amboina the trespasser is smitten with leprosy; and further, the prohibition itself is not rationally grounded; on the same island a rough sketch of a female sex organ—that is, something particularly "potent"—replaces the legal notification.[4] "Property" in

---

[1] *cf.* W. F. Otto, *Religio und Superstitio, AR.* 12, 1909; 14, 1911. Felix Hartmann, *Glotta,* 4, 1913, 368 *f.* Max Kobbert, *De verborum religio et religiosus usu apud Romanos quaestiones selectae,* 1910.   [2] *Faust,* Part I.
[3] Here *Mark* vii. 11 *f.* may be referred to, where the duty of children to maintain their parents is rendered futile by an alleged *tabu* of such support as a sacrifice (*korban*).
[4] J. G. Riedel, *De Sluik- en kroesharige rassen tusschen Selebes en Papoea,* 1886, 62.

its primitive sense, then, is something quite different from what it is with us—it is a "mystical" relation between owner and owned; the possessor is not the *beatus possidens*, but the depositary of a power that is superior to himself.

Once the belief in *tabu* has completely become mere observance, an empty shell, then man breaks his fetters. In the Euripidean *Herakles* neither Nature nor pure humanity can be defiled by the *tabu* of death; Herakles need only take off the veil and show his head to the light:

> Eternal is the element:
> Mortal, thou canst not pollute the heavens.

Again:

> No haunting curse can pass from friend to friend.[1]

This is essentially the "modern" feeling, which opposes power in nature and personality.

R. CAILLOIS, *L'homme et Le Sacre*, 1939, Eng. tr., *Man and The Sacred*, 1959.
J. G. FRAZER, *Taboo and the Perils of the Soul* (*The Golden Bough*, III).
S. FREUD, *Totem and Taboo*.
R. THURNWALD, *Meidung*, in *Lexikon der Vorgeschichte*.

[1] *Herakles*, 1232 *ff*. (Way).

CHAPTER 5

THE SACRED ENVIRONMENT

SACRED STONES AND TREES

1. AT the close of last century, side by side with Animism, arose so-called "Naturism"—that is the hypothesis that the worship of divine beings had originated in a personification of the powers of Nature. The manifold representatives of natural potencies in Greek religion had long been familiar; the variegated and beauteous world of the Vedic deities had just been disclosed; and this also appeared, to a high degree, to have the manifestations of Nature as its basis. Thus the idea readily arose that, in reflecting on the causes of natural events, primitive man had invented gods, spirits and demons as their originators. Even to-day, indeed, every poet does the same; while in so far as language regards natural processes as activities, it likewise appears to assume an agent behind them; we too say that the storm roars, the lightning quivers, the sea rolls. Could not a sort of "disease of language", then, have seduced men into accepting these expressions quite literally? even though primarily they certainly were intended merely metaphorically, just as they are by ourselves. In this way religion could without too great difficulty be explained, since at the close of last century it occupied a comparatively superfluous and poetic position in its relations to science.

To-day, however, the need to "explain" religion has substantially lost ground; at all events we realize that reflection on the causes of natural phenomena cannot of itself constitute religion. Furthermore, it is still more difficult to regard religion as a universal error or (as Durkheim neatly puts it) a "system of hallucinatory images", an "immense metaphor with no objective value". Quite apart from such general considerations, again, the limitation to Nature is wholly untenable since, in the first place, Nature is neither the sole nor even the principal feature in religion; while in the second it is neither Nature nor natural objects that man worships, but always the Power which reveals itself in these.

It cannot therefore be the case that religion arose from "worship of Nature" simply because the concept of "Nature" is quite modern, having been first contrasted with human culture by Rousseau and the romantics. For neither the primitive nor the ancient world was there "Nature", conceived as a realm set over against man and his deeds; nor, again, were the individual objects of Nature in principle distinguished by primitive and ancient man from artificial things.[1] It is therefore not incorrect, although it is undeniably confusing, to extend the term "Fetishism", as was frequently done formerly, to so-called Nature worship; for in "Nature", exactly as in "culture", it is again and again a question of sacred Power, organic and inorganic constituting no antithesis in principle. In this respect the distinction lying nearest to that with which we are ourselves familiar is the contrast between tilled land and the surrounding uncultivated wilderness, as this actually arose first among agricultural peoples. But at that stage the potency was distributed equally between "Nature" and "culture": on the one hand, the ploughed field had its powerfulness in its fertility while, on the other, forest and heath, steppe and "barren" sea had their own powers, uncanny though these were—a distinction to be considered more fully at a later stage. It is never a contrast, however, between Power and impotence, but always between two Powers.

What we moderns call "Nature", in fact, has a prominent rôle in all religions without exception. Yet it is neither Nature, nor natural phenomena as such, that are ever worshipped, but always the Power within or behind. And as we have seen already in so many examples, this Power is substantiated empirically by exactly the same methods, and given its due reckoning in the same way. In other words, the antithesis between sacred and secular, between powerful and impotent, is always more comprehensive than that between Nature and culture, and incessantly cuts across it.

2. That Fetishism and "Naturism" are, however, separated by no unbridgeable chasm should be clear from the example of *stone worship*. With stones of any peculiar size and shape the firm subjective assurance of the presence of Power[2] has ever been associated. When for instance Jacob, his head "resting" on a stone, lay down to sleep and had his remarkable dream, he expressed himself thus—and purely empirically: "How dreadful is this place! this is none other but the house of God,

---

[1] Rudolf Bultmann draws my attention to the fact that even at the dawn of science, in the Ionian philosophy of Greece, the cosmos was apprehended as a "work of art", a product of skill, involving ἔργον and τέχνη; thus Nature's activities were interpreted on the analogy of "artificial" operations. In any case the peculiarity of Greek thought consists precisely in the Greeks being fully aware of this distinction.

[2] Here again *Ahnung*.

and this is the gate of heaven";[1] and he took the stone and set it up for a pillar, anointing it with oil. Even if this narrative is aetiological, and intended to account for the worship of a remarkable stone, still it remains typical of the way in which stones can become most intimately incorporated in man's experience.

The Hellenic peoples who immigrated to Greece from the North, again, were familiar with a stone they called *Aguieus*—"he of the ways"; and when they had permanently settled in Greece the *Aguieus* stone was set up in the market-place, decorated and garlanded: as it had protected the great migration, so it would guard the colony. The stone had the phallic form and was probably, like many other "stones set upright", originally regarded as a manifestation of fertility power. Later in Greece there arose from this stone the phallic *herm*, and eventually the god's image; in Israel, on the other hand, this development was intersected by aversion from the anthropomorphic.

While the latter examples are important with respect to the power of growth, still to be considered, thunderbolts were revelations of celestial power. The *silex* of *Jupiter Feretrius* or *Jupiter Lapis* was preserved on the Capitol and brought into use for ceremonial oaths: it was supposed to smite perjurers like a thunderbolt. The Romans also erected potent stones as boundary posts and dedicated a cult to them: the power residing within them was protective (*termini*). But other powers too could be concealed in the stone; for the ancient Romans a stone, *lapis manalis*, brought down rain—a rain charm, *aquaelicium*, whose echo still resounded in the *chanson de geste*, *Yvain*, in which, as soon as the hero pours water on a stone in the forest of Broceliande, it begins to thunder loudly and rain very heavily.

Metals too are bearers of power, and the rarer these are, the more potent. Gold, which shares its colour with the sun, also possesses something of the sun's vivifying strength; the Greeks prepared death-masks of gold while the Egyptians, for whom the metal stood in direct relationship to life, made in their later eras golden portraits of mummies. With gold, again, the kings divided life among their favourites. The golden apples of the Hesperides, from whose guardianship the fruit later passed into the power of Iduna in Iceland, were for the Greeks the symbol of life.

But *mountains* are of far greater interest. Everywhere in the world there are sacred mountains, whether Power is ascribed simply to them

---

[1] *Gen.* xxviii. 17. We should be mistaken were we to infer a necessary animating of the stone by a spirit or demon from the name *Bethel* (Greek βαιτύλιον). The *El* here is still very general; a power *post festum*.

or is imagined as a demon or god. Remote and unapproachable mountains, often volcanic and repellent, and in any case majestic, stand apart
from the normal and incorporate therefore the Power of the "wholly
other". Japan has its sacred Fujiyama, Greece its Olympus, or rather
several of them, and every region has its own holy peak. Naturally the
mountain is already there in its might before the gods make their entry
into Valhalla; but once there they can hardly reside elsewhere. The
oldest heaven is the mountain-top. Similarly in the Old Testament,
deity dwells on the mount:

> The north and south, thou madest them,
> Tabor (the mount of the gods in the north) and Hermon (the mount
> of God in the south) acclaim thee.[1]

Jahveh appears on Sinai, while in *Psalm* cxxi we find "the hills, from
whence cometh my help".

The mountain, the hard stone, was regarded as a primal and
permanent element of the world: out of the waters of Chaos rose the
primeval hill from which sprang all life. To this ancient eminence,
depicted in many temples, the Egyptians transported their creator-
god; it was looked upon as the "navel" of the earth, as its focal-point
and beginning. In Greek temples, similarly, the *omphalos* was a primitive symbol of earth and of all birth;[2] in ancient thought birth from
stone was as usual as that from the fertile earth. Mithra was regarded
as born from the rock—*ex petra natus*: and the goddess Athene was
born from Zeus' κορυφή, that is from the summit of Olympus.[3] The
story of Deucalion and Pyrrha again, who created their posterity by
throwing "their mother's bones", that is to say stones, behind them,
is universally known.

3. Like stone and mountain, the *tree* too is a power-bearer. Naturism
interpreted the tree as a symbol of celestial phenomena; it was supposed
to be a matter of the cloud-, weather-, or light-tree, whose leaves are
the clouds, its branches the sun's rays, its fruits the stars.[4] More
realistic research, however, has shown that it is not the tree that conceals
the celestial potencies, but these the tree. The incomparable Helen

---

[1] *Ps.* lxxxix. 12.
[2] *cf.* A. de Buck, *De Egyptische Voorstellingen betreffende den Oerheuvel*, 1922. W.
H. Roscher, *Der Omphalosgedanke bei verschiedenen Völkern* (*Ber. ü. d. Verh. d. Sächs.
Ges. d. Wiss. Phil.-hist. Kl.* 70, 2, 1918). A. J. Wensinck, "The Ideas of the Western
Semites concerning the Navel of the Earth" (*Verh. d. Kon. Akad. v. Wet. te Amster-
dam, Afd. Lett. N. R.* 17, 1). [3] H. Diels, "Zeus", *AR.* 22, 1923–24.
[4] W. Schwarz, in Chantepie[1], I, 64 *f. cf.* GENERAL LITERATURE, p. 19 *ante*.

was once a plane in Sparta, and in Rhodos she was styled *dendritis*, "she of the tree". She shares this title with none less than Dionysus, just as Zeus was also a tree on certain occasions. In Greece trees were probably always regarded as the seat of power:—the *hamadryads*, which "are born and die with the trees"[1]; some of these were fortunate and became famous heroines, like Helen and Europa. But the ancient Egyptians were already familiar with the sycamore "which enclosed the god", as well as with the other on which sits the merciful goddess who gives water and nourishment to the dead. Elsewhere in the most ancient Egyptian *Texts* it is recorded that the gods sit on this sycamore. It is remarkable, still further, that in Egypt and Greece it was usually the barren, dead tree that was believed to be the bearer of potency or of the god: the secret of the tree, which so deeply impressed man, was that of the vicissitudes of life and death.

The primitive mind, then, lacked that unquestioning acceptance of the regularity of natural processes which our own intellectual outlook regards as axiomatic. To primitive man life is Power, not Law. Even when it is dominated by a will it reveals itself spontaneously; in this respect, therefore, the comparison of Power with the electric current loses its applicability. To early thought the dying down and reanimation of Nature are indeed no miracle—for where no law is valid, miracle has no place—but nevertheless it is a spontaneous and astounding event which might well never have occurred. And here the power of life in the tree enters into a very peculiar relation to human life. It cannot, as Mannhardt suggests, have been the observation of growth alone that induced man to infer a similarity between his own nature and that of the tree. For though man certainly grows like the tree, still he does not continue to grow through a series of apparent deaths. It was rather the experience of the tree-power, in its constantly repeated defeat of death, which forced itself upon man and caused him to rely on the firmly assured existence of the tree as being the more powerful. The "conjoined-growth" of tree and man, recognized by Mannhardt with his brilliant insight, and which will be subsequently discussed more fully in connection with the religious aspects of agriculture, is consequently not at all a rational parallel, but a mystical union that is the effect of man's desires operating in a magical way. In Mecklenburg it is—or rather was—the custom to bury the afterbirth of a new-born infant at the foot of a young tree; in Indonesia, again, a tree is planted on the spot where the placenta has been interred; in both cases alike

[1] Servius, in *Ecl.* 10, 62.

the child grows up with the little tree; and R. Andree has compiled examples in which the child's life is bound up with that of the tree.[1] We too retain vestiges of this in fairy tales in which the withering or blooming of a small tree indicates the hero's danger or well-being, and also—in the modern way of showing respect—in the limes and the like planted at the birth of a royal child. But all that is merely an echo. In the Bismarck Archipelago "a coconut tree is planted on the birth of a boy. When it bears its first fruit the boy is included in the ranks of the adults . . . when the life-tree of the great Ngau chieftain Tamate-wka-Nene grew, his *mana* became very great also".[2] That is genuine "conjoined-growth".

But the presupposition of such conjunct growth is relationship in essential nature, in fact the presumption of the equivalence of man and plant, which really implies that the concept of "Nature" does not as yet exist.[3] In Indonesia, in fact, there is only one word both for the human soul and for that of the rice plant. Even where the plant world serves man as cultural material it apparently never becomes a thing: man utilizes no material whatever, but invokes the power in his environment, as well as that in himself. This means, still further, that there is actually no "environment" in the strict sense of the word. Woman is a tilled field, the tilled field a woman: and where the vegetative world has not yet been domesticated this holds good in even greater degree.

Not only does the tree grow up with the individual, but it also sustains the power of the life of the whole community. All over the world we find May-poles and Easter branches, adorned with ribbons and fruits like the *eiresione* of the Greeks and the *lulab* of the Jews, which bring new life to the social group; but to this theme I shall return. The Egyptians set up a barren tree with great ceremony, thereby restoring life; and in the days before the Greeks a similar rite occurred in Crete with a holy tree. The tree was a saviour, a life-bearer. The community gathered around it; and the French revolution showed how firmly the symbol of the tree is anchored in human consciousness—and, at the same time, how few symbols even revolutionary humanity commands!—when it set up the tree of liberty, thereby simply continuing the primeval dances around the May-pole.[4]

[1] *Mitt. Anthr. Gesellsch. in Wien*, 14, (62).   [2] Lehmann, *Mana*, 42.
[3] Bultmann kindly informs me that, in his opinion, the idea of the transference of the tree of life to the vine was at the basis of the well-known passage in *St. John* xv.
[4] "This traditional stake, the May-pole, the gathering-point of the peasants on festival days, became the revolutionary symbol in Périgord from May, 1790." A. Mathiez, *Les Origines des cultes révolutionnaires*, 1904, 32.

Ultimately the tree grows together with the whole world as soon as man becomes conscious of its existence, that is as soon as theoretical reflection begins, even when this retains its mythical form. Herakles found a tree of life in the garden of the gods at the end of the world, Adam in Paradise at its beginning; the Egyptians and Babylonians also were familiar with this idea, the former seeking the tall sycamore "on which the gods sit", the "wood of life on which they live", in the Eastern heavens.[1] The Persians and Indians likewise were acquainted with sacred plants which, in the form of a sacrament, brought divine life to the community: *haoma* in Persia, *soma* in India. The *tulasi* plant was regarded as the bride of the god by the Hindu, while to the Romans and the Germanic tribes the ever green leaves of the mistletoe signified the secret of life and death; and for Virgil they still opened the gates of the underworld.[2]

Eventually the world-tree, *Yggdrasil*, emerged from Germanic religious fantasy as a form of the *Vårträd*, the protective tree of the community transformed into the colossal.[3] The sacred tree of Uppsala was looked upon as its earthly image, but was more probably the original from which it had been created. Even if the Christian concept of the cross may have influenced the Germanic idea—*Yggdrasil* means "Odin's horse", that is the stake on which, according to the myth, Odin had hung—we must nevertheless regard this prodigious expansion of the conception of the holy tree as its most forcible expression. *Yggdrasil* enfolds the three worlds, stands there exalted and mighty, and yet decayed both above and below. With it the world passes away. And that it was the gallows of the dying god implies no contradiction of the heathen tree symbol (as Golther suggests),[4] but actually the most acute expression of its meaning: the secret of life and death.

E. DURKHEIM, *The Elementary Forms of the Religious Life.*
MIRCEA ELIADE, *Metallurgy* (Cahiers de Zalmoxis, I) 1938.
A. DE GUBERNATIS, *La Mythologie des Plantes*, 1878–1882.
W. MANNHARDT, *Wald- und Feldkulte*, 1904–1905².
MAX MÜLLER, *Natural Religion*, 1889.
    Physical Religion, 1898.

[1] K. Sethe, *Die altägyptischen Pyramidentexte*, II, 1910, 1216.
[2] *cf.* E. Norden, *P. Vergilius Maro, Aeneis*, Buch VI², 1916, 163 *ff.*
[3] *cf.* the magnificent description of the relationship between the "world" of the home and the World in general, the home-tree and the World-tree, in Grönbech, *Vor Folkeaet*, II, 9.
[4] *Handbuch der germanischen Mythologie*, 1895, 527 *ff.*

CHAPTER 6

THE SACRED ENVIRONMENT

SACRED WATER AND FIRE

1. IN the idea of holy water, too, it is clear that so far as concerns the veneration of the potent surrounding world, it is only in a very limited sense actually a matter of *environment*. For the powerfulness becomes manifested to man in his own experience, while this experience itself implies his developing consciousness of a connection between the essential nature of the object of worship and of the individual as subject. Man feels that his own life is dependent upon, and supported by, the environmental Power. But in his eyes it is not merely the environment, since this concept presupposes an attitude of disinterested observation which is absolutely foreign to the religious man, and recognized least of all by the primitive mind; rather is it the very centre of his life. Just as man and tree grow up together, so in ancient Egypt life fluctuated with the rise and fall of the flood waters; in the old *Texts* reference is often made to the "young water" which was a libation to the dead king and procured new life for him. In scantily watered country, in fact, the most beautiful representation of the after-life that could be formed was that one might drink water there, and that a generous goddess handed down from her tree water to the fainting man.

Incidentally, however, this is by no means restricted to countries poor in water. For the well accompanies the tree, and all over the world the source of living water is accounted a joyous miracle; the "water of life" brings fruitfulness and prosperity. But its potency extends even farther: it bestows eternal life, effects miracles and great deeds, and ultimately means community with the god. It resulted in fertility and increase for primitive man, to whom the animation of the fields by floods, rains and spring water was an experience of the revelation of Power; while to the mind no longer wholly primitive the sacredness was limited to certain particular waters, to definite springs and rivers, such as the holy fountain by which Demeter rested in Greece and the sacred rivers of India; also to special "holy water" endowed with power tested and proved, or guaranteed by consecration; in such cases the potency of the water becomes miraculous. To this countless legends testify, whose heroes are saved by the precious water of life which to others, again, restores vitality; the *eau de jouvence* and the *Jungbrunnen* impart renewed youth, or even chastity. But all the world over, too, the practical rite manipulates the miraculous water. Purifications by water were effective in ancient Egypt as well as for Roman Catholic piety: the *holy water*, freed from all damaging influences by exorcism, defends the person or object sprinkled with it from all demonic sway, drives off spooks and sickness, protects entrance and egress, house and cattle.[1] And finally, in baptism, water expels the devil and pours in sanctifying grace. But to the mind straining onward from Thing to Spirit, like St. John, water becomes the expression of eternal life; and he exalts the well of water, "springing up into everlasting life", above the venerated well of Jacob.[2]

2. *Fire* occupies its proper place between the powers in which (on the one hand) man indeed participates, but which he himself does not activate, and those (on the other hand) which he certainly recognizes as superior, but nevertheless handles as he wills. "All kinds of animal have been acquainted with fire, but to them it has conveyed nothing; only for man has flame had some meaning . . . man alone possesses the genius for fire", says Rémy de Gourmont;[3] or in modern terms: Fire belongs only half to Nature, and the other moiety to culture. Of course primitive thought did not make this distinction, yet it was fully aware that fire is man's property: even if it did come down from heaven, still it was kindled and nourished by man. This is the truth in the Prometheus myth, although the celestial origin of fire is hardly the first and most essential reason for its worship. Flame, on the one hand a power spreading warmth and light, and, as such, a power *par excellence*,[4] is at the same time a human acquisition. Still we can add that the celestial fire of lightning and of the sun was doubtless very soon brought into connection with the kindled earthly flame; this persists in the Hindu belief in the dual birth of *Agni*. But in the fire cult the emphasis is everywhere laid on the terrestrial fire, kindled to flame by man and living together with him.

The oldest fires were kindled by means of a fire-stone or borer, "begotten", as we should say in accord with the primitive sense; and Indian *Agni* speculation repeatedly uses expressions taken from sex

---

[1] *cf.* Fr. Heiler, *Der Katholizismus*, 1923, 168 *ff.* Water, like fire, is regarded as a protection against the dead; *cf.* I. Goldziher, *AR.* XIII, 1910, 20 *ff.* E. Samter, *Geburt, Hochzeit und Tod*, 1911, 83 *ff.*   [2] *St. John* iv. 13, 14.
[3] Quoted by R. Allier, *Le non-civilisé et nous*, 238.   [4] *cf.* Chap. 2.

life. The friction between the two pieces of the borer is regarded as generation and birth; they constitute a mated couple.[1] One ritual prescribes that the officiant should "keep the fire alight this night with shavings, and warm the fire-borer at it towards daybreak. It is exactly as if a calving cow is being mounted by the bull";[2] the two pieces of wood are regarded as pregnant, bearing within them the child *Agni*.[3] For long the old method of producing fire remained the same in popular custom: in Germanic countries the *nodfyr* ("need-fire") was ignited by rubbing wood, while on Midsummer's eve, and at other times when it was extinguished, the hearth fire was revived in that way.[4] This originated from the primeval Indo-Germanic conditions when fire was the most precious of possessions, to be renewed only with difficulty probably not merely because the process itself was arduous, but certainly and primarily because the fire's living power must never be allowed to perish, and could be restored only in a traditional, sacramental manner. On that account, and because of its extremely potent quality, the *nodfyr* in the Middle Ages was looked upon as "sacrilegious", and explicitly forbidden by church councils of the eighth century,[5] just as many other vestiges of the old mightiness had to give way before the new divine Power.

How closely human life and that of fire are interwoven is apparent in the many stories of procreation by fire.[6] Just as the flame is generated by human means, so it itself can also engender man's life; thus a Dyak woman of Borneo accidentally discovered the creation of fire by rubbing a liana against a piece of wood; the same liana presented her with a child, Simpang Impang.[7] In ancient Rome, again, the marital couch, *lectus genialis*, stood beside the fire on the hearth, while old foundation legends, as for example that of Praeneste, relate how a girl sitting by the hearth was impregnated by a spark sprung from the flame, and bore the founder of the city.[8]

[1] H. Oldenberg, *Die Religion des Veda*[2], 1917, 125 *f.*

[2] W. Caland, *Das Śrautasūtra des Apastamba*, 1921, 144.   [3] *ibid.*

[4] Reinsberg-Düringsfeld, *Das festliche Jahr*[2], 1898, 231 *f.*

[5] *Concilium germanicum*, 742; Council of Lestines, 743, *de igne fricato, de ligno, id est nodfyr, cf.* H. C. A. Grolman, *Tydschr. Ned. Aardr. Gen.*, 2. R., 46, 1929, 596.

[6] Ad. Kuhn, *Die Herabkunft des Feuers und des Göttertrankes*[2], 1886, 64 *ff.*

[7] P. Hambruch, *Malaiische Märchen*, 1922, No. 30.

[8] Wissowa, in Roscher's *Lexikon*, Article "Caeculus"; *Cato, Fr.* 59, in H. Peter, *Veterum Historicorum, romanorum reliquiae*, 1, 1870; *cf.* Pliny, *Nat. Hist.* XXXVI, 204. Compare also the ancient ecclesiastical rite, in which the Easter candle is thrust into the baptismal water, to the accompaniment of a benedictory text in which sex expressions predominate (*regenerare, admixtio, foecundare, concipere, uterus, etc.*). Fr. Heiler, *Der Katholizismus*, 1923, 229 *f.*

All these ideas are based on the fire on the *hearth*. In Indo-Germanic countries above all, but elsewhere also, the hearth is the power centre of the house. Its warming glow is a guarantee of all good things and really makes the house—as we, in this era of central heating, are unfortunately learning by its deprivation. To the Hindu, similarly, *Agni* is "the never departing, great lord of the house".[1] We moderns must try to imagine the isolated primitive farm, without fire, as it is depicted in an Iceland folk tale: "Once in Winter the fire died on the island of Grimsö, so that not a single farm had it any longer. The weather was windless and very cold, the sound frozen over so that the ice was thought to be firm enough to cross. Therefore they sent three sturdy fellows to the mainland to bring fire . . .",[2] and Frazer describes the same conditions in primitive Italy. Now I have already indicated that it was not only the difficulty of generating fire anew which made its extinction seem so fateful: fire—and with it life—*dies*, and the house in which the flames expire is thereupon deprived of the life power. The same condition, still further, holds good for the community, the state: only the regulated renewal of its fire assures its prosperity, the forms of power being strikingly transferred from the family to the larger communal group. On Lemnos *e.g.* the sacred fire was extinguished every ninth year and a fresh one brought from the island of Delos: therewith, as they said, "a new life began";[3] and here there prevails that primitive systematization of life which we shall often meet with later. *We* should say that a community or state prospers and then declines. But in this change *we* do not perceive the regular rhythm, the increase and diminution of power, just as little as we can support and as it were nourish this power of the state. We distinguish to-day between life, as such, and vitality, activity, prosperity, *etc.* To primitive man, however, life is life, and he knows nothing of "flourishing civilization", just as he knows little of "living piety".[4]

We find the forms of worship of the power of fire most beautifully and systematically developed in ancient Rome; they originated in the primeval domestic cult, wherein the hearth fire was entrusted to the care of the women (the later vestals), while the father of the family appeared as the priest of the flame and his sons (*flamines*) as the kindlers. Fire is the object of the oldest family worship, wherein the power of

---

[1] Oldenberg, *Rel. des Veda*, 130.
[2] H. u. I. Naumann, *Isländische Volksmärchen*, 1923, No. 22. C. Andersen, *Islandske Folkesagn*, 1877, 201.   [3] Farnell, *The Cults of the Greek States*, IV, 302, 429.
[4] New fire is as it were the renewal of creation; *cf.* Grönbech in Chantepie, II, 573. O. Huth, *Janus*, 1932, 73.

the communal essence is concentrated; and on the first of March, at the commencement of the old Roman year, the fire was extinguished and immediately rekindled. Thereby prosperity was ensured for another year. In the state the hearth fire (*vesta*) became the deepest mystery, on which the community's security depended: "the temple of Vesta, the eternal fire, and the fatal pledge for the continuance of the Roman empire deposited in the shrine".[1] Human life and the life of the fire subsisted in a reciprocal relationship: they participated in each other, and Oldenberg is quite correct in alluding to the friendly connections between man and fire, which gives his life a basis and a home. The returning Indian bard announces his success first of all to the flame on the hearth, while before her death Euripides' Alcestis takes a ceremonial farewell of the hearth, and implores it to protect her children.[2] For the hearth offers safety: it is an asylum; Hecuba leads old Priam to it: "all shall be saved by this altar".[3] In modern Calabria too, in case of death, the fire on the hearth is allowed to expire,[4] while according to old Germanic custom the flame was revived on special festival days, or when "sinking fortune made it evident that a renewal was necessary";[5] and an Indian tribe had to pay, by its gradual decline, for a girl's carelessness in permitting the fire to go out.[6] These examples afford ample proof that the idea of the potency of fire extended very far, and was by no means limited to Indo-Germanic peoples.

Fire's living power protects against evil influences: "*Agni* drives away monsters, *Agni* the brightly flaming, immortal, light, purifying, worthy of reverence."[7] On the other hand, nothing impure or dangerous to life must touch the flame; as the Romans said, "Let nothing of leather be admitted; therefore let no carrion come nigh" (*ne quod scorteum adhibeatur, ideo ne morticinum quid adsit*);[8] the fire must be sustained

[1] Livy, XXVI, 27, 14; *cf.* Fowler, *The Religious Experience of the Roman People*, 68 *ff.*, and *The Roman Festivals of the Period of the Republic*, 147 *ff.*

[2] 168 *ff.*   [3] Virgil, *Aeneid*, 11, 523.

[4] Th. Trede, *Das Heidentum in der Römischen Kirche*, IV, 1891, 415.

[5] V. Grönbech, *Vor Folkeaet*, 11, 1912, 57.

[6] K. Knortz, *Märchen und Sagen der nordamerikanischen Indianer*, 1871, No. 60. On the Saturday before Easter the "new light" is brought into Catholic churches candles being lit at the "new fire" to the accompaniment of the thrice repeated words, *lumen Christi*. When the light of salvation threatens to expire, a fresh one must be kindled; *cf.* J. Braun, S.J., *Liturgisches Handlexikon*², 1924, 86.

[7] Caland, *ibid.*, 144.

[8] Varro, *de lingua latina*, VII, 84; *cf.* Ovid, *Fasti*, I, 629 *f.* "It is not lawful to bring leather into her shrine, lest her pure hearths should be defiled by skins of slaughtered beasts" (Frazer).

> *Scortea non illi fas est inferre sacello,*
> *ne violent puros exanimata focos.*

by pure torches.[1] Its pure nourishment, however, could be strengthened by incantations and gestures: in many German dioceses, similarly, new fire was made and blessed after all the lights had been extinguished on Maundy Thursday, and all fresh lights and candles were lit at the new flame.[2] Such holy fire has purifying power: together with water it is the great means of purification; the "fire of the purifier", indeed, was accounted as much the more potent. John the Baptist speaks of baptism with fire,[3] and in rites of consecration the old lease of life was annulled by fire and a new one rendered possible.

Finally, fire has been transformed into even the World-principle, the idea of the hearth thus being expanded to colossal proportions. This occurred chiefly in India, where *Agni* was regarded as the universally vivifying Power, even in water. It is both human love and divine immortality: "Oh friend of all men, thou art the navel of the peoples, like a pillar standing fast thou supportest man."[4] Further: "One alone is *Agni*, who is kindled at many places; one alone the sun which penetrates all things. One alone the flush of dawn which shines over the whole world. One alone there is, and it has unfolded itself into the whole Universe."[5] To revere *Agni* the sublimest lines of the *Rig-Veda* were composed, while in the speculation of the West fire became, for Heracleitus, the *arche*, the ultimate substance and power of the Universe; and as rites gradually fell into disuse the ancient mode of controlling the renewed life was transposed, by the soul seeking firm rhythms, into the inner world-process; still the ruling force of the world, of the cosmos, is "an ever living fire, with measures of it kindling and measures being extinguished".[6] But at the Christian altar the eternal light, nourished not only by the soul, remained the assurance of an ever self-renewing Love.

KURT ERDMANN, *Das Iranische Feurheiligtum*, 1941.
AD. KUHN, *Die Herabkunft des Feuers und des Göttertrankes*[2], 1886.
M. NINCK, *Die Bedeutung des Wassers im Kult und Leben der Alten*, 1921.

[1] Virgil, *Aeneid*, VII, 71: *castis taedis*.
[2] Mannhardt, *Wald- und Feldkulte*, 503.
[3] *Matt.* iii. 11; *Luke* iii. 16. Here reference may also be made to the Mandean fire baptism.   [4] Bertholet, *op. cit.*, 9, 48.
[5] *ibid.*   [6] *Fr.* 30 (Diels; Cornford).

CHAPTER 7

THE SACRED WORLD ABOVE

1. WHEN man seeks the frontiers of his own being, he finds these within himself, in his environment, and in the world above. "Where heaven is, there is God", said an Ewe tribesman;[1] and it is easy to understand that heaven and its phenomena have not only always taken a prominent place in the poetry and thought of all peoples, but have also been the connecting links with the concepts of the "Wholly Other". For these the forms assumed by the celestial god, or gods, are unnecessary. Heaven, simply as such, preceded its characters or inhabitants. In Mexico, for instance, Preuss found that the concept of heaven, in its entirety, enjoyed precedence over that of the individual stars;[2] and in a different connection the relationship between heaven, or the celestial god, and the cosmic and social order, will at a later stage become more intelligible.[3] At present, however, we are investigating not the laws and ordered processes dominating human life from above, but those dramatic events in the upper world which seem to be parallel, or even akin, to those of the lower world of earth.

2. This implies that primitive man regards celestial events not as the domain of Law. He is by no means certain about the daily return of the heavenly light,[4] and the fear that the sun may some day fail in its course is to him in no way a mere phantom of the brain. The sun indeed, to our minds the pivot of the regularity of the whole solar system, appears to him neither constant nor even single; the Togo negroes, for example, formerly believed that each village had its own special sun, and it was only at a later date that they altered this opinion.[5]

The events of the higher world, therefore, form no completed process, but rather a revelation of Power. Life in the heavens deploys itself spontaneously just as it does on earth. The Cora Indians, for instance, speak of stars as "opening buds",[6] while in an ancient Babylonian hymn to Sin, the moon-god, the orb is styled "the fruit that

---

[1] J. Spieth, *Die Religion der Eweer*, 1911, 5.
[2] K. Th. Preuss, *Die geistige Kultur der Naturvölker²*, 1923.   [3] Chap. 18.
[4] Boll, *Die Sonne*, 9.   [5] Spieth, *ibid.*, 355.
[6] K. Th. Preuss, *Die Nayarit-Expedition*, I, 1912, XXXIX.

forms itself".[1] The old Egyptian heaven- or sun-god, again, was always called "he who originates from himself"; and thus in the world above potent life manifests itself.

But since this life is not yet subjected to any ordered regularity the "naturalness" of Nature, to our own minds so axiomatic, is absent. The powerful is apprehended, therefore, not in its invariability but in its potency, which can most forcibly reveal itself, but which may also withdraw itself or even fail altogether; the way in which primitive peoples interpreted eclipses of the sun and moon is universally familiar, and the Egyptians had a tradition relating how the sun, in its wrath, once deserted men and departed to a foreign country.[2] The primitive or semi-primitive mind, then, regards the daily return of light by no means as a matter of course, but as the subject of perpetual fear and hope. What Chesterton has said of sunrise in a fine passage—that it is no repetition but a theatrical *da capo*, and "that God says every morning, 'Do it again' to the sun; and every evening, 'Do it again' to the moon",[3] is genuinely "primitive" in feeling, just as his association of this type of idea with that of the fairy tale is quite correct.[4]

The feelings of hope and of anxiety connected with sunrise produced the great light myth, as this acquired its form in the most varied cultural circles. Light, the sun, or even the moon, is a conquering hero, a warrior who annihilates the monster of darkness. The sun "rejoiceth as a strong man to run a race";[5] while the magnificent Babylonian hymn addresses this acclamation to the moon:

> O Lord! Who is like unto thee? Who is equal to thee?
> Great hero! Who is like unto thee? Who is equal to thee?
> Lord Nannar! Who is like unto thee? Who is equal to thee?
> When thou liftest up thine eyes, who can flee?
> When thou drawest near, who can escape?[6]

The dawn of light is a triumph over enemies: the dragon, the snake, or some other atrocity of death and darkness is defeated; and this *light myth* dominates extensive tracts of the religious imagination in general: God as victor or as king—this entire realm of ideas is based on the dawn, while with it thoughts of creation are interwoven,[7] and the Christian Christmas symbolism of *crescit lux* is also a reinterpreta-

[1] Lehmann, *Textb.*, 302.
[2] K. Sethe, *Zur altägyptischen Sage vom Sonnenauge, das in der Fremde war*, 1912.
[3] *Orthodoxy*, Chap. IV, "The Ethics of Elfland", 107.
[4] Chap. 60. [5] *Ps.* xix. 5.
[6] H. Zimmern, *Babylonische Hymnen und Gebete*, II, 1911, 6. [7] Chap. 87.

tion of this natural process.[1] Victory and light, lordship and the sun:
they must all be connected together; and the relations between the
Roman imperator's dignity and conquering light have been con-
vincingly presented by Cumont, while in naming Cleopatra's twins
Helios and Selene, Antony designated them as *kosmokratores*—rulers
of the universe.[2]

The light myth, still further, may be concerned with the *sun* just
as much as with the *moon*. There are "moon peoples" as well as "sun
peoples", and in the history of a *single* nation, like the Babylonians,
there are both moon- and sun-periods. Argument over the priority of
sun or moon would be futile; both predominate in various places and
at different times,[3] and in many myths and fairy tales we find competition
between the two orbs.

3. The mighty events of the higher world arouse not merely reverence
on man's part; they are also regarded as a celestial model and source
of power. Between upper world and human world there prevails an
essential kinship, and the primeval sun riddle set by the Sphinx to
Oedipus reflects an even older idea:[4]

> When it rises in the morn
> It has four feet.
> When day turns to noon
> Two feet are granted it.
> As night comes on
> It stands on three feet.[5]

In a Slovak fairy tale the scullion asks the sun why he climbs higher
and higher in the morning, but sinks lower and lower in the afternoon.
The sun replies: "Ah, my dear fellow, ask your master why after birth
he grows bigger and bigger in body and strength, and why in old age
he stoops towards the ground and becomes weaker. With me it is just
the same. Each morning my mother gives birth anew to me as a beautiful
boy, and every evening she buries me as a feeble old man."[6]

In Egypt, where this comparison was familiar from quite early times,
the analogy between the sun's fate and that of man was transformed

[1] Boll, *Die Sonne*, 23.   [2] Boll, *ibid.*, 22.
[3] Ankermann, in Chantepie, *op. cit.*, I, 189.
[4] *cf.* P. Pierret, *Le Dogme de la Résurrection chez les Anciens Égyptiens*, 17.
[5] A fifteenth-century version in R. Köhler, *Kleine Schriften*, I, 1898, 115 *f*. The
Greek in Athanaeus, X, 456 B.
[6] H. Usener, *Kleine Schriften*, IV, 1913, 386 *ff*.

from the authentication of their parallel reviving and decease into a joyful belief in the renovation of human life. Just as each morning the sun renews its life, so it is with man, while death is no actual death but life with Ra, the sun-god. A very ancient *Text* says of a dead king: "His mother, the sky, gives birth to him, alive, each day that it pleases Ra; with him he rises in the East and with him sets in the West; so that on no day is his mother, the heavens, empty of him."[1] Man thus interweaves his own life with the greater and mightier continuity of Nature. Here again, however, this association is by no means regularly ordered, but is a quite spontaneous manifestation of the solar power. To the Romans, *mater matuta* was the goddess of the morning light and at the same time of birth.[2] He "who sees the light of the world" enters thereby into intimate relationship with the light that is his life.

Stars too were regarded as related to man; again and again we find the idea that the dead live again as stars in the heavens.[3] Similarly, the Egyptian custom of sewing a sun amulet into the grave linen is an instance of this way of bringing one's lot into close connection with celestial power.[4] It is just as if one were taking the solar potency with one into the grave.

4. The light of heaven is man's salvation. His life is bound up with the sun in its rising, as his death to its setting.[5] Many peoples sing and speak of the sun's treasure, preserved at the end of the world in the uttermost West, which the hero wins for himself. Thus Hermes steals the sun's cattle: here prosperity implies, in the good old antique way, the possession of cattle; but this can also be interpreted as gold, or a beautiful woman or some other treasure,[6] and countless fairy tales and myths relate how in this way heavenly bliss was attained. In all these narratives, however, the thought of death is always presupposed, since the sun's path of salvation traverses death. Hence the dreadful guardians of the hoard, the gloomy place whence the hero must fetch it, *etc.*

Sun-worship assumed its most magnificent raptures, as celestial

---

[1] *Pyramidentexte* (Sethe), 1835; *cf.* W. B. Kristensen, *Livet efter döden*, 1896, 69 *f.*
[2] G. Wissowa, *Religion und Kultus der Römer*[2], 1912, 97.
[3] Preuss, *Nayarit-Expedition*, XXX *ff.* As regards Egypt, Sethe, *Sage vom Sonnenauge*, 5, Note 2; *cf. Pyramidentexte*, 251.
[4] *Pyramidentexte*, 285: "Thou who in thy bonds seest Ra, who praisest him in thy fetters, as the great amulet which is in thy red linen clothing."
[5] Boll, *Die Sonne*, 17.
[6] H. Usener, *Kleine Schriften* IV, 1913, 44 *ff.*, 226 *ff.*, 464.

salvation, in ancient Egypt. There, under the influence of the priest-hood of the sun-city Heliopolis, immense temples were erected to the sun even as early as the first half of the third pre-Christian millennium; temples that were vastly different from the usual form of sacred Egyptian edifices. Worship was offered in the open at a great altar in the midst of a huge court; neither *naos* nor cult image played any part. Only a gigantic obelisk was erected on a colossal plinth: the old and probably originally phallic symbol of prosperity and fullness of power. Through a passage at first in semi-darkness, and then in com-plete obscurity, representing the sun's nocturnal course, the base of the obelisk was reached where the worshipper, his face turned to the East, greeted the rise of the victorious orb.[1] The Pharaohs of the Fifth Dynasty made this sun-worship their own unique privilege, and bringing their government into direct connection with the sun's triumph, called themselves "sons of Ra". This form of veneration continued to maintain its influence in Egypt until the revolution of the heretical Akhnaton effected its culmination, and procured for it a brief though glorious hegemony.[2] From this group of sun-concepts, still further, originated many beautiful hymns in which the universally nourishing, universally sustaining power, and the splendid victory of the celestial light, are celebrated; the crown of this type of literature, Akhnaton's hymn, interprets the triumph and guardianship of the divine power as truth and love. Nor is the latter lacking in the earlier hymns; for instance, in a hymn to Amon about 1420 B.C.:

> Thy love is in the Southern heaven,
> And thy grace in the Northern heaven.
> Thy beauty conquers all hearts,
> Thy love compels all arms to fall.[3]

While still finer and more impressively developed, we find in Akhnaton's hymn the starry loveliness side by side with victory and love:

> In beauty dost thou shine on the celestial horizon,
> Thou living Aton (sun) who art from of old.[4]

[1] F. W. von Bissing (and L. Borchardt), *Das Re-heiligtum des Königs Ne-Wsr-Rē*, I, 1905; cf. L. Borchardt, *Das Grabdenkmal des Königs Sa'ḥu-Re'*, 1910–13.
[2] G. van der Leeuw, *Achnaton. Een religieuze en aesthetische revolutie in de veertiende eeuw voor Christus*, 1928.—H. Schäfer, *Amarna in Religion und Kunst*, 1931.—A. de Buck, *De zegepraal van het licht*, 1930.—K. Sethe, *Urgeschichte und älteste Religion der Ägypter*, 1930.   [3] Al. Scharff, *Ägyptische Sonnenlieder*, 1922, 50.
[4] My *Achnaton*, 47. Scharff, *ibid.*, 61.

And it was certainly not the heart subduing beauty of sunlight that was the last thing to impress man as powerful; nor was it a mere accident that so many hymns were composed in honour of sun and moon in Babylon. In later times, too, the number of sun-songs was considerable; and in the fiercest stress of battle Aias implores Zeus to save him from the mist and allow him at least to die in the light, although the dramatic "mist" of insanity finally engulfs him; here once more are associated light, life and salvation.[1] Similarly for the poet of the *Antigone* the victorious sun's rays expel the enemy:

> Sunbeam, of all that ever dawned upon
>   Our seven-gated Thebes the brightest ray,
>   O eye of golden day,
> How fair thy light o'er Dirce's fountain shone,
> Speeding upon their headlong homeward course,
> Far quicker than they came, the Argive force;
>   Putting to flight
> The argent shields, the host with scutcheons white.[2]

The *poverello* of Assisi, on the other hand, although he regards the heavenly powers as God's creation and gift to humanity, still feels himself bound to them in a sort of brotherhood of all creatures:

> *Laudato si, mi signore, cum tucte le tue creature*
> *spetialmente messor lo frate sole,*
> *lo quale jorna, et illumini per lui;*
> *Et ellu è bellu e radiante cum grande splendore;*
> *de te, altissimo, porta significatione.*
> *Laudato si, mi signore, per sora lune e le stelle,*
> *in celu l'ai formate clarite et pretiose et belle.*[3]

Of course this relationship is a kind of monastic brotherhood, and no longer the primitive mind's interweaving with Nature. It is only divine *caritas* that sustains the community with Nature; and yet the sun continues to be the expression of the highest bliss:

> *de te, altissimo, porta significatione.*

[1] Boll, *Die Sonne*, 15.   [2] 100 *ff.* (Storr).
[3]   Praised be Thou, O Lord, with all Thy creatures,
In especial my brother, the sun,
Who brings the day, and through whom Thou shinest.
And he is beauteous and radiant in great splendour.
Of Thee, O Highest, he bears the image.
Praised be Thou, O Lord, for my sister the moon, and the stars;
In heaven Thou hast formed them bright, precious and lovely.

5. With the idea of coordinating Time according to the standard of events in the world above there appears, together with the revelation of spontaneous Power, a manifestation of immutably ordered regularity. Instead therefore of being incalculable, and incessantly requiring empirical verification, Power now becomes permanent and immovable.

From this viewpoint the Calendar[1] originated as the most familiar to us of a whole series of instances in which the terrestrial course of affairs has been adjusted to that of the heavens.[2] As it is above, so below:—this school of thought, quite inaccurately monopolized for the Near East as "the ancient Oriental concept of world-order", is in fact encountered all over the world wherever man has ceased to think altogether primitively, and has rendered his life absolute in Time by relating it to the still more potent life above. In one famous *Fragment*, previously cited in another connection, Heracleitus asserts that "the sun will not exceed his measures; if he does, the Erinyes, the avenging handmaids of Justice, will find him out".[3] This is the absolute antithesis of the idea of triumphant light: to all eternity the course of the heavenly bodies is unchangeable.

The stars too follow their immutable paths. Victory is here as it were crystallized into a triumph that knows no strife. The Egyptians were profoundly impressed by the constant presence and the unceasing return of the "everlasting" and "untiring" stars (those surrounding the Pole, and the planets)[4] and identified the fate of the dead with that of these immortal celestial bodies, while in Hellenism they became *dei aeterni*, the immutable controllers of human fate.[5]

The intimate connection between man and the depositories of Power, therefore, still persists. But now the incalculable and spontaneously operating potency has, in principle, become something that can be reckoned with; only it can no longer be resisted, and it is quite futile to curse it or pray to it; it is eternally exalted, arctically above both enmity and friendship. There is indeed, as A. van Gennep says, some kind of consistency in this advance from being linked with the activities in

---

[1] Chap. 55.
[2] *cf.* M. P. Nilsson, *Sonnenkalender und Sonnenreligion, AR.* 30, 1933. Herm. Fränkel, *Die Zeitauffassung in der archaiischen griechischen Literatur (Vierter Kongress für Ästh. u. allg. Kunstwiss. = Beilageheft z. Zeitschr. f. Ästh. u. allg. Kunstwiss.* 25), 1931, 97 *ff.*   [3] Diels, *Frag.* 94 (Burnet).
[4] *cf.* Kurt Sethe, *Altägyptische Vorstellungen vom Lauf der Sonne (Sitz. ber. d. preuss. Akad. der Wiss. phil. Kl.* 1928, XXII).
[5] F. Cumont, *Les anges du Paganisme, RHR.* 36, 1915, 159.

animal and vegetable life to being bound to the movement of the
Cosmos, to the *"grands rhythmes de l'univers"*;[1] and I by no means
dispute van Gennep's estimate of this idea as magnificent. In star-
worship, nevertheless, community with the arbitrarily capricious or
victorious Power became a subjection under the starry yoke. The
upper world was locked away: its life became a process, its might
a fate.

Thereby human life is astrologically predestined. In the earliest
times, for the Babylonians, the stars inscribed the "writing of the
heavens" from which the erudite could read his destiny. That was,
however, the only thing he could do. It is not at all to be wondered
at, then, that man revolted against this celestial tyranny: "The stars
who know in the midst of our laughter how that laughter will end,
become inevitably powers of evil rather than good, beings malignant
as well as pitiless, making life a vain thing. . . . The religion of later
antiquity is overpoweringly absorbed in plans of escape from the prison
of the seven planets."[2] Man hoped for an ascent of the soul from the
realm of the evil "elements of the world" ($\sigma\tau o\iota\chi\epsilon\hat\iota\alpha$ $\tau o\hat\upsilon$ $\kappa\acute o\sigma\mu o\upsilon$) into
the empyrean, the eighth sphere of the Universe, where Power does
not imply arbitrary rule.[3] He sought a *soter* to save him from the might
of the stars; Christ too saves "from the conflict and battle of the powers
and gives us peace from the strife of potencies and angels",[4] and the
Epistle to the Galatians opposes the liberty through Christ to the
former "thraldom of the Elemental spirits".[5] In sublime terms, too,
the *Epistle to the Romans* celebrates the love of Christ, from which no
"archontes", no planetary guardians nor celestial powers, which by
their sevenfold circle bar the way to the other refuge of the eighth
heaven, can ever separate us.[6] "From the moment of birth we begin
to die, and the end of life is closely allied to its beginning":[7] this
wisdom of the Roman poet accords at most with the possibility of a
science, but scarcely of a religion; and while astrology amalgamates
with many religions, it is itself a science,[8] knowledge about Power,
but neither its veneration nor utilization. This science had its origins
wherever, as in China and in ancient Greece, attempts were made to
delimit days and hours exactly, according to the position of the moon,

---

[1] *Les Rites de passage*, 1909, 279.
[2] Murray, *Five Stages of Greek Religion*, 180.
[3] Chap. 46.
[4] Clem. Alex. *Theod. Exc.* 71, 72.
[5] *Gal.* iv. 3; *cf. Col.* ii. 8.   [6] *Romans* viii. 37 *ff.*
[7] Manilius: *nascentes morimur, finisque ab origine pendet.*   [8] Chap. 72, 83.

stars, *etc.*,[1] and it attains its fullest bloom when every event in human
life is subjected to the almighty stars. At that stage no specific revelation
of Power in mankind can be thought of apart from some quite special
star: Augustus, for instance, had his *sidus julium*.[2] "His star", similarly,
led the wise men from the East to the manger at Bethlehem. In contrast
with this, however, the Talmudist explicitly declares: "Israel is subjected to no star, but to God alone."[3]

6. In so-called "Naturism"[4] we found the worship of Power manifesting
itself in the objects of Nature, and subsequently the clear recognition
of regulated order in the course of the Universe. In both standpoints,
still further, there subsist the presuppositions of later speculation.
The earliest Greek philosophers sought the origin and the sustaining
basis of all life in some single natural phenomenon, either water, air
or fire, which in its unity and divinity would include the manifold
diversities of the world as it presents itself to us: the ἀρχή is the essence
of the world, and at the same time its divinity. Here there enters in a
later Naturism, for which natural events constitute the order in life
and are, as such, divine precisely in virtue of this very orderliness.
Rousseau's worship of Nature, Goethe's "Nature in God, God in
Nature", seek the sacredness superior to humanity once more in
totality, in life in its entirety, whose austerely rational order bears
man safely over the confusion of the individual life.

But from the primitive viewpoint the essential distinction is that the
Greeks discovered the concept of Spirit; and any modern Naturism
must relate itself in some way to this Spirit, whether "the living garment
of God" surrounds the psychical core, or Nature ultimately accords
with this spiritual principle (as for Rousseau), or must serve as a
corrective in contrast with the malicious inventions of a degenerate
culture, as for the Encyclopaedists or Wagner.[5] The most recent
"Nature" speculation, however, that of the Nietzsche-Klages school,
appears once again to desire to follow this latter course. But exactly as
with its direct antithesis—the Christian-Greek contempt for "mere"

---

[1] *cf.* M. P. son Nilsson, *Die Enstehung und religiöse Bedeutung des griechischen Kalen-
ders* (*Lunds Univ. Aarsskrift*, N. F. Avd. 1, 14, 21), 35 *f.*
[2] H. Wagenvoort, *Vergils Vierte Ekloge und das Sidus Julium* (*Med. Kon. Akad. v.
Wet. Afd. Lett.* 67, A. 1, 1929).
[3] Troels-Lund, *Himmelsbild und Weltanschauung im Wandel der Zeiten*[4], 1929, 140 *f.*
[4] Chap. 5.
[5] In the first version of *The Ring of the Nibelung*; *cf.* P. M. Masson, *Rousseau et la
restauration religieuse*[2], 1916, 9 *ff.*

Nature—it is dependent on the concept of Spirit, which is completely absent from primitive religious thought.

F. BOLL, *Die Sonne im Glauben und in der Weltanschauung der alten Völker*, 1922.
  Sternglaube und Sterndeutung[2], 1919.
F. CUMONT, *Astrology and Religion among the Greeks and Romans*, 1912.
R. PETTAZONI, *Dio* I, 1922.
TROELS-LUND, *Himmelsbild und Weltanschauung im Wandel der Zeiten*[4], 1929.

CHAPTER 8

THE SACRED "CONJOINED WORLD". ANIMALS

1. WE must now discuss the sacred world of man himself, although the surrounding and the upper worlds must also be considered to be his. But the animals with which man lives pertain to his own domain, to himself, in a still more specific sense than does the rest of "Nature". Once again Chesterton is perfectly correct in saying that "we talk of wild animals; but man is the only wild animal. It is man that has broken out. All other animals are tame animals; following the rugged respectability of the tribe or type."[1] Humanity, however, does not always break loose, while "primitive" man does so far less frequently than "modern".[2] The contrast that Max Scheler and Buytendyk drew between man and animal, therefore, namely that the former objectivizes his environment and stands in an independent and superior relation to it, while the animal belongs to its surroundings, is not at all true of primitive mankind.[3] For he too appertains to his environing sphere and only rarely "objectivizes", it may be solely in magic,[4] and then only with the help of a Power that is superior to himself and to all else. For in this environment with which he feels himself intermingled he perceives again and again the revelation of Power, and as yet no "world", in our sense of the term, exists.

In this respect it is above all what is non-human that impels man to regard animals as being bearers of power. The strong non-human beast, essentially foreign to himself, is at the same moment very familiar to him first of all as hunter, and subsequently as cattle-breeder. This fusion of awe before superiority on the one hand, and on the other intimacy with the wholly familiar, enables us, if not to explain, at all events to understand, animal cults and Totemism.[5]

The animal's superiority can now be appreciated without more ado. For it controls powers wherein man himself is deficient: muscular strength, keenness of sight and smell, sense of direction and ability in tracking, flying, running with terrific speed, [6] *etc.* On the other hand

[1] *Orthodoxy*, 265.   [2] *cf.* van der Leeuw, *La Structure de Mentalité Primitive.*
[3] Max Scheler, *Die Stellung des Menschen im Kosmos*, 1928, 44 *ff.* F. J. J. Buytendyk, *Blätter für Deutsche Philosophie*, 3, 1929, 33 *ff.*
[4] Chap. 82.   [5] Ankermann in Chantepie, *op. cit.*, I, 169.
[6] *cf.* Lévy-Bruhl, *How Natives Think*, 38.

the significant distinction which, despite all evolutionary theories, we moderns presuppose between man and animal in our ordinary feelings and thoughts is not yet present. Thus of ancient Egypt Maspero writes: "The interval separating humanity from animals was almost non-existent. . . . Their (the animals') unions with the human race were fruitful, and it was no matter for surprise that the kings of Egypt should depict the sun-falcon as the head of their line and speak of the egg from which they had originated."[1] We find the same state of affairs to-day in the Indian Archipelago, where the indigenes recognize no essential differences between animal and man, and where marriage with animals, birth from and of animals, and animal descent are regarded as something quite ordinary. A Papuan relates for example: "on that island dwells one of my own relatives; long ago one of my ancestors gave birth to twins, a real child and an iguana; the mother suckled both, and when the iguana grew big she brought him to that island; there he still lives in a cave, and is allowed to survive because of the reverence felt for him. The crested dove and the black cockatoo also belong to my tribe. Towards the latter (adds the missionary who recounts this) he shows less respect, for he shoots them whenever he can and brings them to me, only someone else must carry them for him; he will never eat nor even touch them."[2] In fairy stories, in this respect also a faithful reflection of feeling about life in the past, man stands in a similarly intimate relationship to animals: they too treat animal birth and marriage as quite common events.

Thus the animal is on the one hand the non-human, the wholly different, the sinister or sublime: on the other it is intimately attached and familiar; and this union of both aspects renders the worship of the animal as a numinous object comprehensible.

The repellent and strange animal *par excellence* is the snake. It plays a part in numberless legends as a monster (dragon, *etc.*); its emerging from the ground connects it with the secrets of death, while its resemblance to the phallus, which constitutes it a sex symbol even in modern psychical experience, whenever this is released from repressions as in neurotic cases, relates it to the mystery of racial existence. Its potency is experienced chiefly as calamitous and menacing.

The familiar and most nearly related animal, again, is the domesti-cated beast. With different peoples domestication followed various

[1] G. Maspero, *Études de Mythologie et d'Archéologie Égyptiennes*, 1893–99, II, 213.
[2] A. C. Kruyt, *Het Animisme in den Indischen Archipel*, 1906, 120 ff.

courses. The pig and dog are regarded here as impure (that is as sacred, but sinister), there as friends of mankind. Cattle are the best loved of all domestic animals, and the religions of India and ancient Persia compete in their esteem. Even to-day, as in olden times, cattle urine is the principal Indian means of purification, while the cow's life is sacred. The modern Hindu sends one that has become useless out into the jungle, where it is torn to pieces by dogs, or sells it to the (Mohammedan) butcher; but he will not kill it himself.

The domestic animal ranks as a member of the family. It is not so long ago that in Eastern Holland the death of the farmer was ceremonially announced to his cattle, and even to his bees; similarly the country folk in the province of Gelderland speak of "bees' luck" which is granted to worthy people; the bridal pair, too, entreats the bees for their blessing on the marriage.[1] The ancient Greeks regarded the killing of the ox as the slaying of their own brother, laments for the death of the victim being uttered during the sacrifice.[2] Not so long ago animal trials were actual institutions; the beasts could appear as witnesses, accused and plaintiffs. In 1565 the inhabitants of Arles demanded the expulsion of the grasshoppers, and the contemporary *Tribunal de l'Officialité* dealt with the suit, *Maître* Marin undertaking the representation of the insects and defending their cause with great zeal. But the grasshoppers were sentenced to depart under penalty of excommunication, and even as recently as 1845 an animal trial occurred in France.[3]

Thus if on the one hand the feeling of the equality, or even of the superiority, of the powerful animal proved itself very tenacious, yet on the other attempts have long been in progress to rationalize animals out of these human relationships. It was preferable, therefore, that the wife of Faustulus, Acca Larentia, should be a whore (*lupa*) rather than a she-wolf (*lupa*).[4] As was the case also with potent things, however, the return to primitive feeling can be discovered only by the poet, it may be by the path of longing:

I think I could turn and live with animals, they are so placid
    and self-contain'd,
I stand and look at them long and long.[5]

---

[1] H. W. Heuvel, *Oud-achterhoeksch boerenleven*, 1927, 227.
[2] G. Murray, *The Rise of the Greek Epic*, 86 *ff*. Odyssey, 3, 415 *ff*.
[3] E. Westermarck, *The Origin and Development of the Moral Ideas*, I, 254 *f*.
[4] Plutarch, *Romulus*, 4, 3.
[5] Whitman, *Leaves of Grass*: "Song of Myself", 32.

2. With the idea of the powerful animal Totemism is closely connected. It may be true that a totem may also be a plant, or indeed some
natural phenomenon; yet "the animal totem predominates to such an
extent, and one receives so firm an impression that everything else is
of later origin, that the relationship of man to animal may be regarded
as the real core of Totemism".[1]

There is individual Totemism, and also social; the former, however,
is better termed *Nagualism*, in accordance with the relevant belief of
the inhabitants of Central America or, with that of the North Americans,
Manituism.[2] From the second designation it is clear that it is a matter
of the appropriation of, and connection with, the animal's power;
thus a young Red Indian goes into the wilderness, where in a dream
his totem animal appears to him and unites itself with him, while among
the Eastern Eskimo, Kagsagsuk is a sort of Soft Johnnie, mocked and
ill-treated until on a lonely spot in the mountains he finds the *amarok*,
a demonic beast which endows him with gigantic strength.[3] In Mexican
beliefs, again, the gods also have a *nagual*, a personal protective spirit.[4]

This individual guardian spirit is closely related to the "external
soul" residing in an animal, with which we shall become acquainted
at a later stage.[5] The potency of the superior animal, still further,
becomes experienced as human power; Wundt therefore refers to
"animal souls", and from this idea attempts to derive that of totem
ancestors.[6]

But with this we reach social Totemism proper. The term itself
originated with an English interpreter, John Long, who first employed
it in 1791 in the sense of a well-meaning spirit which guards men in the
form of an animal, and which because of its protection is never killed
nor eaten [7] In modern research, however, Totemism has become the
subject of interminable dispute, in which the expression is used most
variously in the loosest and vaguest senses and with the most arbitrary
limitations. Not only do different investigators arrive at and formulate
diverse conclusions, but a single *savant* like Frazer has contrived in
the course of time to evolve three distinct theories about Totemism.
In spite of all this, as generally recognized features of the phenomenon
there may legitimately be considered: (*1*) the well-being of some human

---

[1] Ankermann in Chantepie, *op. cit.*, I, 165 f.   [2] Chantepie, I, 171 f.
[3] W. Krickeberg, *Indianermärchen aus Nordamerika*, 1924, No. 6.
[4] W. Krickeberg, *Märchen der Azteken und Inkaperuaner*, 1928, No. 4 and Note.
[5] Chap. 42.   [6] Wundt, *Völkerpsychologie*, IV, 358 f.
[7] Reuterskiöld, *Der Totemismus*, (*AR*. 15, 1912) I; A. van Gennep, *Religions,
Mœurs et Légendes*, 1908–1914, I, 51.

community is irrevocably bound up with the totem; and from this we may, but need not necessarily, (a) infer that the group bears the name of the totem: (b) the totem is accounted its ancestor. (2) The totem involves sundry tabus: such are (a) the prohibition of killing, or eating; but in specific cases or under special conditions the command to eat may itself become imperative, because contact between the totem and the social group must be strengthened: (b) the prohibition of inter-marriage within the same totem group (so-called exogamy). By the enumeration of these characteristics, however, we have gained no genuine understanding of Totemism; and this we can achieve, so far as the modern mind can ever succeed, only if we duly consider its religious basis. Of course totems are by no means gods, and they are as a rule not "worshipped" in the sense that sacrifices and the like are offered to them. But it is a failing of modern thought that, in connection with the term religion, it must immediately think of "gods". Totemism, however, needs no gods; but it implies submergence within the power of some animal. "When man in the hunting stage . . . forced by the necessity of life and his unvarying daily occupation, thinks only of animals which are at the same moment his enemies and his food, if as it were he merges himself wholly in the animal, then it is only natural that this content of his consciousness should press for expression";[1] and this submersion in the being of a superior power, which can nevertheless be subjugated, constitutes the essence of Totemism and transforms it into a religion. Everything social is merely secondary, and is the consequence of the experience of Power. The totem animal, as a group, is a sort of reservoir for the potency of the tribe or clan.[2]

On the totem depends the life of the community. The Bantu tribe of the Ba-ronga says of the buffalo, "the magician of the plain" which executes all sorts of tasks: "our whole life depends upon him"; if he dies there is nothing left for the tribe but collective suicide. There is in this instance no question of "Totemism" in the sense of a social system with totem classes, etc., such as is to be found in Australia; all the requisite presuppositions, however, are already present,[3] and we approach a further stage nearer this system when the essential relationship with the animal is indicated in the form of descent. An Amandabele youth, for example, refuses to milk a certain cow: "it is

[1] Ankermann in Chantepie, op. cit., I, 169.
[2] Saintyves, Force magique, 56 and Note 2; Reuterskiöld, op. cit., 20 ff; cf. B. Schweitzer, Herakles, 1922, 82.
[3] Carl Meinhof, Afrikanische Märchen, 1921, No. 20.

too powerful for him, he is afraid to milk his mother".[1] If this point of view becomes systematic, then derivation from the totem can be taken into account instead of mere connection by blood. The totem poles, therefore, bearing the animal at the top and beneath this a series of ancestors, are (as Wundt remarks) a sort of impersonal family tree;[2] with other instances, they occur in North America.[3] It is mainly in Australia that we find any very intricate totem system in which the totem provides the standard for the entire social organization of the community.

If, however, we start not from this system, but from the idea of the accumulation of power in some animal species, then we can understand the many residues of this standpoint persisting in less primitive cultural complexes. To say, for example, that the ancient Egyptians were totemists is undeniably nonsensical, if we mean by this that they accepted a totemistic system. But it is not absurd if we mean merely the idea of essential relationship with the animal and the possibility of subsisting upon this animal's power. In this latter sense the Egyptians, as we have already seen, were certainly totemists, and a similar state of affairs holds good for the bear and wolf tribes in the old Germanic world.[4]

3. For in the intimate relationship between animal and man the former can be man, and man animal. Thus in fairy tales the animal, which was originally merely such, has become an enchanted prince, while whoever allows himself to be duly impressed by the stories of the Indians of North and South America, must feel that to their minds there was no distinction whatever between the animal and the human being. Marriage and birth, war and treaty bind them together; and hardly any metamorphosis is necessary to make an animal out of man, or conversely. This transposition becomes more imperative as the contrast between the two is more clearly grasped, and then so-called *Lycanthropy* comes into existence. Although this is best known under the form of man moving about in the guise of a wolf, the fusion of animal and man is by no means pure lycanthropy in the proper sense. In Indonesia the crocodile and dog, the cat, but above all the tiger, are "werewolves",[5] while in ancient Germanic times we find the *berserkr*, the "bear-skinned man" who can transform himself into the bear's

---

[1] Fourie, *Amandebele*, 106.   [2] Wundt, *op. cit.*, IV, 331.
[3] Besson, *Le Totémisme*, 1929, Plates XXIII *ff.*
[4] Grönbech, *Vor folkeaet*, II, 1912, 98 *ff.*   [5] Kruyt, *Animisme*, 190 *ff.*

shape. But here too the genuine werewolf occurs; Sigmundr and Sin-fjötli lurk in the forest in wolf form; this belief, indeed, was influential until quite recently, and crimes were perpetrated with it as a cloak.[1] Behind it there lies an ecstatic experience; the animal is the completely "Other", to which man flees for refuge when he is satiated with humanity. The women of the Dionysian cult sought the divine in the animal. They lived themselves, as it were, entirely into the animal not from love of "animalism" in any modern sense, since the idea was not then in existence! but only in order to gain freedom from them-selves. As in Euripides' magnificent description:

> And one a young fawn held, and one a wild
> Wolf cub, and fed them with white milk, and smiled
> In love, young mothers with a mother's breast,
> And babes at home forgotten.[2]

In the cult of Dionysus the animal was precisely the god with whom man sought to unite himself.

The same thing occurred in regularized worship. Animal masks were everywhere used in sacred games and dances to invest the performers with the characters of the (divine) animals. One played the animal, therefore, in order to be identical with it and to utilize its power. The "bees" was the name given to the priestesses of Demeter, and "fillies" to others, while the girl dancers of Artemis Brauronia were regarded as "she-bears".[3] From animal mask-dances, in fact, Greek tragedy originated.

Worship of animals, as ascribed by us and by the ancients to the Egyptians above all other peoples, is found among almost all races even if only in its rudiments. The Power that makes itself known to man in field and forest, in mountains and water, was very frequently perceived in animal form, the spirit of the corn being a buck or hare when it is not an old woman. It is then no matter for surprise that many of the "high gods" also exhibit animal characteristics, and this not in Egypt only. Demeter, whose priestesses were fillies, was herself a mare which foaled the colt Areion by the stallion Poseidon;[4] similarly Dionysus was a bull, and was invoked in that form by the women of Elis.[5]

---

[1] Charles de Coster gives a most realistic description, *La légende d'Ulenspiegel et de Lamme Goedzak*; *cf.* Bruno Gutmann, *Volksbuch der Wadschagga*, 1914.

[2] *The Bacchae*, 699 *ff.* (Murray).

[3] *cf.* van der Leeuw, *Goden en Menschen in Hellas*, 1927, 37.

[4] Pausanias, VIII, 24, 4.   [5] G. van der Leeuw, *ibid.*, 112.

Thus the slaughter of the animal-god had the same sacramental character as the killing of the totem. In ancient Rome the October horse (*october equus*) was sacrificed by the *flamen martialis* after it had won the race. The blood from the tail was in part allowed to drip on the sacred hearth of the *regia* and in part preserved in the sanctuary of Vesta (*penus Vestae*), while its severed head was contended for by the men belonging to two wards, the *via sacra* and the *subura*, being nailed by the victors to the *regia* or to the Mamilian tower, *turris mamilia*, until the next festival; the animal was the bearer of the harvest plenteousness, and from its neck a garland of cakes was suspended *ob frugum eventum*—for the vigorous growth of the fruits.

Not only the potency of vegetation was thus sustained by animals: in every sphere they were the superior and the wise. Animals played a part in the foundation legends of very many cities, as did the she-wolf in Rome, the pig in Alba, *etc.*; they were permitted to go their own way, leading where no human wisdom could ever reach. Similarly two "milch kine" that had borne no yoke carried the ark of the covenant back to the land of Israel so that it became dangerous to the Philistines.[1]

Animals now remain potent only in fairy tales, and only on coats of arms do they still retain their ancient magnificence; but these escutcheons were once the symbols of a life that linked itself to a stable form of superhuman existence.

M. Besson, *Le totémisme*, 1929.
J. G. Frazer, *Totemism and Exogamy*, 1910.
A. van Gennep, *Religions, Mœurs et Légendes*, 1908–1914.
V. Hehn, *Kulturpflanzen und Haustiere*[8], 1911.
E. Reuterskiöld, *Der Totemismus* (*AR*. 15, 1912).
    Die Entstehung der Speisesakramente, 1912.

[1] 1 *Samuel* vi. 7.

WILL AND FORM

1. THE principle that the environing and the higher worlds form the world conjoined with primitive man, and that their sacredness can be experienced only in a most intimate community of essential nature, finds yet another expression besides that implied by the term "Power". For Power acquires *Will*. The environment, that is to say, not only shares man's life and exercises an intense influence over him, but also "wills" something with regard to man, who on his own part desires something therefrom.

A hint of these conditions subsists in the *theory of Animism* as, in its classical form, it dominated speculation for a long time, chiefly owing to Tylor's outstanding research. But actually it is little more than a hint; for in its entire structure and tendency this theory suits the second half of the nineteenth century far better than it does the primitive world!

It sets out from psychological data. While Dynamism attempts to understand the experience of the environment in its potency, Animism aims at interpreting it as an encounter between two wills, or souls or spirits:—those of man and of his surroundings. This is its core and its permanent significance. But unfortunately much more than this was appended to it, starting from dream experience. For in one's own dream we make long journeys; in another person's dream we can also appear to other people, since others can see me in dream exactly as I am. Conversely, I can meet others if I dream about them. But during the dream my body and theirs demonstrably remain quietly in the same place. There must then be a certain "Something" that can release itself from the body:—the Soul. Besides the dream, again, there is another condition in which this soul appears to have left the body:—Death, when the body lies apparently lifeless. Nevertheless the "Something" must continue to live somehow or other. For dead people too meet us in our dreams, appear to us, and we speak to them. There must therefore be an existence of the soul after death.

Such is the psychology of Animism. But the animist requires a cosmology as well, since he is surrounded by a spontaneously active world. Now human motion always depends on the soul's presence, apart from which torpidity sets in. The movements of Nature, therefore, waves in the waters, the flame of fire, but also the rustling in tree-tops, and rolling stones, have now to be explained similarly to man's movements. "Their (primitive men's) own personality and feelings are . . . the sole causally connected material for observation at their disposal for forming their ideas about Nature; with these observational data they put together their picture of Nature . . .";[1] and thus man argues from himself to the world and concludes that not he alone, but also all objects which move of themselves, have souls.

The whole world, then, is full of "spirits". Seas, lakes, waters, mountains, caverns, trees, forests, villages, towns, houses, the air, the heavens, the underworld: all these things and places are regarded as possessed of souls, as for example by the inhabitants of the island of Nias, near Sumatra.[2] And thus it is with countless peoples.[3] But when we go on to ask how primitive humanity came to regard not only animals as possessed of souls, but also all kinds of objects that manifestly never even have life, then the animistic theory gives two different answers. In the first place, a sort of malady of thought is supposed to have induced man to do this, just as it leads our own children to speak of the "naughty table" which has hit them, and to look on Teddy Bear as an actually living creature. But it may also well be that this malady of thought was caused by a disease of language; for this itself presupposes personification. We say—and must say: the storm howls, the sea glitters, the sun shines; but we know that the storm, the sea and the sun are not really active agents. The primitive mind, however, did not know this, but was led into personifying by language which had become accustomed to divide the surrounding world into male and female —masculine and feminine—beings.[4]

All this is of course a regrettable error, from which man recovers as soon as he has reached the grown-up era of the nineteenth century! But if we leave the erroneous, indeed the pathological, aspect aside for a moment, then little objection need be raised against Animism as an explanatory theory of the world. Tylor, indeed, admired its logical conclusiveness; in his opinion Animism is "a thoroughly coherent and rational philosophy", supported too by the conviction, familiar also to ourselves, that effects presuppose causes; the "effects" are the phenomena of movement, the "causes" are the "spirits". These spirits

---

[1] Nieuwenhuis, *Die Wurzeln des Animismus, Int. Arch. Ethnogr.* 24, Supp., 1917, 61.

[2] Wilken, *Verspreide Geschriften*, 1912, III, 233 f.

[3] Alviella, *L'Idée de Dieu*, 1892, 107.   [4] Alviella, *op. cit.,* 60 ff.

are really nothing other than "personified causes". And Nieuwenhuis still regards Animism as essentially the same primitive science, refers to "syllogisms" and looks upon the necessity for causality as its basic ground.

2. But it is quite incomprehensible how this theory about the inter-connectedness of the world should be a religion, indeed the origin of all religion. For "the soul cult" and "the cult of ancestors" are evidently something more than philosophical interpretations of the causal nexus. The animistic theory, in fact, attempted to explain primitive conscious life according to the model of Anglo-French Positivism, and in so doing simultaneously to account for the origin of religion! and by this failure duly to estimate religion it was wrecked. This was realized on many sides—even on the positivistic itself. Söderblom in Scandinavia, Marett in England, Durkheim in France, Preuss in Germany, Kruyt in Holland and a series of other investigators have accumulated a whole arsenal of objections to Animism. They are mainly the following: (*a*) Animism does not make it comprehensible why souls suddenly become worshipped after death; and incidentally, that is not the case at all with a great many "souls". This omission arises, however, from: (*b*) the fact that Animism did not recognize the concept of Power; it failed to realize therefore that worship always depends on the sub-stantiation of Power. Because of this it also overlooked the fact that the universal animation of Nature and in artificial objects, or the possibility of their being charged with potency, is by no means always bound up with the idea of "soul"; for something can live and be power-ful, can indeed be worshipped, without having any "soul" whatever attributed to it.[1] But the soul theory—and this is probably the chief defect—(*c*) is treated in a one-sided rationalistic way; Animism failed to perceive that, in the concept of souls or spirits, something like faith must be present. It forgot too that dream theory cannot be the origin of belief in souls and in the dead, in spirits and gods, unless these ideas have already been introduced into the dream from other sources; further, it overlooked the fact that primitive man, who had to struggle with dire necessity to wring sustenance from his surroundings, was hardly inclined to "philosophize" about "causes". It also completely misunderstood the intimate fusion of every *Weltanschauung*, and of all religion, with experience. Still further: (*d*) the relationship between the spirits of the dead and those of Nature is by no means clear. Of

[1] *cf.* here Otto, *Gefühl des Überw.*, 68.

course it does happen that spirits of the departed lurk hidden in mountains, *etc.*, but this is no justification for setting up the worship of the dead as a general principle to explain the endowment of Nature with a soul. Again, (*e*) the entire construction of the idea of "universal endowment with souls" rests on a gigantic error, so that according to Animism it must be supposed that humanity began, like the child, with untruths, whilst ultimately (*f*) even the analogy with the child cannot be maintained, since the child knows quite well that Teddy Bear is not alive and only makes the animal live from time to time under the stress of emotion. It would be astounded, as Durkheim remarks, if the bear actually bit it!

3. That, roughly, is the record of the sins of Animism: and it is undeniably a long record. But if only we release the facts with which it begins from the theory itself, then it becomes evident that Animism has great and permanent significance. For we can now start afresh with the child who endows its toys with life. As has just been seen, it does this under the influence of emotion. It desires to have life around it and to find another will opposed to its own; so it personifies its toys, or even things not intended as toys at all. "Personifies" is actually too calculated, too rationalistic an expression; we had better say: it grants to the lifeless and soulless object *Will and Form*. Even the latter: perhaps the cushion represents an elephant, or the broom an aunt! But the child does not wish to explain anything thereby, and to him the assigning of will is the expression of his own "immediate childish world-experience".[1] The question as to why "primitive man and the child see the world as a picture of personal life", then, is quite futile. "On the contrary, we must ask ourselves: Why do we ever lose this natural mode of observation, so that we can restore it only by artificial means?"[2] But the motive for so-called personification, at all events, lies in experience. And by the investigators of so-called pre-animistic tendency this experience was universally discerned in the necessity, in the incessant danger and the constant crisis, which threatened primitive life. These arouse the feeling of dependence upon an arbitrary will (as with the "animist" Nieuwenhuis);[3] they awaken the consciousness that someone, spirit or god, is either inimical or well disposed towards man. In this there is undoubtedly much truth, although we should

[1] A. A. Grünbaum, *Zeitschr. f. pädag. Psychologie*, 28, 1927, 456.
[2] *ibid.*, 457.   [3] Nieuwenhuis, *op. cit.*, 15.

do better not to imagine too much about primitive man's life in his primeval forest!

For this need still exists in our own case in the modern world. We too are animists, though we do our best to forget it! And children and poets are not victims of any maladies, nor mentally deficient, but human beings whose emotional life casts off certain artificial constraints. And in this respect the human experience which evokes the animistic endowment with will and creation of form appears to be a very general one: *Solitude*. He who lives in subjection to Powers is solitary. Whether Power stands confronting him, or whether he knows himself to be one with it, or indeed understands how to control it in some magical way— it still leaves him lonely. In his environment, then, man seeks not merely "the world of mankind", but his own equal, a will:

> Unlocked the spirit-world doth lie,
> Thy sense is shut, thy heart is dead![1]

"It is not that the child begins to endow the moon, which was originally presented to him as inanimate Nature, with psychic charac- teristics, but the moon is presented to the child from the outset as a being . . . endowed with a soul."[2] In the crisis of solitude therefore, which probably bore very severely on primitive man even though it is only too well known to ourselves, he succeeded in giving the Powers a will and a form. And this induced all the possibilities of objectification, of speaking and being addressed, of malediction and entreaty, of revela- tion and of the self-concealing God.

For primitive man, just as for our peasants, the changeful seasons were the really important factors in life together with the great events of birth, marriage and death. That Winter, like Spring, is a power which one can control by observing the rites, was for that reason something self-evident to the primitive mind. At all events the malicious or beneficent potencies of the season now became a will, a demon of fertility or a god of the harvest, which could be invoked, encountered or expelled. This is Animism. Few examples are necessary here, as we shall discover an abundance in later chapters. For in the three terms *Power*, *Will* and *Form*, there lies practically the entire concept of the Object of Religion.[3]

---

[1] *Faust*, Part I.   [2] Grünbaum, *ibid.*, 459.

[3] The term "Form", *Gestalt*, is one of the most important in the present work. It is best understood by referring to recent "*Gestalt* Psychology", which maintains that every object of consciousness is a whole or a unit, and is not merely constituted by the

In Suabia, Sweden and the Netherlands the fruit trees are wrapped in straw at Christmas time so that they shall bear heavily;[1] this is an attempt to retain and concentrate the potency of the trees, and consequently an instance of Dynamism. But if the farmer goes into the orchard, as in Pillersee, to strike the trees and call out to them: "Wake up, tree! To-night is Christmas Eve, bear many apples and pears once more", then that rests on presupposing a will and a possibility of persuading the tree, and therefore constitutes Animism, although certainly of a rudimentary type. A more fully developed Animism emerges, again, when the power of the tree is regarded as a "tree spirit", a dryad or woodsprite or whatever else it may be styled, and acquires the potentiality of free movement.

Here, however, we must guard against stating the relationship between Animism and Dynamism in such a way that the former is looked upon as the successor of the latter in point of time, as often happened owing to the gratification arising from the early discovery of "Power" and the influence of the unfortunate term "Preanimism". In many cases, certainly, we can show how impersonal power received will and form. But at all periods there has been Dynamism as well as Animism, while both still exist to-day side by side: the saint, who hears prayer, is a form and has a will, while his wonder-working relics are a power. Animism and Dynamism therefore designate not eras, but structures, and are as such eternal. It is a cheap amusement to point out the "error" that consists in regarding holy water as being especially potent, or in ascribing the growth of crops to a will. It is just as easy to smile at the "mistaken" belief in the power of baptism, or at the pious delusion that disease is cured by some superior will interfering. Poets and children, none the less, to whom it is quite natural to be confronted by power and will, know that this "error" is no error at all, but rather a living vision of reality. And just like children, poets are

elements that analysis may discover; the English name of this system is usually "Configuration Psychology". "Endowment with Form", and again "Form Creation" in this sense, will appear in what follows as equivalents for the allied term *Gestaltung*. But it is vitally important to observe that, throughout this volume, all Forms are visible, or tangible, or otherwise perceptible; and thus Endowment with Form, or Form Creation, indicates the gradual crystallization of the originally formless feelings and emotions into some kind of perceptible and unified Forms; *cf.* further Chap. 65, Section 2.

[1] O. von Reinsberg-Düringsfeld, *Das festliche Jahr*[2], 1898, 460. H. W. Heuvel, *Oud-achterhoeksch boerenleven*, 473: in Gelderland the farmer went *met bloote gat*—in his shirt—into the orchard: an example of the nakedness rite often found in fertility customs.

accustomed to look more deeply into Reality than anthropologists and historians!

4. With penetrating insight, Söderblom has given prominence to the profound significance of Animism in its connection with Dynamism and so-called primal religion. "In the impersonal Power of the *mana*-type there dawns the realization that the divine penetrates the whole Universe and is in its essence supernatural. The belief in souls and spirits initiates the apprehension of a spiritual presence which, more closely defined, is a realm of will: at first of capricious and arbitrary individuals but subsequently, as the result of prophetic influence or some other ethico-religious achievements, of a more rational, more personal and more moral Being acting from inner laws."[1] Certainly "spiritual" should not be interpreted in our sense. For Power which acquires a Will also receives a Form: Will and Form together constitute "personality" as this dominates mythical modes of thought, exactly as the most up-to-date science of "substance and force", or "energy and atom", is unable to dispense with it.

The distinction between Dynamism and Animism may also be stated thus: the "extraordinary" in Dynamism is the "unexpected" in Animism. Now what is unanticipated emanates not from Power but from Person. Thus man can complain about the incalculability of the events of the world in accordance with animistic ideas and, if this is done in such fine terms as Alviella employs, we will listen gladly: "There was nothing but chance, caprice, at most custom (in natural processes). They (primitive men) were not certain that the light of day, once it had disappeared, would return in the morning, and just as little sure that Summer would follow Winter. If after the sun has departed it approaches again each Spring, if the moon each month reassumes its lost form, if rain ends drought, if the wind dies away— all this occurs because these beings so desire it; but who knows if they always will desire it, or will always be capable of it?"[2] But I scarcely feel inclined, with Alviella, to prefer the fixed order and the brazen law of a modern *Weltanschauung*, "based on the natural sciences", to this arbitrariness. For we must realize how there subsists in this capriciousness the possibility of the good, as well as of the evil, will— of the devil as of God, of sin as of grace, of the drama of God and man.

We have been reminded too, and with perfect justice, that without that affirmation of Will in the Universe and in man which constitutes

---

[1] *Gottesglaube*, 283.   [2] *L'Idée de Dieu*, 178 *f.*

Animism, Plato's philosophy could never have been formulated; while to this Kant's may be added, and if we consider Form, Pheidias and Raphael too. From this fertile mother, whose name is *Form-creation*, spring morality, psychology, theory of knowledge, poetry and painting; but if we wish to insult her we call her Mythology! More important than Plato and Raphael, however, are Moses and St. Paul: Jahveh is an animistic God not so much because He originates from the mount, or personates the wind, but because He is nothing other than Will, than burning passionate activity. Supreme activity, again, allied with lowliest form—but what a form!—appears to us in Jesus. And with his fine feeling for primitive values, Chesterton has here too expressed beautifully how intimately connected are arbitrary will and love, fear and adoration: "For a man walking down a lane at night can see the conspicuous fact that as long as nature keeps to her own course, she has no power with us at all. As long as a tree is a tree, it is a top-heavy monster with a hundred arms, a thousand tongues, and only one leg. But so long as a tree is a tree, it does not frighten us at all. It begins to be something alien, to be something strange, only when it looks like ourselves. When a tree really looks like a man our knees knock under us. And when the whole universe looks like a man we fall on our faces."[1]

A. BERTHOLET, *Von Dynamismus zu Personalismus;* in *Pro Regno Pro Sanctuario*, studies for van der Leeuw's 60th year, 1950, 35 *ff.*

CTE. GOBLET D'ALVIELLA, *L'Idée de Dieu*, 1892.

A. C. KRUYT, *Het Animisme in den Indischen Archipel*, 1906.

G. VAN DER LEEUW, *La Structure de la mentalité primitive*, 1928.

L. LÉVY-BRUHL, *How Natives Think.*

A. W. NIEUWENHUIS, *Die Wurzeln des Animismus*, Int. Arch. Ethnogr. 24, Suppl., 1917.

R. OTTO, *Das Gefühl des Überweltlichen*, 1932.

K. TH. PREUSS, *Die geistige Kultur der Naturvölker*[2], 1923.

E. B. TYLOR, *Primitive Culture*[4], 1903.

G. A. WILKEN, *Verspreide Geschriften*, 1912.

[1] *Heretics*, "Science and the Savages"; Chap. XI, 152.

CHAPTER 10

THE FORM OF THE MOTHER

1. "SEARCH out the ancient mother", old Bachofen warned us years ago.[1] Science has never wholly ignored this admonition, although the peculiar and profound, yet somewhat obscure, theories of this romantic *savant* have only very recently gained due attention. "There is nothing more sacred on earth than the religion of the mother, for it leads us back to the deepest personal secret in our souls, to the relationship between the child and its mother"; in these terms Otto Kern has crystallized the essence of our theme.[2] Believing that behind Power he decries the outlines of a Form, man recognizes therein the features of his own mother; his loneliness when confronted with Power thus transforms itself into the intimate relationship to the mother. Modern psychoanalysis has opened the eyes of many of us to the weighty and all-dominating significance of the mother-form in adult life; while the poets, the sole genuine animists and realists in the midst of a theorized world, have felt the need of this somewhat forced awakening, bound up though it is with so many disagreeable new speculations. Similarly St. Francis, in the marvellous hymn already quoted, speaks of "our sister Mother-earth, who sustains and cares for us, and produces so many kinds of fruit together with grasses and beautifully coloured flowers".[3]

World events are now no longer any play of potencies: they are all reduced to the one great and mysterious happening: *Birth*. Movement and change, coming into being and passing away, are now a being born and a return to the womb. The Mother is the all-nourishing earth: life is to be born of Mother-earth, death is to enter in to her; and this too the poets have never forgotten: the old man who cannot die, in Chaucer's *Canterbury Tales*, sighs and groans:

> Thus walke I, lyk a restelees caityf,
> And on the ground, which is my modres gate,
> I knokke with my staf, bothe erly and late,
> And seye: "leve moder, leet me in!"[4]

[1] *Urreligion und antike Symbole*; *antiquam exquirite matrem.*
[2] *Die griechischen Mysterien der klassischen Zeit*, 1927, 24.
[3] *Laudato si, mi Signore, per sora nostra matre terra,*
la quale ne sustenta et governa
et produce diversi fructi con coloriti flori et herba.
[4] *The Pardoners Tale.*

In Greece the oldest divine forms were Earth-mothers. Men, and likewise fountains, stones, plants, *etc.*, were all regarded not as created nor made, but as born, autochthonous.[1] To the Greeks the earth was a form, only not in the plastic Homeric sense: she was a woman with half her body above the ground; and she lacked the mobility of the later great celestial gods: she was half Power, half human. But she *was* human, and bore her progeny in human fashion. She was styled Pandora—when not simply *Ge*, the earth—because she poured out all from her rich treasure, her coffer, which became a dangerous miracle box only to the eyes of a moralizing age. And although her motion was restricted, one movement was always assured to her: her uprising in Spring, when to all creatures she brought new life.

Many were her names: she was called Athene, *kourotrophos*, the "great mother", the many breasted: in Asia, Ephesia: by the Greeks, Artemis, Diktynna or Britomartis; she was a wild natural power, at home in forest and mountain. Probably pre-hellenic Greece already knew her as Mistress of Animals, ποτνία θηρῶν. She was the oldest and the most revered, and at the same moment the most mysterious, of divine forms; and when they spoke of her poets lighted upon the exotic and violent clang of the rarest primeval sounds:

> And the eldest of deities Earth that knows not toil nor decay
> Ever he furrows and scores.[2]

Aeschylus, again, imitates the child's babbling:

> O Mother, Mother Earth, I am sore afraid;
> Beat back my fear!
> O Father, her first birth, Great Zeus![3]

The Mother, then, is anything but a theoretical invention intended to explain the world process. She is Form, just barely outlined; and everywhere that Nature gives or takes something, there is the Mother. The "god bearing fountain" became an epithet for the Madonna, and ἡ ἐν τῇ Πηγῇ (She in the well), now the title of honour of the *theotokos*, was once a suggestion of nameless Form, still half identical with the

[1] Ninck, *Die Bedeutung des Wassers im Kult und Leben der Alten*, 20.
[2] Sophocles, *Antigone*, 339 (Storr).
> Θεῶν τε τὰν ὑπερτάταν, Γᾶν
> ἄφθιτον, ἀκαμάταν, ἀποτρύεται . . .
[3] *The Suppliant Women*, 890 *ff.* (Murray).
> μᾶ Γᾶ μᾶ Γᾶ, βόαν
> φοβερὸν ἀπότρεπε,
> ὦ πᾶ, Γᾶς παῖ, Ζεῦ.

water from Earth.[1] There were, too, many mothers, called by the
Greeks nymphs:—not maidens but young women, who were invoked
at marriages for their blessing.[2]

From the Greeks the Mother passed to ourselves as the Sacred
Three—and at the same time as a warning that here genuine personality
has not yet been achieved; and thus the *eumenides, semnai, moirai,
charites* and *horai* find their counterparts in the three fairies or *Holden*
of Celtic or German popular belief.

2. As we have learnt to recognize her thus far, the Mother is the
Form of untouched wild Nature, the "mountain mother", as the
Greeks styled her; under the names of Artemis, Cybele, *etc.*, she retained
this character, while on Germanic territory *Holda* or *Frau Holle* is a
similar figure. But side by side with this appears the mother-form of
the tilled and cultivated earth. And again we must be careful not to
make any theoretical distinction, and it maybe try to interpret this
new Mother-earth as some "goddess of cultivation"; gods and goddesses
"of" something or other prolong their miserable existence only in
works of reference and decorative paintings! To primitive humanity,
then, cultivation was Nature as directly experienced, while the goddess
was the form assumed by this experience.

The earth, still further, offers not only rich gifts and marvellous
ornamentation, but she nourishes too. To the Greeks she was *Gaia
kourotrophos*; and the *kouroi* were the young, of plants as well as of the
animal and human world; to her knees she drew children, young
animals and flowers.[3] She was, however, not always a form; and folk
customs, from ancient Egypt to those of modern husbandmen, have
faithfully retained the old idea of the receptacle of Power. In many
places the "last sheaf" was, and indeed still is, the object of some
special rites or other; ceremonially bound or threshed, it is the holder
of the potency of the ploughed field, exactly as the May-pole sustains
the strength of wild Nature. The granting of form begins whenever
some animal, harvest cock or goat, takes the place of the purely vegetative power reservoir; and then this develops into dressing the last of
the corn as a woman or, as in La Vendée, the farmer's wife being
threshed and winnowed in fun.[4]

This indeed is no "personification" in our sense of the term. Natural

[1] Otto Kern, *Die Religion der Griechen*, I, 1926, 89.   [2] Ninck, *Wasser*, 13 *f.*
[3] G. van der Leeuw, *Goden en Menschen in Hellas*, Fig. 1.
[4] Mannhardt, *Baumkultus*, 612; Frazer, *The Golden Bough*, VII (*Spirits of the
Corn*, I), 149 *f.*

occurrences are not allegorized—this again is done only by decorative painters!—but the essential community between human and terrestrial life is experienced. The earth, for instance, is regarded as woman, and woman as pertaining to the earth; this is the significance of the Polish custom of calling after the man who has cut the last of the grain: "Thou hast cut off the navel cord"; while in Scotland the corn spirit is reaped under the name of "the maiden".[1]

In Greece Demeter was the corn-mother, the grain-producing earth.[2] She has her sisters all over the world, from the German and Dutch *Roggenmuhme* (Dutch *roggemeuje*), to the rice-mother in Java and the mother of the maize in Mexico. In her mysteries the ceremonial cutting of an ear of corn was the climax; to her the plough was sacred, and she herself was once impregnated on the thrice-ploughed field.[3] She had a daughter called Kore, "the maiden", just as in Scotland; originally she was probably alone, and the "maiden" was another earth-mother from elsewhere, who later became her daughter; both are actually only variant forms of Gaia.[4] The first is the mother in complete motherhood, the ripe fruit; the second, the maiden, the flower. The fate of both is the same: the grain must fall into the ground and die, so that it may bear fruit; subsequently the myth transformed this descent into the underworld into the rape of youth and the mother's sorrow. But in the countryman's festal calendar the *katagogia*, the "going down", still correctly signifies the transference of the seed to its underground receptacle.[5]

The birth and death of corn and men are intimately connected: "arising" and "going down", *anhodos* and *katagogia*, are the eternal crises, the sudden changes of fortune, in life. Kore-Persephone is not only the dying youth of the grain, but also the beauteous leader of the village youth, with whom she picks flowers on the meadow, and who must also grow old and die. And Demeter is the assistant at birth, Eileithyia, Eleutho, Eleusia;[6] on the other hand the dead were called after her: Δημητρεῖοι:—"Demeter's People."[7]

---

[1] Frazer, *ibid.*, 155, 164.   [2] Euripides, *The Bacchae*, 276.

[3] *cf.* Chantepie, *op. cit.*, II, 301.

[4] Farnell, *The Cults of the Greek States*, III, 116 *ff*.

[5] Farnell, *ibid.*, III, 114.—M. P. Nilsson, *A History of Greek Religion*, 123.

[6] Probably the name is not to be divorced from Eleusis and Eleusinia; *cf.* S. Wide, *Lakonische Kulte*, 1893, 175, and W. Roscher, *Ausführliches Lexikon der griechisch-römischen Mythologie*, Article "Kora".—Chantepie, *op. cit.*, II, 318; *cf.* also: F. Muller, *De "Komst" van den hemelgod*, Meded. Kon. Akad. v. Wet. Afd. Lett. 74, B, 7, 1932.

[7] Harrison, *Prolegomena to the Study of Greek Religion*, 267. Plutarch, *On the Face which Appears on the Orb of the Moon*, XXVIII.

To this corresponded a very close relationship of woman to the tilling of the land; the cult of Demeter was the affair of the women. And everywhere in the world it is woman who concerns herself with husbandry and its rites. In all this, too, very ancient social conditions play their part. Many tribes represent a transition from the hunting to the settled stage—the agricultural, the men being occupied in hunting and fishing while the women cultivate the fields. This state of affairs, however, which has its repercussions in agriculture for long periods, should be ascribed neither to indolence nor to the masculine desire to rule, and just as little should a hypothetical substitution of patriarchal conditions for matriarchy be assumed here. Women and the soil are in fact associated in the religious sense: woman is the ploughed field, the field a fertile woman: "In some parts of India, naked women drag a plough across a field by night";[1] and all this can be understood only if woman's greater potency is recalled. Like the tilled field, she too is the bearer of life, and like it she conceives and gives birth.[2]

That woman is a ploughed field is indeed familiar to the poetry of all ages and regions. To the mind of the old Egyptian sage, Ptahhotep, "she is a goodly field for her lord",[3] and in the Egyptian love song the beloved assures her swain:

> I am thy favourite sister.
> To thee I am as a garden
> Full of sweetly scented herbs.[4]

Similarly, the *Vendidad* asserts that the land "is unhappy that for long is left untilled: here wanders a beautifully formed woman who has long remained childless",[5] and that the earth bestows her riches like "a loved woman lying on her bed who produces a son for her dear husband".[6] The Hindus, like the Greeks, were aware that the phallus is a plough;[7] to the Greek poets, in fact, the image of the tilled field

---

[1] Frazer, *The Golden Bough*, I (*The Magic Art*, I), 282 *f.*; *cf. AR.* XI, 1908, 154 *ff.*

[2] *cf.* Farnell, *op. cit.*, III, 106 *ff.*—Lévy-Bruhl, *Primitive Mentality*, 316 *ff.*

[3] A. Erman, *The Literature of the Ancient Egyptians*, 61.

[4] M. Müller, *Die Liebespoesie der alten Ägypter*, 1899, 27.

[5] Lehmann, *Textbuch*, 164; *cf.* GENERAL LITERATURE, p. 19 *ante.*

[6] *ibid.*; *cf.* also the Vedic marriage formula: "This woman came as a cornfield endowed with life. Ye men, sow in her the seed"; in Bertholet, *op. cit.*, GENERAL LITERATURE, p. 19 *ante.*—Conversely, in the twelfth-century church hymn the Blessed Virgin is referred to thus: *terra non arabilis, quae fructium parturiit*; *cf.* F. J. E. Raby, *A History of Christian Latin Poetry*, 349.

[7] E. Abegg, *Das Pretakalpa des Garuda-Purana*, 1921, 200 *f.*—E. Fehrle, *Die kultische Keuschheit im Altertum*, 1910, 170 *ff.*—Dieterich *Mutter Erde*, 46 *f.*

was extremely vivid: Sophocles refers to a wife whom the husband has seen

> E'en as the tiller of a distant field
> Sees it at seedtime, sees it once again
> At harvest, and no more.[1]

Modern popular poetry too still clings to this image, just as the barren queen in the fairy tale complains: "I am like a field on which nothing grows",[2] while in the rough humour of comedy the cuckold consoles himself: "he that ears my land spares my team".[3] A later romantic period also, which prefers longing to power, can yet discover no other than the primal simile of the fruitful field, even when the uncouthness of earth and fruit is replaced by the more tender flower and bud.

But this leads to a yet wider perspective wherein the maternal form was perceived. I must begin by stating definitely that Mother Earth is very human. Demeter is the loving and sorrowing mother and her most beautiful image, the Cnidian Demeter, unites something of the tearful expression of the *Madre Dolorosa* to the joyfulness of the corn-goddess;[4] Isis again is the typical "housewife", devoted to her husband and son. Indeed, in the maternal divinities is found the entire scale of feminine possibilities: the lover, and not seldom the beloved of all the world (Ishtar-Aphrodite type), together with the virgin (Artemis, Mary).[5] But she is always the mother even when she is a maid, and even when, as in the Western Asiatic religions, a peculiar relationship subsists between the mother and a young god, to whom the feelings of both lover and mother seem to be devoted.

This singular relationship, certainly, has its social presuppositions. We know little of the origins of matriarchal law. We can, however, feel assured that a hunting social organization is connected with masculine predominance, just as is the agricultural stage with that of women. Still, it seems to me that in the combination of matriarchy and agriculture the social element appears not to be the original so much as does the religious: it is very unlikely that matriarchal law began in the intimacy between women in the course of their common agricultural pursuits. This intimate feminine intercourse and the subsequent social segregation of women, much more probably, were initiated by the

---

[1] Sophocles, *Trach.*, 31 *ff.*; *cf. Oedipus Rex*, 1257.
[2] *Kinder- und Hausmärchen*, No. 144.   [3] *All's Well That Ends Well*, I, 3.
[4] Farnell, *op. cit.*, III, 277; *cf.* also his *Outline History of Greek Religion*, 77.
[5] *cf.* the utterance in this spirit of Ramakrishna in Bertholet, *Lesebuch*, 14, 83 (*cf.* GENERAL LITERATURE).

"eternal feminine", the peculiar and mysterious power of woman, which appertains to the earth as does the earth to it.[1]

3. It has already become clear that virgin and mother stand in no antithetical relationship. Only for a culture no longer quite primitive, but influenced by the ideal of virginity, does the unity of maid and mother become a problem, an offence and a marvel; the ancient world, on the other hand, regarded the maiden either as the daughter, or as about to become a mother. And here too it was Hellas that generated the ideal form of the maiden as well as of the mother.[2]

For Faith, the virgin forms are the exponents of feminine youth in everyday life. Since times immemorial the young village girls have been beloved figures as they assemble, above all around the village well: the future mothers at the springing womb of the earth. It is an eternal event: "The young maidens come from the town to fetch water— innocent and necessary employment, and formerly the occupation of the daughters of kings. As I take my rest there, the idea of the old patriarchal life is awakened around me. I see them, our old ancestors, how they formed their friendships and contracted alliances at the fountain-side; and I feel how fountains and streams were guarded by beneficent spirits."[3] Young Werther perceived correctly: at the well arises new life; according to the Greeks, there dwelt the nymphs who bless birth, and the manifold dances of the virginal goddesses or demons took their form from the village roundelays.[4] In Sicily they were the youths whom a "queen" supervises, ($\pi\alpha\hat{\imath}\delta\epsilon\varsigma$ and $\check{\alpha}\nu\alpha\sigma\sigma\alpha$), exactly as at a festival one of the village girls appeared as the leading dancer and queen.[5] Artemis had her train:

> Once Hermes, the god with the golden wand,
> Stole me from the dance of Artemis,
> The virgin with golden arrows and rustling raiment;
> Many were sporting there, young maids and noble girls.[6]

Persephone too had such a chorus; and the many Madonnas of Christian times owe their plurality to their predecessors in antiquity.[7]

---

[1] cf. F. Gräbner, *Das Weltbild der Primitiven*, 1924, 33.
[2] Farnell, *Cults of the Greek States*, III, 278.
[3] *The Sorrows of Werther*, Goethe's *Works*, VI, 6 (Nimmo); Book I, May 12.
[4] G. van der Leeuw, *Goden en Menschen*, 26 ff.
[5] Nilsson, *History of Greek Religion*, 112.　　　　[6] *Hymn. Homer. in Ven.*, 118.
[7] Probably also of Celtic origin occasionally; cf. U. von Wilamowitz-Möllendorf, *Griechische Tragödien*, II⁸, 1919, 215 ff., on the Three Maries on the Island of la Camargue, Provence; cf. further Trede, *Heidentum*, II, 120, IV, 241, and Heiler, *Katholizismus*, 189.

The relationship between virgin and mother is intrinsically temporal: the maid becomes a wife. Hera is maiden, bride and wife; Artemis, virgin and mother. Often an annual bath was supposed to restore the girlhood of the goddess, as is also related of the old Germanic Hertha. This of course implies not that virginity is retained, but that fertility is constantly and miraculously renewed.[1]

The adoration of the Madonna first became a cult of sacred virginity in the Roman church. To antiquity, on the other hand, fertility was far more potent and holy than chastity, although the latter too possessed power. Demeter and Isis are mothers; Mary, their successor, is mother and maiden. But despite the ideal of virginity, the church was just as little able to dispense with the mother's form as was later Buddhism in the case of Kwanyin in China and Kwannon in Japan.[2] It is true that side by side with the mother, Mary, who has borrowed her form and even her attributes from the mothers of the Mediterranean basin, Christianity recognized another mother also, the church.

4. To primitive man, still further, his environment is not a summation of vastly different things, but a unity that is experienced as such. Therefore the mother too is not Earth alone and nothing else. The Cora Indians, for instance, worship Nasisa, "our mother", the goddess of the earth, the maize crop and the moon. In the Near East, again, the fertility mother is at the same time "queen of heaven", and this title was subsequently transferred to Mary; for heaven and earth are not severed from one another; and this experience receives its most forcible expression in the idea of the *holy marriage* between these two domains, this group of forms also being developed to the highest degree of perfection by the plastic genius of the Grecian people: "Beneath them the divine earth made fresh-sprung grass to grow, and dewy lotus, and crocus, and hyacinth, thick and soft, that upbare them from the ground. Therein lay the twain, and were clothed about with a cloud, fair and golden, wherefrom fell drops of glistering dew."[3]

Thus Homer, singing the nuptials of Zeus and Hera: yet even this brilliant scene has preserved the primeval feature of the bridal couch on the ploughed field ensuring fertility. Similarly, on the night before

---

[1] cf. A. G. Bather, "The Problem of the Bacchae", *Jour. Hell. Studies*, 14, 1894, 244 ff., and Fehrle, *Kultische Keuschheit*.

[2] Compare the sober indictment by L. Coulange, *La Vierge Marie*, 1925, with the lyric by Th. Zielinski, *La Sybille*, 1924, which makes the Mother theme, reinterpreted as the idea of love, the principal feature in Christianity.

[3] *Iliad*, XIV, 346 ff. (Murray); cf. also the magnificent Aeschylus *Frag.* 43.

Midsummer's Day the farmers of Moon, in Esthonia, take girls from the ring-dance into the wood, where they simulate intercourse, while in the Ukraine the rudeness of this custom became harmless joking, though nevertheless it was connected with the conviction that a good harvest would result;[1] and in the Dutch province of Groningen, even to-day, a struggle called *waolen*, between youths and maids on the ground, is still a permanent incident during harvest.[2] In Java, however, intercourse actually occurs on the rice field; and with such customs we are once again transported to the very heart of Dynamism. As a Form, man still suffices for himself and feels as yet no need for projection beyond himself. But when the magical confidence in his capacity for directing the course of events by his own activities begins to wane, then he creates figures in his stead to perform the sacred actions for him. Just as the sheaf and the farmer's wife were transformed into the mother, so was the harvest custom into the sacred marriage.

But for the nuptials a bridegroom is also required. And with this we meet an extremely momentous phase in the history of religion. We can understand the attachment to the mother; but similarly, and in accord with Freud's theories, the intimate relationship to the father is probably no longer a secret to anyone. To every man his mother is a goddess, just as his father is a god. In the history of religion this has resulted in two great groups—the religions of the *Father*, who dwells in heaven and begets and acts, "outward force applying" (again to quote Goethe); and side by side with these the religions of the *Mother* living and giving birth in the Earth, in whose womb all process has both its beginning and its end. In no religion whatever is the mother or the father completely lacking.[3] Judaism and Islam have mercilessly expelled the mother, but to Christianity she returned as *mater gloriosa*. The Old Testament, however, recognizes the image of the mother only in its moral and spiritual sense: "as one whom his mother comforteth, so will I comfort you" (*Isaiah* lxvi. 13); but in the second chapter of *St. Luke* it has returned once more in its true significance. It seems irrefutable that here racial as well as religious types are con-

---

[1] Mannhardt, *Wald- und Feldkulte*, 1, 468, 480.

[2] H. C. A. Grolman, *Tydschrift K. Ned. Aardrykskundig Gen.*, 2. *Reeks*, 46, 1929.

[3] On the disputed question whether Mother Earth occurred among the Semites, *cf.* Th. Nöldeke, *AR.* 8, 1905, 161. Ef. Briem, *AR.* 24, 1926, 179 ff. B. Gemser, *Stemmen voor Waarheid en Vrede*, 62, 1915, 919 f. All in all, it appears to me just as certain that the Semitic representation is not the same as that of the Indo-Germanic peoples, as that the Semites by no means lacked the Mother Form, and indeed that it exerted no slight influence even on Greek ideas.

cerned. Religions that are intensely oriented towards Will turn away from the mother to the father. The relation to the father, again, can be spiritualized and moralized; that to the mother never completely so. From the Lord's Prayer all natural relations are remote, but not from the *Angelic Salutation*.[1] When he may no longer be the fructifier, the father may be creator; the mother can only bear offspring. The father acts with power: the mother is merely potent. The father leads his people to their goal: the mother's child-bearing renews the cycle of life. The mother creates life: the father history. She is Form and Power: he Form and Will; and Animism and Dynamism carry on their final struggle with the aid of the forms of both father and mother.

Thus we can understand how, in the history of mankind, one form never completely supplants the other; and the form of the mother lives on in religion because it is alive in our hearts:

> Thou—despite thy minor rôle—
> Goddess of possibilities,
> Of ultimate tragedies,
> Of ultimate happiness and sorrow—
> Mother and loved one—Both . . .[2]

J. J. BACHOFEN, *Urreligion und antike Symbole;* selection edited by C. A. BERNOULLI, 3 vols.

R. BRIFFAULT, *The Mothers: A Study of the Origin of Sentiments and Institutions*, 3 vols.

A. DIETERICH, *Mutter Erde*[3], 1925.

Eranos Jahrbuch, 1938, "Vorträge über Gestalt und Kult der grossen Mutter".

L. FRANZ, *Die Muttergötten in vorderen Orient u. in Europa*, 1937.

J. E. HARRISON, *Prolegomena to the Study of Greek Religion.*

K. LEESE, *Die Mutter als religiöses Symbol*, 1934.

G. VAN DER LEEUW, *Goden en Menschen in Hellas*, 1927.

EWALD ROELLENBLEACK, *Magna Mater im alten Testament*, 1949.

---

[1] *Luke* i. 28.   [2] Chr. Morgenstern, *Kleine Erde.*

CHAPTER II

POWER. WILL. SALVATION

1. THE Title of the present Chapter requires brief explanation, "Salvation" having been selected as the most suitable English equivalent for the German *Heil*, together with the occasional alternative "Deliverance"; unfortunately, neither word can be regarded as an exact rendering for the wealth of ideas implied by *Heil* itself, even though we possess many closely associated terms derived from the same root, such as heal, health, hail, hale, holy, and whole; while the Latin *salus* and the French *salut* may be added in order to clarify the very wide meaning, throughout this volume, of Salvation as always implying such concepts as whole, complete, perfect, healthy, strong, vigorous, welfare, well-being, as contrasted with suffering and misery, and in some connections bliss, both earthly and heavenly. It is in fact essentially characteristic of *Heil* itself that it may involve any one of these ideas, and sometimes all of them simultaneously; it is, in other words, universal in its significance, and indicates one of the principal sources of the religious life in all its manifestations. For the same reasons terms derived from *Heil* must be accorded a far wider range of meaning than is usual. "Saviour" (*Heiland*) thus denotes one who effects the spiritual conditions implied by the foregoing equivalents of *Heil*, or any one of these. Similarly "Holy" and "Sacred" (*Heilig*) mean being in some of these conditions, or being their cause or stimulus; "Sanctuary" (*Heiligtum*) any situation where they are aroused and experienced, while finally "The Story of Salvation" (*Heilsgeschichte*) will speak for itself; in short, the accepted, but definitely limited, English significance must be invariably expanded in the directions just indicated, so as to preclude any too rigid connotation confined to Christianity alone.

In this sense, therefore, possession of the powerful object, of the potent animal, means *salvation*. Water and trees, the fruit of the fields and the beasts in the forests, are all Bringers of Salvation; the force issuing from their power transforms the gloom of life into joy and happiness. But when felicity thus comes from without, from some potent situation, it is termed *Salvation*. "Salvation has come to us"— the cry of faith of the Reformation had its dawn in the primitive conception of a deliverance wholly unearned by man himself: Salvation therefore is Power, experienced as Good.

For a long time, however, salvation lacked form. The first saviour was the phallus which brings fertility, or its female equivalent; and subsequently, all sorts of powerful entities. For many peoples the last sheaf is the receptacle for the power of all the corn; in Värmland in Sweden, again, the housewife bakes a cake out of the flour from the last sheaf in the shape of a woman:—thus Power begins to assume definite human form; and the cake is distributed as the bread of strength to all the inmates of the household.[1] Even to-day, many a festival loaf in animal or human form has a similar origin.[2]

For long, too, the animal form remained inseparable from salvation. A very ancient invocation of the women of Elis, for example, mentions the bull Dionysus, who is to come with the *Charites*, the bearers of fertility. Elsewhere it is a green branch, or a stake adorned with vegetative symbols, that incorporates fertility. The Greeks celebrated the *daphnephoria*, and their *eiresione* resembled our palm catkins and *Palmpaschen*:

> Eiresione brings
> All good things,
> Figs and fat cakes to eat,
> Soft oil and honey sweet,
> And brimming wine-cup deep
> That she may drink and sleep.[3]

In ancient Egypt, similarly, water was salvation, the fertilizing water of the Nile floods; and this saving water became one of the chief components of the figure of Osiris the saviour, whose wanderings in the floods were probably an original feature, not introduced in the myth of his murder.[4] To rivers, in fact, sacrifices were offered long before man became conscious of any river gods.[5]

In the same way the grain often received animal form, the corn-

---

[1] Reuterskiöld, *Speisesakr.*, 116.   [2] *cf. Jer.* vii. 18.

[3] J. E. Harrison, *Prolegomena*, 80; *cf.* A. Dieterich, *Kleine Schriften*, 1911, 324 *ff.* and Zielinski's version, *The Religion of Ancient Greece*, 56,

> Eiresione brings figs, and eiresione brings loaves;
> Honey it brings in a jar, and oil to rub on our bodies,
> And a strong flagon of wine, for all to go mellow to bed on.

[4] *cf.* J. Frank-Kamenetzky, *AR.* 24, 1927, 240 *f.*

[5] *cf.* W. A. Murray, *Zeitschr. f. ägypt. Sprache u. Altert.*, 51, 1914, 130. *ERE.* Sethe, "Heroes".

stag, or cock or hare, springing from the imagination.[1] But the intense emotion of willing and suffering is also transferred to the potent or weakened fruit without any form at all; thus folklore relates the "pains of the flax".[2] Everywhere seed-time is a season of mourning, an echo of this surviving in the ballad of the afflictions and death of John Barley-corn, as modernized by Burns.

2. In the succeeding phase the human form emerges on all sides from the hitherto amorphous Power; thus the last sheaf becomes the mother of the corn, whether called Demeter or by some other name, while henceforth the tree's potency, as each year it returns to life, is styled Dionysus; and vase paintings portray this god with a human head projecting from the stake.[3]

But the salvation form expands most profusely in the representations depicting the annual renewal of growth in general. Thus Spring is a "return", or a new birth, of the saviour; and the laurel branch, which a boy brought to Delphi, was soon displaced by its bearer as repre-senting the god.[4] Folk customs again, which have preserved the primi-tive for us, continue to celebrate the May king or queen. The Greeks called such a god, who arose from the seasonal changes, *kouros*, which means a youth; and certainly youth in itself, then its leader, and only ultimately its mythical type, has been accepted as saviour—not in Greece alone. The young seed, the young herd, the village youth:— all this compellingly invaded the idea of *kouros* or *kore*, whether it came to be styled Apollo or *Pfingstlümmel*, Persephone or May queen.

Several powers, moreover, may receive only a single form. It is impossible, for instance, to say that Apollo is merely the god of Spring, since he is also much more; Osiris, similarly, is the god of self-renewing vegetation. His figure was frequently constructed from fertile soil out of which ears of corn were sprouting—*Osiris végétant*.[5] We have already seen that he was, too, the god of "young" water;[6] he was also the primeval king, the bringer of culture, the god of the dead and the granter of good life in the hereafter. Thus he is actually a "saviour"

---

[1] Frazer, *The Golden Bough*, VII (*Spirits of the Corn*, I), 272 *ff.*

[2] *e.g.* M. Boehm and F. Specht, *Lettisch-litauische Volksmärchen*, 1924, 248 *ff.*

[3] J. E. Harrison, *Prolegomena to the Study of Greek Religion*, 42 *ff.* Farnell, *Cults of the Greek States*, V, 118 *f.*, 241.   [4] G. van der Leeuw, *Goden en Menschen*, 90 *f.*

[5] A. Wiedemann, *Muséon*, N.S. 4, 111 *ff.*

[6] *Pyramidentexte*, Sethe Edition, 589: "Thou art young in thy name 'young water' "; *cf.* 767, and H. Junker, *Die Stundenwachen in den Osirismysterien*, 1910, 5. *Nachtstunde*, 63.

in the fullest sense, best expressed by σωτήρ; the rescuer in case of
need, and this not merely in occasional but equally in regularly recurring
necessity. For the primitive mind, then, "rescuer" and "preserver"
merge into one.[1]

3. Many potencies compose the form of the saviour—not that of
Nature alone. Culture too is a "salvation", that is a deed that is willed
or volitional. We moderns accept this as a matter of course and honour
the discoverer, the author of peace, the sage. Primitive man also revered
them; but he placed them on the same level as sun and Spring, as rain
and animals; for to his mind, what was willed and achieved by man
was in principle no different from natural events and processes. Nature
and culture were one: both impelled by *a single* power and willed by
a single will.

Thus everywhere we find prehistoric forms that taught man to
plough or mine and gave him laws, but also fixed the sun in its course
and rid the world of monsters and plagues of every kind. Herakles is a
saviour of this type (ἀλεξίκακος), but he is at the same time *kouros*,
who wins eternal life. No distinction whatever is made between occasional and permanent necessity: every necessity is in fact occasional,
just as each sunrise and each Spring signify salvation. And the struggle
for salvation against disaster takes on similar forms, whether it is a
question of bringing a swamp under cultivation (Herakles' conflict
with the Hydra), or the expulsion of darkness by the sun; fights with
dragons therefore provide perhaps the most universal *motif* in the
saviour myth. Whoever reads the expositions of Breysig and Ehrenreich
can hardly escape the impression that the first of these investigators,
in desiring to explain the idea of god as derived from some historic
form of a bringer of salvation, is just as one-sided as the second, who
regards the personification of Nature's power as its basis.[2] Only a
combination of these two viewpoints is in fact adequate to the com-
plexity of the actual situation.

4. God, as I have previously observed, is a late comer in the history
of religion. And the remarkable thing is that, if appearances are not
entirely deceptive, God the son subsisted before God the father;[3] the

---

[1] *cf. RGG.* Kurt Latte, Article *Heiland.*

[2] K. Breysig, *Die Entstehung des Gottesgedankens und der Heilbringer,* 1905. P.
Ehrenreich, *Götter und Heilbringer, Zeitschr. für Ethnol.* 38, 1906, 536 *ff.*

[3] *cf.* J. E. Harrison, *Epilegomena to the Study of Greek Religion,* 18 *ff.*

saviour is thus a primeval form subsisting side by side with that of the mother. At all times (except during the rationalistic period) it has been easier for man to believe in the son than in the father, in youth and the future rather than in age and the past; and the saviour form is exquisitely adjusted to that of the most beautiful human figure, that of youth, whilst his will is the equivalent of youthful buoyant impetus. This is the grain of truth in the contentions of Xenophanes and Feuerbach, that man has created a God after his own image. In fact he did so create the mother and the saviour, but not the father.

K. Breysig, *Die Entstehung des Gottesgedankens und der Heilbringer*, 1905.
P. Ehrenreich, "Götter und Heilbringer", in *Zeitschr. für Ethnol.*, 38, 1906, 530 *ff.*
H. Lietzmann, *Der Weltheiland*, 1909.
A. Van Deursen, *Der Heilbringer*, 1931.

CHAPTER 12

THE SAVIOUR

1. THE *Son* brings salvation. He is not only the hope of the living, but also the consolation of the dead; and the potency of the family and the tribe is preserved by the son. When we wish for a son as the sustainer of the race we too desire salvation: we crave life, which surpasses ourselves and our own age, persists after us and is more powerful than we. Life is not only continued in the son: it is (to fall back on mathematical terms) raised to a higher power.

Where there exists a family or tribal cult, the son is its priest; this is most clearly perceived in ancient Egypt. There the *sa mr-f*, the "son whom he loves", was the administrator of the rite of sacrifice to the father and regularly brought gifts to his dead parent, thus prolonging his life in the grave. The god Horus became the prototype of the good son by safeguarding the life of his father Osiris; just as the young god imparted salvation to the old, so every good son bestowed it on his father, who had become an Osiris. He thus addressed him: "Lift up thy countenance, that thou mayest see what I have done for thee: I am thy son, I am thine heir; I have grown corn for thee, for thee I have mown wheat; the grain for thy *Wag*-festival, the corn for thy yearly feast";[1] and elsewhere: "How beautiful is it to see, how blissful to regard and view Horus when he gives life to his father, when he imparts strength to Osiris."[2]

The Egyptians expressed these acts of the good son by the word *nd̲*, usually translated by "revenge", but which means revenge on the father's enemy, Set, as well as all the good and the life that the son can bestow on his father:—salvation, therefore, in its most comprehensive sense.[3]

2.　　　　To another thou art child, friend;
　　　　　　I see in thee the god
　　　　　　Whom with awe I recognized,
　　　　　　To whom flows my devotion.[4]

Into human life the saviour enters in very different forms, but his coming is always felt as the experience of Spring:

[1] *Pyramidentexte* (Sethe), 1879, *cf*. 1950.　　　　　　[2] *ibid*., 1980.
[3] *cf. ibid*., 1558.　　　[4] Stefan George, *Der siebente Ring, Maximin, Kunfttag*, I.

> Now Spring has come once more . . .
> Thou sanctifiest the road and the air,
> And us also, on whom thou lookest—
> Therefore I stammer forth my thanks to thee.[1]

This is because the periodic *salvation of Spring* was probably the strongest root of belief in the saviour: in the young god's form life renews itself. His epiphany, his "day of coming" (*Kunfttag*), is the newly awakening life; and thus the saviour-god lacks that eternal constancy which is the attribute of the god of heaven and of other deities; his potency, rather, is perpetually changing, an ascending and declining power. Nature's cycle, in fact, is at one and the same moment the most saddening and the most joyous that we know. Not only the melancholy of Autumn but also Winter's famine, not merely the poetry of Spring but equally Summer's superfluity, all cooperate in the mighty form of the saviour who dies and rises again, who slumbers and awakens, who departs and reappears. Of Dionysus, for example, it was said that he had his lulling to sleep and his rising up (κατευνασμοί, ἀνεγέρσεις), and all the fully developed saviour forms show similar characteristics.[2]

But it is only rarely that Power remains merely Nature-power for long periods. To primitive man life was ever one and indivisible; and thus the visionary feelings of the mystic stimulus attached themselves to the old *kouros*-form of Dionysus, feelings that inundated Greece in early historical times; and from the periodic epiphany of the saviour there developed the historic event of the god of ecstasy's entry, overcoming the resistance of prosaic and suspicious people.[3] Thus the old Italian god of Spring, Mars, was at the same time the war-god because the commencement of the fruit year simultaneously signified the beginning of another harvest, brought in by the people as the army (*exercitus*).[4] But wherever the saviour appears the breath of Spring always dominates, whatever its narrower or later meaning may be.

3. The saviour-form appears, however, not only in the experience of the son or of Spring; there must also be considered the other type of event, already discerned in dealing with the development of the form of Power. Salvation, then, is connected not only with racial continuance,

---

[1] Stefan George, *Der siebente Ring*, *Maximin*, *Kunfttag*, III.
[2] Plutarch, *Of Isis and Osiris*, 69.
[3] Chantepie, *op. cit.*, II, 320; van der Leeuw, *Goden en Menschen*, 115 *ff.*
[4] Contrast here Kurt Latte, *AR.* 24, 1927, 251.

nor merely with the eternal repetition of Nature's life: it lives too in the inestimable boon, bestowed once for all, which is linked by memory to some single historic individual. While suffering from its childish maladies, it is true, the history of religion transformed almost all personalities that have been regarded as historical into moon-gods or some other projections of myth; but fortunately that stage has now been passed, and we see that not only many bringers of salvation actually have their roots in history, but also that at some time gods can have existed, no matter how much their human forms may be entwined with legends. This is the truth in *Euhemerism.*

But the main point here is that independently of the question, always so difficult to answer, whether a saviour has actually lived, to have existed constitutes an essential feature in his texture. Thus attempts have been made to secure a historical form for the Egyptian saviour-god Osiris,[1] and it is in fact not impossible that such a form has co-operated among the diverse components of his figure—the prehistoric god of death, the god of the Nile, the *kouros.* Still more important is it that in any case the structure of Osiris required the features of a historic man. This man was a king, or if not a king, he should have been one; for he taught men agriculture, gave them laws and culture in general,[2] as did Demeter and Triptolemus in Greece and so many more or less primitive figures to other peoples.

But we cannot assert that the bringer of culture and salvation, and the saviour, exhibit the same structure so far as Phenomenology is concerned. The bringer of salvation may also develop into a quite different form—that of the Originator.[3] This depends on whether he more resembles a son than a father, whether the characteristics in his figure have been derived from the power of age or that of youth. But this much is certain in any case:—that salvation may be historic just as well as cosmic, and that in this respect primitive man made hardly any distinction. Rites, "culture" and cosmic phenomena—all alike pertain to salvation: Jeshl or Yehl, the salvation-bringing raven of Tlingit, brings both fire and sunlight;[4] Osiris inaugurates culture, and also life from death; Herakles, again, casts down the powers inimical to culture, and overcomes death, while Christ institutes baptism and communion, bestows salvation in its most comprehensive sense, and even mediates creation.

---

[1] Frazer, *The Golden Bough,* VI (*Adonis, Attis, and Osiris,* II), 159 *f.*
[2] Plutarch, *Of Isis and Osiris,* 13.
[3] Chap. 18.   [4] Wundt, *Völkerpsychologie,* 5, 300 *ff.*

4. One root of the saviour idea, finally, springs from the experience of being healed; when man falls ill, whoever cures him is his saviour, and thus healing pertains to the operation of salvation in its most essential sense. Jesus heals: "The blind receive their sight, and the lame walk, the lepers are cleansed, and the deaf hear, the dead are raised up, and the poor have the gospel preached to them."[1] Salvation of body, and of soul, merge in the New Testament fulfilment of the prophecy of the Old Covenant: "The Spirit of the Lord is upon me, because he hath anointed me to preach the gospel to the poor; he hath sent me to heal the brokenhearted, to preach deliverance to the captives, and recovering of sight to the blind, to set at liberty them that are bruised, to preach the acceptable year of the Lord."[2] To-day too the soul's salvation still demands the cure of the body just as, conversely, every successful physician is regarded as one who, in a sense, bestows salvation. The Christian churches, however, have to some degree forgotten this connection, and are consequently penalized by the success of so many movements and prophets, like "Christian Science", that achieve faith cures. For man realizes that, despite all artificial isolation, conversion and healing go together, as will become still clearer with reference to holy men.[3]

5. The saviour myth, then, is constituted in the main by the following features:—

A. Birth, Epiphany. The saviour's appearance is miraculous; and this supernatural aspect may also be attributed to his conception. A fixed train of thought, especially among Mediterranean peoples, makes the holy child the offspring of the mother and of the divine father; and long before virginity was esteemed a moral quality, parthenogenesis was the accepted method of explaining the uniqueness of the newly born saviour—or rather of emphasizing this. Thus for the gift bestowed on the world in Plato Apollo, as well as Perictione the mother, was held responsible. Isis, again, conceived Horus, the son *par excellence*, by Osiris, only after the latter's death. For salvation rises even from death. Very beautiful in its grandiose *naïveté* is the description of Isis' joy: "Isis the excellent, who protected her brother (Osiris), who sought for him without wearying, who crossed over the whole land in her affliction without resting till she had found him; who created shade with her feathers (Isis originally had the form of a bird) and air with her

---

[1] *Matt.* xi. 5.   [2] *Luke* iv. 18 *f. Isaiah* lxi. 1, 2.   [3] Chap. 27.

wings; who cried out joyously when she brought her brother (who had been drowned) to the land; who raised the weary (*sc.* phallus) of the benumbed body (the dead man); who stole his seed and produced an heir; the child was suckled in the wilderness, the place where he was being unknown; she who, when his arm grew strong, brought him within the palace of Keb (the king of the gods)."[1]

Birth and epiphany, still further, are intrinsically the same. An old Christian tradition relates that the life of Christ as saviour commenced with His epiphany at Jordan, and cites the text: "Thou art my son, the Beloved, to-day I have become thy father."[2] Thus this is a duplicate of the account of the birth in *St. Luke* ii which follows the ordinary scheme of divine birth even though, in accordance with Hebrew feeling, it substitutes the Holy Spirit for God.[3]

But like birth, epiphany too is a springing forth from death, from the realm of the unattainable. Apollo comes from the country of the Hyperboreans: yet "neither by ships nor by land canst thou find the wondrous road to the trysting-place of the Hyperboreans".[4] It is the land at the end of the world, the fabulous country far beyond all others, whence the saviour comes. In Greece, therefore, the foreign origin of certain saviour-gods, like Apollo and Dionysus, was interpreted as an epiphany, and conversely. On the one hand Apollo is the intruder who appropriates for himself the cults of other divinities, *e.g.* that of Mother Earth at Delphi. He is the god of the victorious immigrant Hellenes, the "god of migration" (*Aguieus*) and thereby a historic saviour-form. The *paian* again, the song of victory celebrating the defeat of the python, the primeval Delphic earth snake, is the echo of a historical event; and the road which the god follows in the guise of the boy bearing the laurel, at his epiphany, is the "sacred way" of the immigrants from the North. But at the same time the country whence he comes is the mythical realm of the dead, and his unique arrival becomes a periodical event, a sojourn, *epidemia*, soon followed by a departure, *apodemia*; while the combat with the dragon is one instance of the eternal struggle between the old and the new salvations. Thus the two salvation myths, the historic and the mythical-natural, intercross, so that one becomes the expression of the other. The occurrence of salva-

---

[1] *Hymnus Bibl. Nat.* No. 20, 18th Dynasty.
[2] *Luke* iii. 22; *cf.* H. Usener, *Das Weihnachtsfest*, 1911, 40 *ff.*
[3] M. Dibelius, *Jungfrauensohn und Krippenkind* (*Sitz.-Ber. d. Heidelb. Akad. d. Wiss.* 1931–32, 4, 1932).—G. Erdmann, *Die Vorgeschichten des Lukas- und Matthäus-Evangeliums und Vergils vierte Ekloge,* 1932.
[4] Pindar, *Pyth.* X (Sandys).

tion bears the traits of Spring, while the experience of Spring remains eternally new and unprecedented.[1]

The epiphany is, of course, just as miraculous as the birth. The saviour performs miracles too—and not miraculous cures merely. In the Roman breviary the baptism of Christ in Jordan (that is, His epiphany) and the miracle of Cana are still linked together: before the newly appearing saviour water is converted into wine. The date of the feast of the Epiphany, January 5, was already that of the god Dionysus before it was connected with Jesus;[2] and wherever Dionysus appears, striking the earth with his thyrsus, flow forth milk, honey and wine:

> And one would raise
> Her wand and smite the rock, and straight a jet
> Of quick bright water came. Another set
> Her thyrsus in the bosomed earth, and there
> Was red wine that the God sent up to her,
> A darkling fountain. And if any lips
> Sought whiter draughts, with dipping finger-tips
> They pressed the sod, and gushing from the ground
> Came springs of milk. And reed-wands ivy-crowned
> Ran with sweet honey, drop by drop.[3]

In the struggle which the saviour must undertake, too, miracles are profuse.[4]

Miracles are portents of a new era, whether of Spring or of the World-Spring, as in Virgil's *Fourth Eclogue*. There the characteristics of the wondrous vegetation are combined with the great miracle of peace;[5] a new age of happiness dawns for the world. We too experience Spring as a marvel and understand how, conversely, the longed-for miracle of a new salvation must bear the hues of Spring.

B. Deed of Salvation. This consists in overcoming powers hostile to life, and usually bears therefore the stamp of the combat: Apollo, for example, slays the python. Similarly, Herakles' gigantic labour in performing the twelve tasks is now a cultural deed (the defeat of the hydra, *etc.*), and again a completely mythical event (procuring the

---

[1] cf. my Article, *Über einige neuere Ergebnisse der Psychologischen Forschung und ihre Anwendung auf die Geschichte, SM.* II, 1926, 36 ff.

[2] cf. H. Gressmann, *Tod und Auferstehung des Osiris (Der Alte Orient*, 23, 3), 1923, 22 ff. K. Holl, *Der Ursprung des Epiphanienfestes. Sitz.-Ber. d. preuss. Akad. d. Wiss.*, 1917. Ed. Norden, *Die Geburt des Kindes*, 1924. W. Bousset, *Kyrios Christos*², 1921, 62.

[3] Euripides, *Bacchae*, 704 ff. (Murray).

[4] *ibid.*, 750 ff. and cf. 142 ff.   [5] Lietzmann, *Der Weltheiland*, 1909, 2 ff.

apples of the Hesperides, *etc.*), but always a struggle against death whose treasure he wins for himself—Geryon's herd, the golden apples, the horn of Achelous—by overthrowing and terrorizing death (Hades and Persephone in the underworld, Eurystheus).

But *Death* is very often linked with the deed of salvation: in the struggle the saviour himself succumbs. Here the Nature basis is perfectly clear: life in the heavens and in vegetation periodically perishes. Salvation, then, must die. Osiris, the good and just king, and at the same time the self-renewing life of the Nile, is slain by his enemy *Set*; and he shares this fate with a whole series of salvation-gods conforming to the pattern of dying Nature: *Tammuz, Adonis, Attis* in the cults of the Orient, *Hosain*, the saint of the Shiah sect, *Baldur* in the Germanic myth. "Except a corn of wheat fall into the ground and die, it abideth alone: but if it die, it bringeth forth much fruit."[1]

The saviour's death is the great sorrow, μέγα πένθος, which Egyptian *Texts* avoid naming, but which can be made good again by joy in the resurrection. In the Osiris myth joy and sorrow are divided between father and son: Horus' deed of salvation is his revenge for his father and also his resuscitation; Horus is the living and victorious saviour. But usually life and death are united in a single form.

Christianity alone, however, has transformed death itself into salvation. All saviour religions proclaim life from death, but the gospel of the Cross preaches salvation *in* death. Here complete impotence becomes the utmost development of Power: absolute disaster becomes salvation; and thus what the mystery religions dare not speak of, nor mourn, is changed to highest bliss. Death annihilates death.

C. Resurrection. Parousia. Great joy follows the great sorrow, the rejoicing of Easter morn the despair of the burial: Osiris is found by Horus or Isis and awakened from the dead. The lament for Attis precedes the *Hilaria.*

> Those who are sowing in tears
>   shall reap with shouts of joy;
> sadly they bear seed to the field,
>   gladly they bear home the sheaves.[2]

Seed-time is a time of sorrow: harvest brings an outburst of rejoicing.

Resurrection and *parousia* are interrelated as are birth and epiphany, birth and resurrection being conceived rather as mythical and periodic, epiphany and *parousia* more as unique and historic. At the end of time the saviour returns and rightly orders all. Saoshyant, for instance,

[1] *John* xii. 24.   [2] *Ps.* cxxvi. 5, 6 (Moffat).

the Persian "helper", even appears to be limited to eschatological activity, if he is not the prophet Zarathustra himself—ancient *Texts* seem to indicate this—as whose son he is usually regarded, that is in the *parousia*. Of miraculous birth, he performs the great act of salvation called *frasho kereti*, the restoration of all things, but first of all of men, who in a general resurrection receive back their bodies.[1] Many bearers of salvation remain thus concealed until the end of time, the time of greatest need: then they will appear and bring deliverance to their people. This is related of the last of the twelve Imams, one of the descendants of Ali, who disappeared in 879: bringing rescue, he will return as the *Mahdi*; and the sagas of the Emperor Frederick Barbarossa in the *Kyffhäuser* ("are the ravens still flying about the mountain?"), of the Emperor Charles in the *Unterberg*, of the three Tells in Switzerland, are all eschatological forms of one and the same yearning. To the consummating and perfecting saviour is given "all power in heaven and in earth".

6. The saviour, whose being is not of this world—for just as he "returns", so also he has existed from the beginning (*Pre-existence*)—is born when the time is "fulfilled". It is this fatefulness of the time of salvation that links the periodic form of the saviour with the historic. The May king and the *kouros* are bearers of salvation for their periods—but happiness, even if it repeats itself, is unique in our experience, and the poet knows that each Spring is equally unique, while *every* year "*everything* changes".[2] Salvation, which was granted only once and for

---

[1] Chantepie, *op. cit.*, II, 253 *f*.

[2] An ancient German *epiclesis* expresses a marvellous deliverance, and at the same time a glorification, of the Nature element in the saviour image, by connecting in its own superb yet naïve way the misery of sin and that of Winter—

> Open the heavens, O Saviour,
> From heaven, descend, descend!
> Break down the gates and doors of heaven,
> Cast off their bolts and bars!
>
> O Earth, blossom forth, blossom forth, O Earth!
> Let all be green in hill and dale!
> O Earth, bring forth this floweret,
> Arise, O Saviour, from the Earth!
>
> Here we suffer diremost need.
> Before our eyes stands eternal death.
> O come and lead us with thy powerful hand
> From misery to our Fatherland.

Everything is here: Old Testament prophecy, the hope of salvation in the new covenant, the child-bearing Mother Earth and the opening heavens, the scion of Spring and the Lord from above.

all, is nevertheless extended in festival and celebration, in sacrament and liturgy, endlessly in time and space. Around the figure of the "suffering servant of Jahveh" are united the periodic lament for Tammuz and the mourning for the lost people, the rejoicing over reawakened Nature and the cheerful hope in the descendant of David. For the outstanding factor in all salvation is that it is present, that the time is fulfilled. Thus the modern poet too finds all the ancient tones of the end of time and of new beginning, of salvation and fulfilment, in the wondrous song:

> You had eyes dimmed by distant dreams,
> And cared no more for the sacred inheritance.
> Through all space you felt the breath of the end . . .
> Now lift up your heads. For salvation has come unto you.
> In your burdened and arctic year
> A Springtime of new miracles has now burst forth.
> With flowering hand and gleaming hair
> A god has appeared and has entered your home.
>
> Now mourn no more—for you too have been chosen—
> That your days ebb away unfulfilled . . .
> Praise your city that has given birth to a god!
> Praise your days in which a god has lived![1]

[1] Stefan George, *Der Siebente Ring, Maximin.*

CHAPTER 13

POWER AND WILL IN MAN. THE KING

1. *LE premier qui fut roi, fut un soldat heureux.* Despite all its superficiality Voltaire's old maxim contains some truth, if only it is taken in its "primitive", and not in its original, sense. Chesterton is unquestionably right in saying that the idea of the strongest man forcibly making himself king is merely "current cant", if we disregard the mystical element of admiration which creates the ruler.[1] Yet for primitive man it is precisely power and luck that possess this mystic significance; power and will do not, as for ourselves, unite to constitute a "personality", a character, but rather an *office* or status that someone assumes; and our own expression, "his majesty", still indicates this impersonal dignity of the power which is imposed on the man and fuses with his own will. In ancient Egyptian it is called *hm-f*, which means literally "his club".[2] The club is both an implement and a weapon; and we have already seen that the power, emanating from the tool, meant to the primitive mind something far more than mere efficiency. It is indeed very likely, *a priori*, that the original kings were sturdy fellows who could smite hard with their clubs. But it is certain that their potency, whether attached to their clubs or their wisdom, was experienced as a power "from elsewhere". In the primitive world, then, the king is the power bearer, the saviour; and for quite a long time he remained so, while when kings *dei gratia* became constitutional monarchs, the mystic dignity became assigned to the "potent" successors, the Rienzis and Napoleons, down to the *duce* of our own time.

Thus in Melanesia the son inherits not his father's chieftainship but, if the father can so arrange affairs, that which gives him the chief's dignity, his *mana*.[3] The ruler's *mana* can, however, also be lost. When the Maori chief Hape was dying, he summoned his tribe and asked who might be in the position to stand in his footsteps and lead the people to victory. He really put this question for the benefit of his own sons, hoping to give them an opportunity to ensure the chieftainship for them-

---

[1] *The Everlasting Man* (People's Library Edition), 67.
[2] *cf.* L. Borchardt, *Die Hieroglyphe ḥm, Zeitschr. f. äg. Spr. u. Altert. K.* 37, 82. Erman-Grapow, *Wörterbuch der äg. Sprache.*
[3] Codrington, *The Melanesians*, 56 *f.*

selves; but they hesitated so long that finally a chief of low rank gave the answer, and thus they lost the authority, the *mana*.[1] Scandinavian sagas, too, tell us of a king's "luck" to which pertain victory in battle and invulnerability, healing power and good weather, particularly during sea voyages. To struggle against the king's "luck" is difficult, but "with God's help and the king (Olaf's) luck", on the contrary, one can achieve much. The king's "luck", as it were, overflows, so that under the rule of Jarl Haakon the corn grew everywhere it was sown, and herrings were to be found all round the coast; a Gothic definition of the king, again, calls him "he in whose luck we conquer". But if the harvest was bad the peasants blamed the king. Here again the "luck" is not heritable: a foundling seized the spear of the Lombard king Agilmund, and therewith the king's "luck" passed over to him, so that he was adopted and succeeded the king in the government.[2]

In describing the royal office, however, our modern expressions cannot be employed; "strong personality" is unsuitable, while "dignity" in our debased sense of a good position is equally inadequate. The term "office", or "official status" (*Amt*), then, still represents most explicitly the primitive combination of power and will that constitutes the king a saviour. How irrelevant are our present-day ideas is obvious from the familiar stories about royal children taken into combat; thus, by Tjostol Aalesön young Inge in Norway, and by Queen Fredegond young Clotaire in France, were conducted to decisive battles as guarantors of luck.[3]

The Roman *Imperium* too was regarded as an office borne by the person of an emperor or magistrate; and in the later worship of the emperors, the soul of the monarch received the *imperium* in the course of its descent through the planetary spheres. To the office, still further, corresponded potent objects as the *insignia* of kingship; the Egyptian Pharaoh was adorned with a snake, the bearer of his devastating might; and the mace and sceptre are still familiar to us to-day.

The kingship, as a power superior to its bearer himself, has been very characteristically depicted by Gerhart Hauptmann in a scene where rebels, pressing king Prospero hard, fall down before his face. Then Prospero asks:

> What has befallen me?
> Why is all dark around me? Why
> Is all my body bathed in death's cold sweat?

[1] Lehmann, *Mana*, 22.
[2] S. Grönbech, *Vor Folkeaet*, I, 146 ff., 194; III, 49 ff.   [3] *ibid.*, I, 197.

and Oro the high priest replies:

> That Power, which from him struck, is all too strong
> E'en for the very soul that houses it.[1]

2. Since kingly potency is no personal capacity, all conceivable salvation is expected of it. The king's power ought to overflow; and the next most closely related consequence of this is that he should bestow gifts. "Forsooth, the king deserves the name of king only *if he distributes gifts*, rules justly, is merciful and leads a noble life before his subjects", as it says in *The Arabian Nights*. Among the old Icelandic and Anglo-Saxon *kenningar*, again, we find as poetic synonyms of "king": "dispenser of gold", "of swords", "of rings", "giver of treasures";[2] like the ancient rulers of the Orient, the German monarch too was expected to display his power by giving presents, and thus it was probably no advantage for the life purpose of the Egyptian prophet-king Akhnaton that, as we can still perceive from his monuments, he had as ruler to bestow many gifts. Those whom he favoured in this way knew how to appreciate his influence as long as it subsisted, but as soon as the royal authority had declined they allowed the king's religion to meet an ignominious end. Primitive kingship and prophetic capacity were very difficult to unite.

But royal power likewise manifests itself in matters which we moderns consider quite beyond human attainment. As a genuine saviour the king also *heals*; and until fairly recent times the "king's touch" was regarded in England as a cure for scrofula. Shakespeare describes his restorative influence, to which throngs of unfortunate people fly for aid and

> at his touch—
> Such sanctity hath heaven given his hand—
> They presently amend.[3]

Cosmic events too are subject to kingly power. The famous ruler of Bangkara in Sumatra, Si singa Mangarajah, who caused so much difficulty to the Dutch authorities, governed the rain and sunshine and blessed the harvest.[4] Similarly, the Masai king not only destroys the enemy but makes rain also, his power residing in his beard; and like Samson he loses this if he is robbed of his hair.[5] The chief of Etatin

---

[1] *Indipohdi*, Act III.   [2] A. J. Portengen, *Revue Anthr.* 35, 1925, 367.
[3] *Macbeth*, IV, 3.   [4] Wilken, *Verspreide Geschriften*, III, 166 f.
[5] Frazer, *The Magical Origin of Kings (Lectures on the Kingship)*, 112 ff.

in Southern Nigeria, again, was never permitted to leave his own house: power must be concentrated and carefully guarded. He was forced into office, and had been shut up for ten years when he gave the following description of his activities: "By the observance and performance of these ceremonies I bring game to the hunter, cause the yam crop to be good, bring fish to the fisherman and make rain to fall."[1] The curse, or the blessing, of the *datu* of Luwu in Celebes settles the prosperity of the rice harvest as well as human well-being; similarly with the sultan of Ternate in the Moluccas,[2] while Rajah Sir James Brooke (1803–1868), the ruler of Sarawak in North Borneo, was not only worshipped as a divine deliverer from the Malay power but also influenced the success of the rice crop, the water with which the women washed his feet being preserved and distributed among the farms so as to ensure a rich harvest.[3]

The classical land of royal power, however, was ancient Egypt, where the king was addressed as follows: "Thou art indeed he who canst veil the horizon; the sun rises at thy pleasure; we drink the water of the river when thou willest it, and breathe the air of heaven when thou permittest";[4] and the king makes Egypt's frontiers as wide as those "which the sun encircles". This is no swaggering nor exaggeration of a flattering Byzantinism: the king actually rules the world. Man strove to combine in one single individual all secular power and all conceivable prosperity, and the good king is thus described in excessive, yet at the same moment realistic, terms: "He illuminates the Two Lands (Egypt) more than the sun-disk. He makes the Two Lands green more than a great Nile (a plenteous flood); He hath filled the Two Lands with strength. (He is) life cooling the nostrils. . . . The king is food, His mouth is increase. He is the one creating that which is; He is the Khnum (the god who forms out of clay) of all limbs; The Begetter, who causes the people to be."[5] One of the most usual epithets applied to the monarch was "he who gives life", an expression with a double meaning since it might also signify "he on whom life was bestowed".[6] In relation to men, then, the king was the power bearer, while in

---

[1] Frazer, *The Magical Origin of Kings* (*Lectures on the Kingship*), 118.

[2] Kruyt, *Het Animisme in den Indischen Archipel*, 229 f.

[3] Wilken, *ibid.*, III, 167 f. Kruyt, *ibid.*, 231; *cf.* Lévy-Bruhl, *How Natives Think*, 252 ff.

[4] *Geschichte von Sinuhe*, 232 ff. *cf. Popular Stories of Ancient Egypt* (Maspero), 68 ff.

[5] Breasted, *Ancient Records of Egypt*, I, Sect. 747; *cf.* further Lietzmann's compilation, *Der Weltheiland*, 51 f.

[6] *cf.* A. Moret, *Le Rituel du Culte divin journalier*, 1902, 101.

relation to power itself he stood in need of it; and in occupying this dual position he became the original type of all the mediators between God and man.

The idea of the good king who ensures the well-being of the world is practically universal; for Confucius also knew that the general weal should be anticipated from a good prince, while the reproach for every failure could be laid on a bad one. Thus the inclination, still operative to-day among simple people, to place the blame for everything "on the government" has very old and religious roots: God, Power, really bears all the blame; only since He is too remote, man seeks some bearer of power who is nearer and can also be the scapegoat when necessary. In the Nyanza district, for instance, a hereditary king was banished from the country because of a lasting drought;[1] and Oedipus, again, had to listen to the complaint that although the land might once have extolled him as its deliverer, still it did not see why it should die of plague under his rule, and definitely expected a remedy from him.[2] Homer's description of the government of the good king is well known: "the black earth bears wheat and barley, and the trees are laden with fruit, and the sheep bring forth and fail not, and the sea gives store of fish, and all out of his good guidance, and the people prosper under him".[3] In precisely the same sense the regal power of Cyrus ensured that his soldiers, in crossing a river, should arrive safely on the other side: "the passage was considered a miraculous thing; the river had manifestly retired before Cyrus's face as for the king".[4]

In the Hellenistic era these ideas about kings received universal significance, and centred particularly upon Augustus; later, the whole of the Middle Ages is replete with them. The famous "canon attributed to St. Patrick enumerates among the blessings that attend the reign of a just king 'fine weather, calm seas, crops abundant, and trees laden with fruit' ".[5] Further, the German emperors, especially during the struggles with the Pope, stressed again and again the religious and indeed cosmic basis of their own rulership. Royal raiment, too, had possessed religious significance even when, in remote times in Egypt and elsewhere, it was only a simple primitive loin cloth. The cloak dedicated to St. Denis by Hugh Capet's consort was called *orbis terrarum*, while the emperor Henry II adorned his robe with sun,

---

[1] Frazer, *op. cit.*, 116 f.
[2] Sophocles, *Oedipus Rex*, 49 f.   [3] *Odyssey*, XIX, 109 ff.
[4] Xenophon, *Anabasis*, I, 4, 18; *cf.* H. Smilda, *Mnemosyne*, 1926.
[5] Frazer, *op. cit.*, 125.

moon and stars; Frederick II, similarly, "can give no completer expression to the fullness of his authority than by adorning his royal seal with a crescent couchant and a star since 1211".[1] The king's power, then, is no human might, but *the* power, the potency of the world; his imperialism is not covetousness, but an assertion of his world status, and his garb "the living garment of God". By the ancient Egyptians the "two lands" were regarded, as a matter of course, as constituting the world, while the princes of later antiquity and the Middle Ages regarded the world as their realm—no longer, however, so much as a matter of course.

3. The king, then, is a god: indeed he is one of the first and oldest gods: Power has been embodied in a living figure. For the king is no rigid god; he is rather a living, active, changeable power, a god who walks among men. But undoubtedly a god. Of course it was known all the time that this bearer of high rank was a quite ordinary man. Even the Egyptians joked about the drunkenness of the Pharaoh, Amasis,[2] and when someone called Antigonus a son of the sun and a god, he himself jocularly remarked: "Of that my bedchamber attendant knows nothing."[3] But after all it is not the man who is revered, but the official status, the power that has assumed form; and it is adored not as an immobile greatness, but as living salvation. The institution of kingship signifies, indeed, a forcible and thorough change in human life: everything was waste and misery, but now all is well. Once again the breath of Spring is wafted: "What a happy day! Heaven and earth rejoice, (for) thou art the great lord of Egypt. They that had fled have come again to their towns, and they that were hidden have again come forth. They that hungered are satisfied and happy, and they that thirsted are drunken. They that were naked are clad in fine linen, and they that were dirty have white garments. They that were in prison are set free, and he that was in bonds is full of joy."[4] That is the good tidings as it was announced at the accession of Rameses IV: the *Gospel* (*evangelium*), as people said later on.

In a still more literal sense than he is a god, the king is the son of god; and in this also he is a saviour-form. So Pharaoh declared of him-

---

[1] F. Kampers, *Vom Werdegang der abendländischen Kaisermystik*, 1924, 8 *ff*.

[2] G. Röder, *Altägyptische Erzählungen und Märchen*, 1927, 298 *ff*.

[3] Plutarch, *Of Isis and Osiris*, 24. Thus, when Alexander was wounded, he was astonished that his blood was not *ichor* "such as flows in the blessed gods". E. Bickermann, *AR*. 27, 1929, 25, Note 2.

[4] A. Erman, *The Literature of the Ancient Egyptians*, 279.

self: "I am the god, the beginning of being, nothing fails that goes out of my mouth";[1] and in the temple of Soleib Amenhotep III may still be observed adoring himself.[2] But above all the king of Egypt was literally the *son* of god, whether he appeared as the son of the sun-god, like the kings of the Fifth Dynasty, or Amon was assigned to him as his own father; and at Deir el Bahari and Luxor the temple walls exhibit in word and design a formal account of the king's birth; Amon approached the queen, and from the union of the god with mortal woman the young king sprang. Even *Psalm* ii cannot apprehend the king's intimate relationship to God otherwise than as sonship: "Thou art my Son; this day have I begotten thee".[3] Thus for the monarch a miraculous birth is quite natural.

As in birth, so at death. Even during his life the Egyptian Pharaoh was regarded as dead and endowed with eternal life. He was probably the first to whom the idea of immortality was applied; the funereal *Texts* were originally composed for him alone.[4] Similarly among the Indonesian tribes the personal continuance of life after death is thought of in connection with office, that is as limited to the tribal leaders.[5]

Naturally the sacred king is surrounded with every kind of *tabu*, to such a degree indeed that frequently kingship very closely approaches captivity, as in the case of the African ruler whose words were quoted previously. The Roman *rex* again, divested of his temporal power, of all his grandeur retained only the burdensome *tabus* as *rex sacrorum*; while in Hawaii the king was seen only by night, and whoever saw him by day was put to death; nor was he permitted to touch food with his own hand.[6] Power, concentrated in the king, must be protected.

4. The king becomes a god at the moment of his appearance; for it is precisely this *appearance* that changes the world and introduces a new era. To appear as a form is indeed the royal glory; and this we find expressed very beautifully in the song sung for the epiphany of Demetrius Poliorketes and preserved by Athenaeus: "For the other gods are too far removed from us, or they hear us not. Either they do not exist at all, or they do not concern themselves about us. But thee

---

[1] Breasted, *Records*, II, 293.
[2] G. Maspero, *Au Temps de Ramsès et d'Assourbanipal*, 1912, 46.   [3] *Ps.* ii. 7.
[4] Thus the king was the sole officiating person in worship. The Babylonian *Penitential Psalms* were composed for the king—of course in his capacity as the representative of the people—and only later used by the common folk. M. Jastrow, *Die Religion Babyloniens und Assyriens*, II, 1, 1912, 117.
[5] Kruyt, *op. cit.*, 4.   [6] Frazer, *The Belief in Immortality*, II, 388 *f.*

we can see with our own eyes. Thou art neither wood nor stone, but here in the very flesh. Therefore to thee we pray."[1]

The Roman cult of the emperors, too, was directed to the "god present on earth in the body, ἐπιφανής, praesens."[2] In him was salvation revealed and apparent; in his own era the king was the saviour. Thus in him also are to be met those historic and periodic-natural tendencies already described in dealing with the saviour. These trends even intersect most tragically. For the prince who saves his people, who has been manifested, becomes again and again the ruler who has lost his power and must depart. Far from being an "important", or even an unimportant, "personality", the king rises and sets as often as the orb with which he is frequently so intimately connected; and in *The Golden Bough* Frazer has brought out the tragic original meaning of *Le roi est mort, vive le roi* in an unforgettable manner.

Royal power, then, is world-power, but like that of the sun it is valid only for its own period. We date according to kings. In the imperial era their assumption of the government was regarded as the commencement of the world, ἀρχὴ τῶν παντών;[3] the Egyptians likewise treated the accession as a constant parallel to the commencement of all things. Thus the gospel of the new monarch is of cosmic range: he is σωτήρ in the most comprehensive sense. But he is the eternal son, and as saviour he is always the young prince; the old deposed ruler is presupposed, so that the king's first proud year succeeds the sad last year of his predecessor.

With these years of the kings a peculiar feature is associated. In Babylon the king celebrated every year a new accession day. "His reign was reckoned from the first new year's day after the death of his predecessor; his first accession he held on the first new year's day; the rest of the initial year was assigned to his dead forerunner and designated as *rêš šarruti* or the beginning of the kingship";[4] and in the earliest Egyptian era we find exactly the same procedure: on the Palermo Stone, inscribed with the oldest chronicle, the last uncompleted years of a reign are not called after any event.[5] On this feature Eduard Meyer remarks: "Here therefore full and proper years of rule are

---

[1] Bertholet, *Lesebuch*, 4, 85.
[2] H: Usener, *Dreiheit, Rh. Museum*, N. F., 58, 23. On the peculiar and mediatory character of Roman emperor worship cf. E. Bickermann, *Die römische Kaiserapotheose*, AR. 27, 1929.   [3] Lietzmann, *Der Weltheiland*, 14 f.
[4] S. Mowinckel, *Psalmenstudien*, II, 1922, 7.
[5] cf. K. Sethe, *Beiträge zur ältesten Geschichte Ägyptens*, 1905, 70 ff. But he ascribes this peculiarity to the purely chronological purpose of the enumeration.

reckoned beginning with the day of the king's accession and ignoring the calendar year, just as at present, in charters, the years of the reign of the pope and of the king of England are calculated".[1] Each king thus begins anew, after he has put a score under the reign of his predecessor; each has his own era. Now we can understand this if we regard the monarch as the bearer of power; for the power is always new, and the king always a new king. He is never a mere continuation, but always an appearance, a new beginning; and this point of view concerns itself just as little with the particular events of any period as with the "important" personality of the ruler. Life is imprisoned within a dogma to which it must adapt itself; a net is extended over life in order to hold fast the power; its circulation is sustained by notches in the tally of time, just as is the circulation of light by the change of night and day. The king, then, signifies permanence in change.

The Egyptians said of him that he "renews life"; and this was intended in a very literal sense. For change, as it was actually experienced —and here the historic line intersects the periodic—occurred apart from the fixed times for change; but any such accidental and unforeseen waning of the power that revealed itself in the king could not be tolerated, since bodily or mental weakness in the monarch might be detrimental to the whole of life. Hence that assignment of a time limit to the monarchy, to which Frazer has devoted a great part of his work, and which found clear expression in the ancient Egyptian feast of *Sed*. Usually this is interpreted as the jubilee of a reign; but it has in fact a deeper meaning. Eduard Meyer, again, referred to "an imposing of limits to kingship", which began, as it were, for a second time with this feast.[2] During the festival a sort of coffer stood before the king in which, just as at burials, there lay a veiled form probably representing the embryo, thereby symbolizing in a drastic way the king's rebirth.[3] The "old" king, who actually wore funereal dress, was thus confronted by the new one; the king, as it were, succeeded himself.

Regal power, still further, is confined within its human form only for an appointed period. The name of the ancient Roman festival,

---

[1] In Sethe, *Beiträge zur ältesten Geschichte Ägyptens*, 1905, 73.

[2] *Geschichte des Altertums*, I, 2³, 1913, 153.

[3] Yet this muffled form was also otherwise interpreted—*e.g.* as a little princess. But it is not clear how the princess could serve as a permanent requisite of the regal ceremony. P. E. Newberry gives a very clever, but somewhat far-fetched, explanation in *Ägypten als Feld für anthropologische Forschung* (*Der alte Orient*, 27, 1), 1927, 21. On the feast of *Sed*, *cf.* W. B. Kristensen, *Meded. Kon. Akademie van Wetenschappen, Afd. Lett.* 56, B. 6, 1923, 16.

regifugium, was interpreted by Frazer as a vestige of a time when the ruler actually had to take flight after the expiration of his time limit or else, as can still be proved of the *reges nemorenses*, the kings of the woodlands, of Aricia, had to defend himself against a pretender to the throne. Even at the coronation of English kings, until that of Edward VII, a herald challenged all those to come forward who might question the sovereign's right to the throne.[1] The issue, then, is clear: Power must manifest and maintain itself, and this not only at the accession but perpetually. We must of course recall the fact that Power is no affair of mere theory, but always an empirically authenticated and experienced greatness. I do not wish, however, to cite all the examples of time-limited kingship, of which Frazer has compiled a large number:[2] I shall draw attention only to essentials.

After a certain interval therefore, after power had departed from him, the king must actually die. Of this the Egyptian feast of *Sed* and the Roman *regifugium* were modifications; and many primitive peoples are known who actually killed the "old" king. Here too the saviour must suffer and die. He might wait till he was killed, but also he might himself surrender to death; and of this too Frazer has compiled many instances. In all this the conception of sacrifice plays a part; the king should sacrifice himself for the good of his people. But yet another idea arose—that of the substitute, which attained the highest significance in the development of the concept of the saviour.

Thus once again two originally and basically different ideas are united in one. Actually, the king is always the substitute: he supervises his people's salvation, performs sacrifices, leads to war, *etc.*, and when he dies he dies for the people in order that its power should be preserved. Even his corpse could bring salvation: the body of the Swedish king Halfdan the Black was distributed to four districts, so that it might ensure a rich harvest for them all.[3] But side by side with this idea another emerges: the old custom is mitigated; the king does not actually die, but allows a substitute to be executed. This is the mock king who exercises the princely power for a brief time, usually for only one day, and is then killed; later, he is merely maltreated. This king-for-a-day, generally a slave or war prisoner, is to be found as early as Babylon, and still played his part at the Roman Saturnalia. In an Assyrian pantomime there occurs a dialogue between the mock king and his

---

[1] Frazer, *The Magical Origin of Kings* (*Lectures on the Kingship*), 275.
[2] *The Golden Bough* IV, (*The Dying God*), 14 *ff*, 46 *ff*.
[3] *Ibid.*, VI (*Adonis, Attis and Osiris*, II), 100 *ff*.

lord; the *pseudo*-king now gives orders to his master; he desires to eat, drink, love a woman, *etc.* Everything is granted him; but the end of the story is that his neck is broken and he is thrown into the river; thereby he assumes the place of the god Bel, who also dies to rise again.[1] Probably the king himself had to die originally as the substitute for the god, that is for the country's power; and then the two "substitutes" gradually fused into a single form.

For a long time this type of the innocent king-for-a-day, suffering in a ridiculous manner, vividly persisted in Literature. We recall Christopher Sly in Shakespeare's *Taming of the Shrew*, allowed as master to give orders and enjoy things for a day, but then thrown into the street again.[2] "Behind the disgraceful mask of the fallen or transient king, our ancestors perceived the tragic figure of the God-Man who died for the well-being and life of his neighbour."[3] The substitutive sacrifice for man's salvation gradually expanded into one of the great world-moving thoughts, and became linked to the change of kings. To preserve this salvation the figure of the saviour must be broken; and Frazer and other investigators have advanced the view that Jesus was maltreated by the Roman soldiers in the character of the mock-king already familiar to them from the Roman Saturnalia.[4] But even if this cannot be proved, still the King of the Jews on the Cross bears all the features of the king dying for the salvation of his people; and he still remains a king in the apotheosis, in St. John's Gospel: "Art thou a king then?—Thou sayest that I am a king."[5]

That the king must suffer is involved in the conception of the periodic change of life. The Old Testament was aware that when life is regarded historically, and when its periodic vicissitudes have been replaced by the rule of the sovereign Will, then whoso brings salvation must also suffer. The "suffering servant of Jahveh" too, particularly when he is the representative of the people, exhibits all the traits of the king.[6]

[1] E. Ebeling, *Keilschrifttexte aus Assur religiösen Inhalts*, 1917, *Nr.* 96. *cf.* F. M. Th. Böhl, *Stemmen des Tyds*, 10, 1920, 42 *ff.* H. Zimmern, *Berichte über die Verhandl. der sächs. Gesellsch. der Wiss.*, 1906, 1918.
[2] In other Literatures also: Dutch, *Krelis Louwen* (Langendyk); Danish, *Jeppe fra Bjerget* (Holberg).   [3] A. Moret, *Mystères Égyptiens*, 1913, 273.
[4] *cf.* P. Wendland, *Hermes*, 33, 1898, 175. H. Vollmer, *Jesus und das Sacaeenopfer*, 1905. J. Geffcken, *Hermes*, 41, 1906, 220 *ff.* Frazer, *The Golden Bough*, IX (*The Scapegoat*), 412 *ff.* Further in R. Bultmann, *Die Geschichte der Synoptischen Tradition²*, 1931, 294. E. Klostermann, on *St. Mark* xv, 16 *ff.* in *Handbuch zum Neuen Testament*.
[5] *John* xviii. 37.
[6] F. M. Th. Böhl, *De "Knecht des Heeren" in Jezaja* 53, 1923. Böhl kindly writes to inform me that, in his opinion, the manner in which, in *Isaiah* xlix. 7, 23, liii. 15, the kings of the nation are compared with the "servant" who is identified with Israel,

5. In accordance with his type, still further, the bringer of salvation for his era always comes "again", whether as the son or as his own successor; and this hope of a definite return is also attached to the king-experience. This longing is constituted by the expectation of periodically renewed salvation and the yearning for happy "last days", for the harmonious fading away of history under a "good king".

Of such a king the ancient Egyptians had a vague anticipation: "A king will come from the South . . . the people of the days of this son of man will rejoice . . . they will remain far from evil. The godless too will humble their faces because of fear before him . . . the uraeus (royal snake) on his forehead will appease the rebels . . .";[1] the "good king's" reign was always a messianic era.[2] But as soon as the historic consciousness developed, and the idea of periodicity gave place to that of the end of the world, this epoch of salvation became transferred to the end of time, transposed to the far off and happy distance. What the Jews longed for from the branch of the line of David is universally known, and is most beautifully expressed in *Psalm* lxxii by the song of the good king:

> May he prove the champion of the weak,
>   may he deliver the forlorn,
>   and crush oppressors!
> Long may he live, long as the sun,
>   as the moon that shines for ever!
> May his rule be like rainfall upon meadows,
>   like showers that water the land!
> Justice and welfare flourish in his days,
>   till the moon be no more!
> From sea to sea may his domain extend,
>   from the Euphrates to the earth's far end! . . .
> all kings do homage to him,
>   all nations yield to him!
> For he saves the forlorn who cry to him,
>   the weak and helpless;
> he pities the forlorn and weak,
>   he saves the lives of the weak,

involves that the "servant" must also be conceived as king. "Servant" is the counterpart of "king". At the New Year Festival the king assumes the rôle of the servant, and the latter that of the king.

[1] W. Golénischeff, *Rec. de Travaux*, 15, 1893, 87 *ff.* (*Pap.* 1116 *Ermit. St. Petersburg*). *cf.* J. W. Breasted, *Development of Religion and Thought in Ancient Egypt*, 211 *f.* L. Dürr, *Ursprung und Ausbau der israelitisch-jüdischen Heilserwartung*, 1925, 1 *ff.*

[2] *cf. e.g.* Lietzmann's description of the reign of a Babylonian king, *op. cit.*, 20 *ff.*

> he rescues them from outrage and oppression—
> they are not cheap to him . . .
> May the land be rich in waving corn,
> right up to the top of the hills!
> May the folk flourish like trees in Lebanon,
> may citizens flower like grass in the field!
> For ever blessed be his name,
> sure as the sun itself his fame!
> All races envy his high bliss,
> all nations hail him as the happy king![1]

In the Middle Ages these ideas became connected with the great emperors Charlemagne and Frederick II (Barbarossa); they were not dead, but were waiting in the mountain for the day of the nation's direst need, to deliver it. Perhaps owing to the general belief in a definite limit fixed for Frederick's life, in the thirteenth century people doubted that he was actually dead, and indeed on several occasions false Fredericks successfully appeared.[2] Reformation of the church, again, was included in the universal welfare to be realized by the emperor. Thus when Power can no longer be linked with any actually visible form, the saviour-form of the ruler is placed at the close of time, as was supposed to have been inscribed on king Arthur's grave:— *Hic jacet Arthurus Rex quondam Rexque futurus*: "Here lies Arthur, sometime king, and king to be."

The kingly figure, then, is one of the most momentous of all those that man has depicted for himself. To derive the entire belief in God from the deification of rulers, however, would be just as stupid as to ignore the prominent rôle which the saviour-king has played in evolving that concept of God which tends to assume the form of a *numen praesens*, a son. Again and again humanity has sought to base the transient form and changing will of man upon the changeless essence and the eternal Will controlling the Universe; and thus the Chinese mystic also assigns to the ruler a place in direct relationship to *Tao*:

> There are four great ones in the space of the world,
> And the ruler of men is one of these.
> As his prototype Man has the Earth,
> As its prototype Earth has Heaven,
> As prototype Heaven has *Tao*—the Universal Order—
> And as prototype *Tao*, this Universal Order, has itself.[3]

[1] Moffat.
[2] Fr. Pfister, *Die deutsche Kaisersage und ihre antiken Wurzeln*, 1928.
[3] *Tao-teh King*, 25; cf. Chap. 2.

CHAPTER 14

THE MIGHTY DEAD

1. EARLY Animism derived religion from the cult of ancestors; and in so far as, in fact, the dead are accounted powerful, this was quite correct. It is, however, not their "souls" which possess power but they themselves, their living-dead forms; and to Animism Form is always indispensable. The dead man, then, is no soul without body, but another corporeality which may be more potent even than the living, but can also lose some of its power; for the event of death, which will be discussed later,[1] enhances, but also enfeebles, power.

In no case, however, can the cult of the dead be regarded as the outcome of any primitive psychology. It is derived, rather, from an actual *experience*: its roots lie in the meeting with the dead.[2] Such an encounter is by no means rare in our own still superstitious days; but probably the theorists of Animism have seen no spectres!

It is not, however, a fact that *all* the dead are powerful. It depends on the influence they enjoyed during their life-time, and also on the circumstances under which they died. In virtue of their rank, for instance, tribal leaders usually possess power after death also, and there are even cases where continued life after death is limited to the bearers of power;[3] originally the ancient Pharaohs appear to have been alone in their enjoyment of immortality. The conditions attending death are also important: women dying in child-bed often have a specific power after death. But in many cases a special potency is ascribed, by gradual stages, to all the dead.

2. So far as *Form* is concerned, however, the might of the dead is thought of as dwindling away. They lead a shadow life; the fixed outlines and concrete substance of Form have given place to something quite nebulous and misty. On Ceramlaut, for example, the recently dead appear as a white mist, and those who have been dead for some time as shadows.[4] The dead, again, cannot be grasped, but can be seen

---

[1] Chap. 22.

[2] cf. K. Th. Preuss, *Glaube und Mystik im Lichte des höchsten Wesens*, 1926, 19.

[3] Söderblom, *op. cit.*, 28; Preuss, 30.

[4] J. G. F. Riedel, *De Sluik- en Kroesharige rassen tusschen Selebes en Papoea*, 1886, 163.

through; they have no bones.[1] Occasionally they are imagined as being
smaller than the living.[2] But even though the form has disappeared to
a great extent, it is still there: the dead man resembles the living; he
can be recognized, seen and spoken to.

3. Opposed to the annihilation of power that thus affects Form,
however, is an enhancement that applies to Will; and thus the opinion
that the living are always "on the right side of the fence" is neither
primitive nor religious. In pantheistic vein, a Dutch poet renews the
honouring of the dead in writing of his dead son: "From my own
immediate feeling I understand now the essence of the worship of the
dead which was common to all civilized peoples. Even in his last days
my child was sacred to me, when he had found peace. Now, after his
departure, he is a being of a higher order: he has become divine, he is
my mediator; through him the Being of the Universe became tangible
and personal, something which I can love and to which I can speak,
not a mere ceremonial sound nor a vague auto-suggestion."[3] The
dead, then, are more potent than the living: their will imposes itself:
it is irresistible. They are superior in strength and insight, they are
the κρείττονες;[4] this concept is particularly explicit in Scandinavian
culture, and in this connection suicide, in order to gain power to
execute one's threats against the living, is a wholly practical idea.[5]

To the dead, still further, is ascribed cosmic power; here too Animism
was correct in asserting that in their effectiveness Nature-spirits and
the dead are not to be separated. Yet they themselves are not "spirits",
but simply deceased. In New Zealand, for example, a dead medicine-
man or chief is invoked for rain and fertility,[6] while in Indonesia the
dead can protect in the perils of war, guard from misfortune at sea
and make fishing and hunting highly productive.[7] The Greek *trito-
patores*, too, were at the same moment dead ancestors and demons of
the wind.[8]

Yet when human life is placed on the same level as vegetative life,
and the dead are intimately allied with the grain dying in the earth
and then springing up from it, Power is always a mere *unity*. The

---

[1] N. Söderblom, *Int. Review of Missions*, 1919, 533.

[2] Fr. von Duhn, *AR*. 12, 1909, 179 *f*., Table III, on the sarcophagus of Haghia
Triadha.   [3] Frederik van Eeden, *Paul's ontwaken*.

[4] E. Rohde, *Psyche*, I [5-6], 1910, 246, and Note 2, who refers to Plutarch, *Cons. ad.
Apoll.* 27. English Translation, 166, 201.

[5] H. and I. Naumann, *Isländische Volksmärchen*, 1923, Nr. 64.

[6] Alviella, *Idée de Dieu*, 113.

[7] Wilken, *op. cit.*, III, 190.   [8] B. Schweitzer, *Herakles*, 1922, 75 *f*.

altar of Consus in the *circus maximus* was simultaneously a granary and the dwelling-place of the dead.[1] Burial is a sort of seed sowing. The Roman family *lar*, again, expanded from a domestic god and family ancestor to the god of a district: *lar compitalis*, the deity of the cross-roads.[2]

4. The dead exercise their power over man in both a propitious and a disastrous way. They are terrible, and at their approach men are filled with dread. Of women dying in child-bed I have already spoken, while in Indonesia the *pontianak* is a gruesome figure: hollow backed, it sits in the tree-tops in the guise of a bird, causes miscarriages, and at midnight robs men of their masculine vigour. On the Island of Borneo again, before the founding by Abdu 'l Rahman of the town named after them, one was compelled to shoot for two hours at the *pontianak* lurking in the vicinity before approaching the settlement.[3] In ancient Egypt, similarly, there were formulas to protect the pyramids from the attacks of the dead.[4] Greece too had its dreadful dead, who worked evil on the living and dragged them down to death; tormenting spirits of this type were the harpies and sirens. Hecate's gloomy retinue raged through the night, Dionysus too being regarded as the leader of a "wild hunt". This notion was later developed during Germanic antiquity and the Middle Ages: Wotan, "the furious", dashes about with his wild company on stormy nights; he and the *Perchta* are the exact counterparts of Dionysus and Hecate with their *thiasos* or *komos*,[5] while in the Middle Ages the dead bore off the living to a gruesome dance or the most wretched nuptials.[6]

From time to time this belief in the dead leads to a sort of fatalism, especially among primitive peoples: the power of the dead is so much stronger than that of the living that one surrenders completely to them; they thus control custom and usage, so that any deviation draws their anger in its train, as *e.g.* among the Bataks.[7] The excessively powerful will of the dead dominates the whole of life; the "living exist under the shadow of the dead".[8]

---

[1] A. Piganiol, *Recherches sur les Jeux romains*, 1923, 2; *cf.* 13.

[2] *cf.* S. Wide in Gercke and Norden, *Einleitung in die Altertumswissenschaft*, II², 1912, 241. Chantepie, *op. cit.*, II, 435.

[3] Wilken, *op. cit.*, III, 223 *ff.*   [4] *Pyramidentexte* (Sethe), 1656.

[5] *cf.* Beth, *Einführung in die vergleichende Religionsgeschichte*, 92.

[6] *cf.* my Monograph: *In den hemel is eenen dans*, 1930, 20 *f.* (*In dem Himmel ist ein Tanz, Munich.*)

[7] *cf.* J. C. van Eerde, *Inleiding tot de Volkenkunde van Ned. Indie*, 1920, 190 *f.*

[8] N. Adriani, *Het animistisch heidendom als godsdienst*, 44. *ibid.*, Posso, 64.

But they can also exert a beneficent influence: I have previously observed how they rule the elements to the advantage of the living. Usually they protect their own people; thus the Greek *heros* was a sort of domestic demon; buried under the threshold, he occasionally showed himself to the inmates of the house in the guise of a snake.[1] In Vedic India, again, the young wife sacrificed to the ancestors and implored them to bless her with children.[2] For the dead are either the forbears, the heads of the family, whose power over their people has been enhanced by death (as will be observed later) or else they are that sinister troop, the throng of the dead. But the ghost of anyone, whether related by blood or not, can inspire dread and oppress; and with this we return to the experience of:

5. *The encounter with the dead*, which lies at the base of every form of their worship. Nordic and Icelandic sagas afford marvellous examples of the horror and devastating power emanating from the dead, as for example in the story of Grettir the Strong and the spectre Glam. The shepherd Glam, a sinister fellow, is slain by a ghost. Then he too begins to haunt the place and many people meet him: "that brought them great hurt, for when they saw him some fell fainting, and others lost their reason". He commenced to straddle the ridges of the roofs of the farm and walked both by day and night; people hardly ventured to come into the valley any longer. He continued, however, to kill cattle and people till at last he was slain once more by Grettir the Strong; but his victory procured him only bad luck.[3]

On certain days hosts of dead invade the settlements of the living:— on Ceramlaut, every Thursday, they visit their relatives from sunset to cockcrow. A meal is prepared for them: if this is omitted they lay a curse on the house.[4] In Cambodia, likewise, little boats filled with rice and cakes, *etc.*, are made for the dead, and floated on the river so that they may travel in them;[5] while on All Souls' Day a sacrifice of food or candles should be offered, lest the dead become hurtful to us. But when they have eaten their fill they are driven away: "Out of the door, ye souls, the anthesteria is over"; in Greece they were with these words ejected through the door, and with almost the same formula in

[1] *cf.* S. Wide, *Lakonische Kulte*, 1893, 280. J. E. Harrison, *Prolegomena to the Study of Greek Religion*, 325 *ff.*

[2] H. Oldenberg, *Die Religion des Veda*², 1917, 332, *cf.* 308.

[3] Naumann, *Isländische Volksmärchen*, Nr. 69.

[4] Riedel, *Sluik-en kroesharige rassen*, 163.

[5] Frazer, *The Golden Bough*, VI (*Adonis, Attis and Osiris*, II), 61 *f.*

Vedic India.[1] On days when the departed walk there is power in the air: we should take care, there are "polluted days"; thus in ancient Rome there were some days during which *mundus patet*, that is the ancient vault, into which also the first fruits were thrown, remained open. Then the dead walked, especially in February, the month of purification; the temples were closed, marriages should not be celebrated, the graves were adorned with flowers and sacrifices offered to the dead. For three days during May, again, the *lemures* were about; at midnight the farmer appeared at his door and threw black beans over his shoulder to buy off the terrible power: "when he has said nine times, 'Ghosts of my fathers, go forth'! he looks back, and thinks that he has duly performed the sacred rites".[2]

The *twelve nights* too were potent times, each of them deciding the weather for one month of the coming year; work was at a standstill, for spirits walked; and in Mecklenburg people avoided calling animals by their names from fear of the wild huntsman.[3] During All Souls the Tyrolese leave the uneaten cakes on the table together with burning candles for the poor souls, who are said to come from Purgatory to earth at the angelus on All Souls' Day, while in ancient Prussia it was the custom to hold a wake some days after the funeral: afterwards a priest swept the house and chased out the souls with the words: "Ye have eaten and drunken, ye departed, go out, go out."[4]

Thus in the first place sacrifice to the dead is a payment of ransom; but its purpose is also their sustenance, and if they are generously disposed they even appear as benefactors; at the Greek funeral feast the dead man was the host, ὑποδέκτης, and the saying *de mortuis nil nisi bene*, which we have converted into an affair of piety, was seriously observed.[5]

It is, however, when intercourse with the dead is interpreted as marriage that it assumes its most dreadful form: Antigone had to descend into the *thalamos* of Hades, while Iphigenia, Helen and Cassandra were regarded as brides of Hades.[6] In popular belief it is not death, but a dead man, who is the bridegroom: and Bürger's *Leonore*

---

[1] Rohde, *Psyche*, I[5-6], 236 *ff.* English Translation, 168, 197. Oldenberg, *Religion des Veda*, 550: "Avaunt, ye fathers, ye friends of *soma*, to your deep and ancient ways. But return a month hence to our home, rich in posterity, in male offspring, to eat the sacrifice."

[2] Ovid, *Fasti*, V, 429 *ff.*   [3] Reinsberg-Düringsfeld, *Das festliche Jahr*, 464 *f.*

[4] E. Samter, *Geburt, Hochzeit und Tod*, 1911, 32.

[5] Rohde, *Psyche*, I, 231 *f.*: ἐιώθεσαν οἱ παλαιοὶ ἐν τοῖς περιδείπνοις τὸν τετελητεύκοτα ἐπαινεῖν, καὶ εἰ φαῦλος ἦν. E. T. 170.

[6] L. Malten, *Der Raub der Kore, AR.* 12, 1909, 311.

has given this theme its classical form. But even in the horror of the encounter with the departed there still lives the conviction that life comes from them. The Greek festival of All Souls is called the "festival of flowers", and even marriage with death has been transformed by mysticism into a form of bliss:

> Death calls us to the nuptials—
> Brightly the lamps are burning—
> The virgins are at hand—
> There is no lack of oil.[1]

[1] Novalis, 5. *Hymne an die Nacht.*

THE AWFUL FORM, THE EVIL WILL: DEMONS

1. "ANIMISM" was right, too, in maintaining that the boundary between the dead and every kind of spirit, even gods, is always plastic. But the spirit world is by no means confined to the realm of the departed. Admittedly, many demonic forms originated from belief in the dead and in spectres; I need say no more about this at present. But Power was experienced in other forms also; and in so far as the potent *will* is here again decisive in creating these forms, belief in demons is animistic. The powers of life are felt and perceived as terrifying, often indeed as devastating, and always as incalculable; and World-power, divided among many petty rulers, is placed in the hands of despotism and inconstancy. If this belief in demons predominates, a persistent fear haunts human life, as was the case among many primitive peoples; but if it can merely assume its position among other opinions—as *e.g.* in our own civilization—then it leads to superstition.

2. Neither fear nor superstition, however, is ever the outcome of reflection. Belief in demons does not mean that chance rules the Universe, but rather that I have experienced the horror of some power which concerns itself neither with my reason nor my morals;[1] and it is not fear of any definite concrete terribleness, but vague terror of the gruesome and the incomprehensible, which projects itself objectively in belief in demons. Horror and shuddering, sudden fright and the frantic insanity of dread, all receive their form in the demon; this represents the absolute horribleness of the world, the incalculable force which weaves its web around us and threatens to seize us. Hence all the vagueness and ambiguity of the demon's nature: "the characteristic of the *troll* is the malicious lack of plan which adheres to his whole way of acting, as opposed to that of man, who in all his deeds, for good or evil, is conscious of his own purpose . . . his eyes are so wicked that one glance from them suffices to burn away the fertility of a province, and it is this psychic chaos that results in his mere proximity invoking gloomy delusions".[2] The awe-inspiring character of demons is impres-

---

[1] *cf.* Otto, *The Idea of the Holy*, 126 ff.
[2] V. Grönbech, *Vor Folkeaet i Oldtiden*, II, 1912, 180.

sively described in the Babylonian *Prayer Against the Seven Evil Spirits*:

> Seven are they, seven are they,
> In the Ocean Deep seven are they,
> Battening in Heaven seven are they,
> In the Ocean Deep as their home they were reared,
> Nor male or female are they,
> They are as the roaming windblast,
> No wife have they, no son do they beget;
> Knowing neither mercy nor pity,
> They hearken not unto prayer or supplication.
> They are as horses reared among the hills;
> The Evil Ones of Ea,
> Throne-bearers to the gods are they.
> They stand in the highway to befoul the path.
>
> From land to land they roam,
> Driving the maiden from her chamber,
> Sending the man forth from his home,
> Expelling the son from the house of his father,
> Hunting the pigeons from their cotes,
> Driving the bird from its nest,
> Making the swallow fly forth from its hole,
> Smiting both oxen and sheep.
> They are the evil spirits that chase the great storms,
> Bringing a blight on the land. . . .
> Upon themselves like a snake they glide,
> Like mice they make the chamber stink,
> Like hunting dogs they give tongue.[1]

The malicious inadequacy of all that happens and the irrationality at the very basis of life receive their form in the manifold uncanny and grotesque apparitions that have inhabited the world from time immemorial. The demons' behaviour is arbitrary, purposeless, even clumsy and ridiculous, but despite this it is no less terrifying. In Lithuania, for instance, the *Laumen* can work very quickly, but they can neither commence nor finish anything.[2] The *trolls* again, as is well known, are hollow backed, and utter duffers. Even the Devil is absurd, the "stupid" devil who is outwitted and whom the hero of the fairy

[1] R. Campbell Thompson, *The Devils and Evil Spirits of Babylonia*, I, 1903, 77, 31, 33, 155; *cf.* O. Weber, *Die Literatur der Babylonier und Assyrier*, 1907, 166 *ff.* K. Frank, *Babylonische Beschwörungsreliefs*, 1908, 20 *f.*

[2] W. Böhm and F. Specht, *Lettisch-litauische Märchen*, 1924, No. 9.

tale reviles just as valiantly as the modern pietist.[1] Nevertheless this laughing at demons never rings true; there is too much horror mixed with it, as Ibsen, in spite of all his modern irony, understood and expressed so marvellously in the scene in *Peer Gynt* where the Hall of the Old Man of Dovrë, and the goings on of the *trolls*, are described. Otto and Karl Jaspers,[2] again, have indicated the demonic in Goethe, and whoever wishes to understand the experience of the demon will find his best teacher in the modern poet. None better than Goethe has experienced the contradictory, terror-inspiring and incomprehensible side of life and rendered it vivid to us—of course completely freed from the forms of primitive mentality. Towards the close of his *Autobiography*[3] he looks back on the life of the boy and youth which he has just depicted:—"whilst he wandered to and fro space which lay intermediate between the sensible and suprasensible regions, seeking and looking about him, much came in his way which did not appear to belong to either; and he seemed to see, more and more distinctly, that it is better to avoid all thought of the immense and incomprehensible. He thought he could detect in nature—both animate and inanimate, with soul or without soul—something which manifests itself only in contradictions, and which, therefore, could not be comprehended under any idea, still less under one word. It was not godlike, for it seemed unreasonable; not human, for it had no understanding; nor devilish, for it was beneficent; nor angelic, for it often betrayed a malicious pleasure. It resembled chance, for it evolved no consequences; it was like Providence, for it hinted at connection. All that limits us it seemed to penetrate; it seemed to sport at will with the necessary elements in our existence; it contracted time and expanded space. In the impossible alone did it appear to find pleasure, while it rejected the possible with contempt." We may designate this demonic aspect—again with a typical term from Goethe—the *inadequate*: it is at the same moment the criticism advanced by the logical human will upon the frenzy of events, and by the colossal higher Power on the feeble will of man. In the demon form, then, man's will shatters itself against the irrational harshness of the Universe, while in the demon's own will the hard world crushes the form of humanity. And the end is grotesque distortion, nightmare, madness.

---

[1] For an example of the latter *cf.* Fr. Zöller, *Die Möttlinger Bewegung, Religionspsychologie*, 4, 1928, 74, in which the leader of a sect refers to the devil as a "miserable sow".   [2] *Psychologie der Weltanschauungen*[2], 1922, 193 *ff.*
[3] *Works*, V, 422, 423; *Truth and Fiction*, Book 20. (Nimmo's Edition).

3. The demonic figure emerges from extremely diversified experiences: the wildness and fearfulness of uncultivated land, the solitude of mountain regions far from fruitful valleys :—these are the *experiences of Nature* that have contributed most towards the creation of this form. Within enclosed human dwelling-places security holds sway; but outside, in field and mountain, live the *trolls*, the *utukku* of Babylonian religion, the *jinns* of Islam; and in a Jewish legend spirits which have crept into a house are cast out into the desert, their true realm, by a decree of the courts; they too take refuge in forest and wilderness.[1] Between the Nature-demons and man rules enmity, with the sole exception that man, aware of his own superiority over the helpless figures, renders them occasional service, as for example when the human woman succours the demon woman in child-bed. Apart however from the contrast between cultivation and the desert, between subservient and arbitrarily ruling power, the experience of Nature with her manifold mysteries also tended to induce the creation of this form. Thus the power of time unites with that of place: awe-inspiring midnight is haunted by the horrid forms of the wild hunt, while sultry noon heat awakens dread in the heart of the lonely shepherd whom the *meridianus daemon* torments and who has seen the fearful and fantastically distorted figure of Pan.[2] In addition to these, again, there are all the greater and lesser fears of forest and field. Each Thing has its own mysterious and incalculable aspect, each experience of Nature its own demon: pixies, moss and wood fairies, elves, dwarfs, *etc.*, inhabit waters and forests, fields and the subterranean caverns of the mountains, in German popular belief, and to this analogies can be found everywhere.

Side by side with Nature, again, is the *experience of Dreams*. It is not so-called "free imagination", formerly held to be responsible for the creation of every form, that generates demons, but rather the organically articulated imagination of the dream, which appears with all the force of actuality therein. First of all there is the dream of *dread*: the Greek *empusa*, which has one leg of ass dung and the other of iron,[3] is a creature of the dream of dread. All the bogeys that terrorized our childhood dreams had for us the same reality as they possess in popular belief; all the fears of the day have crept into our sleep and there exert

---

[1] *Der Born Judas*, VI, 277.
[2] The "rye-aunt" too wanders at midday in the cornfield to terrify men; H. W. Heuvel, *Volksgeloof en Volksleven*.
[3] *cf.* L. Radermacher, *Aristophanes' "Frösche"*, 1922, 175 *f.*

their power in terrifying form. The Greek *Lamia*, for one, the child murderess: the Babylonian-Assyrian *Labartu* too, who lurks in morass and mountain, and against whose calamitous influence children wore amulets around their necks. The *nightmare* is an intensification of the experience of dread: in Greece *Ephialtes*, in German countries the *trude, etc.* Similarly, the sudden night attack of the demon that shuns the day (*Genesis* xxxii) is probably correctly interpreted by Roscher as the description of a nightmare.[1]

With the dream experience is connected the *sexual* root of the idea of the demon; for the sexual or ejaculatory dream called into existence the countless forms of *incubi* and *succubi*. Thus the Babylonian *ardat lile*, the "maid of the night", persisted in Jewish tradition as Lilith, "Adam's first wife".[2] In popular narrative, too, the *motif* of the dream marriage (the so-called *Märtenehe*) played a great part; union with a demonic being—Melusine, in Islam *jinn*-marriage, in Scandinavia marriage with *trolls*, in Celtic lands with fairies—may well be understood as a dream event, even though we must not overlook the fact that a practical proof of power is no less completed in the dream—even if this is subjectively or autistically distorted—than in waking experience; and unavowed fear, as well as suppressed shame, of sexual potency takes its revenge in sleep.

In other respects also it is difficult to divorce the experience of Nature from that of the dream; the satyr, for example, is certainly a Nature form, but it is equally a fantasy of the sexual day dream. Nor are the experiences of Nature and dreams the sole basis of the belief in demons; for sickness, lunacy and ecstasy are ascribed to demonic influence. Man has lost power over himself, and so another and mightier being must have taken possession of him.

Since belief in demons finds its sustenance in so many sources, it is not to be wondered at that most primitive and semi-primitive peoples think of the world as being inhabited by a multitude of demons; "they cover the earth like grass", says a Babylonian *shurpu-Text*.[3] If then a belief in God definitely establishes itself, if some attempt is made to regulate and concentrate the Power of the Universe, evil spirits must somehow or other be cleared out of the way, if not for

[1] W. H. Roscher, "Ephialtes", *Abh. der K. Sächs. Ges. d. Wiss. Phil.-hist. Kl.*, 20, 1903.

[2] The belief in the *Incubus* was admirably and vividly depicted in Charles de Coster's *Légende d'Ulenspieghel et de Lamme Goedzak*; *cf.* O. Weinreich, *AR*. 16, 1913, 623 *ff.*; Taufik Canaan, *Dämonenglaube im Lande der Bibel*, 1929, 48.

[3] Morris Jastrow, *Die Religion Babyloniens und Assyriens*, I, 1905, 283.

every-day affairs (here they rule even to-day!) at least so far as the conception of the Universe is concerned. In this respect a few spirits were lucky and made their way to divine rank. For taking everything into consideration, no essential difference can be admitted between demon and god; the idea of a god certainly has many other roots besides belief in demons, but one of these may become a god—if he does not become a devil. The Greek *daimon* does not of course mean the same as *theos*,[1] but neither does it by any means imply an inferior being; indeed, in its function as a characterization of the irrational, it leads to a peculiar conception of gods that I designate "momentary gods".[2] How little was often necessary to effect the ultimate separation between god and demon can be observed in the relation of the Iranian gods to Hindu demons, and conversely: for the Iranian designation of the devil, *Daeva*, became the title of the gods in Sanskrit (*deva*),[3] while the Iranian title of the supreme Being, *ahura*, serves in India as that of a specific and ancient type of god (*asura*), but for the enemies of the gods also. Many "great" gods of a developed pantheon still bear clear demonic features: Apollo causes plague, and at his approach the gods start in terror from their seats.[4]

Everywhere demons are older than gods; and they become evil only when they are brought into contrast with the latter. Originally just as "demonic", the gods subsequently become rational and ethical, while the evil spirits, at first merely purposeless and malicious, become the enemies of the gods, become devils. They form the horde of naughty boys held in check by the great lords, to whom a prank is frequently permitted but who are also often severely punished. As intermediate beings, again, they rule a kind of world midway between deities and men. Of course this occurs only in the religions of the higher cultures, wherein poets and theologians have co-ordinated and rationalized the domains of gods and men; while in so far as the demons have not been condemned outright they must be content with a sort of vassalage.[5]

But grievously do they revenge themselves. For the experience of the inadequate and terrifying in the world still goes far too deep. Contrasted with their God, therefore, the serious Persians were compelled to set up a demon of almost equal rank, and the Jews to transfer

---

[1] According to M. P. Nilsson (Chantepie, *op. cit.*, II, 347) the word $\Theta\varepsilon\acuteo\varsigma$ expresses a definite individuality, and the term $\delta\alpha\acute\iota\mu\omega\nu$ an undefined power.

[2] Chap. 17; *cf.* M. P. Nilsson, *Götter und Psychologie, AR.* 22, 1923-24, 377 *ff.*

[3] Chantepie, *op. cit.*, II, 19, 214.   [4] *Hymn. Hom. in Ap.* 1 *ff.*

[5] *cf.* Plato, *Symposium*, 202; "and like all spirits he is intermediate between the divine and the mortal" (Jowett).

all sinister forms to the essential nature of Jahveh, who still shared much in common with the demon. In Islam and Christianity, too, evil spirits are recognized chiefly as powers inimical to God but subject to Him; even the gods of Greece were forced to see themselves reduced to the level of deceptive demons! Yet in the very concept of God the demonic continues to proclaim its presence, whether as absolute incalculability (predestination), or as inestimable mercy.

But even if the Devil is still a demon, whose form is moulded on the Grecian Pan, in popular belief he yet remains the "stupid" and inadequate, yet awful, Devil. But more and more he became the figure of the radically evil which can never be assimilated to the idea of God, the will that opposes itself to God's Will.

CHAPTER 16

THE SPECIAL FORM OF POWER: ANGELS

1. ANGELS are soul-beings: that is, not independent Power forms, but potencies which emanate from some other Power and appear as forms. Gods can thus send forth angelic beings, but men also; and the idea of the angel is intimately connected with that of the external soul.[1] Angels, then, are Powers that have widened outwards in their extension.

Even the name, ἄγγελος, מלאך, indicates that they are sent forth. We still speak of the angel who protects children, but we seldom realize that it is not an angel sent by God that guards the little one, but the power which the child itself has emitted. The beautiful saying of Jesus: "Take heed that ye despise not one of these little ones; for I say unto you, That in heaven their angels do always behold the face of my Father which is in heaven",[2] indicates the correct interpretation. These beings are not confined within themselves, in the sense of any modern Atomism. Each has not only relations to its environment, but part of itself therein; in other words, this is as yet no environment. Its life may thus subsist not only in its body, nor only in a "soul" supposedly immaterial, but also externally. We may recall certain fetishes, the tree of life, etc.; and then we perceive that the power exercised by man in the world is not to be regarded as a mere operation concentrated in the *ego*, but advances towards man, or stands over against him, as a form. Later I shall refer specifically to wraiths and soul-beings, but already we perceive the soul as a guardian spirit.

Babylonian hymns recognized a god and goddess of their own for each individual, playing no part in the pantheon but praying for their possessor and necessary to his good fortune.[3] In their absence a sick person suffered; here, then, the angels were almost gods. In Egypt on the other hand, where the *ka* formed the very condition of life and the assurance of security, the angel remained a soul.[4] In Iran, again, each thing had its *fravashi*, a concept bearing a closer relationship to the

---

[1] Chap. 42. [2] *Matt.* xviii. 10.

[3] A. H. Edelkoort, *Het zondebesef in de babylonische boetepsalmen*, 1918, 138. *cf.* further A. M. Blackman, *Journal of Egypt. Arch.* III, 1916, 239 *f.*

[4] *cf.* my Article, *External Soul, Schutzgeist und der ägyptische Ka, Zeitschr. f. Ägypt. Sprache und Altertumsk.*, 54, 1918.

protected object than is expressed by the term guardian spirit. The *fravashi* was the power of a dead or living man, and subsequently of any being in general, but leading an independent existence. The gods also had a *fravashi*; and as a portion of its possessor, the *fravashi* had no separate existence.[1] The *fravashis* thus constitute an extremely instructive example of how ideas intersect in primitive religion: the soul, the dead, angels, guardian spirits, with these and other terms are they designated; but little is to be achieved with general theories here!

In Jewish popular belief, too, we find a similar outlook: the maid Rhoda claimed to see Peter, but the others did not believe her and asserted that "it is his angel".[2] The Talmud also speaks of guardian angels,[3] while in the legend about the emperor Jovinian, in the *Gesta Romanorum*, the guardian angel appears as the emperor's wraith. In ancient Germanic folklore, again, the *Fylgja* is the bearer of a man's power, who appears to him in a dream in the form of an animal or woman and announces his death;[4] families too have their *Fylgjur*. And although Wagner dealt very arbitrarily with the old sagas, still he had a sensitive comprehension of the essentials of the ancient faith and created, in his Brunnhilde, a magnificent angelic being in the primitive sense: she is "Wotan's Will", the soul sent forth by the god, and in relation to the hero she is the genuine *Fylgja*, the "death warning":

> Death-doomed are they
> Who look upon me;
> Who sees me
> Bids farewell to the light of life . . .
> Nay, having looked
> On the Valkyrie's face
> Thou must follow her forth.[5]

It is the profound idea that whoever sees his own power taking shape before him must die.

2. The *angels of the god*, then, are potencies emanating from him. When the vulture, in an Egyptian animal fable, has stolen the cat's

---

[1] N. Söderblom, *Les Fravashis*, 1899, 32 *ff.*, 60. H. Lommel, *Zarathustra*, 1930, has coined the fine term *"Heilküre"* for the *fravashi*.   [2] *Acts* xii. 15.
[3] A. Kohut, *Über die jüdische Angelologie und Dämonologie*, 1866, 19.
[4] *cf.* Hugo Gering, *Vollständiges Wörterbuch zu den Liedern der Edda*, 1903, 300. In Iceland, during the transitional period before the introduction of Christianity, people believed in a kind of form intermediate between the *valkyrie-fylgja* and the five angels of God who protect man; *cf.* A. Olrik, *Nordisches Geistesleben*[2], 1925, 97.
[5] *The Valkyrie*, Act II (Armour).

litter, the god Ra sends a "power" to exact vengeance for her.[1] As yet this liberated fragment of the god has no form, but in the true home of angels, Persia, it is very different. For the *Amesha Spentas* are energies sent forth by Ahura Mazda: their names designate his qualities: *Vohu Manah*, the good thought, *Khshathra Vairya*, divine dominion, *Ameretat*, immortality, *etc*. Under the influence of the religion of Zarathustra, however, with its strict ethical and spiritual character, a certain degree of abstraction became attached to this angelic being. But that the theoretical intellectualism of Christian speculation on the attributes of God did not prevail here is clear from their ancient description as "rulers who by their glance alone are effective, the sublime superior forces, the mighty ones":[2] this is no abstraction in our sense, but a powerfulness that has not attained a completed form because it is still too closely bound up with the supreme Power. For the effectiveness of Ahura Mazda is due to these energies which are severed from him: with his "good thought" (*Vohu Manah*) he rules, in virtue of his "divine dominion" (*Khshathra Vairya*) and in accord with his "radiant righteousness" (*Asha*).[3] Subsequently, however, the forms of these angels received outlines of constantly increasing clarity; *Vohu Manah* became the guardian of the gates of Paradise and the heaven of Ahura Mazda the court of an oriental prince surrounded by his *divan*. In this form angelology passed over to Judaism and Islam. But there too the angels still remained the concrete attributes of God: *Uriel*, the glory of God, *Raphael*, God's salvation, *etc*.[4] At the same time they became, like the Persian angels, more and more the messengers of God, his satraps and couriers. But it is scarcely to be doubted that all these angelic powers were originally independent revelations of the one Power, and only attached themselves to a single divine figure later as his ambassadors. In the case of Persia this is very clear: *Asha* is the world order, in the guise of a power, which we have already considered. For the angels are older than the gods.

Of this a different kind of proof is provided in the pre-Persian Jewish belief in angels, which is bound up with the מלאך יהוה, the angel of the Lord. Actually, this is not the servant of Jahveh but his external soul, identical with him, and yet in itself a form. In *Genesis* xlviii. 15 *f.*, "angel" is used simply as another expression for the God who has

---

[1] Günther Röder, *Altägyptische Erzählungen und Märchen*, 1927, 303.
[2] Edv. Lehmann, *Zarathustra, en bog om Persernes gamle Tro*, 1899–1902, 138.
[3] *ibid.*, 67.
[4] Kohut, *op. cit.*, 25.

led Jacob.[1] In this respect, however, we need consider no reluctance to humanize Jahveh as having induced the idea of the angel. And the מלאך (angel) too is no pale copy. He is Jahveh himself, or rather a fragment of the mighty will that has assumed form. Only later does he become a messenger.

And the more the angel takes this status, the more is he severed from the idea of Power and soul. For Power and Will disappear, and there remains only the form: imposing, it is true. The Greek Iris and Hermes are messengers of this type, while Hermes (and also the *angelus bonus* in the cult of Sabazios[2]) still remains loosely connected with the soul in his character, as its conductor to Hades, of *psychopomp*. Odin's ravens are similarly attributes (*Hugin*, thought, and *Munin*, memory) and external souls at the same time. Jupiter, again, can send forth his eagle in precisely the same way as the magician or witch can send out soul-animals.[3]

3. Thus angels become intermediate beings, powers of subordinate rank. To the Jews, according to St. Paul, they were the mediators of the Law as an addition to the promise of God.[4] To Mary they announced that the Saviour was to be born of her: to the shepherds the "great joy" of the miracle that had occurred, and to the women and disciples the resurrection. In Christianity, still further, their task is to praise God to all eternity,[5] while in Islam their food is "Praised be Allah", their drink "Allah is holy".

In those religions that apprehend God as personal Will the angels remained servants whose work it was to announce or execute God's Will. There may also be rebellious, fallen and evil angels; but all are dependent on the sovereign Will which ultimately decides their fate. Their forms may be those of Nature, but it is Nature dominated and swayed by God's Will. This is most beautifully expressed in *St. John* i. 51: "Ye shall see heaven open, and the angels of God ascending and descending upon the Son of Man". The angelic power, then, must always have a bearer.

But it could also once again become "power" completely, as with the

---

[1] A. Lods, *L'ange de Jahvé et l'âme extérieure*, (*Zeitschr. für die Alttest. W. Beih.*, 27, 1914), 266 *ff*.; van der Leeuw, *Zielen en Engelen*, *Theol. Tydschrift*, N.R. 11, 1919; *cf. Exodus* xxiii. 21, where the name—that is, the essence of Jahveh—is in the angel who goes before the Israelites.

[2] F. Cumont, *Les Anges du Paganisme*, RHR. 36, 1915.

[3] S. H. Hubert and M. Mauss, *Esquisse d'une Théorie générale de la Magie*, Année Sociologique, 7, 78 *ff*.   [4] *Gal.* iii. 19.   [5] *Rev.* vii. 11.

belief in stars in the Hellenistic era, which has its echo, too, in the New Testament.[1] The "visible gods",[2] who tried to hinder the soul's journey to heaven, were powers that strove amongst themselves and which, in relation to man, constituted an inexorable necessity; while in magic angels and demons were invoked as *nomina barbara*.[3]

But power devoid of any bearer can be valued differently too, and in this sense, again, there are good angels and evil; the "powers celestial, rising and descending" of Faust's *Monologue*,[4] are the classical instance of this, while in Fechner's speculations belief in angels attained an apotheosis with later dynamistic colouring: the potencies—and this in the true spirit of Goethe—are not dead but living beings. The earth, just as in Hellenism, is "an angel who is so rich, fresh and radiant, and at the same moment so steadfast and serene as he moves through heaven, his vivacious countenance turned wholly towards heaven and carrying me with him on his journey".[5] Even the *psychopomp*, the conductor of the soul, is not absent. But whether good or evil, terrifying or beautiful, these angels have lost their soul-character and are powers devoid of all relation to any bearer; they are no longer actual angels, that is to say, but demons.

For the belief in angels reverts to the dual experience of Form, in the first place *in actu*, either as one's own, or as some foreign, power, yet lacking form, and in the second *idealiter*, as a power released and having some definite form. Exactly as man experiences himself dually, once as himself—and in this way he can imagine nothing and represent nothing to himself—and a second time as a wraith-soul-angel, so he experiences God in the same dual way, first as a Power and a Will that can neither be imagined nor represented, and again as a presence with definite form.[6] The belief in angels, therefore, is equally momentous for the idea of revelation and for the type of the concept of God.

And it is no mere matter of chance that fundamentally Christian ideas still retain something of the angel concept: thus Christ was called an angel, and in *The Shepherd of Hermas* the expressions "Son of God", "Holy Spirit", the Archangel Michael, and the "glorious" or "most holy angels" are so employed that they cannot be distinguished. Justin, again, calls the heavenly Christ "the angel of great counsel", "the Son of God", "angel and messenger of God", "Lord of the powers"

[1] *cf.* Chap. 7. [2] Cumont.
[3] *cf.* E. Peterson, *Rh. Museum*, N. F. 75, *Engel- und Dämonennamen*.
[4] *Faust*, Part I. [5] *Über die Seelenfrage*, 1861, 170.
[6] G. van der Leeuw, *Psychologie und Religionsgeschichte*, 11.

(that is of angels), and "wisdom" (another angel idea), while *The Ascension of Isaiah* mentions "the angel of the Holy Ghost".[1] The Holy Spirit also has the form of a dove, that is of a veritable external soul, and the *Logos* finds its prototype in "Rumour, the messenger of Zeus", *Ὄσσα Διὸς ἄγγελος*:[2] but after all the Word was the purpose of the Gospel mission. We should therefore feel no astonishment at all this, since the essence of all Christian preaching is ultimately the imparting of God through a Form which is with Him one Being, and in this way a "dual experience" of God. Hence it is no accident that, at the climax of Christian adoration, the great eucharistic hymn of praise is taken up by both men *and angels*; for the powers have only one task—to praise God Who has assumed Form: "Therefore with Angels and Archangels, with Thrones and Dominions, and with all the company of heaven, we laud and magnify thy glorious Name".

[1] G. van der Leeuw, *Zielen en Engelen*, 228 f.   [2] *Iliad*, II, 93.

CHAPTER 17

POWER AND WILL GIVEN FORM IN THE NAME

1. WE have already had occasion to observe that the idea of a god who is in some way or other personal is not an absolutely necessary element in the structure of religion. On the whole, the concept of "personality" is fairly modern and artificial; in the sphere of religion, therefore, it is more advisable to retain "Will" and "Form", while Form, again, is not always bound up with Will. Still further, the man who must come to some understanding with a power, and who therein experiences a will, attempts by every possible means to give an outline to this experience, in order to delimit it from other similar experiences; and this he does by assigning to it a *Name*. For the Name is no mere specification, but rather an actuality expressed in a word. Thus Jahveh creates the animals and leads them to Adam; he says something to them, and that is their name.[1] The names of things subsist before they acquire a "personality"; and the name of God is there even before "God" exists.

In the Name, then, is reflected experienced Will: but experienced Power also. For the extraordinary, the striking, when it receives a name, generally remains nevertheless often *mana*-like. Giant cedar trees, for example, are "cedars of *El*".[2] The vocabulary of execration, indeed, has retained this primitive application of the name as an indication of the super-potent; while whoever encounters something peculiar cries: "my God": *nom de Dieu*; or he describes anything striking as "*sakermentsch*", and quite fails to realize how much primeval experience he thus utters! Power is thus authenticated and assigned a name; plural forms being intended to express the indeterminateness wherein the experience is more powerful than form creation: God is *Elohim*. Similarly the Germanic peoples experienced the power of the *Waltenden* who rule in sea, forest and field:[3] Greece too was familiar with such collective powers whose impersonality was expressed by the plural, and who only rule together, as a genus: the nymphs in wells and woods, *semnai*, muses, *moirai*, *horai*, *artemides* (these also in the plural originally!), *panes*, *silenoi*, *anakes* (rulers), *etc.* The Celtic world, again, knew of the "mothers" who appear in threes, persisting in popular belief as the "three Marys". Even ancient Egypt had its seven Hathors, female

---

[1] *Gen.* ii. 19.   [2] *Ps.* lxxx. 10.   [3] Nilsson, *AR.* 22, 1923–24, 384.

predecessors of the *Eileithyias* and the seven fairies who stand by the cradle of the newborn child.

This, however, is neither polytheism nor polydemonism. It is a creation of form for Power and Will, the chorus of the drama as it were; only the actual *dramatis personae* are still absent. Just as man fashions his own power into a plurality of "souls",[1] so the Power of the Universe reveals to him not the sharp outlines of any single person but the dance of the *charites*, the stormy procession of the *horai*.

But whenever a second and self-moulded experience thus follows the immediacy of the experience of Power, personal features become sharpened. The actual numinous experience itself is formless and structureless: it is the collision with Power, the encounter with Will. Only the dual experience of Form produces demons and gods, and it would therefore be incorrect to ascribe any considerable rôle to "imagination"; for no unregulated play of fantasy predominates here, but the creation of Form. In this manner formless Power and purposeless Will are endowed with structural relations which fuse to constitute a unity stamped with individuality.

The name at first borne by the divinity is just as general and collective as is the divinity itself; it is not yet a proper name, but merely adjectival. Man first names his experiences according to their type, exactly as Adam named the animals: "the dark or fair, the wild or winterly and the radiant person are far older pairs than Aegeus and Lycus, or even than Lycurgus and Dionysus, Nestor and Lyaeus".[2] The name assigns to Power and Will a definite form and some settled content, and is therefore by no means any abstraction. Quite the contrary: it is not simply essential, but is also concrete and even corporeal. The ancient Egyptians, indeed, regarded the gods' names as their limbs: "It is Ra, who as the lord of the ennead created his names. Who then is this? It is Ra, who creates his own limbs: thus arose the gods who follow in his train".[3] Only by virtue of their names, then, do gods attain to story and myth; for myth is nothing other than "dual experience of the form", that is the experience of the god encountered anew, but henceforth indirectly, structuralized, and endowed with form.[4] That is why man

---

[1] Chap. 40.   [2] H. Usener, *Göttliche Synonyme, Kleine Schriften*, IV, 1913, 304.
[3] *Totenbuch* (Naville), *Kap.* XVII, 6 *f.*
[4] Lévy-Bruhl probably implies this in his excellent suggestion: "Can myths then likewise be the products of primitive mentality which appear when this mentality is endeavouring to realize a participation no longer directly felt—when it has recourse to intermediaries and vehicles designed to secure a communion which has ceased to be a living reality?" *How Natives Think*, 368.

longs to know the god's name; for only then can he begin to do something with his deity, live with him, come to some understanding and—in magic—perhaps even dominate him. The children of Israel, said Moses, will ask what is the name of Him that has sent him.[1]

The condition for all intercourse with deity therefore is to know its name. Thus the Roman distinguished *di certi* from *incerti*: the former he knew by name, he could invoke them, their power invaded his life. But the second category should not be ignored. For there are countless powers, and if we are not sure that we know their names correctly, then we should at all events leave for them an empty space, an altar dedicated to the unknown god", ἄγνωστος θεός, a formula like *sive deus sive dea, sive quo alio nomine fas est appellare*:—"whether god or goddess, or by whatever name it is lawful to call".[2] Then we shall have made due provision for them, and there will be no power whatever that can elude the prayer. Thus it became possible for an entire hymn to consist of merely two phrases, like the ancient Egyptian: "Awake in peace; thine awakening is peaceful", while all the rest is constituted only of twenty-nine names; the intoner could then vary and extend it himself.[3] In many hymns to the gods the names are like the *basso continuo* executed by the suppliant according to his own judgment.

2. In their *indigitamenta* the Romans had secret lists of divine names which were introduced during the official invocation of the gods; similarly the names of the domestic and family gods were kept secret. It is indeed chiefly the ideas of the Romans that are the principal source of our deepest insight into the essence of divine names and their functions as the creation of forms of Power. But this must not be interpreted as though there was nothing else of significance in this respect: for the structure of the gods' names, or of particular or individual gods, is everywhere an indispensable intermediate link between formless Power and the completed god-form. An intermediate link, of course, not in the chronological sense, but in the structural and psychological; or still better: a structural relation.

Everywhere, too, extremely different powers reveal themselves. The Greek term *daimon* "is merely a mode of expressing the belief

[1] *Exodus* iii. 13.

[2] Gellius, *Attic Nights*, II, 28, 2 *ff*. G. Appel, *De Romanorum precationibus*, 1909, 14, 76 *ff*. E. Norden, *Agnostos Theos.*[2] 1926, 143 *ff*. *Theol. Wörterb. zum Neuen Test.* Ἄγνωστος.

[3] A. Erman, *Hymn to the Royal Serpent*, *The Literature of the Ancient Egyptians*, 12.

that a certain effect is produced by a higher power".[1] Actually, then, every experience of power, and every encounter with a superior will, should have led to the formation of some divine form; and this indeed is often the case. But not always; and therefore we need not regard the individual or special gods as indispensable members of the evolution of the idea of God, but merely as a structural relation which, whether it actually occurs or not, is necessary to the structure. From the many, nay the innumerable, potencies which reveal themselves to man in forest and field, in home and work: from the "rulers" which in popular belief are frequently designated simply as "he" or "she": from the infinite diversity of the sheaves (does not each conceal a marvellous power?): from mountains (does not each separate peak awaken its own feeling of awe?): from labour (does not each individual type demand its specific strength?): there arises by means of the name a possibility of denomination and of enumeration.

All this, however, is no process of abstraction. The endowment with form by means of names is often incorrectly confused with allegory as *we* understand this;[2] but there is a vast contrast between our hope that Pluvius will not be too unreasonable, and the invocation of a rain god by primitive and ancient peoples. In our eyes the "rain god" is an abstraction from a reference book on mythology, but to men of the primitive and classical eras he was a living power, to which by a name had been given some kind of sketchy form.

An experience, then, does not belong to the god, but rather has its "god pertaining to it"; when for example the plague was devastating Attica Epimenides, the prophet and purifying priest, released black and white sheep on the Areopagus. Where they lay down sacrifice should be offered τῷ προσήκοντι θεῷ, to the god concerned; and the altars of these deities were "nameless altars".[3] When Odysseus, again, is cast on the coast of Scheria he arrives at the mouth of a stream and invokes its god: "Hear me, O King, whosoever thou art, as one to whom prayer is made."[4] No abstraction, then, but a most concrete experience: not theory, but the empirical verification of Power, created the "particular" or "special gods". There is here no question of Power in general, still less of any abstract idea of Power, but of *this* actual power with which one is at this very moment concerned and which

---

[1] Nilsson, *A History of Greek Religion*, 166.

[2] Thus Heiler, *Prayer*, 42 *ff.*

[3] Diog. Laert., *Epimenides*. C. Pascal, *Il Culto degli Dei gnoti a Roma, Bull. della Comm. arch.*, 1894, 191.   [4] *Odyssey*, V, 445.

"the situation demands". Thus when Horatius Cocles leaped into the Tiber he implored not the divinity, but simply the river itself: "Holy father Tiberinus, I pray that thou wouldst receive these arms, and this thy soldier, in thy propitious stream."[1] Horatius knew the name of the river: Odysseus knew it not and had to content himself with the general title ἄναξ. As the Greeks would say, the name gives consistency to "some good spirit", Θεός τις, and facilitates the possibility of invocation.[2]

In this connection, Usener has introduced the expressions "momentary gods" and "special gods"; and especially as regards the first of these, we must always realize (to repeat) that it by no means represents any definite phase in the evolution of the concept of God. For there would be only few genuine "momentary gods", since the major part of such momentary experiences pass away, it may be with the invocation of some unnamed "good spirit". But occasionally this gained a name: the god who compelled Hannibal to retreat from the *Porta Capena*, for instance, received a fane as *Rediculus*, and the voice which proclaimed the Gauls' approach an altar under the name of *Aius Locutius*.[3] Usener interprets the creation of the god of lightning as follows: "He was the god who in the lightning flash travelled to earth and there took up his abode. It is a clear example of what I have termed a momentary god, that is of a religious idea aroused by a single phenomenon and not extending beyond this." Then the single *keraunos* might have become an individual or "special" god of lightning in general, and eventually under the epithet *keraunios* absorbed by some more comprehensive divine form—*e.g. Zeus keraunios*. This holds true also of Rome, where *Fulgur* appears side by side with *Jupiter Fulgur* and *Jupiter Fulminator*.[4] Now it is true that, apart from isolated cases of actual worship, the momentary god is an "abstraction in so far as the primitive capacity of conception is, as it were, being purely bred".[5] The expression "structural relations", however, is better than the term "abstraction", which involuntarily stresses the theoretical aspect. Thus by means of the "momentary god", or god of "momentary function" (to adopt Fowler's term), we apprehend the transition from the solitary and instantaneous experience to the permanent form.

[1] Livy, II, 10 f. (Spillan).
[2] Θεός τις guided Agamemnon's ship in the storm: Aeschylus, *Agam.* 661.
[3] G. Wissowa, *Religion und Kultus der Römer*[2], 1912, 55.
[4] H. Usener, "Keraunos", *Kleine Schriften*, IV, 481 ff.
[5] M. P. Nilsson, *Primitive Religion*, 1911, 41 ff.; cf. also Wundt, *Völkerpsychologie*, IV, 560 ff.; R. M. Meyer, *AR.* 11, 1908, 333.

Nevertheless Usener is fundamentally correct: "The feeling of the Infinite can enter only into finite, limited phenomena and relationships. Not *the* Infinite, but *something* infinite and divine, manifests itself to man, is grasped by his spirit and expressed in his language."[1] In the paradox of this "something infinite" lives the whole marvel of religious comprehension; in it is depicted the limitation not only to anthropomorphic form but also in dogma and in words in general.

It is, then, the name that makes the actual "special god". It is this that compels the form to persist and guarantees that man can always rediscover it. The number of these numinous entities is unlimited: every action in life, every experience, has its god. "Thus the moment in which an object, or its striking characteristics, appears in human feeling and life in any perceptible relationship, whether agreeable or repulsive, is to the consciousness of the Ewe native the birth hour of a *tro*";[2] and thus he worships a mother of the market, *Asino*, the market itself, *Asi*, and also riches, *Ablo*.[3] To our minds the market is a very concrete thing, wealth merely an abstraction; but to the Ewe native both alike are living powers which he can approach through the medium of a name.

As has already been observed, the Romans possessed to a high degree the genius for this endowment with form by means of the name;[4] and in fact they associated the slightest event with the invocation of a "special god". Since the field was ploughed thrice, agriculture recognized three gods of the plough, *Vervactor, Reparator, Imporcitor*. *Insitor* watched over seed sowing, *Sarritor* the eradication of weeds, *Messor* the reaping, *Conditor* storing in the granary, *Sterculinius* the manuring, *etc.* Seed growth in the soil was under the guardianship of *Seia*; germination and sprouting were protected by *Proserpina*; *Segesta* took care of growth above the surface, *Volutina* of the development of the bud, *Flora* of the blossoms and *Matura* of the ripening. The other cares of the husbandman too all had their specific or individual gods: cattle breeding had *Bubona*, horse rearing *Epona*, bee keeping *Mellona*, while *Pomona* superintended arboriculture.[5] In human life it was exactly the same: *Domiducus* watched over the bringing home of the bride, *Liber* assisted the husband in sex intercourse and *Libera* the

[1] Usener, *Götternamen*[2], 276.
[2] J. Spieth, *Die Religion der Eweer in Süd-Togo*, 1911, 8.
[3] *ibid.*, 132 *ff.*   [4] Bertholet, *Götterspaltung*, 10.
[5] S. Wide, *Einleitung in die Altertumswissenschaft*, II, 1912, 240 *f.* (4th Edition, S. Wide and M. P. Nilsson, 1931).

wife.[1] The newborn babe, too, was as it were divided between potencies down to the minutest trivialities: *Alemona* nourished the fetus, *Vagitanus* opened the child's mouth at its first cry, *Levana* raised it from the ground, *Cunina* protected the cradle, *Statanus* taught it to stand, *Fabulinus* to speak, *etc.*[2] But concrete things too became powers in virtue of their names, powers that could be invoked: in the house *Janus* was the door, *Vesta* the hearth, while *Cardea* and *Limentinus* pertained to the threshold.[3]

The religion of the special gods is therefore far more practical than abstract, the severance from actual experience being still very slight. Of Rome Wissowa asserts that "all the divinities are, as it were, thought of in a purely practical manner as operative in all those things with which the Romans had to do in their ordinary life. . . . The great number of gods' names, and the unlimited multitude of divine beings, which we meet with in ancient Roman religion, therefore depend by no means on any special many-sidedness of the religious imagination, but only on the necessity, in the most immediate and everyday affairs, of recognizing the divine governance and bringing oneself into accord with it."[4] In this sense, then, we must also interpret those deities who to our mode of thought appear as *pure* abstractions, as so-called attribute-gods.[5] Instead of saying: these deities are nothing but attributes, that is abstractions, we should rather express ourselves as follows: The "attributes" that we still recognize in the deities, in the God of Judaism and Christianity, their strength, loving-kindness and justice, are actual experiences that have been transformed into ideas; originally they possessed some specific form, however sketchy and mediated through the name this may have been. First of all there were attributes of the god: subsequently, the god himself; just as there were at first shady trees, sunlit fields and blue skies, and only later the landscape. This is what Usener discovered, even if the experiential character of the idea of god had not become clear to him, when in a lecture following a sleepless night, he contradicted his opinion that the plurality of deities had arisen by splitting away from a single one, by the view that the multiplicity subsisted first, while from this the individual "great" gods had gradually developed.[6] Of course here too we must understand the expressions "originally" and "at first" not in the purely historical, still less in the chronological sense, but merely structurally and psycho-

[1] Lehmann-Haas, *Textbuch*, 221 *f.*   [2] Wide, *op. cit.*, 241.
[3] *ibid.*   [4] *Religion und Kultus*, 20 *ff.*   [5] Wissowa, *op. cit.*, 271 *ff.*
[6] *cf.* A. Dieterich, *Kleine Schriften*, 1911, 354 *ff.*

logically. Here as always we are concerned with understanding the structure of the idea of God, not with the facts of its origin.[1]

To the Greeks, similarly, *Paian* was the healing power, or rather the potency involved in the exorcism of the sick: or as we should say, the prescription personified. *Damia* and *Auxesia* similarly appear to us as "personifications" of growth, the second with her eloquent name at least being very transparent; but in Aegina and the Peloponnese they possessed an ancient cult.[2] For us, again, *Nike* is the "goddess of victory", that is a decorative figure; but to the Greeks she was the concrete power of victory.

So, too, the most real *Brahman*, the potent sacrificial formula, became the supreme deity to the Hindus, and as connected with it the power of isolated objects was indicated by compounds of *pati*: *Brahmanaspati* (*Bṛhaspati*), the lord of prayer, *Kṣetrasyapati*, lord of the field.[3] This again is no development of concepts, but an elementary endowment of form (*Gestaltung*). Medieval allegorical figures also, which we are inclined to condemn as mere bloodless metaphors, actually had something of the vivacity of the special gods; for to a great extent in the Middle Ages every thought, every experience, still assumed form. "It is only with difficulty that we could imagine anything by *Bel accueil, Doulce Mercy, Humble Requeste* (characters in *Roman de la Rose*). But for their contemporaries they had a reality clothed with living form and coloured with passion, which brings them wholly into line with the Roman special gods."[4] We should therefore not be surprised at *Quarème* being a figure in Literature and Painting,[5] since *Karneval, Kirmes, etc.*, still live as such in popular customs.

The Romans carried the reality of attributes so far that they could think of a large number of the gods only as linked to a bearer, so that we cannot decide whether we are concerned with gods or with souls. Thus there were divinities of the army: *Bonus Eventus, Fortuna, Victoria*, which could have Augustus, the army (*exercitus*), the *legio*, etc., as bearers.[6] Every imperator, again, had his own *Victoria*:[7] every power was immediately specialized. Power in general became that of

---

[1] *cf.* further Wundt, *Völkerpsych.* VI, 8.   [2] Usener, *Götternamen*, 129 *ff.*

[3] Beth, *Einführung*, 20; (*cf.* GENERAL LITERATURE); *cf.* E. Cassirer, *Philosophie der symbolischen Formen*, II. *Das mythische Denken*, 1925, 256 *f.*, with reference to the termination *tar* (*savitar*, etc.). Oldenberg, *Rel. d. Veda*, 63 *ff.*

[4] J. Huizinga, *Het Herfstty der Middeleeuwen*, 1919, 351.   [5] *ibid.*, 354.

[6] A. von Domaszewski, *Abhandlungen zur römischen Religion*, 1909, 104 *ff.*

[7] A. Piganiol, *Recherches sur les jeux romains*, 1923, 122 *f.*, 139. A. von Domaszewski, *Die Religion des römischen Heeres*, 1895, 37. Wissowa, *op. cit.*, 127 *ff.*

victory, and this again the power of victory of a definite leader or some specific legion: thus there was a *Victoria Sullana, Victoria Caesaris* and *Victoria Augustana*. Similarly with the potencies *Honor, Virtus, Pietas, Disciplina*; and to what a slight degree our modern distinction between concrete and abstract subsisted is clear from the fact that Jupiter, Mars, *Victoria*, the *Genius, Virtus*, the *aquilae sanctae* and the *signa* of a *legio* were all alike worshipped as *di militares*.[1] According to our ideas, however, these comprise two "great gods", a sort of protective-spirit-soul (*genius*), two abstract concepts (*Victoria* and *Virtus*), and a kind of fetish (the eagles and the ensigns). But to this difference the Romans attached no meaning whatever.

For a moment, certainly, we might suppose that an exception must be made so far as concerns a partial creation of form in the Roman belief in gods. For in Gellius[2] divine pairs are to be found which at first sight seem to presuppose divine marriage. *Nerio Martis, Salacia Neptuni, Lua Saturni:* were not these simply the spouses of the gods so named, and was not the whole specific Roman creation of form by means of names an error? But a second glance shows that *Nerio Martis* was only the masculine strength of the god, *Salacia Neptuni* the flux of water, *Lua Saturni* the seed's potency of germination.[3] We too still find a tendency to this creation of form by the name when we speak of the king's majesty, the holiness of the pope or the excellency of a minister. But this is assuredly no affair of attempting to transform personalities so named into abstractions. The title is rather a compromise between individuality and power, an intermediary between the special form of the bearer and the superpersonal power which he carries.

But when the name is no longer regarded as a living potency, then the special god decays or declines, and becomes an epithet of some "great god", that is really of some special god who has had better fortune: it becomes one of the retinue of the great god.[4] The "mistress", who originally had her own realm of authority as the local goddess of the surrounding dells, thus became a title of Demeter, Isis, Cybele or Mary, as δέσποινα, *domina, Donna*.[5] Meilichios again, "*He of appeasement*", "is nothing else. He is merely the personified shadow or dream

---

[1] von Domaszewski, *Religion des römischen Heeres*, 44, 19.

[2] *Noctes atticae*, 13, 23.

[3] von Domaszewski, *Abhandl.*, 104 ff. Wissowa, *op. cit.*, 134 ff. W. Warde Fowler, *The Religious Experience of the Roman People*, 481 ff. G. van der Leeuw, *God, Macht en Ziel, Theol. Tydschr.* 1918, 123 ff. Kurt Latte, *AR.* 24, 1927, 253 f.

[4] Usener, *op. cit.*, 272.   [5] *ibid.*, 216 ff.

generated by the emotion of the ritual—very much, to take a familiar instance, as Father Christmas is a 'projection' of our Christmas customs";[1] he became an epithet of Zeus Meilichios. In the same way *Aphiktor* ("the Suppliant"), the name form of the prayer of the community and of the cry of the commonwealth, likewise passed as a title to the Olympian deity.[2]

Thus the construction of form by means of the name simplified the eternally changing experience of power, the encounter with ever new superiority. From the many hearth fires arose one *Vesta Publica*, one *Janus* on the Forum from the numberless doors, ultimately one *Terminus* on the Capitol from the many boundary stones, and one *Juno* out of the thousandfold soul-like guardian spirits of the women.[3] At first an event is just itself; and so long as it is apprehended as it originally occurred it opposes any endowment with form. In primitive languages, for instance, the man who arrives is another than the man who leaves; and in primitive religion, similarly, the god who appears is another than the god who departs: the experience in its original momentariness is still present.[4] But religion was also concerned when, "for every propitious event, the ancients endowed the god to whom this pertained with a specific epithet and erected to him a special temple; they had apprehended an activity of the Universe, and designated thus its individuality and its character".[5]

3. "God", therefore, is not the specialist of the works of reference. In these we find "gods" of trade, love and knowledge. Each has his own calling. But the god is not the director of such affairs: he is an actual experience. Thus we understand how indubitably polytheistic religions, such as the ancient Egyptian or Greek, speak simply of "god" whenever it is a case of regarding some definite event as the revelation of superior power. Thus "God" preserves the life of the shipwrecked mariner and brings him to safety on an island;[6] that is precisely the god "whom it concerns", "some good spirit", $\Theta\epsilon\acute{o}s$ $\tau\iota s$.

This practical or empirical significance of belief in a god is what von Wilamowitz implied in calling "god" the exponent of a belief or

---

[1] Murray, *Five Stages of Greek Religion*, 30.
[2] *ibid.*, 43; "the assembled prayer, the united cry"; *cf*. Wide, *op. cit.*, 176 *f*.
[3] E. Samter, *Die Entwicklung des Terminuskults, AR.* 16, 1913, 142 *ff*.
[4] Usener, *op. cit.*, 317 *ff*.
[5] Thus wrote Schleiermacher in 1799, in his *Discourses upon Religion*, with admirable powers of observation even if in romantic terms. (First German Edition, 56 *f*.)
[6] A. Erman, *The Literature of the Ancient Egyptians*, 30.

a feeling:[1] "god" is above all the name for some experience of Power. From the emotions of the young maidens of Troezen, for instance, who before marriage sacrificed their tresses, there arose the name and later the form of Hippolytus. This, however, implies no anthropomorphic theory nor Feuerbachean wisdom. The power in the experience leads to endowment with form. Surrender of maidenhood involves contact with some strange power, and this contact receives name and form.

A more suitable appellation, however, for the semi-formalized potency than the much too personal term "god" is the Roman *numen*. A *numen* is, first of all, only a nod of the head: that is the will element therein. But further, it is also power, and has a name. It is, however, still so vague that it exhibits no human features at all, and can also be ascribed to some power as an attribute.[2] But the "attributes" are nearer to the experience than is the fully developed god.

Indeed it almost appears that the Romans were familiar with the structure of this semi-formalized will-power, as it were, in its "pure culture". For they also had an adequate term instead of "person", which would here be too copious and modern; they spoke of *capita*, meaning by *caput* a legal person, and therefore someone with whom relations are possible and who himself can do something.[3] Bickel has rightly stressed the fact that this juridical personality was no abstraction, but always remained connected with the demon;[4] that is, probably, that the powerful will had received a name, and that this legal personality was attributed to the gods.[5] In connection with what has been previously observed,[6] we might also describe these divine personalities as offices: just as the king's power is his status, so divine power is something "official". Just as the monarch, as such, is no acquisitive nor cowardly personality, but always shows kingly courtesy, generosity, *etc.*, so the god is not some good or wise person but, simply as god, ever divine. His name is known—that is to say, men know what they require him for and what they expect from him. He was *deus certus*, and in Rome indeed was included in social relationships as *pater or mater*. It was, then, from these conditions that the possibility of a cult first of all arose; and whatever is addressed to nameless Power is *magic*.

---

[1] U. von Wilamowitz-Möllendorff, *Griechische Tragödien*, I[8], 1919, 100.

[2] Chantepie, *op. cit.*, II, 444. Latte, *AR.* 24, 1927, 256. G. van der Leeuw, *Theol. Tydschr.*, 1918, 123 *ff*.   [3] E. Bickel, *Der altrömische Gottesbegriff*, 1921, 35, 63.

[4] *ibid.* Whether his historical construction of the *di certi* from the ancestral spirits of the Italici, as connected with the juridical "person" of the Romans, is correct, is dubious.   [5] *ibid.*, 40 *f.*   [6] Chap. 13.

"*Les Saints successeurs des dieux*"[1]—the structure of special gods is still realized to-day: the *saints* of the church have become their successors.[2] "If someone has toothache, he fasts and extols St. Apollonia; if he fears danger from fire he makes St. Laurence his helper in his distress; if he is afraid of plague he makes his vows to St. Sebastian or Ottilia; Rochus is invoked for eye disease, Blase in case of sore throat, while St. Anthony of Padua returns lost objects."[3] Thus the successors of the *genius* and the *lares* as house and family deities are the saints, whose altars in houses and whose statues at cross-roads persist in giving form to the ancient isolated experience;[4] and as the cult of St. Thaddeus shows, even the momentary god still arises spontaneously: "In her special need some pious woman or other has turned to a new saint and been successful; she praises her helper and then others follow her example— thus is to be explained how the apostle Thaddeus, who a few years ago was practically unknown in Catholic circles, possesses to-day in countless churches devotional statues surrounded by votive tablets."[5] The church has always been very well able to reconcile itself to the indestructible structures of the idea of God, and has adopted and christianized them rather than sacrifice them to a barren Monotheism. In fact, in the sixth century Gregory the Great expressly recommended that the cults should be retained in the ancient places of worship, and merely the holy martyrs set up instead of demons, in accordance with the wise principle that "he who seeks to ascend to the highest point climbs not by leaps, but by steps or strides".[6]

H. Usener, *Götternamen*[2], 1929.
A. Bertholet, *Götterspaltung und Göttervereinigung*, 1933.

[1] P. Saintyves, 1907.
[2] In origin, the sheiks of Mohammedan popular piety are also divinities to some degree; *cf.* C. Clemen, *Die nichtchristliche Kulturreligionen in ihrem gegenwärtigen Zustand*, 1921, II, 87 *f.*
[3] Luther in *The Large Catechism* in N. Söderblom's *Einführung in die Religionsgeschichte*, 1920, 52; *cf.* Heiler, *Prayer*, 47. H. Usener, *Sonderbare Heilige*, I, 1907, 34. Heiler, *Katholizismus*, 190 *f.*
[4] Wide, *op. cit.*, 242.   [5] Heiler, *Katholizismus*, 191.
[6] The pope's letter to the abbot Mellitus; *in extenso* in J. Toutain, *RHR.* 40, 1919, 11 *ff.*

CHAPTER 18

THE SACRED WORLD IN THE BACKGROUND

POWER AND WILL IN THE BACKGROUND

1. THE History of the History of religion is just as meagre as the History of religion itself is profuse. It seems as though only very few ideas could arise within it; even till to-day, unfortunately, a more profound historical comprehension has but seldom been applied to it. In this respect investigators have too often been content to smile at Hegel as an arbitrary constructor and oppressor of History, while in the interval they themselves have done naïvely and badly what they reproached Hegel for doing, and what at all events he self-confidently and brilliantly executed.

Thus the dominant but shallow Evolutionism of the nineteenth century led to the concept of God, as held in the recent past, being regarded as the climax of a long development from quite crude beginnings: while in accordance with this, every ancient or primitive idea of God was estimated by the standard of this ultimate achievement. And then a reaction set in, equally superficial according to the ideals of the Philosophy of History, which while announcing itself as "anti-evolutionism" nevertheless restricted itself merely to inverting the development, so that it placed the concept of God of the "Enlightenment" and the nineteenth century, which to the reaction was also a matter of course, at the summit and derived everything else from this beginning by way of "degeneration". Both tendencies, however, are completely unanimous in holding that "God" can be applied only to what a modern Western European, descended from the Christianity of the age of "Enlightenment", is accustomed to designate by this name without further philosophical or phenomenological reflection.[1]

It is true that in the course of this controversy one important discovery was made; for it became clear that another belief prevailed among many primitive peoples besides that in spirits and fetishes, which had hitherto been almost the only one known. This belief was regarded by its first exponent, Andrew Lang, as the idea of a supreme being, a

[1] *cf.* my Review of Fahrenfort's *Het hoogste Wezen der Primitieven, Deutsche Lit.-Ztg.*, 1929, I *Heft*.

"high god". In the main this supreme being resembles the God whom the "proverbial plain man" imagines to himself even to-day: the Creator, the sustainer of the Universe, eternal and primal, benevolent and the Father of men, invisible, omniscient and the guardian of morality.[1] With Animism, whose orthodox doctrine Lang henceforth vehemently opposed, although he had himself previously supported it, this supreme being had of course no connection: such a God could never have originated from any spirit of the dead. By Animism, then, people had been led astray; even in the past, in barbarism, humanity had to a great extent believed what it still believes, even though it neither theologizes nor philosophizes: a God to whom there is no need to sacrifice (cults implying degeneration), who is no revengeful spirit (like the Jahveh of the Old Covenant) but a Lord of the heavens (like the Jahveh of the prophets), and a loving Father (like the God of Jesus). He has created all things: the Eskimo believes that there must be some being that has made all,—"Ah! if only I could, how I would love and honour this being"; and this is confirmation of St. Paul's doctrine that man knows God through creation.[2] Again, he has given moral commands and watches over their observance: the inhabitant of Terra del Fuego believes that killing brings rain, snow and hail; there is a "big man in the wood" who dislikes that, and whom it angers. And such a children's bogey stands higher, despite all the crudeness in the idea, than the Jewish God who permitted Agag to be slain: "The black man of shivering communistic savages is nearer the morality of our Lord than the Jehovah of Judges."[3]

To all these contentions Evolutionism naturally opposed itself, and insisted on ascribing the development of the worship of a supreme being to the influence of Christian missionaries. It seemed altogether too insane to suppose that the end should subsist at the beginning. But gradually it became clear that the supreme beings are indeed, in the great majority of cases, original and autochthonous. And the anti-evolutionists endeavoured to show that the beginning was a beginning in fact, and that what until their day had been so regarded was merely the product of mythical luxuriance and animistic degeneration. With an extensive equipment of knowledge, facts and cooperators, and with passion and scientific self-reliance, Father W. Schmidt undertook to vindicate the honour of the supreme being. He attempted to show that amongst those primitive peoples who really possess the oldest culture (the so-

[1] Lang, *The Making of Religion*, 173.   [2] *Romans* i.
[3] Lang, *ibid.*, 175 *f.*, 183 *ff.*, 192 *ff.*, 203 *ff.*, 218 *ff.*, 237, 271 *ff.*, 280 *f.*, 294.

called pygmy tribes), there subsists in its purest form the belief in a single sublime Creator-God, combined with an elevated moral order sustained by that God. With the assistance of the theory of so-called cultural cycles prevalent in Ethnography,[1] he believed himself able to prove that these oldest peoples, nourished by the herbs they collect, possess the belief in a supreme being, a moral code of a high status and monogamous marriage. And that section of their ideas and customs which does not agree with this is then to be explained by the influence of neighbouring cycles of culture, which have had to pay for their higher civilization (cattle breeding, hunting and agriculture) by a degeneration of their belief in God into mythical-animistic-magical concepts, and of their moral code to polygamy and licentiousness, *etc.*

Schmidt herewith transfers the controversy to historical territory, where I do not wish to follow him.[2] I need observe merely that the idea of the supreme being has amalgamated everywhere with animistic and dynamistic viewpoints, and that a genuine Monotheism has nowhere been proved, while the chronology of cultural cycles has remained matter of dispute until to-day.

But one thing is certain: there does exist a primitive worship of some Being, which can be interpreted neither as Power nor as Will, and which possesses a remarkable similarity to the God of the "proverbial plain man" so dear to Lang.

2. How then must this Being be interpreted? The constructions hitherto offered were influenced to a great extent by three errors: (*1*) That it is historically important to discover the oldest, because this is the most significant; (*2*) That in any case there pertains to religion a "God" as he is depicted in the Catechism or perhaps in the *Confession du Vicaire savoyard*; (*3*) That, as was taught in ancient church doctrine, there is a "natural" religion which contains the genuine belief in God and was originally common to all men, upon which through a special revelation Christendom erects the specific Christian religion of salvation in Christ. If however we free ourselves from these errors and from the pursuit after the historically demonstrable God—or still better—one God, then we find:

The Semang, a pygmy tribe on the Malacca Peninsula, worship a thunder-god *Keii*, who has created all things except the earth, this being made by another god *Ple*, who had formerly been a man. *Keii*

---

[1] *cf.* F. Gräbner, *Methode der Ethnologie*, 1911.
[2] But *cf.* Clemen and Fahrenfort, *op. cit.*

punishes sinners; his son—for he has a wife—is his policeman who
roves about in the form of a tiger: among other things he punishes
incest and want of respect for one's parents. He is invoked only occasionally, and has no fixed cult, the other creator, *Ple*, being the racial ancestor
of the Ple-tribe.[1] Here we must note: the connection with thunder,
with morals and creation, and with tribal origin together with occasional
invocation.

Among the Kurnai in South-East Australia again, where (as Father
Schmidt also concedes) the belief in a supreme being is still retained
in its purity, *Mungan-ngaua* is worshipped. Formerly he lived on
earth and taught men how to make nets, canoes and weapons; now he
lives in heaven, where he is a chief as he was previously on earth. He
too has a son who is the ancestor of the Kurnai; he speaks with the
voice of the bull-roarer (the imitation of thunder). The betrayal of the
secret rites he punishes by flood amongst other things, and is called
"our father". To the Kurnai, however, "father" means uncle as well
as father, and also all those who were initiated at the same time as they.
Here then we observe: the connection with the origin of the tribe,
with thunder and heaven, the moral code, rites and the arts.

In Northern Central California there are again two creators; one
created the earth and the other bestowed culture, but the former has
left the earth and now lives "above" in heaven. He is sublime, kindly
and weak, while the other, identified with the prairie dog or coyote,
is the trickster or adventurer, with traits of Owlglass as well as those
of the hero. The creator *Olelbis* has a wife and many relations, being
invoked only occasionally, principally in time of need; and because
he is in heaven, he sees everything but is not omniscient.[2] Here are
to be noticed: the connection with heaven, with creation, culture, the
sun and moon (the eternal "two brothers" in the myth all over the
world), the occasional cult only in case of need and the fact that the deity
sees all.

Similarly *Baiame*, the supreme being of the Kamilaroi of Central
Australia, once lived on earth as a benefactor and then went with his
two wives towards the East and dwells invisible in heaven, occasionally
appearing in human form. He is regarded as creator in a careless and
let-well-alone way; a Kurnai when asked, "who has made this?"

---

[1] Fahrenfort, *op. cit.*, 42 ff.

[2] R. Dangel, *Der Schöpferglaube der Nordzentralkalifornier*, in *SM*. III, 1927. For the
remainder of the citations, *cf.* the relevant works of Beth, Fahrenfort, Clemen, Söderblom and Schmidt; further, C. Strehlow, *Die Aranda- und Loritja-Stämme in Zentral-
Australien*, 1907 ff.

replied, "*Baiame*, I think". He rules the rain and speaks in the thunder, is eternal and punishes transgressors. *Alchera*, the god of the Arunta, is a strong giant with the feet of an emu. His wives have dogs' feet, his sons being emus and his daughters dogs, which corresponds to the division into Emu and Dog clans. His dwelling too is in heaven, which, however, he did not create, but which it would appear he protects from collapse. Side by side with him there is an entire series of forefathers, *alcheringamichena*, who are also cultural heroes and participate in eternal uncreatedness with *Alchera*.[1] Here we observe a clear connection with totemistic ideas, together with the features already enumerated.

Among the African Bantu tribes, again, where the rule of magic (*juju*) is supreme, a god *Nzambi* is recognized who has withdrawn into heaven and does not trouble himself about terrestrial affairs; he is looked upon as creator, but possesses no cult. In times of direst need he is invoked by the tribes, but they are not at all surprised if he does not hear them.

With *Kitshi Manitu* in the next place we were familiar from youth as the "great spirit" of the Algonquins. He is closely connected with the *mana*-power *Manitu*, already discussed, and also stands in intimate relationship to the totemistic ideas of Nagualism, while the significance of *Manitu* itself appears to vacillate between impersonal power, protective spirit and supreme being.

The classical land of the supreme being, however, is China. *Shang-Ti* is the lord in the heights, the supreme lord who is concerned with heaven, although not identical therewith, but merely a personal being dwelling on high. He stands on the same level as the ancestors, the emperor being called "the son of heaven". But he himself is not an ancestor, while fatherhood only indicates origin; he is, however, closely linked with the heavens and also the origins of the empire and dynasty. He represents the moral world order, and justly rules the world he has created and maintains; in contrast to *Tao*,[2] he is conceived as personal, but is scarcely any more anthropomorphic than is this Power: only once does an ancient *Text* say: "the lord spoke to king Wen".[3] As creator he was neglected, but his moral significance became the standard for Chinese religious sentiment; he has proclaimed laws and prohibitions and punishes evil-doers. In the cult, only the emperor

[1] Beth, *Religion und Magie*; *cf.* also J. Wanninger, *Das Heilige in der Religion der Australier*, 1927, 192 *f.* [2] Chap. 2.
[3] What this implies with respect to the Phenomenology of belief in God may be estimated by comparing it with the endlessly repeated "Thus spake Jahveh" of the Old Testament.

approaches him when worshipping the "imperial heaven", the "supreme emperor", at the "altars of heaven". It is true that all can pray to him; but Confucius significantly asserted that he could hardly remember the last time he prayed.[1] Söderblom is right, therefore, in saying that only in China has the structure of the idea of the supreme being attained a culture of its own:

> Be in awe of Heaven's wrath,
>   No idle dallying venture!
> Be in awe of Heaven's course,
>   Risk not too long your idle ways!
> High Heaven sees everywhere,
>   With you it goes forth, and returns;
> High Heaven sees all clearly,
>   And ever goes with you.[2]

In Vedic India *Varuna* and *Mitra* are the chief figures of the *Adityas*, a type of god which, while maintaining its own place in the Hindu pantheon, is probably of different origin from *Indra* and his companions. The *Adityas* are connected with the kingdom, with heaven and the sun; further, they are intimately related to the path of life, to *Ṛta*[3]; sometimes *Varuna* is accounted its creator, at other times its chief attendant. His character, as contrasted with that of the drunken swashbuckler *Indra*, is described by Oldenberg as "the tranquilly shining sublimity of a sacred kingship that preserves the order of the cosmos and punishes sin". "The one slays the enemy in battle, the other always upholds the laws." *Varuna* sees all, has ordained all and appointed each thing its place. To him one prays: "What was then the grievous sin, O *Varuna*, which makes thee wish to destroy thy friend who praiseth thee? Reveal it to me, thou who art not to be deceived, thou who art mighty in thyself! With obeisance would I implore thy pardon, that I may be free from the guilt of my actions."[4]

3. I believe that all these examples, adduced from cultures most widely separated in time and space, fully justify the Title assigned to this Chapter:—"The Sacred World in the Background: Power and Will in the Background". The God in whom, to his astonishment, man had now discovered his own enlightened ideas, and whom he again

[1] Bertholet, *op. cit.*, 6, 67.
[2] Lehmann-Haas, *Textbuch*, 11.   [3] Chap. 2.
[4] Bertholet, *op. cit.*, 9, 51; *cf.* 40 *ff.*, 45. Oldenberg, *Die Religion des Veda*, 96 *ff.*, 178 *ff.*, 200 *ff.*, 299 *ff.*, 322 *ff.*

jubilantly greeted as the sole God of primal revelation, but whom, as Söderblom perceived, he could more easily have found in eighteenth century Deism—this God is a God in the background, and his sublimity and remoteness from the world are those of a passive pre-existent being who is taken into consideration only occasionally. The concept itself originates with Preuss, whose *Glaube und Mystik*, together with Söderblom's *Gottesglaube*, probably form the most important contributions to the understanding of the structure of belief in the supreme being.[1]

Man, then, exercises power, particularly in the rites which he performs and which rule his world; they subject to him, at least partially, other powers, rain and wind, animals and plants. By means of rites he can dominate the world; there might therefore be no power but his own, and his potency might have subsisted from the very beginning: to quote *Faust*, "the world was not, till I created it". But these conclusions he hesitates to draw; for he experiences the need of setting up a higher court, even if only in the background, some Power from which he can derive all others, including his own, a Power that as it were authorizes his rites but does not concern itself overmuch about him, nor disturbs him in his own fullness of power: only what has been instituted by the supreme being, rites, laws and prohibitions, should be observed. To this it gives close attention, and in order to be able better to do so it goes to heaven, where originally it did not exist: from there it can see everything and take care that the world does not run off the rails. Thus it is God as preserver rather than as creator, although at the same time the entire existence of the world may be derived from the divine predecessor, the Power in the background. But the creative process very often advances no farther than the individual objects that it is supposed to have created; it does not act continually, but initiated once for all, although all further activity is inconceivable without its own. Hence the name "originator" assigned to it by Söderblom, which indeed indicates one of the principal features in its nature.

Thus it approximates both to the bringers of culture and salvation[2] and to tribal ancestors. As originator of rites it is as it were the original medicine-man, and also the first lawgiver:[3] in this manner it ensures the order of the world and is responsible for its emergence. "Probably *Baiame* made it!": so man indicates the Power in the background.

---

[1] *cf.* my Review, *Deutsche Literaturzeitung*, 1928, 13 *Heft.*   [2] Chap. 12,
[3] *cf.* further Father Schmidt, *Settimana intern. di Etnol. relig.*, IV. *Sess.* 1925 (1926), 247 *ff.*

"Actually the primeval-father is superfluous, since it is merely the moon's phases that are magically represented in the festivals; but man requires an originator to make the world, to organize it and introduce ceremonies";[1] the "background" character of the primal father could not be better emphasized. Hence, too, the lack of cult worship; only in time of need, that is when all other means have failed, is he invoked, although even then one hardly expects a hearing. Thus far Lang is quite correct: the religion of the supreme being is certainly that of the "proverbial plain man", even though it is scarcely that of Jesus and the prophets.[2] Man blasphemes in his name, and also calls on him in pious exclamation; he emerges, too, in proverbs, that treasure of the "plain" man.[3] All this means that he is the God in the background, to whom one refers but does not bring down from heaven, and who also does not come forth from there spontaneously.

In this connection, then, two features are of the utmost importance: but *not* the relationship between the highest being and Nature: Söderblom is quite right in regarding this as of merely secondary significance. The originator is a god of neither the heavens nor the sun although, residing as he does in sublime remoteness, he is naturally closely linked with both phenomena. But for the historical consciousness his significance is very great, since here—and this is something fundamentally new—Power is placed in relationship to History: "there are narratives about them", asserts Söderblom of the originators.[4] But the Power-activity does not become a living actuality in history: it is transferred instead to the beginning; it is reserved, antecedent Power, and the Australian tribes have a special name for the "primeval age, unattainable in time" (*Alcheringa* among the Arunta).[5]

The second highly important characteristic of this belief is the intimate union between Power and morality, although the necessity of submitting one's actions to a certain order, and the further need of adapting events in general to a fixed rule, assume in the supreme being a somewhat vague form. It is, however, the court of appeal for human conduct and the guarantee of the orderly world process.

4. Thus in the concept of the supreme being the "appertaining god" becomes the background of the Universe. He is the Will in the

---

[1] K. Th. Preuss, *Religion und Mythologie der Uitoto*, I, 1921, 32.
[2] G. van der Leeuw, *Struktur der Vorstellung des höchsten Wesens.*
[3] Thus among the Bataks: "all depends on God", "we are in God's hands", etc. Nieuwenhuis, *Das höchste Wesen*, 33.   [4] *cf.* Preuss, *Glaube und Mystik*, 58.
[5] K. Beth, *Primitive Religion*, in *Die Religionen der Erde*, 1929, 8.

world behind us, but not an articulate and active Will; he is also the Power in the world of the background, but only meagrely personified.[1] He subsists in all cultural religions; and also in Judaism and Christianity, where, however, the fundamental activity of God prevents the full attainment of his characteristic attributes. The God in the parable of the Prodigal Son might be the supreme being, except for one feature: that of the Father hastening to meet the penitent sinner. The originator hastens not: he has done so once, but has become weary!

In eighteenth century Deism the worship of the supreme being attained its highest prime. The God Who, in the Incarnation, in sacrament, was too near, thus became a God in the background who sustained morality and gave, in immortality, a further guarantee of the reward of virtue and the punishment of evil-doing. A Voltaire's sceptical police-belief, like the warm enthusiasm for virtue of a Rousseau, turns to the Power in the background; while by Robespierre it was honoured as *l'Être Suprême*, in whose name he had his political opponents, people of evil conduct—guillotined!

When devoutness accompanies this belief, however, it assumes the form of *humility*: it is not we that rule the world, for what are we in contrast to the eternally sublime Father, the venerable background of the Universe? and this lowliness has found its most touching expression in Goethe's poem:

> When the All-Holy
> Father Eternal,
> With indifferent hand,
> From clouds rolling o'er us,
> Sows his benignant
> Lightnings around us,
> Humbly I kiss the
> Hem of his garment,
> Filled with the awe of
> A true-hearted child.
>
> What doth distinguish
> Gods from us mortals?
> That they before them
> See waves without number,
> One infinite stream;

[1] Although the expression "*mana*-gods", which I applied to the supreme beings in my *Einführung in die Phänomenologie der Religion* (1925), may seem to stress the aspect of Power too exclusively, still this factor cannot be allowed to remain unnoticed. We should remember *manitu*!

But we, short-sighted,
One wavelet uplifts us,
One wavelet o'erwhelms us
In fathomless night.[1]

In these few lines is contained the complete structure of belief in the Originator, as it lives on through the ages.

C. CLEMEN, *Der sog. Monotheismus der Primitiven, AR.* 27, 1929.

J. J. FAHRENFORT, *Het hoogste Wezen der Primitieven,* 1927.

H. FRICK, *Über den Ursprung des Gottesglaubens und die Religion der Primitiven, Theol. Rundschau,* N. F. 1–2, 1929–30.

A. LANG, *The Making of Religion*[3], 1909.

G. VAN DER LEEUW, *Die Struktur des Glaubens an höchste Wesen, AR.* 29, 1931.

A. W. NIEUWENHUIS, *Das höchste Wesen im Heidentum, Int. Arch. f. Ethnogr.* 27, 1926.

R. PETTAZONI, *Allwissende höchste Wesen bei primitivsten Völkern, AR.* 29, 1931.

K. TH. PREUSS, *Glauben und Mystik im Schatten des höchsten Wesens,* 1926.

P. W. SCHMIDT, *Der Ursprung der Gottesidee* I[2], 1926, II, 1929, III, 1931.

[1] *The Limits of Man* (Dwight).

CHAPTER 19

POWERS

1. THE indefinite and nameless multitude of Powers assumes Form in a plurality of personalities which, each endowed with a name and a sphere of activity of its own, are interconnected by organic relationships. *Polydemonism* becomes *Polytheism*. But these, of course, are not periods in the evolution of belief in God which in due sequence succeed each other. Rather are two different structures to be understood by the two terms. The one comprises the chaotic world of the many potencies with which we are already familiar: sacred beings whose realms of power are separated in either place or time, *numina* of the night and day, of Spring and Winter, of this activity or that. The other embraces precisely the same world, but as oriented according to definite viewpoints: thus the chaotic plurality becomes an ordered whole. Both structures alike are timeless, and in no case settled stages on the highway of mankind: to a great extent, indeed, Polytheism remains always Polydemonism. When for example the several corn-mothers of Greece had already been fused for some time into the single form of Demeter, the "black" Demeter of Phigalia still remained, with her ancient cult and crude myths, as a different form from that of the mother of Eleusis, just as the "black" madonna of some Italian town or other is radically different from the madonna figure of another locality.[1]

The process leading repeatedly from Polydemonism to Polytheism is termed *Syncretism*. In the development of culture man finds the Universe becoming steadily smaller; his world is no longer limited to his own village, but extends to a number of such communities linked together by manifold connections, and ultimately to a province, a state, to neighbouring states. The many potencies of the next village and the nearest state thus become familiar to him, whether in goodwill or in war. Then there arises some kind of understanding between his own and foreign powers, so that those exhibiting the closest mutual relationship unite under one name and a single form, while the remainder acquire definite reciprocal interconnections. Thus a Pantheon comes into being, although of course it is never completed: the *Adityas* in

[1] Bertholet, *Götterspaltung*, 6.

India, the *Vans* in Scandinavia, Dionysus and his circle in Greece, are never entirely merged in the world of the gods but maintain their own status and character.

One point must, however, be added: it concerns the concept, "God". Or rather *a* concept, "God". For here again we must not rest content with Christian or any other generally accepted ideas. At this stage, however, "God" is something other than simply Power or fetish, spirit or demon. The gods of Polytheism are indeed wills and forms in the animistic sense; but they are distinguished from other potencies that are likewise endowed with Will and Form. They possess something that is specific in its type, which it is not easy to include within any concept whatever, because here again we run the risk of imposing our own ideas. On that account we should not yet say that the deity is "sublime", even though what we mean thereby is not far removed from our own concept of sublimity. What should now be added to the character of complete Otherness, which the idea of God shares with all the objects of religion, is best indicated by an example: the ancient Egyptians, then, ascribed golden flesh to the gods. "Gold (is) the flesh of the gods . . . Rē said at the beginning of his words: My skin is of pure gold";[1] here the Greek idea of *ichor*, the blood of the gods, is relevant. By gold, then, very much is expressed which we too ascribe to deity: difference in nature, sublimity, beauty, immortality, since gold signifies eternal life. But the image is actually such:—it is quite concrete and no affair of concepts at all.

2. There are, again, several interconnections between powers that correspond fairly exactly to the prevailing conditions of human society; these are designated by the general expression *Theogony*. Thus the various types and ranks of the gods are brought together in relations resting on affinity, the simplest form being probably that of the *Triad*:— Father, Mother and Child: this existed in ancient Egypt:—Osiris, Isis, Horus. Horus is an older celestial god, who originally had nothing to do with Osiris: in the triad, however, he appears as the typical faithful son, just as Isis is the typical Egyptian loving sister-wife. And the family triad is so very powerful a factor in the human spirit, in so far as it thinks in patriarchal terms, that even Christianity could not dispense with it, so that the trinity of Jesus, Mary and Joseph may be regarded as the "trinity of Catholic popular piety".[2] But there are other

---

[1] B. Gunn and A. H. Gardiner, "The Temple of the Wady Abbad", *Jour. of Eg. Arch.* 4, 247.   [2] Heiler, *Katholizismus*, 192.

conditions also: for the matriarchal state is reflected in the duality Mother and Son, or Lover. Here the Near East is typical:—Cybele and Attis, Ishtar and Tammuz; and if the paternal god is combined with them there arises another triad. The groups of gods on the bas-reliefs of Boghazköi should probably be explained in this sense: the bearded father-god meets the mother on the lion, who is followed by the young god on a panther.[1]

Together with the Triad, of course, there appears *Duality*, predominantly as a pair of twin brothers whose unity and estrangement, based on the relationship of the sun and moon, have given occasion to many myths. The connections of the most diverse gods to some larger group, such as we find in Egypt, are more independent of Nature. the so-called Great *Ennead* includes, besides the already independent composite Osiris triad, the other important gods too, and shows indeed a tendency towards the development of the concept of totality. Here the same mystic urge manifests itself that has rendered the Christian dogma of the Trinity, which originally and essentially emphasizes the unity of the Christian "Powers", again and again the starting point of monistic and pantheistic speculation,[2] and has similarly reduced the three gods included in the *Trimurti* of post-Vedic India, Brahma, Rudra and Vishnu, to forms of the incorporeal Absolute.

But powers also unite to form an association exhibiting the traits of either a Greek *polis*, a warrior tribe or an oriental despotic state, as the case may be; in hierarchic organization, lesser powers are subjected to the more important. One is the chief, whether as father of gods and men, Zeus, whose lordship is patriarchially conceived, or as the great king surrounded by his *divan*, an image still extant in later Judaism. Demons and angels became either vassals and ministers, or rebels; and the Persian divine state had its viziers and satraps, the Jewish its grandees, among whom the rebellious were not lacking, and the Germanic its court skalds.

3. Beside these connections, however, various divisions occur in the manifoldness of powers. Thus the time distinction into periods according to two gods, one succeeding the other as in the case of Apollo and Dionysus, is actually based on natural events; similarly the delimitation of powers according to place and nation corresponds to natural and cultural conditions. Cosmically, again, Power subdivides into celestial

---

[1] Haas, *Bilderatlas*, Part 5, Fig. 2; *cf.* Zimmern's *Text*.
[2] *cf.* H. Groos, *Der deutsche Idealismus und das Christentum*, 1927, 107.

and earthly or subterranean (chthonian), while in accord with Form, into male and female, father and mother, and sometimes child also. Then there are distinctions relevant to their spheres of operations, the "offices", or τιμαί, as Herodotus says. Aeschylus, too, was familiar with a formal classification of the gods:

> Of every god
> That guards the city, the deep, the high,
> Gods of the mart, gods of the sky,
> The altars blaze.[1]

But we must guard against reducing these divisions to the currency of works of reference which speak about gods like a *Who's Who*; for the traits of the form, the attributes and τιμαί, the cosmic or social links, are all to be understood only in the light of the numinous basis of Power. That is the truth misapprehended in *Henotheism*: man never has to deal with some community of gods as if it were a foreign superior state with which he comes into relation, but always only with Power, Will and Form as they become actual, impressive and visible at any given moment; and what has been revealed to him at that moment he afterwards co-ordinates according to his own standards.[2]

4. The Power that endows with sacredness the objects of man's environment, of the conjunct and the upper worlds, can withdraw itself into the background. But it can also come more and more prominently into the foreground. And in any case it is linked with the world; what is regarded with amazement as "Wholly Other" belongs nevertheless to the events of the world. Still further, the more thoroughly it is brought within the series of other phenomena so much the greater is the danger of its losing its original sacredness and becoming "world". In so-called Polytheism, then, there goes on an incessant struggle for the independence of the sacred Power over against the world; but in a wholly logical Polytheism world and god would fuse into one.

This, however, is no fault of Polytheism. It is rather the rendering apparent of the limits demanded by God as over against the world; although of course we can also say: the limits necessary to the world as against God. For neither the plurality of powers, nor the imaginative intensification of the outlines of the form, is in itself to blame for the fact that God threatens to become now world, and again man. For a God who is actually one, in the sense that there is no other Power

---

[1] *Agamemnon*, 88 *ff.* (Murray).   [2] *cf.* H. Schmalenbach, *Logos*, 16, 1927, 322.

whatever except him, would be wholly identical with the world; and Christianity allows the world and its overlord, the Devil, to exist in contrast to God.[1] Powers reveal themselves to us, and the ultimate unity is essentially the affair of faith, not of religion; for the religion of Power in general would be the worship of the Universe.

Anthropomorphism, too, is not wholly evil; for along with the fetish and the animal form, one possible expression of the Something Other is abandoned. But the human form of power also indicates distance; man has been unable to discover in the world any power higher than his own, and he now creeps, as it were, into this power himself.[2] He thereby renders some fragment of the world powerless, but does not necessarily make himself super-powerful; and it is precisely those attributes of the god, which raise it highest above man, that can be expressed no otherwise than in human analogies: strength of will, spirituality of outlook, certainty in fixing a goal.[3] Physical anthropomorphism, then, can be overcome, even though it is never conquered completely; but psychical anthropomorphism is given at the same time as human ideas and thoughts, and whoever desired to abandon it must remain absolutely silent about the god. For all speech is human and creates human forms; and even if animals and fetishes do seem to endow the Wholly Other with peculiarly adequate form,[4] still this is only because animals and things are themselves observed by man. The god of the animal, in fact, would first of all be a man.

"Whence the gods severally sprang, whether or no they had all existed from eternity, what forms they bore—these are questions of which the Greeks knew nothing until the other day, so to speak. For Hesiod and Homer were the first to compose *Theogonies*, and give the gods their *epithets*, to allot them their several *offices* and *occupations*, and describe their *forms*; and they lived but four hundred years before my time, as I believe."[5] In these words of Herodotus there lies the whole of classical Polytheism: the interconnection of the powers, the limitation of their operations, the development of their personality and creation of their form. This Polytheism is indeed to be found in

[1] Together with a whole host of "powers", φθορά, θάνατος, ἁμαρτία (corruption, death, sin), of the Pauline world; cf. O. Piper, *Die Grundlagen der evangelischen Ethik*, I, 1928, 127.

[2] cf. H. Werner, *Einführung in die Entwicklungspsychologie*, 1926, 272.

[3] cf. Kurt Sethe, *Amun und die acht Urgötter von Hermopolis, Abh. der preuss. Akad. der Wiss.*, 1929, phil.-hist. Kl. 4, §235.   [4] Chap. 3, 8.

[5] *Herodotus*, II, 53 (Rawlinson); my italics; cf. van der Leeuw, *Goden en Menschen*, 163 f.

many places, but nowhere so consistently and completely developed as in Greece.[1] Where it is an affair of names and forms it has become for ourselves a matter of course, and it is only recent decades that have perceived other possibilities, and also that the Greeks themselves were not content with the gifts of their own poets. For the criticisms of Xenophanes, of the Tragedians and the Sophists upon the Homeric idea of god, were passionately and quite seriously intended, and Plato knew full well why he excluded poets from his community.[2] In these criticisms fear of the humanizing of Power extends ultimately to its identification with the world. "Homer and Hesiod have ascribed to the gods all things that among men are a shame and a reproach—theft and adultery and deceiving one another." Thus says Xenophanes,[3] and he believes that he can draw the conclusion that man created gods in his own image: "If oxen or horses or lions had hands and could draw with them and make works of art as men do, horses would draw the shapes of gods like horses, oxen like oxen; each kind would represent their bodies just like their own forms." Again: "The Ethiopians say their gods are black and flat-nosed; the Thracians, that theirs are blue-eyed and red-haired."[4] We have already observed, however, that this anticipation of Feuerbach cannot be correct. But that a certain danger threatened here was again and again repeated by all the great Greeks in confirmation of Xenophanes. Thus Euripides is most severe with the beautiful Olympian forms; his gods are often mere machines, empty schemata with which men can screen their own deficiencies.[5] And even when they are real forms they exhibit so much human pettiness that they can merit only the poet's indignation, and not a single breath of adoration.

> Thine is unwisdom, or injustice thine,

says Amphitryon to Zeus; and Theseus substantiates this:

> Have they not linked them in unlawful bonds
> Of wedlock, and with chains, to win them thrones,
> Outraged their fathers? In Olympus still
> They dwell, by their transgressions unabashed.

Scornfully, again, Herakles asks:

> To such a goddess who shall pray now?[6]

---

[1] Nilsson, *A History of Greek Religion*, 144. [2] *Republic*, 377 *ff*. and elsewhere.
[3] *Fr.* 11 (Diels; Cornford). [4] *Fr.* 15, 16 (Diels; Cornford).
[5] *e.g. Troades*, 969 *ff*.; *cf.* U. von Wilamowitz-Möllendorff, *Griechische Tragödien*, III[5], 1919, 281 *f*. [6] Euripides, *Herakles*, 345, 1316 *ff*., 1308 (Way).

Here we see quite clearly where Theogony and endowment with Form have led. In the last resort neither the human gods nor their all-too-human poets were at fault, but rather the powers themselves. Who can help it if they clash with each other continually, if their will appears to be pure arbitrariness, if their rule must appear a tyranny? Poetic endowment with form by the Greeks merely gave its keenest expression to that question, addressed to the powers, which agitates many peoples, and in which the whole problem of *Theodicy* is contained: "What do ye powers desire? and why do ye desire it?" Much is presupposed here: that Power has Will: that man also has will, and indeed a will that does not operate by magic: that he has recognized some norm to which he ascribes absolute value. We shall discuss all this later; but we are now concerned with the fact that man can tolerate no plurality of forms and wills. And this indeed not merely because of the intractability of imagination—think of the Greek poets!—but because of the undeniable existence of forms and powers as such, quite apart from all fantasy. It was in fact the *Universe* that, under the form of gods, oppressed the Greeks; and it is *man* himself who causes himself this deep anxiety as to the gods' will.

Therefore the Greek attempted to free himself from gods: Euhemerus accounted for them as being men of an earlier age.[1] But the Greek mind chose a yet more resolute attitude: multiplicity and form had to give way to the Impersonal. The gods with human emotions, θεοὶ ἀνθρωποπαθεῖς, are after all too much like the world and men:

> For God hath need—if God indeed he be—
> Of nought: these be the minstrels' sorry tales.[2]

Nature itself is divine and requires no gods.[3] This indeed by no means yields any satisfaction to the poet's cry for a god "to whom one can pray", as Wilamowitz well remarks, since the divine Power in Nature, too, hears not. But from the far-reaching consequences of this flight from the Universe the Greeks were, of course, saved by their feeling for the principle, "Nothing in excess" (μηδὲν ἄγαν). But in India personal existence appeared more and more indefensible and despicable; even the existence of gods is, if not wrong, as in Greece, at least suffering: "in the unshakeable, the immovable, my heart rejoices".[4]

---

[1] Bertholet, *Lesebuch*, 4, 80 f.
[2] Euripides, *Herakles*, 1345 f. (Way); cf. U. von Wilamowitz-Möllendorf, *Herakles*², 1909, 481.
[3] *ibid.*, 1232; also *The Trojan Women*, 884 ff.; cf. my Article *Een dramatische Geloofsbelijdenis, Hermeneus*, 2, 1929.   [4] Bertholet, *Lesebuch*¹, 225.

This led ultimately to the disappearance of Form, to the eventual defeat of all will to live in Brahmanism and Buddhism—that is to religious *Atheism*.

Thus the development of Form and the humanizing of Will are not the basis of the question as to the claim of the gods. For everywhere that Power and man encounter each other, at the limits of human nature, this question appears, in ancient Babylon and *The Book of Job* just as with the Greek tragedians. Power no longer possesses its intrinsic claim; it must substantiate it; but in Polytheism, and above all in its most beautiful and profoundest revelation—the gods of Olympus—the question is shirked. Power and Nature, Nature and human life, all flow into each other: to the Homeric Greeks "the divine is neither a justifying explanation, nor an interruption and suspension, of the natural course of the world: it is the natural course of the world itself".[1]

Thus Power becomes our own life, numerability becomes intelligibility, the god's image becomes that of man. Here in fact lie the presuppositions of Greek, and at the same time of modern, science and art. But here too, ultimately, all worship ceases: Aristophanes is wholly right in his conservative criticism, in so far as he reproaches Euripides for causing the poor widow who plaited myrtle chaplets to lose half her customers by his disavowal of the gods.[2]

By relinquishing Form or Will, therefore, the solution can never be obtained, not even by simply erasing plurality. Only belief in the Creator escapes the consequences of Anthropomorphism: God created man after His own image. Only belief in Incarnation those of Polytheism: God becomes man, not world.

[1] W. F. Otto, *Die Götter Griechenlands*, 1929, 218.
[2] *Thesmophoriazousai*, 443 ff.

THE FATHER

1. FORM and Will, then, can fail to such a degree that they are abandoned; and man can calm himself by the belief that his God is the world, is humanity, "growing with the world".[1] As we shall see,[2] he can even worship himself as humanity, as the human type: he can also take refuge in the Impersonal, in the Absolute, which "neither acts nor suffers, nor loves nor hates; it has no needs, desires or aspirations, no failures or successes, friends or enemies, victories or defeats".[3] After Greece, India has its say.[4]

And only that concept of God which renounces completely the specific potency of humanity can escape these consequences. For as long as man's own power attempts to destroy, to use, admire or enjoy external power, Form and Will must fail, since man is thereby compelling, using, admiring and enjoying himself over and over again. At most he can completely deny Form and Will: but that does not help him very much, since the world offers them to him every day in confusing plenteousness. And the tranquil background—as James saw quite rightly—can mean only "a moral holiday" and not a moral common round.[5] He himself took refuge in a modernized Polytheism; but recognition of manifoldness can avail just as little as its denial. Only where it is believed that Omnipotence—"all Power"—belongs to God does Form live and Will rule. Anthropomorphism need no longer be dreaded, because it is not we that impart Form to God, but He to us; anthropopathy is no longer a danger where all dominion comes from God and arises out of His Will; and plurality need no longer be destroyed by a desperate, colourless and unreal unity where His unity, to Whom all Power belongs, is comprehensible in itself, as is also the plurality of power that He has created. Thus we have expressed the essential principle: Form and Will have their real and divine life in God, *in the Creator*. But of course we do not mean that creator whom we have found reposing in the background of the Universe; rather do we think of the God Who imparts Himself in His creation, and Who even gives Himself.

[1] Typically, H. A. Overstreet, "The Democratic Conception of God", *Hibbert Journal*, XI, 1913, 394 ff.   [2] Chap. 37.

[3] James, *A Pluralistic Universe*, 47 f.   [4] Chap. 21.   [5] *ibid.*, 116 ff.

2. In this connection we naturally feel tempted to consider solely the Monotheism of Israel, to which indeed our description of fearless anthropomorphic belief in the Creator applies in the first instance. But it is imperatively necessary to inquire into the intelligible basis of Form and Will, and not to hesitate before anything less exalted. For man calls this God "Father", and hitherto we are familiar only with the Mother.

In this respect, too, Frazer remarks that it is chimerical to imagine that women invented the worship of goddesses, since "if women ever created gods, they would be more likely to give them masculine than feminine features".[1] But the second hypothesis would be just as false. It is true that both male and female elements, and the dominance of either at any given period, play a great part in the structure of the idea of God. But there is too much of the feminine in every man, and of the masculine in every woman, for precedence to be conceded here to either the one or the other sex. The religion of the Mother, therefore, is that of humanity exactly as is that of the Father.

In a way that produces on us moderns an almost amusing impression, we perceive the enormous interval separating the two, when in ancient Babylon we find our familiar name "father" replaced by "uncle";[2] the god is "uncle", that is the wife's brother, the most important male figure after the primarily important woman. This is a vestige of an all-embracing motherliness. But the distance in question finds its basis first of all in the contrast between father and mother, that is between active and passive: the mother gives birth, the father generates; the mother receives, the father gives. Thus next to the maternal figure there appears the paternal. And just as woman resembles the field, so does man the plough—to the Greeks Erichthonius, Erechtheus, "the earth opener".[3] Of course, the myth of the holy marriage, as has been observed,[4] has the mother as its principal person; and the father-spouse can be at the same time son. Here, where mother-earth is supreme, lie the roots of the Oedipus myth which, in our day, has been raised almost to the rank of a dogma by the Freudian school.[5] An ancient Egyptian divine title runs: "The Bull, that is, the spouse of his mother".[6] But the aspect of activity, of the giver, cannot be mistaken

[1] *Man, God and Immortality*, 129.
[2] B. Gemser, *De beteekenis der Persoonsnamen voor onze kennis van het leven en denken der onde Babylonieërs en Assyrieërs*, 1924, 102 ff.
[3] cf. E. Fehrle, *Die kultische Keuschheit im Altertum*, 1910, 185 f.
[4] Chap. 10.   [5] cf. C. Clemen, *Arch. für die ges. Psychologie*, 61, 1928, 26.
[6] cf. A. Wiedemann, *AR.* 21, 1922, 453.

in the figure of the father-spouse even when it subsists in the closest
proximity to the main factor of receptive passivity. For primeval—
and only to blind eyes, rude—sex symbolic language mediates theological creation of Form: most beautifully expressed in the words of
Tao-teh King:

> The spirit of the Deep never dies.
> It is the eternal feminine.
> The sallyport of the eternal feminine
> Is the root of heaven and earth.
> Eternally it urges itself forward, and yet remains steadfast.
> In its operation it remains effortless.

The "deep" is the "valley", the empty space between the walls of the
hills, matter without form, the mere possibility of being, while the
"spirit" is the active, the form-imparting.[1] The complete form would
therefore be not that of the mother, that is of "possibility"! but of
the willing and creating father.

But of course we must not interpret paternal form and will in terms
of the generative act alone; therein lies the onesidedness of Freudian
doctrine.[2] In the light of this lack of balance, also, it would be difficult
to understand how Christianity could take over belief in the Father
from the religion of Israel, wherein the Father form, as husband and
generator, is almost completely lacking. "Doubtless thou art our
father, though Abraham be ignorant of us, and Israel acknowledge us
not: thou, O Lord, art our father, our redeemer; thy name is from
everlasting. But now, O Lord, thou art our father; we are the clay,
and thou our potter; and we all are the work of thy hand."[3] This is
not the figure of the generator but of a creator, whose relations to man
are the precise opposite of those of kinship, and before whose will
man bows in deep but trustful dependence.

For many primitive and ancient peoples, that is to say, the term
"father" does not mean the same as it does for us, the "father" being
the representative of an age level, that of the older as contrasted with
the younger. For the term is older than the modern family, and presupposes a social organization in which a group of seniors was distinguished from a group of juniors. Here, then, much less importance

[1] R. Wilhelm, *Laotse, Tao Te King*, 1921, 8, 92. The creation of the form "Heaven-
earth" (male-female) is also connected with these ideas; *cf.* H. Th. Fischer, *Het heilig
huwelijk van hemel en aarde*, 1929.

[2] R. Thurnwald, *Ethnologie und Psychoanalyse*, in *Auswirkungen der Psychoanalyse
in Wissenschaft und Leben* (edited by H. Prinzhorn), 1928, 125 *ff.*

[3] *Isaiah* lxiii. 16; lxiv. 8.

attaches to the act of generation than to authority, fullness of power, the wisdom of the oldest men who, as is well known, were among many primitive societies the guardians of the secret rites. Even the Roman idea of *pater familias* regarded this power of the *pater* as independent of his actual fatherhood: "he who rules in the house is called *pater familias*, and is rightly so named even if he has no son". Power is limited to *domus*.[1] It is therefore in the light of this dual activity, firstly as generative-creative, secondly as authoritative-ruling, that the Father-form of God is to be understood: the indubitably superior, from which all Power is derived, but which communicates and imparts itself.

3. For this form the unity of God is not so important, at least not as a negation of plurality; and it is absolutely wrong therefore to conceive the history of religion as a development leading up to "Monotheism". Even for "developed religion, concepts like 'Monotheism' and 'Polytheism' are empty numerical schemes, by which the value of a religion can be measured just as little as can the worth of a marriage by the number of children sprung from it".[2]

It is a question then not of the unity, but of the uniqueness, of God: a form like that of God has nowhere been seen by our eyes: with a Will like God's we have never at any time come into contact. Who is like God? The uniqueness of God is no mere negation of His plurality, but a passionate affirmation of His potency. So deeply indeed has God's self-imparting activity bitten into human life that man must say to his God:

> Whom have I in heaven but thee?
> On earth I care for nothing else.[3]

Thus the Monotheism of Islam also was not a protest against Polytheism, but an enthusiastic belief in God's omnipotence.[4] For "omnipotence" is no bloodless "attribute" of a theoretically conceived ruler of the world or originator, but the conviction that all Power belongs to God, and none to man except what he receives from God. Here we are just as remote from the "supreme being" as from the manifold powers of Polytheism. Perhaps even farther: for here it is a case not of a "highest" being, but of *Being* itself, the sole reality, unique existent actuality, unique significance.

[1] G. May, *Eléments de Droit romain*[13], 1920, 103.
[2] Wundt, *op. cit.*, IV, 320.   [3] *Ps.* lxxiii. 25 (Moffat).
[4] A. Bertholet, *Die gegenwärtige Gestalt des Islams*, 1926, 8.

"God is One" therefore is to be regarded not as an assertion or conviction, but simply as an expression of faith in the sense of the classical acclamation εἷς θεός, "God is One".[1] God is One because from Him comes salvation, Power that has been turned to good. God is One because He is omnipresent in the inexhaustible activity of His Will: "If I ascend up into heaven, thou art there: if I make my bed in hell, behold, thou are there."[2] This burning activity of the Will of God is supremely vivid in the Old Testament, no less in quite primitive features such as in the story of Jahveh's sudden attack on Moses,[3] than in the battle-song of the Israelites, in which their joy in the active God who fights and saves, who descends from His mount to take their side, is unmistakably and resonantly heard:

> Blest be the Eternal One, my Strength,
>   who trains my hands to war,
>   my fingers how to fight!—
> my Crag, my Stronghold, my Fortalice and Deliverer
>   the Shield behind whom I shelter,
>   the subduer of nations before me!
>
> Eternal One, come down upon the bending heavens,
>   touch the mountains till they smoke,
> flash lightning out to scatter my foes,
>   shoot thine arrows to discomfit them;
> reach from on high to raise me from these floods,
>   rescue me from these alien hordes,
>
> O God, I would sing thee a new song,
>   and play to thee on a ten-stringed lute,
>
> May our sons be straight and strong like saplings,
> our daughters like cornices carved in a palace!
>
> Happy the nation that so fares!
> Happy the nation whose God is the Eternal![4]

But the all embracing activity of the Will, and the complete Father form, are declared by Christianity in the Incarnation. Unperturbed by the reproach of either Anthropomorphism or Polytheism, it beholds the figure of Him Who has come that He may perform the Will of Him who has sent Him.

[1] Chap. 63.
[2] *Ps.* cxxxix. 8.
[3] *Exodus* iv. 24 ff.
[4] *Ps.* cxliv (Moffat).

CHAPTER 21

THE ABSOLUTELY POWERFUL

1. OUR second Chapter dealt with Power theorized, rendered absolute, having attained dominance with no creation of form nor inclusion of will. Here, form and will having been abandoned as inadequate, we shall discuss Power unsustained by any person; Power that is not the outcome of will and that does not display itself, but absolutely *is*. Obviously the Power considered in Chapter 2 was not "previously" existent: just as little is the Power now in question only a late fruit of maturer speculation. But from the outset there is a tendency to Power simply as such, which at first concerns itself with neither will nor form; and also to the reattainment of Power after the creation of form has failed, as can be observed most clearly in the case of the Greeks. This produces a considerable structural difference, which induces me to devote a specific discussion to this flight to absolute Power.

It can be regarded, then, as an attempt to cling to the experience of Power purely in itself, while escaping from the "dual experience of form". Power overcomes us—herein all religions agree. But whoever has been undeceived in the divine will, and evaluates the second formalized experience of Power as mere appearance, tries to retain this experience in itself, as pure Power. Forthwith he hits upon the idea of *Fate*. Thus did Aeschylus: and thus did Goethe's Prometheus:

> I honour thee! For what?
> Hast thou the miseries lightened
> Of the down-trodden?
> Hast thou the tears ever banished
> From the afflicted?
> Have I not to manhood been moulded
> By omnipotent Time,
> And by Fate everlasting,
> My lords and thine?[1]

One alone is powerful: the force that here, and at this moment, binds me, the law according to which I have come into being. There may be other powers, forms and wills besides my own: but like myself

---

[1] The poem *Prometheus*.

these too are subject to that primeval determining Power which roots
me to this very life, this very time and place. The riddle as to why I
was born and why, just here and now, my life rolls on, is insoluble:
it is just my lot, and the Power apportioning it my fate. Whatever
holds good of me holds good also of the whole Universe: its potency
too is limited and conditioned, its "Being-now", as its "Being-thus",
a mystery.

Now I experience this Power of fate as pure Power only as soon
as I not merely verify it, but also surrender myself to it. Then I abandon
all personal adjustment to Power, I despair of any interference of
Power on my own behalf, I relinquish the thought of *salvation* and
deliver myself up to *Fate*.[1] I may turn out to be a failure: if so, Destiny
receives demonic attributes and, as in later Greek times, I long for
the "saving fate, for mercy".[2] But the old Greeks achieved this. The
idea of the rightness of the Universe took the place of the idea of
salvation: we have not understood God's will: his form appears dubious
to us: nor can we justify his deeds. Nevertheless Fate is always right;
and we address no demands to it because it is the absolutely powerful.
Thus Euripides' "Natural Law" led all "to the right goal". The
problem of a theodicy cannot arise, just as every personal desire from
Power is excluded. So Plato thought: "God, as the old tradition
declares, holding in His hand the beginning, middle, and end of all
that is, moves according to His nature in a straight line towards the
accomplishment of His end. Justice always follows Him, and is the
punisher of those who fall short of the divine law."[3] Against *ananke*
neither magic—human power—nor the art of healing, neither cult
nor even Zeus—the power of the willing god—can do aught.[4]

2. We found that uniformity of the person and constancy in form
were dependent on the *Name*; we need hardly be surprised, therefore,
that the abandonment of will and form implies also a loss of the name
of the power; Euripides, for instance, calls his god "Zeus" or "Natural
Law" or even "world reason". The name has now become "empty
sound", and far from being competent to guarantee essence—as was
the case in the structure of primitive thought—it has sunk to the
level of an unreality, or at least an inadequacy. The Greeks, who
turned from the gods to the divine (θεῖον), derived from the proper

[1] *cf.* further Otto Piper's observations, *Die Grundlagen der evangelischen Ethik*, I,
1928, 108 *ff.*   [2] P. Tillich, *Philosophie und Schicksal, Kantstudien*, 34, 1929, 302 *ff.*
[3] *Laws*, IV, 715e (Jowett); *cf.* Tillich, *ibid.*, 301 *ff.*   [4] Euripides, *Alcestis* 962 *ff.*

name "Zeus" a significance which probably expressed something more general than when we say "God".[1] Thus it is primarily intended by Aeschylus in the famous apostrophe to Zeus in *Agamemnon*:

> Zeus! Zeus, whate'er He be,
> If this name He love to hear
> This He shall be called of me.
> Searching earth and sea and air
> Refuge nowhere can I find
> Save Him only, if my mind
> Will cast off before it die
> The burden of this vanity.[2]

From doubt and care, then, the poets find rest in the god who has no name—or has every name. And later reflection sees powers scattered throughout the world and invoked by different names, while only the one God is intended whose actual name no one knows.[3] Henceforth the name is regarded as a limitation; it can certainly offer a footing in the turmoil of the infinite manifold and provide firm outlines in the dissolution, but what has thus been won is not the divine. "If I called him by a hundred names, like a Turk, I should yet fall short and have said nothing in comparison to the boundlessness of his attributes."[4]

3. Thus from Form and Will man flees to the impersonal, the nameless; but also to the *Inner Life*; and then Power operates not from without, but from within. In relation to the human it is of course transcendent (otherwise it would no longer be the object of religion), but its superiority is that of the whole as over against the part. The god who is invoked in Euripides' Prayer of Hecuba, which has already been frequently quoted, is the air, the world principle advanced by Diogenes of Apollonia, the ἀρχή, which is the life-creating force in both man and beast.[5] The concepts "God" and "soul" affect each other: God becomes the world-soul; and with this the human spirit

---

[1] Therefore not "exactly the same as when we say God", even if "much less the proper name of one among countless gods other than Jahveh", and indeed "no longer a person". Wilamowitz, *Griech. Tragödien*, III[5], 1919, 283.

[2] *Agamemnon*, 160 *ff*. (Murray).

[3] Thus Maximus of Madaura, in F. Cumont, *Les religions orientales dans le paganisme romain*[2], 1909, 307.   [4] Goethe, *Conversations with Eckermann*, March 8, 1831.

[5] *cf.* Karl Joel, *Der Ursprung der Naturphilosophie aus dem Geiste der Mystik*, 1906, 112 *f*.

consciously turns back to extremely primitive paths. Power, as we saw, was "stuff" that could impart soul, the frontier between god and soul being indistinct, and the idea of *mana* comprising both. Now Power is made absolute from within as the world-soul, in conscious contrast to the powers which intrude from without:

> What were a God, who, outward force applying,
> But kept the All around his finger flying!
> He from within lives through all Nature rather,
> Nature and Spirit fostering each other;
> So that what in Him lives, and moves, and is,
> Still feels His power, and owns itself still His.[1]

Here, side by side with the humble worship of the Whole, there rings in Goethe's words a note of fear in face of the incalculability of the divine Will, which bestows its power and its spirit but which also, when it so pleases, withdraws them.

4. The Power which, nameless, moves within the Universe, is ultimately *One*; that is, there is none other beside it. Here—not in Monotheism—unity receives its full stress. The form of the Father, standing opposed to the world, is unique, while the Power which, like air, penetrates everything, is One—in the sense of One and All; and in the ancient world we find such pantheistic impulses. The name of the Egyptian god *Atum*, for example, was explained as: "Atum, that is, all the gods", while the dead were deified and each of their limbs identified with a god; thus a funeral *Text* quotes the dead man as saying that his hair is Nun, his countenance Ra, *etc.*, and "there is no member of my body which is not the member of some god".[2]

It is well known, further, how the Hindu spirit derived all individual powers from the twofold unity of *Brahman* and *Ātman*. The interval between object and subject is thereby completely annulled, and the absolute otherness, the transcendence of Power, can persist only in the feeling of submersion and plunging within the Universe. In the *Bhagavad-Gita* speaks the Sublime:

> And others, sacrificing with the sacrifice of knowledge worship me as one or as several, in many ways—so they worship me, who face every way.
> I am the oblation, I am the sacrifice, the offering to the fathers am I; I

---

[1] *God, Soul, and World* (Dwight); *cf.* H. Groos, *Der deutsche Idealismus und das Christentum*, 1927, 71 *f.*, on the derivation of Goethe's lines from Giordano Bruno, *De Immenso*, IV, 15.   [2] *The Book of the Dead*, Chap. 42, 10.

am the herb, the sacred formula; I am also the melted butter, I am the fire, I am the burnt offering.

I am the father of this universe, the mother, the supporter, the grand-father, that which should be known, the purifier, OM, the Rigveda, the Samaveda, the Yajurveda;[1]

The way, the supporter, the Lord, the witness, the abode, the refuge, the friend, the origin, the dissolution, the abiding-place, the storehouse, the changeless seed.

I give heat, I hold back the rain and send it forth; I am the immortal and also death; being and non-being am I, O Arjuna.[2]

Here every form, every particularity, every individuality fails. God too is superfluous, since the divine within man is all: "Who ranks the higher, he who offers sacrifices to his own self (*ātman*) or he who sacrifices to the gods? We should reply, he who offers sacrifice to himself."[3]

Unlike the Hindu, however, the Greek could never completely dispense with Form. But even Zeus does not *have* all Power—he *is* all Power; and this conception is already found in Aeschylus:

> Zeus is air, Zeus is earth, Zeus is heaven;
> Zeus is all things and whatsoever is higher than all things.[4]

The Stoics absorbed this idea: mythology is deceitful: "but though repudiating these myths with contempt, we shall nevertheless be able to understand the personality and the nature of the divinities pervading the substance of the several elements, Ceres permeating earth, Neptune the sea, and so on . . . under the names which custom has bestowed upon them".[5]

Thus Power becomes increasingly limitless, and constantly richer:

---

[1] *Om* is the sacred magic syllable, followed here by the three canonical Vedas.

[2] *The Song of the Lord: Bhagavad-Gita*, IX, 15. (E. J. Thomas); *cf.* also the pantheism of romanticism:

> Argatiphontidas and Photidas,
> The citadel of Cadmus and Greece.
> Light, ether and the waters,
> What was: What is: What shall be;

(Heinrich von Kleist, *Amphitryon*, III, 11), and the objection of that typical animist, Alcmene!

> Shall I pray to this white marble block?
> If I am to think of him at all
> I need some recognizable features (II, 5).

[3] Oldenberg, *Lehre der Upanishaden*, 33.

[4] Cornford, *Greek Religious Thought*, 109; *cf.* H. Diels, *Zeus*, AR. 22, 1923–24, 11 *f.*

[5] Cicero, *De Deorum Natura*, II, 72. (Rackham).

"The heavens become a house, the stars chambers for the god who has grown rich."[1] Power becomes more and more absolute Power: each barrier, each limitation, collapses. Everything reposes on the one indivisible Potency: all longing is appeased, all struggle suppressed. All is within, nothing remains outside: except Him who came to bring not peace, but the sword.[2]

[1] G. Th. Fechner, *Über die Seelenfrage*, 1861, 197.
[2] Chesterton, *Orthodoxy*, "The Romance of Orthodoxy".

P. TILLICH, *Philosophie und Schicksal* (*Kantstudien*, 34, 1929).

PART TWO

THE SUBJECT OF RELIGION

A. THE SACRED MAN

CHAPTER 22

SACRED LIFE

1. JUST as the Object of religion, to faith, is Subject in the sense of "the active and primary Agent",[1] exactly so for Subject and Object. The sciences concerned with religion observe a person who practises religion, who sacrifices and prays, *etc.* Faith sees a person to whom something has happened; and Phenomenology describes how man conducts himself in his relation to Power. But it must never be forgotten that this person himself first decides, or alters, his attitude after he has been affected by Power. In this all believers are unanimous, from primitive man who experiences the nearness of Power and calls out "Tabu!", to the apostle who exhorts us to love God because He "first loved us".[2]

For this reason I now turn to the consideration of the life called "sacred", because human life, in directing itself towards Power, "first" of all was touched by Power: in orienting itself to the sacred, that is to say, it itself participates in sacredness. On the other hand, we must not for one moment forget that man is himself active, so that whoever speaks of faith is at the same time dealing with religious culture. The question whether animals possess faith is meaningless; the question whether they have religion can be answered merely in the negative, simply because they have no culture. How Power affects animals we know not; but we do know definitely that they do not react to Power. In this respect man, in his humanity, appears on the scene independently.

2. In its relationship to Power, then, human life is first of all not the life of the individual, but that of the *Community*; and this will be discussed later. But neither is it life in its variegated manifoldness such as we observe in the Press or the modern novel. Rather is it life in a form simplified and abbreviated to its essential factors: life, that is to say, as it is lived by all without exception, and quite apart from any differences in manner of living, talent, temperament, *etc.*: that is,

[1] *cf.* Chap. 1, Section 1.   [2] 1 *John* iv. 19.

Birth, Marriage and Death: Life as it directs itself to Power and is seized upon by Power; therefore not the personal life of feeling, not the life of thought, but simply Life in its stark nakedness. Of this we must constantly remind ourselves, even when we are dealing with conditions only semi-primitive, or indeed not primitive at all.

Actually, even birth, marriage and death are still too ample. Birth and death suffice. For whatever else occurs in life, marriage, war, initiation and the bestowing of names, all can be included in the great polarity of life and death. As over against Power there is no history, neither collective nor individual. Whatever there is in life that is variable or contingent is forced into definite, stereotyped and diversified rites as much as is at all possible; rites which all, without exception, aim at the transition from life to death and from death to life. If, in the mood of modern mankind, we represent our life as a straight line, then at its beginning and its end we draw thick transverse strokes: what lies before birth does not belong to our life, and as to what follows death, we may cherish a belief; but "life after death" differs in every respect from the life we possess, and is at the very least a new beginning. The line between the two heavy transverse strokes we next divide into sections by finer strokes which indicate the great transitions: maturity, marriage, commencement of a career, retirement, a severe illness, *etc.* But in sacred life each stroke is equally heavy, each section equally important, each transition is one either from death to life or from life to death. This means that our secular life has the form of a line, but the sacred life the form of a circle. It is as the poet imagines Death to speak to man:

> If, with swift convulsion,
> Aught overwhelming has shown itself akin to thee,
> And thou, abandoning thyself in the great dance,
> Receivest the Universe as thine own—
> In every so truly great an hour,
> Which awed thine earthly form,
> I have touched thee in the very ground of thy soul,
> With sacred and mysterious Power.[1]

3. The important affairs in life therefore are not events as we understand them, but "transitional rites" (*Rites de passage*) as van Gennep calls them. Birth, naming, initiation, marriage, sickness and recovery, the start and the end of a long journey, the outbreak of war and con-

---

[1] Hugo von Hofmannsthal, *Der Tor und der Tod*.

clusion of peace, death and burial, are all points of contact between Power and life, and hence must not merely be experienced and then remembered, but must actually be *celebrated*. *In transitional rites, life affected by Power turns towards Power*. Instead of "events" or "experiences", therefore, the content of life is better styled "celebrations".

4. The first of these is *Birth*. This is not merely an event that occurs only once: it is rather an entry into life, the entering of a power which can be furthered, impeded and even frustrated. In China, celebrating birth is called "the passage through the gate"; a bamboo archway is erected first of all in the middle, and then in each of the four corners, of the room; then the *Tao* priest, the father and children step through these. This ceremony is repeated every year, or every third or sixth year, according to the family, until the rite of "the cessation of childhood"; but it is performed also when the child is ill, or repeated several times in the course of the year or month.[1] The celebration is intended to ensure contact between Power and life; the ordered induction of Power is necessary, and in cases of waning power the solemnizations must be more frequently repeated.

If no celebration takes place, in fact, birth does not become definitive, does not become an event. Thus the Central Australians believe that a child killed immediately after birth can afterwards be brought forth again by the same woman;[2] child murder is therefore not murder, but merely a sending back of life which has not yet been admitted to power; for one is "born" only when all the rites have been completed. Immediately after coming into the world one is still "only partially born"; what has occurred has such slight power that it can easily be reversed.[3]

The rites here in question are of various kinds. Laying the newborn infant on the ground was customary among the Romans; and elsewhere, *e.g.* in the Indonesian Seranglao Archipelago, the child is placed in contact with the earth, and as it were baptized with it.[4] Here therefore the new life is directed towards the power of Mother-earth. In Greece, again, a naked man ran around the hearth with the infant,[5] the fire's potency being thereby extracted. But since the induction of power

---

[1] A. van Gennep, *Les rites de passage*, 82 *f.*
[2] Spencer and Gillen, *The Native Tribes of Central Australia*, 51 *f.*
[3] Lévy-Bruhl, *How Natives Think*, 342 *f.*
[4] Riedel, *Sluik- en kroesharige rassen*, 175.
[5] *Amphidromia*; Samter, *Geburt, Hochzeit und Tod*, 113; *cf.* S. Reinach, *Cultes, Mythes et Religions*, 1, 1905, 137 *ff.*

first makes birth an actuality, it is never really perfected; new rites are continually necessary; and thus it is intelligible that certain initiatory rites, such as circumcision and baptism (naming), are equally birth rites.

Birth then is never perfected; but it also is not an actual beginning. The sacred life indeed knows neither beginning nor end, but strives after continuity by means of power. Birth is therefore rebirth: birth and death pertain to each other, and rites at birth are often exactly similar to the customs to be observed at death.[1] In case of miscarriages or still-births, for instance, the East African Wazaromo say "he has returned". But here we should not think of any theory of pre-existence. For there is nothing theoretical in this apprehension of life, which progresses not in a linear direction but in cycles, returning ever again upon itself.[2] Life is here no series of facts, but a stream in which it is always an affair of surmounting the perilous obstacles where power may fail, but where it may also become overwhelmingly strong. Birth time is a critical time, an exposed stage; and the woman who has just given birth is regarded as impure, that is as either powerless or under the influence of a foreign and dangerous potency. In Sweden, between child-bed and her first visit to church, a woman was formerly called "heathenish"; she had to be careful and to carry some steel about with her, so that the *trolls* could obtain no power over her.[3]

As the revelation of Power, however, every birth is a miracle: the extraordinary, the "Wholly Other", announces itself in the crisis of birth, in the newly appearing life. Actually, then, every birth is a "miraculous birth", this expression of course not being understood in the sense of supernaturalism; for in the transition from death to life, in the cycle of life regarded in its abbreviated form, Power reveals itself. Thus arose the myth of the origin of man, which assumes the form of "issuing from elsewhere" even where the physiological conditions of generation are known; a myth which was connected above all with great men like kings *etc.*, and which still persists in nurses' tales of Frau-Hollenteich or the stork.[4]

---

[1] A. van Gennep, *op. cit.*, 68 *f.*, 74, and Note 3.   [2] J. E. Harrison, *Themis*, 273.
[3] Klara Stroebe, *Nordische Volksmärchen*, I, 1919, No. 18.
[4] It is impossible to agree with Frazer (*Totemism and Exogamy*, IV, 57 *ff.*) in deriving the idea of marvellous birth from the ignorance of primitive man about the relationship between conception and birth. It is no matter of lack of knowledge but—positively—of the experience of arrival from elsewhere. Ignorance may certainly have furnished the condition for this, which then attained a positive import by "transposition"; (on this term *cf.* p 610.).

5. Man, however, cannot rest content with mere life: he must seek sacred life, replete with Power. Rites guarantee him power: he himself creates salvation; and the great majority of these rites are *purifications*.[1] Potent water or fire must assist man to surmount some critical situation, must neutralize the disturbing power and grant admission to the beneficent influence. *Bathing* and *Baptism*, then, first make life "true" life; and the *baptism of fire*, one of the most frequent initiatory rites among primitive peoples, still survives in the fairy story about the dwarf rejuvenated by flame,[2] and also in the Eleusinian legend of the deification of Demophoon by fire through the agency of Demeter.[3]

Beating also has lustrative value, especially the "stroke with the rod of life", a freshly cut twig that bestowed fertility; the *accolade*, again, is an initiation, a puberty rite.[4] Here the idea of purification approximates to that of mutilation, which leads anew to the profoundest ideas about death and revivification, since mutilation is an intimation of death. Again and again must sacred life be commenced anew, and each *rite de passage* is a rite of birth, but of death also. Thus *circumcision* is certainly a weakening of the man, but is nevertheless an enervation with more potent life as its aim. In Buru in the Dutch East Indies the boys who are to be circumcized are kept apart, and may eat only foods which have been prepared by virgins;[5] this indicates the critical situation, the contact with power, to which the boys expose themselves by this rite. But circumcision, which occurs principally among Malay-Polynesian and Semite-Hamitic peoples, must not be isolated; for it is only one of various rites having as their purpose the induction or renewal of power. Thus life is not accepted simply as it is, but is changed, mutilated, so that it will become capable of Power; and circumcision is a charm of the same character as filing down the teeth, tattooing, the perforation of the maiden's hymen, the boring of the nasal bone, *etc.*,[6] in Central Australia this last operation being performed on the men on the occasion of the maturity ceremonies, and on the girls immediately after marriage. For women, indeed, marriage is the entrance into life proper.[7] Similarly among the Mandan Indians, at puberty rites, the youths have the little finger of the left hand chopped off on the skull

---

[1] Chap. 49. [2] *Kinder- und Hausmärchen*, No. 147.
[3] Lang, *The Homeric Hymns*, 197; *cf.* Murray, *The Rise of the Greek Epic*, 350 *ff.*
[4] *cf.* J. Huizinga, *Het herfsttty der Middeleeuwen*, 1919, 129.
[5] Riedel, *Sluik- en kroesharige rassen*, 6.
[6] *cf.* further E. J. Dingwall, *Artificial Cranial Deformation*, 1931.
[7] Spencer and Gillen, *Native Tribes*, 214 *ff.*

of a buffalo by an old man with a hatchet;[1] and the Yoruba natives of West Africa call circumcision "the cutting that saves".[2] Most of these mutilations, moreover, occur not only at so-called puberty rites but also at marriage, during mourning and the like; and thus the whole of life is apprehended only as a crisis of Power.

The various *tests* and *purifications*, then, which those must undergo who are to be initiated into manhood and unrestricted tribal member-ship, are also approximations to death leading to new life, moral considerations and tests of courage and endurance actually occupying only second place. Similarly the harassing still in vogue among ourselves, for example among seamen and in student circles, is no affair of moral ends, even though these are subsequently advanced; a crisis must be gone through, as in Sparta when the *ephebi* were scourged at the altar of Artemis Orthia till the blood ran; "from the outset this custom was intended not as a test of endurance, but as purification and propitia-tion".[3] Even the instruction imparted to the novices at the ceremony was by no means the principal concern. Occasionally, it is true, informa-tion is imparted on religious topics such as the nature of the bull-roarer used by Australian tribes, or the content of the rites, or on moral affairs like conduct towards parents. But the real aim is always the renewal of life, the induction of that power which makes possible a new era and with which actual adult life first begins, just as with ourselves ecclesiastical confirmation, despite all the stressing of instruction in the practice of the Reformed churches and the pietistic emphasis on the inner life, has remained a genuine *rite de passage*.

Even the new clothes which confirmation candidates in the country procure for themselves (at least in Holland) find their prototype among primitive peoples. "In Korea, on the fourteenth day of the first month of the year, anyone who is entering on a 'critical year of his life', makes an effigy of straw, dresses it in his own clothes, casts it on the road . . . 'Fate is believed to look upon the individual clothes as another man.' "[4] And the connection of celebration with the idea of complete renewal still persists to-day in the sphere of religious ritual: monks and nuns adopt new costume, and even lay rites retain something of this attitude; for when Marie Antoinette came to Strassburg as the *dauphin's* bride

[1] E. Samter, *Familienfeste der Griechen und Römer*, 1901, 78 f.

[2] Crawley, *The Mystic Rose*, I, 170.

[3] M. P. Nilsson, *Griechische Feste*, 1906, 192; *cf.* Webster, *Primitive Secret Societies*, 35. A very life-like description of the initiation of boys by the indigenes themselves is to be found in Paul Hambruch, *Südseemärchen*, 1921, No. 9.

[4] Crawley, *The Mystic Rose*, I, 327 f.

she was completely undressed by her ladies and, according to old custom, clothed in new garments of French origin; she had to relinquish her Austrian clothing down to the minutest detail.[1]

With renewal of life conduct also is changed. A novice of the Kwakiutl tribes of Columbia, for example, acts as if he had forgotten ordinary human behaviour and must learn everything anew from the beginning.[2] In other cases the initiated man receives a new name: after circumcision the Amandebele youths in South Africa cross a river and are given fresh names,[3] the ceremony being called *wela*— "the transition", while on Nias boys change their names at marriage and girls at puberty. Similarly, at the conclusion of initiation the Tasmanians whisper a secret name to the boys,[4] just as the Hindu *Upanayana* ceremony of introduction to the teacher includes the reception of a fresh name in addition to the one normally used.[5] Here too secularized rite has preserved much: in Frisia for example, in the Netherlands, men leaving home to seek work receive an additional name, formerly an ordinary baptismal, to-day usually a historical, appellation like Alva *etc*.

This alteration of name indicates a complete change, a total renewal of life.[6] In the sources already cited this is repeatedly and unmistakably perceptible; thus the *Upanayana* ceremony is regarded as a rebirth, and the initiate as a "twice-born man", this idea being carried out with true Hindu precision: "by laying his right hand on the boy the teacher becomes pregnant; on the third day, in the invocation called *Sāvitrī*, a prayer to the inciting god *Savitar*, a genuine 'special god', the Brahman is born".[7] The Liberian *Vai* tribesmen, again, bring their young girls, at about the age of ten, into a shady grove called the *sande*, where they remain till the commencement of menstruation or till they are engaged; like the boys in the *belli* they, and the old women who attend them too, are looked upon as dead. They receive instruction in domestic and sex affairs; but this in itself is not the principal matter, the festival of their emergence being a rebirth,[8] while at Kikuyu in Kenya there is a ceremony, *ku-chiaruo ringi*, that is "to be born again", which must be observed before circumcision; the child must then lie down beside

---

[1] "The official ceremony took place in a wooden structure on one of the islands in the Rhine. In obedience to the requirements of etiquette the *dauphine* was almost completely unrobed and then clothed in garments brought from her new country." P. de Ségur, *Marie Antoinette*, 1921, 20.

[2] Webster, *Primitive Secret Societies*, 40.   [3] Fourie, *Amandebele*, 128 *f.*, *cf.* 137.

[4] Crawley, *The Mystic Rose*, I, 320 *ff.*   [5] Oldenberg, *Religion des Veda*, 466.

[6] Chap. 17.   [7] Oldenberg, *ibid.*, 466 f.   [8] A. van Gennep, *op. cit.*, 197 *f.*

its mother on the bed and cry like a newborn infant.[1] In West Africa
the *Belli-Paaro* is death, rebirth and incorporation in the community
of spirits or souls; "the initiated receive the sign *Belli-Paaro* (several
rows of incisions on the neck and the shoulder-blade) every twenty or
twenty-five years, by which they are killed, roasted and completely
changed, dying to their old life and nature and receiving new reason
and knowledge".[2] In the Congo too this same reference to death and
rebirth in connection with puberty rites is to be met with; there also
the young people receive a new name and pretend to have forgotten
their previous life and not to recognize their old acquaintances,[3] while
in Ceram, in Indonesia, the novices take a most moving farewell of their
friends, since they are going to meet death: the *nitu*, the spirits of the
departed, will tear out their hearts, and give them back only on the
entreaty of the grown-up men. On returning they walk with unsteady
gait, look distracted, enter their houses by the rear doors and avoid the
light, just as though they were coming from the other world.[4]

That initiation means death, and the renewal of life its surrender,
can still be seen in many rites quite apart from specifically primitive
culture. The novice who enters a Benedictine brotherhood, for instance,
prostrates himself on the ground between four candles; he is covered
with a shroud, and the *Miserere* is sung over him; then he rises, embraces
all those standing around him and receives communion from the
hands of the abbot.[5]

The rites that renew human life are therefore the very antithesis of
mere ornaments. I become of age whether I celebrate the day or not:
the psycho-physical process of puberty is completed in my own case
whether I accompany it by ceremonies or not. But the primitive rite
is by no means an ornamental ceremony; it is on the contrary a real
development of power, a creative deed, executed by the community.
He who has no name, then, has not been born, and whoever has not
been initiated remains all his life a child;[6] no matter how aged he
becomes he cannot even "grow old", since he has never grown up!
Similarly, the fate of children who have died unbaptized is a sad one,
because they have no names; they belong nowhere, properly speaking:

---

[1] C. W. Hobley, "Kikuyu Customs and Beliefs", *Journal As. Soc.*, 40, 441 *f*.

[2] Th. Achelis, *Die Ekstase*, 1902, 56 *f*.   [3] Crawley, *The Mystic Rose*, I, 325.

[4] Riedel, *Sluik- en kroesharige rassen*, 108 *ff*.; *cf.* Webster, *Primitive Secret Societies*,
39 *ff*.

[5] Comte Goblet d'Alviella, *L'Initiation, RHR.* 81, 1920, 17, Note 1.

[6] Thus in Fiji no distinction is made between uninitiated men and children; both
groups are called: "they, the children". Webster, *Primitive Secret Societies*, 25.

they cannot really come into existence, either "here" or "there". Thus on one of the Twelve Nights a Tyrolese farmer sees the *Perchta* passing by with her train of unbaptized children; the last child in the line keeps treading on his little shirt which is too long for it, and can hardly keep up with the others. So the farmer shouts: "*Huderwachtl!* come here and I'll tie up your little dress for you"; the child replies: "Now I must thank you, for I have a name", and disappears.[1] At Whittinghame, again, the spirit of a child murdered by its mother haunted the district, and one night a drunkard greeted it with the words "How's a' wi' ye the morn, Short-Hoggers?" The child ran joyfully away, crying out:

> Oh, weel's me now, I've gotten a name;
> They ca' me Short-Hoggers of Whittinghame.

According to church doctrine, as we know, the unbaptized dead[2] go to the *limbus infantium*: certainly not to hell, but neither to heaven; while in the Middle Ages an oath sworn to anyone unbaptized was regarded as not binding, and hence the German princes held themselves released from the oath they had sworn to the child who afterwards became Frederick II.[3] Existence, then, is no fixed possession, but a possibility that becomes a reality only by the induction of power.

6. The Greeks regarded *marriage* as a dying and a resurrection, and called it a τέλος, a consecration; but the mysteries-consecration was a rebirth.[4] Only those who enjoy stupid jokes about the married state can smile at this; and in so doing they never realize that their jests are in themselves no more than a pitiful vestige of the awe that has always accompanied the complete union of two persons in a new life. Marriage is therefore a transition, a crisis; and in sacred life every crisis is one of death. The Greek marriage ritual resembled that of the mysteries to the very details; and although this may have been due in part to the mystery cults having sprung from the domestic cult, still it does not explain the use of the mystery formula, "I have fled from evil, I have found good", ἔφυγον κακόν, εὗρον ἄμεινον, in the marriage

---

[1] W. Mannhardt, *Die Götter der deutschen und nordischen Völker*, 1860, 291.

[2] W. H. F. Basevi, *The Burial of the Dead*, 117 *ff.*

[3] Ranke, *Weltgeschichte*, VII[4], 1921, 182.

[4] Fustel de Coulanges, *La cité antique*[20], 1908, 43; *cf.* Jane E. Harrison, *Epilegomena to the Study of Greek Religion*, 16. But *cf.* here H. Bolkestein, Τέλος ὁ γάμος, *Meded. kon. Ak. v. Wet. Afd. Lett.*, 76, B, 2, who rejects, however, only the equivalence between τέλος and marriage, and not the other facts.

ritual. That is no eulogy of matrimony, but an expression of the consciousness that a new life is opening with new power. Thus we can understand why thoughts of death are frequently so much indulged in at the time of marriage; in Upper Bavaria a mass for the dead is said the day before the wedding, and in the Eifel district the day following, while in Thuringia the bridal pair decorated the graves of their relatives and godparents with their own hands. In Lower Bavaria, again, the best man says after the wedding breakfast: "Since we have eaten and drunk, we must not forget the poor souls", whereupon the guests proceed to the grave weeping and praying.[1] In all this we apprehend the family unity on the one hand, and on the other the proximity of death to life, the latter being very clearly expressed in the Frisian custom of women being wed in a widow's mourning habit; and I do not feel too inclined to accept the relater's rationalistic interpretation of the custom being intended to impress the women with the fact that death alone can part them from their husbands.[2] In Gelderland the shroud, and sometimes even the coffin boards, are made at the time of the wedding.[3]

As transition, as crisis, marriage is exposed to dangerous fullness of power. The potencies revealed in sex intercourse arouse anxiety and inspire fear: they must be restrained; and hence the custom of robbing cohabitation of its power by pre-marital defloration of the bride. For this a stranger or priest is selected, who possesses sufficient power to be able to take some risk.[4] The ceremonial *ruptura hymenis* may also be sufficient, while cohabitation with a child is a mitigation of this practice,[5] as is the observance of the so-called Tobias nights when the bridal pair abstain from marital intercourse.[6] Whether the so-called *jus primae noctis* has a religious basis (the lord or tribal chieftain being the powerful one!) or is a mere survival of the rule of the king or father, appears dubitable.[7]

The transition to marriage, still further, demands not only measures of defence, but implies also an induction of power likewise subjected

[1] Samter, *Geburt, Hochzeit und Tod*, 213.
[2] C. van Alkemade, *Inleidinge tot het Ceremonieel der Begraavenissen*, 1713, 152.
[3] H. W. Heuvel, *Volksgeloof en Volksleven*.
[4] Crawley, *The Mystic Rose*, II, 66 *ff*.
[5] *cf. e.g.* the marriage customs of Naxos, E. Kagarow, *AR*. 26, 1928, 362.
[6] In Vedic India, for example: Oldenberg, *Religion des Veda*, 253. A staff separates the couple, as did a sword among Germanic peoples.
[7] K. Schmidt, *Jus primae noctis*, 1881. On the landowner's consent as necessary to the marriage being a vestige of *jus primae noctis*, *cf*. Heuvel, *Oud-Achterhoeksch boerenleven*, 450.

to definite rules. Thus the communal meal at the wedding is wide-spread; the oldest form of Roman marriage included the custom of *confarreatio*, the bridal couple eating together from the sacrifice of spelt to the accompaniment of a fixed and solemn formula, *certa et sollemnia verba*. In Loango (West Africa), husband and wife and their parents each cut off a small piece of tobacco, place this in a pipe and then all smoke it one after the other.[1] This implies community; but it is just as much sacrament as it is *communio*.[2] A power is introduced into life and at the same time controlled: for rites are always creative, but also always regulative; they signify not only the piercing of a fountain, but further the laying of a channel for its stream. Thus in Russia the bridal night is spent in the store-room in order to ensure the fertility of the marriage,[3] while among very many primitive peoples we find phallic marriage rites, medieval *epithalamia*, and the coarse jests which even to-day the bridal pair are not spared in more primitive circles, being the vestiges of this. Both word and deed are intended to conduct power to the new life.

Hence it is no matter for surprise that like birth (as rebirth) and death (the relinquishing of the old sinful life) marriage also has very often become a symbol of the relationship with divine objects. "For this cause shall a man leave his father and mother, and shall be joined unto his wife, and they two shall be one flesh. This is a great mystery: but I speak concerning Christ and the church."[4] This means that life is regarded here also in its ultimate simplification, and reduced to its utmost and final significance: in his transition to the new community man achieves contact with power, and definitely recognizes this as ultimate.

7. *Death*, again, is not a fact, but a state of transition; no hard matter of fact, but a process that can be advanced or controlled by reflection and action. He is dead who is declared dead: opinion and estimation take the place of fact. Thus the *Talmud* prescribes a thanks-giving prayer on seeing a friend again after an absence of over twelve months: "Praised be Thou, O Lord, King of the world, that makest the dead live again."[5] According to Roman custom, similarly, he who had been proclaimed dead and then returned must avoid the door and

---

[1] A. Bastian, *Die deutsche Expedition an der Loango-Küste*, 1874 to 1875, 170 *f.*, *cf.* Riedel, *Sluik- en kroesharige rassen*, 350 *f.*

[2] Chap. 52.   [3] A. von Löwis of Menar, *Russische Volksmärchen*, Nr. 35.

[4] *Ephesians* v. 31, 32.   [5] K. Kohler, *AR.* III, 1900, 79 *ff.*

enter the house over the roof.[1] It is possible, then, to declare someone dead, to regard him as non-existent; and this has the same effect as actual death: in the Scandinavian sagas the *niding* is actually dead, for there can be life only within the pale of the community, where the powers are operative.[2] The subjective attitude and celebration are in complete agreement. Only proper burial makes death valid; he who has not been buried is not dead. In Calabar Miss Kingsley found the dead predecessor of a tribal chief in his successor's house; the sly chieftain did not wish to allow him burial, because after the completed rite he would of course be properly dead, and then would be able to return to the world; and his successor was so convinced of the persistent value of the chief's *mana* that he did not want to subject himself to any competition. Thus the poor man was simply kept there "outside life but not inside death".[3]

Death too is subjected to rites, and pertains to life's periodicity. It can thus occur only "when the time has come", when the period of life has been fulfilled and the power consumed. Therefore the death which overtakes a man is no "natural" death; that we die is no natural affair, and for this reason man refuses to permit it. With some difficulty he fastens on a "cause", even where in our opinion matters are quite clear; and when the natives of the Melbourne district lose a member of the tribe by a "natural" death, they are dissatisfied with that explanation, and set up a sort of ordeal of God[4] in order to discover the "murderer". Some power or other must have been employed, which they find out; they then resort to the alleged perpetrator's hiding-place and slay him. Therewith the power situation has once more been cleared up: but not for the relatives of the man who has just been killed. Although they know full well who has executed the attack, they too set up on their own part an ordeal of God, and themselves slay a "killer" who belongs to yet a third tribe and has had nothing whatever to do with the affair.[5]

In this procedure, however, "killing" implies nothing ultimate. If only the rites assure the continuity of power he who is dead goes on living, so that what we call death, and what for us is an absolute fact that we cannot evade, is to primitive man merely a transitional state which can be avoided. As long as *burial* has not taken place, therefore, the crisis has not been overcome. That is dangerous, especially for the

---

[1] Plutarch, *Quaestiones romanae*, V.   [2] Grönbech, *Vor Folkeaet*, II, 172 *ff.*
[3] *West African Studies*, 146 *f.*
[4] Chap. 54.   [5] Lévy-Bruhl, *How Natives Think*, 280 *f.*

dead man; but it has its good side also, since the deceased cannot return immediately, and this reappearance is often feared. Here too lies the reason for the *Mourning Period*.[1] Life, as it were, holds its breath, not only in the person of the dead but also in the whole community. For death, as a weakening of power, concerns not merely the dying man but likewise all those belonging to him. The fairy tale of the Sleeping Beauty in the thorn hedge, which is also found beyond Europe, is a reminder of this period of grieving in which life stands still. The dead has taken power with him, and now it is necessary to infuse life with new potency.[2] The *annus luctus*, the mourning period, is accordingly the actual process of death itself; if it is not observed the dead person finds no rest but remains in an intermediate state; in other words, not yet quite "dead";[3] in ancient Iran the three days of mourning were dangerous equally for the dead and the living.[4] Thus we can understand the joy at the burial also, the frequent abandoned festivities accompanying interment of which the wake, still observed among ourselves in country districts, is a vestige; it is necessary to "assist life over a critical situation in safety".[5] Hence the great expansion of power, its transformation into nourishment for the community. Similarly must the sexual licence be regarded that usually occurs during death ceremonies and, among primitive peoples, not infrequently leads to promiscuity.[6] On the Aru Islands, off New Guinea, phallic ceremonies were observed and obscene songs sung, singing and dancing being continued until the widow had discarded her mourning garb.[7] The *Funeral Games* which we find in classical antiquity also had the same purpose: the combats were intended to succour the stagnating life, and are to be found from the gates of Troy to the Tonga Islands.[8] Naturally not only the continuity of the communal life, but also the (renewed) life of the dead man himself, depend on the correct accomplishment of the grieving period and mourning customs: for him new life is effected by the rites, as will be later noted.[9]

The great extent to which life is governed by rule and fixed in

---

[1] Hertz, *Mélanges de Sociologie Religieuse et Folklore, passim.*

[2] N. Adriani, *De schoone slaapster in 't bosch, Versl. en Meded. kon. Ak. v. Wet., Afd. Lett.*, 5e Reeks, 2, 1917, 171 ff.

[3] cf. Wilken, *Verspreide Geschriften*, III, 532 ff.

[4] N. Söderblom, *Les Fravashis*, 1899, 10 f., cf. Spencer and Gillen, *The Native Tribes*, 497 ff.

[5] Grönbech, *Vor Folkeaet*, IV, 58 f.

[6] As in Hawaii, J. G. Frazer, *The Belief in Immortality*, II, 422 ff.

[7] Riedel, *Sluik- en kroesharige rassen*, 267 f.

[8] Frazer, *Immortality*, II, 140.   [9] Chap. 24.

periods is clearly shown by the institution of provisional burial, as this frequently occurs in Indonesia, where the corpse is interred for the time being and is finally buried only a long time, not infrequently several years, afterwards, when only the bones remain. The so-called *tiwah*, again, customary among the Borneo Dyaks, has no single meaning, but so long as it has not been completed the deceased is not regarded as really dead.[1] Death, always a precarious affair, becomes still more ticklish when it concerns persons who are bearers of a particularly dangerous power. In Indonesia, once more, the victims of certain maladies, those who have been forcibly deprived of life (including suicides and the drowned), those who have died as babies, as virgins or in child-bed, princes and priests, are frequently not properly interred —that is not with all the requisite rites. To this, however, nothing dishonourable is attached, only the people fear that the extremely powerful life might again be set in motion, and therefore prefer to leave it in the transitional condition.[2] Among the Dyaks only those who have died of illness are buried and despatched to the realm of the dead, while those who have died in child-bed or war, suicides, victims of accidents and stillborn children are merely placed underground.[3]

8. Human life, made sacred and endowed with power by rites, can also be absolutely and entirely stifled by them. It has already been observed how power seizes upon life in its critical situations and reduces it within their confines; and sacred life is life in this foreshortened form.

But this may be carried so far that nothing individual, nothing distinguishable, nothing really alive remains in life: Power has killed it. The most far reaching example of this tendency, which is, however, present everywhere, is to be found in Buddhism: there birth is merely an unessential incident in the endlessly advancing and essentially empty cycle of life. Buddhist fairy stories, at the end of which Buddha ties the knot of the so-called *Jataka* (Birth-story), speak very clearly in this respect: "At that time the foolish carpenter was Devadatta . . . but the wise carpenter was I." Here nothing further happens, nothing occurs in life, which has become a vacuum; only the sacred master still lives:

---

[1] Hertz, *op. cit.*, 1 *ff.* Wilken, *op. cit.*, III, 436.
[2] van Ossenbruggen, *Bydr. Taal-, Land- en Volkenkunde*, 70, 1915, 280 *ff.*; *cf.* G. van der Leeuw, *Primitieve religie in Indonesie, Tydschrift van het Kon. Ned. Aardrykskundig Gen.*, 2. Serie XLV, 1928, 873 *ff.*
[3] A. W. Nieuwenhuis, *Quer durch Borneo*, I, 1904, 90.

Power has suffocated life;[1] even the specific situations, wherein human dread and will to power had been concentrated, lose their hold.

E. CRAWLEY, *The Mystic Rose*[2], 1927.

A. VAN GENNEP, *Les rites de passage*, 1909.

V. GRÖNBECH, *Vor folkeaet i Oldtiden*, 1912.

R. HERTZ, *Mélanges de sociologie religieuse et folklore*, 1928.

I. und O. VON REINSBERG-DÜRINGSFELD, *Hochzeitsbuch*, 1871.

E. SAMTER, *Geburt, Hochzeit und Tod*, 1911.

J. WACH, *Typen religiöser Anthropologie*, 1932.

E. WESTERMARCK, *History of Human Marriage*, 1891.

[1] Oldenberg, *Buddha: His Life, His Doctrine, His Order*, 193 and Note 1. Else Luders, *Buddhistische Märchen*, 1921. Sylvain Lévi, *Les Jatakas, Conférences faites au Musée Guimet*, 1906, 1 *ff.*

THE GIVEN AND THE POSSIBLE

1. THE sacredness of life is a matter of either *What is given*, or *Possibility*: two viewpoints which must be distinguished, even though they seldom appear in practice in their pure forms. The first of the two asserts that, together with life itself and as such, Power is given. The expansion and expression of life are the development of Power: potencies lie in the given life itself.

But this by no means implies that man has ever accepted life simply as sacred. "Reverence for life" is in fact wholly modern, and perhaps presupposes moral, though not religious, motives. For apart from some kind of criticism of life no religion whatever is conceivable. Religion means precisely that we do *not* simply accept life; it is directed always to the "Other"; and although it has sprung from human life, religion cannot orient itself to this life as such. But it can bring into prominence specific aspects of this existence as being "sacred", and give emphasis to certain phenomena in life as being potent. One part of life is thus accepted, but always at the expense of another, and in life, which is powerless, potency then reveals itself in certain situations.

Thus the *right hand* enjoys preference over the left; possibly this priority is connected with some organic asymmetry, but it is evaluated in the religious sense: the sanctuary, again, is entered with the right foot: with the right hand sacrifices are offered and blessings bestowed. Even children must learn the difference between the "nice" and the wrong little hand—in French, *bonne*, *belle* and *vilaine main*: Dutch, *mooie* and *leelyke handje*; while marriage with a person of inferior rank is contracted with the left hand. God's "right hand" is mighty and carries victory;[1] with the right hand the oath is sworn.[2] The seat on the right hand too is the place of honour: "Christ sitteth on the right hand of God".[3]

The difference between the sexes is similarly esteemed a disparity in Power, emphasis falling now on man and again on woman; life, as it were, may be sacred in either its masculine or its feminine aspect, just as from masculine, or feminine, "experience" originates the form of the Father

[1] *Ps.* cxviii. 15 *f.*   [2] *Ps.* cxliv. 8, 11.
[3] *Col.* iii, 1; *cf.* R. Hertz, *Prééminence de la main droite*, *Mélanges d'Histoire des Religions*, 99 *ff.*

or the Mother.[1] Where the masculine or paternal power predominates, the entire life is ordered accordingly (Patriarchy), while where the potency of the mother or the maid prevails their life-form furnishes the standard for the whole of existence (Matriarchy). Thus when many primitive tribes allocated clearing the forest to the men and the management of cultivated land to the women, this was based on the diversity in what has been "given" to man and woman. The cultural stage of tilling with the hoe recognized this division of labour, in which hunting and warfare fell to the men; and this is not masculine laziness, but the correct allocation of feminine power to those activities connected with the secret of development and growth, and so of birth. When agriculture expands, however, the field work of sowing and reaping is transferred to man because for this the plough is employed, and this is regarded not as an indifferent piece of mechanism but as the phallus; here then it is not birth that is in the foreground, but generation.[2] But wherever it is a matter of approaching close to the power of the earth, as in rites of pulling the plough around and at harvest, then women and girls resume their ancient privileges even at the agricultural stage, and execute ritually and symbolically what has been withdrawn from them in their ordinary occupations. In this division of potency, still further, the psychology of man and of woman is quite clearly recognizable: "The man says 'Look, I am thus and so'; the woman, 'I, too, am thus and so, but don't look.' "[3] The experience of power in generation and birth, in prominence and concealment, is thereby finely characterized in its eternal antithesis, which has its origin in the physical aspect but subsequently extends far beyond this. Thus we understand the awe of man before woman and the fear of woman before man, both of which have religious foundations.[4] Each experiences in the other the fullness of power, as well as the completely antithetic type of diversity from their own being.

Much is "given". What appear to us as human characteristics are really gifts. The king's joy, the hero's conquering power, the warrior's courage, are accounted in German myths, as in Greek, practically as

---

[1] Chap. 20, 10.

[2] cf. Rich. Thurnwald, *Psychologie des primitiven Menschen* (*Handbuch der vergleichenden Psychologie*, edited by G. Kafka, I, 2, 194); cf. Rose, *Primitive Culture in Greece*, 84.

[3] K. Groos, *The Play of Man*, 268.

[4] A fear which can be intensified into terror; the Maori affirmed that "what destroys men is the *mana* of the female organ"; they called this *whare o aitna*, that is "the location or origin of death and misfortune". E. Arbmann, *AR.* 29, 1931, 341.

gifts pertaining to status, which must be accepted just as their opposites, cowardliness and ill luck, *etc.*, are to be accepted.[1] The "world" too is "given" and is scarcely to be severed from the inner life. Each individual has his own world according to what has been "given" him, woman, child, old man, hero, free man, slave, *etc.* But towards and within his own world each experiences the powerful, to which he gives preference over all the rest of his experience. And in this selection there again prevails that criticism which, in spite of everything, refuses simply to "accept", and ever seeks the "Other". Colours, for example, are "given": but some specific colour is impressive, is distinguished and experienced as powerful. Thus with red, the sole colour that occurs everywhere in painting the body;[2] some other hue, again, refers to another potency.[3]

The givenness of sacred life attains its most explicit expression, however, in the manifold myths concerning man's origin. Life is not only something that is to be filled with power: it contains power from the beginning and essentially. It comes from elsewhere, from some potency. That children grow on trees is a childish belief, but it was also a primeval human conviction. Similarly with the origin of man from mountain or stone, from water (*Frau-Hollen-Teich*), the interpretation of birth as a journey from the other side of the sea (in popular belief from "Angel-land", England), *etc.*

Finally life, already powerful in itself, can be accounted as absolutely holy or divine. Wanton joy of life is exhibited in many fairy story figures, from Hans the Strong who fears nobody and terrifies even the devil, to his Hellenic transfiguration in the form of Herakles, in whom the mortal becomes the mighty witness to the immortal:

> Having been a man,
> Now become a god,
> Having endured pain,
> Having gained heaven.[4]

Life as given, further, can become a symbol of the divine even in those religions which must reject its own divinity. I refer here to Hosea's marriage: and also to the beautiful, because unsought, fusion of human and divine life that occurs in Newman's sermon delivered in the small church at Littlemore, when he quitted the Anglican communion: "O my mother, whence is this unto thee, that thou bearest

---

[1] *cf.* Grönbech, *Vor Folkeaet*, I, 24. Otto, *Die Götter Griechenlands*, 245 *ff.*
[2] Grosse, *Die Anfänge der Kunst*, 58 *ff.*
[3] *cf.* Thurnwald, *op. cit.*, 234.
[4] B. Schweitzer, *Herakles*, 1922, 238 *f.*

children, yet darest not own them?"[1] In this lament the "mother"
is the church; but Newman's mother was buried at Littlemore too.

2. As we have seen, sacred life is never accepted as given without
further ado, but is always regarded as something which is also to be
filled with power, as Possibility. And not infrequently this consideration
has settled the precedence. Man must succour feeble life with his own
magic rites, or implore the powers so to do; Pandora, the Earth-mother
who bestows all life, is looked upon as a deceiver. "In human terms,
our life is a deception. But that means only that we deceive ourselves
if we think that life is nothing more than life."[2]

For this reason man made *Tools* for himself in order to correct life.
Certainly he does not dominate these implements as his own pro-
ductions, as their superior,[3] but as *homo faber* he sets to work with
them and succours the weak life. As *homo formans*, indeed, he even
gives life a new form from the very earliest times: *Art* perceives in life
only the possibility of a new and potent creation of form; "Art is the
signature of man".[4] He also enriches the treasure of these signatures
of his, creating for himself a "culture". With the nakedness into
which he was born, and which is "given" to him, he is satisfied no
longer and makes for himself clothes,[5] the apron serving both as a
protection and as an indication of genital potency. Shame is nothing
more than the consciousness of the imperilling of this power, just as
the king and other power bearers are surrounded by apotropaic tabus,
intended to avert evil. To this there must of course be added the
necessity for cover in colder regions; and in fashions, even to-day,
the two tendencies of protecting and indicating still merge.[6]

Work again is first the discovery, and afterwards the utilization,
of possibilities. Thus hunting leads to robbing and robbery to trading.[7]
Every gift conceals some possibility. Things receive value: the wild
beast is domesticated, and its sacredness rests on the gifts "of Nature"
which it brings with it, as well as on the possibilities of its utility.[8]

The idea of value, in its turn, creates the further conceptions of profit

---

[1] *The Parting of Friends.*

[2] W. B. Kristensen, *De goddelyke bedrieger. Meded. der Kon. Akad. van Wetensch.,
afd. Lett.* 66, Serie B, 3, 1928, 23.

[3] Chap. 3.

[4] Chesterton, *The Everlasting Man*, Part 1, Chap. 1.   [5] Chap. 9.

[6] So as not to charge everything against women *cf. e.g.* the diatribe on men's clothing, which shamelessly stresses the genital region, in Chaucer, *The Persones Tale.*

[7] Thurnwald, *loc. cit.*, 205.

[8] *cf.* R. Dussaud, *La Domestication de la Race Bovine, RHR.* 95, 1927.

and compensation. "Compensation" in commerce and in criminal law are one, as Nietzsche perceived,[1] although indeed he failed to add that both alike are of sacred origin. Whoever possesses something "valuable", then, ought to redeem it; and on Buin a fine drum arouses the envy of those who lack such an instrument, so that its fortunate owner must provide a "compensation gift" lest his drum be destroyed for him.[2] War too is the creator and adjuster of values; in Rome, as elsewhere, the seasons for agriculture and for war were identical. War yields power, even where God is believed in: it is help (תְּשׁוּעָה).[3] Property, finally, is the name given to the realization of possibilities; hence the sacredness and the inalienability of possessions. Culture thus provides life with a firm basis.

3. Or is everything futile? Does neither rite nor labour bear fruit? is not merely the given disillusion, but also every value that we attempt to instil therein? Cultural pessimism, in fact, is very ancient: not, however, because civilization itself, nor the life on which it is founded, produces no fruit, since this they do repeatedly. Rather it originates from the fact that neither the given life, nor the culture erected upon it, neither the country nor the tilled field, brings *salvation*. Despite all endeavour it is quite impossible to escape from oneself and lay hold on the Wholly Other. There is certainly fullness of life, but no commanding power of life.

Especially against the inventions of mankind does this pessimism direct its opposition: civilization is a sort of Tower of Babel, sheer wantonness. Man therefore turns away from it and towards "Nature". The Israelite Rechabites, for instance, cherished a nomadic ideal, building no houses but living in tents and forbidding cultivation of field and vineyard; their cry, "Back to the desert", is an anticipation of Rousseau's maxim: "*Revenons à la nature*",[4] of course with a specific religious tinge. During the festival of the Thesmophoria in Eretria the Greeks too lived the primitive life, βίος ἀρχαικός, cooking without fire by the sun's heat.[5] This refusal to accept any creation of form for life may lead further to the disparagement of rites—obedience is better than sacrifice—and even beyond this to the denial of life in general in

---

[1] *The Genealogy of Morals*, II, 4, 5; *cf*. B. Laum, *Heiliges Geld*, 1924.
[2] R. Thurnwald, *Reallexikon der Vorgeschichte, "Vergeltung"*.
[3] Fr. Schwally, *Der heilige Krieg im alten Israel*, 1901, 7.
[4] A. Bertholet, *Kultur und Religion, Festrede*, 1924, 15.
[5] Plutarch, *Quaestiones graecae*, 298 B.

favour of a pure subjectivity.[1] Both the givenness and the possibility of powerful life are thus disavowed, death being greeted as a friend.

> Death is before me to-day
> As when a sick man becometh whole,
> As when one walketh abroad after sickness.
>
> Death is before me to-day
> As when a man longeth to see his house again,
> After he hath spent many years in captivity.[2]

The finest of all types of this despair of life, however, is identical with that which the Greeks elaborated as the very symbol of life's joy— Herakles: but now in his Euripidean transformation. Divinely born, he has exhausted in the travail of his twelvefold labour every one of life's possibilities, and so in his "thirteenth task" of destruction he falls into despair.[3]

[1] *cf.* Ed. Spranger, *Lebensformen*[5], 1925, 107: "The religious *ego* means either elevation to boundless fullness of life, or the negation of existence and a retrogression to the primal values of formless inner life."

[2] The ancient Egyptian *Dialogue of him who is weary of life with his soul*: Erman, *The Literature of the Ancient Egyptians*, 91, 92.

[3] G. van der Leeuw, *Goden en Menschen*, 81 *ff.*

CHAPTER 24

THE DEAD MAN

1. WE moderns are inclined to erase the dead man altogether from our roll: he no longer counts. But in the sacred life he is never omitted. Quite apart from any "soul" that he is supposed to have, and from any "immortality" he is believed to receive (the latter demanding conditions quite different from those hitherto considered), the dead counts just as much as the living man, since neither givenness nor possibility as yet deserts him; and precisely because it is assured by rites, his continued existence becomes a matter of course. Thus *burial in the crouching position*, frequently occurring in prehistoric and early historic ages, was probably a preparation for rebirth, the dead man being placed in the position of the embryo, so that new life commenced from the time of burial.[1] Thus many primitive peoples regard a newborn child as a dead man who has returned, and the Eskimo give the child the name of someone who has recently died; this assignment of a name is called "the resuscitation of the dead", and ends the period of mourning.[2] Similarly, when a child is born in West Africa, objects that have been used by deceased people are held out to it; if it tries to seize one they say: "Look, so-and-so recognizes his pipe", or if a child misbehaves its mother may say: "We made a bad mistake when we thought you were so-and-so".[3]

For death is not a fact nor event, but merely a condition different from life. In Melanesia, *mate* is the state which begins with illness or senile feebleness; nevertheless life after death is just as real as the existence we call life. The conditions preceding death are no more impressively distinct from those after death than is existence before

---

[1] Disputes still prevail as to the correct significance of burial in the crouching posture. But neither Virchow's hypothesis of economizing labour and space, nor Böklen's theory of the imitation of the crescent moon, and just as little Andree's idea that it was sought to prevent the dead man's return by trussing him up, are very illuminating, and least of all the suggestion that it was intended to give the dead the "natural" sleeping posture; cf. M. Hammarstroem, *AR.* 26, 1928, 146 ff. A. Scharff, *Grundzüge der ägyptischen Vorgeschichte*, 1927, 19; Haas gives a description of an Assyrian embryo-burial, *Bilderatlas*, Part 6, 1925, Fig. 43. Egyptian burial ritual provides confirmation of the embryo hypothesis, since the embryo (*tknw*) played a prominent part in it; cf. A. Moret, *Mystères égyptiens*, 1913, 36 ff.

[2] Hertz, *op. cit.*, 119.   [3] Kingsley, *West African Studies*, 145.

initiation into manhood from adult age.[1] Thus Lévy-Bruhl depicts
life as a cycle which, repeatedly set in motion anew by rites, moves on
from death through burial to the end of the mourning period, and then
into new life, rebirth, naming, initiation of the youth, manhood,
and once more to death again, *etc.*[2] This is certainly somewhat schematic,
and must be modified for each individual case. But in its essence
death is simply a transition like any other, and the dead man is not one
who has been struck off the roll, nor even one who has been reincarnated
(since reincarnation presupposes the dualism of body-soul!) but at
most one who has returned and, as a rule, who is still present.

2. The dead man, on the one hand the object of religious worship,[3]
pertains on the other to those forming the community of worshippers,
the religious Subject.[4] And with this the consideration of the dead
leads us once again to the idea of the sacred community. In Greece the
dead were originally buried in, or near, the house,[5] the provision of
power-giving nourishment being of value to the dead as well as to the
living; and although they can bestow power, the dead none the less
require its supply, since after all they are only "poor souls".

[1] W. H. Rivers, "The Primitive Conception of Death", *Hibbert Journal*, X, 1912,
393 *ff.*
[2] Lévy-Bruhl, *How Natives Think*, 255 *f.*   [3] Chap. 14.
[4] Chap. 32.   [5] E. Rohde, *Psyche*, I[5-6], 1910, 228 *f.* E. T. 166.

REPRESENTATION. THE KING

1. WE have already repeatedly encountered the idea of representation, of official action and existence, which very clearly illuminates the relationship between Objectivity and Subjectivity in religion. Man places himself over against God; but this is not his merely subjective attitude; much more is it an objective action, a being appointed. The relation to Power, then, whether as mere approach, subjection, acquisition or any other relationship, always rests only on the possession of Power. The man who seeks God is himself impelled by God.

But he is "impelled" as a *"representative"*: not, that is, as an individual and still less as a "personality", but simply as a bearer of power. In him is completed the apportioning of power to the totality, to the community. *In* him: *through* him merely in the instrumental sense. For he is no religious genius, no religious virtuoso: he is only the hand that Power utilizes, and it is his official status that sustains him.

2. The oldest representative is the king, whose office has been dealt with in detail in Chapter 13. In ancient Egyptian royal epithets the formula *di ankh* occupies an important place: usually translated by "endowed with life", it might equally well be understood in the active sense of "he who imparts life", and it must be so translated in certain cases;[1] for that the king already possessed divine life was, according to the Egyptian viewpoint, precisely the condition of his ability to impart it. He received power, and also exercised it. The Egyptian sacrificial formula, again, commenced with the stereotyped wording: "A sacrifice which the king offers", or "May the king be gracious and offer". This meant that whoever might bring it, every sacrifice was really offered by the king; private individuals could offer only a royal sacrifice, and actually only the king could sacrifice.[2]

Thus the official aspect of representation necessitates the complete severance of person from power. The Matabele king prays to the spirits

---

[1] *cf.* R. Weill, *Les Origines de l'Égypt pharaonique*, 1908, 76 *f.* W. M. Flinders Petrie, *The Royal Tombs of the First Dynasty*, 1900 *f.* II, 23, 199. A. Moret, *Le Rituel du culte divin journalier*, 1902, 101. G. J. Thierry, *De religieuze beteekenis van het aegyptische koningschap*, I, 1913, 79. [2] A. Moret, *Sphinx*, 11, 31.

of his ancestors, but to his own spirit as well,[1] while the Egyptian Pharaoh Amenhotep III is depicted as worshipping himself.[2] Sometimes he represents Power, sometimes the people, and thus he meets himself as it were. This relationship also occurs on a totally different plane: for when in the liturgy the priest says *dominus vobiscum*, the congregation responds: *et-cum spirito tuo*. In official status, then, to apportion and to receive have become identical.[3]

[1] Frazer, *The Magical Origin of Kings* (*Lectures on the Kingship*), 32.
[2] G. Maspero, *Au temps de Ramsès et d'Assourbanipal*, 1912, 46.
[3] The charismata of the Christian community, similarly, imply no *personal* distinction; *cf.* Piper, *Ethik*, I, 332.

CHAPTER 26

REPRESENTATION. MEDICINE-MAN AND PRIEST

1. The objectivity of religion has been exhibited in the capacity of representation resting on the possession of power, the representative being effective by virtue of his official status. Thus we can understand why masks play such a great part in the primitive world. Mask dances are very popular and imply far more than mere mummery: on the contrary, the masks in our everyday amusements are vestiges of official action alike in form and in intention; the *bal masqué* grants not only liberty in general, but also sets people free from their personality. It is, still further, hardly a matter of chance that exactly those who possess an "office" in the old sense of the term have deliberately retained their official garb—clergy and judges: and with the raiment very often the official facial expression too! The person acting officially, then, plays a part; and Preuss describes how during their festivities the Cora Indians are at one moment themselves, while they pray, and at the next they personify the gods and their followers;[1] the participants in the celebration are demons, and its performance is an activity of the powers. Here again therefore it is an interchange of *dominus vobiscum* and *et cum spirito tuo*, uniting the human rôle with the official divine. Especially in the case of phallic dances, and what appear to us to be most immoral sexual excesses, it must always be borne in mind that it is really demons who are acting, and that the superhuman power reveals itself in the human union. Thus we can understand how tribes, which normally adhere strictly to certain limitations in sex intercourse, nevertheless transcend all bounds in their feasts.

It is only in the light of these presuppositions, still further, that we can estimate the notorious deceit of which bearers of power have at all times been guilty. A shallow view might readily interpret all this pious fraud as a kind of priestly offence, and even derive a great proportion of religious ideas and institutions from such sacerdotal deception. Of course there have always been liars and men of doubtful honour, who have misused the objectivity of this official activity for their own ends. And the remark of the haruspex who smiled on meeting

---

[1] *Geistige Kultur, Kap.* 6.

his colleague has at all times found its justification.[1] But this certainly cannot be said about medicine-men and priests in general. This holds good, in the first place, of the former: "the mystery-monger is likewise a mystery to himself".[2] If they feel that their power has deserted them they frequently resign their position voluntarily. The Australian medicine-man, for example, removes from a sick person's body the darts that are believed to have caused the illness. Actually he takes some small stones from his own mouth; and this seems an obvious deception. But if the same medicine-man falls ill he sends for a colleague who performs the same process on him; he is "the actor who forgets that he plays a part".[3] Such an actor, however, is the only genuine one; absorbed· in his rôle, he ceases to think of his own personal temperament and characteristics, and weeps real tears over the fate of Hecuba! The power bearer may even despair of his own potency, while nevertheless still firmly believing in that of others,[4] since if his own exercise of power produces no effect, this may be due to some more potent countercharm being in operation, or to his own capacity declining. On Ysabel Island in Melanesia, for instance, a weather wizard had promised fine weather; but the same day his own hut was unfortunately overturned by a storm. Yet nobody doubted his meteorological skill on that account; they were merely convinced that there was a weather doctor on another island who possessed more *mana*![5]

We are confronted here, therefore, with the same relationship as we have already encountered in the case of the king: man bows before a power, residing within himself, which does not require his own self-confidence in order to be believed in.

2. In the primitive community the bearer of power, besides the king, is the *medicine-man*; here the term "medicine" is to be understood as power-stuff in general, although this can be medicine in our own sense also. Hence the medicine-man is a doctor; but he is also weather wizard, priest, bard, wise man, *etc.*

He is not, however, an institution to the same degree as is the king

---

[1] *cf.* R. R. Marett, *Faith, Hope and Charity*, 145: "It is often maintained by shallow persons that all savages are thorough humbugs, though more especially their chiefs and medicine-men. Much the same, however, is said about the leaders of modern society by those who, as Aristotle expresses it, get their view of the play from the cheap seats."

[2] Marett, "The Primitive Medicine-Man", *Hibbert Journal*, XVII, 1918, 103.

[3] H. Hubert and M. Mauss, *Esquisse d'une Théorie générale de la magie*, *Année sociologique*, 1902–03, 93 *ff.*

[4] Spencer and Gillen, *The Native Tribes*, 130.   [5] Söderblom, *Gottesglaube*[1], 37.

or priest. Certainly his activity also is thoroughly official, but in his person power reveals itself far more spontaneously; and there are of course schools and orders of medicine-men, though their power is of the empirical type. This is shown principally in the case of those magicians whom we are accustomed to call by their North Asiatic name, *shaman*; their potency is based on the ecstasy into which they drum and dance themselves. With these *shamans*, still further, we find ourselves on the road to prophets, but of course only in the sense in which Saul too was "among the prophets", that is as regards the ecstatic frenzy that renders possible a superhuman development of power.

But in any event their knowledge is a power that is superior to themselves. It is transferable from father to son, from teacher to pupils, or is acquired by protracted exercises, especially dancing; but it may also originate directly from a demon; the South American Arawaks relate how one medicine-man obtained his knowledge and his "bull-roarer" from the mother of the waters, exactly as the Roman king Numa was taught by the nymph Egeria.[1] In the community, medicine-men constitute a power beside that of the kings and often competing with this, somewhat as prophets partly complete the fulfilling of the priest's office and partly render it superfluous and oppose it. They are the precursors of doctors and scientists,[2] but of priests also. In Icelandic fairy lore the magician plays a prominent rôle, and now that the Icelandic world has been christianized, he is almost always a priest.

3. Having arrived at the end of this chapter, I shall discuss *priests*. As has previously been observed, originally the king is the priest too. For primitive man, whose life still remains a unity, requires no special representation for religious purposes; the social unity is always religious also. The position of the priest, side by side with that of the king, is thus the commencement of a differentiation of power, although the impossibility of the king's executing all religious functions in person will certainly have played a great part, while the activity of the medicine-man was also concerned in the development of the priestly status: the priest, therefore, is just as much the successor of the kings as of the magicians.

But he is at the same time their competitor. The struggle between priesthood and kingship, in fact, is very ancient: the Pharaohs had to combat the priests of Amon at Thebes; Samuel, Saul; the emperor,

[1] Th. Koch-Grünberg, *Indianermärchen aus Süd-Amerika*, 1920, No. 16.
[2] Chap. 27.

the pope. In Rome, again, the three dignities of the king—as judge, as priest and as commanding the army—were divided between the consuls and the *rex sacrorum*; but against the predominance of the *pontifices* the latter could maintain only the name of the ancient majesty. Thus it can be understood that the priests were not only administrators of the actual cult: the power they represented extended over the whole of life. The name of the Roman *pontifex* can mean only "builder of bridges", *qui pontes facit*, and we know how the Romans regarded the erection of bridges as sacred;[1] the priests originated in this instance, then, from primitive engineers who applied "bridge medicine". In Rome they were also interpreters of the law, and for a long time jurisprudence remained their prerogative, civil law being deposited in the priestly archives.[2]

Even the medicine-man's ecstasy is not always lacking in the priest; there are inspired priests like those of Tonga who, with trembling and perspiration and in a very altered tone of voice, utter the declaration of the god in the first person.[3] But this is restricted chiefly to the most primitive religions, while the priest usually differs from the medicine-man—and also from the prophet—precisely in the ecstasy, the being filled with the god, being in him as it were frozen or crystallized, the occasional miracle incorporated in ordered official actions and the cries of ecstatic possession in the monotonous intonation of the liturgy. In priestly functions, that is to say, power is fixed, while it breaks out, as it were, in medicine-man and prophet. The priest is thus bound to fixed times and places, actions and words, while prophet and medicine-man interfere where and when the spirit drives them or necessity manifests itself. The priest stands for the ordered, the prophet and medicine-man for the occasional, representation of power and of mankind. Prophet and medicine-man operate empirically and pneumatically, the priest dogmatically in faith; and in this description the dangers as well as the superiority of the two positions are brought into sufficient prominence.

But the priest, no less than the king and medicine-man, is a bearer of power. On Mangaia (Cook Island) the priests are called "god-boxes",[4] the impersonal aspect of their power being thereby well expressed. The brahmins again are, in virtue of their birth alone, bearers

---

[1] Chantepie, *op. cit.*, II, 453. Plutarch, *Numa Pompilius*, 9.
[2] May, *Droit romain*, 30 *f*. The priests of our own day have also retained many "civil" functions, particularly the marriage ceremony.
[3] Frazer, *The Belief in Immortality*, II, 78.
[4] Frazer, *The Golden Bough* (*The Magic Art*), I, 378.

of the divine *Brahman* power; and the deification of the priest is just as little an invention as is the cult of the emperors: as power bearer the priest is filled with the god. It is true that all sorts of perils threaten his potency: hence he is surrounded by tabus which sometimes almost obstruct him in his ordered activity, and which have certainly contributed also to the ultimate severance between kingly and priestly dignity. Thus the *flamen Dialis* must be descended from a confarreate marriage (its most ancient form), and himself contract one; he was *cotidie feriatus*:—that is to say, his whole time was festal and dedicated to the god; on festivals he must not even see anyone else working, and must always wear his priestly garb; the fire from his hearth could be used only for sacred purposes, his hair might be cut only by a freeman, while his shorn hair and nail parings were buried under an *arbor felix*; he could swear no oaths, nor wear fetters on his body, while he was forbidden not only to touch or eat all sorts of tabued things but even to speak about them.[1] The priest's life is restricted, power being as it were confined within his life. Official costume, celibacy, strict fasts, regular reading and discharge of the breviary, *etc.*, all have the same end: the representative has to undertake all the guarantees of power of which the community is incapable.

Within the priesthood, too, power is sometimes stronger and sometimes weaker. There are occasions when it is, as it were, concentrated: thus the *hierarchy* arose. Power is then disseminated downwards from the chief, from pope or Dalai Lama, through the ranks of the office-bearers. But the hierarchy, too, once again stresses impersonality, since its fullness of power is present in every priest; even in the humblest holder of sacerdotal office the full wealth of power subsists, even though it may make no brilliant display.

What the priest does, accordingly, has supermundane value: above all, in *sacrifice*. The idea of sacrifice has attained its most magnificent development in India, where the sacred activity has become the movement of the Universe itself as modified by the priest, "where the events and motions of the life of the Universe correspond to the figures of the sacrificial rites and liturgies, and are directed by the magic power residing in the Veda-word. All this is regarded with the eyes of one who feels this very power as subsisting within himself from birth, and who knows that 'the *kshatra* is formed from Brahman: but Brahman is Brahman in virtue of his own self' ".[2] In Christianity too the priest

---

[1] Wissowa, *Religion und Kultus*, 506 *f.*
[2] Oldenberg, *Die Lehren der Upanishaden*, 50.

is the custodian of the life of God, and with this the life of the Universe:
"Where in heaven is there such an authority as that of the catholic
priest? . . . Mary brought the divine child into the world once, but
the priest does this not once only but hundreds and thousands of times
as often as he celebrates. . . . To the priests He has transferred the
right over His sacred humanity, and as it were given them dominion
over His body."[1] "To serve at the altar, and to celebrate the divine
sacrifice, is the proper function of the *sacerdos dei*." The bishop represents God as over against the community and offers its sacrifice to Him,
while as God's representative he bestows divine grace on the community, or refuses this.[2] The church has in fact always been conscious
of the internal tension accompanying the priestly status, the people
just as much as the theologians; thus the Bavarian countryman says:
"Our passon be a real villun, he be, 'cept for t' holy consecration."[3]
The church had to defend the efficacy of priests' orders in severe
struggles against the Donatists, who regarded the consecrations administered by traditores, and baptisms by heretics, as invalid. The *character
indelebilis* received at his ordination permanently qualifies the priest
to administer the sacraments in a valid, even though perhaps illegal
and self-condemning, way; and that the office can damn its bearer is
an important idea which will be encountered at a later stage. The
ministry of the Word should be *obedience*; if it is not this, then certainly
the minister is condemned, but the ministry itself is not invalid. As a
priest observes in one of Sigrid Undset's books, "God's Word cannot
be defiled by the mouth of an impure priest; it can only burn and con-
sume our lips".[4]

G. van der Leeuw, *Deus et Homo*, 1953.

G. van der Leeuw, *Pia fraus* (*Mensch en Maatschappij*, 8, 1932).

J. Lippert, *Allgemeine Geschichte des Priestertums*, 1883–84.

R. R. Marett, "The Primitive Medicine-Man" (*Hibbert Journal XVII*, 1918).

Aake Ohlmarks, *Studien zum Problem des Shamanismus*, 1939.

[1] Pastoral Letter of the Cardinal Archbishop Katschthaler of Salzburg, Feb. 2,
1905, in Heiler, *Katholizismus*, 226.   [2] Harnack, *History of Dogma*, II, 128 ff.
   [3] Heiler, *Katholizismus*, 180.   [4] *Kristin Lavransdatter*, II.

CHAPTER 27

REPRESENTATION. THE SPEAKER

1. ACCORDING to the Greek derivation, a prophet is a *speaker* who relates the cult legend at festivals,[1] so that his action, as a representative, is in the first place a speech which, in Greece itself, generally had a technical and semi-priestly, semi-theological cast. We usually presuppose, however, that a prophet experiences his rôle in a much more ecstatic and more *shaman*-like way, such that representation involves a tension of personality which we call *possession*, and which excludes everything individual, at least so far as the mode of experience itself is concerned. A mentally deranged man, referred to by Karl Jaspers, may be cited in illustration of this; he asked the presiding court official, "most politely, that your honour would have my own thoughts returned to me".[2] Had this schizophrene only regarded his "own thoughts" as being slightly less valuable, he might have been a prophet; he was obviously a relative of the Melanesian demoniac who called himself not "I", but "we two!"[3]

Both types of prophet, however, the calm equally with the ecstatic, speak the word of someone other than themselves: from time to time, as it were, their own personality is totally switched off, so that they are representatives absolutely and completely. The prophet is then a mere tool of Power, "filled with the god" and emptied of himself—literally an "enthusiast". Of this the story of Balaam provides the finest example.[4] Bribed by Balak to invoke a withering curse on the people of Israel, he spoke the word "which the Lord hath put in my mouth". Balak, fearing that the malediction would be converted into a blessing on his enemies, entreated the prophet to remain quite silent instead. But for Balaam that was impossible: "Balaam the son of Beor hath said, and the man whose eyes are open hath said: he hath said, which heard the words of God, which saw the vision of the Almighty, falling into a trance, but having his eyes open." This angered Balak, and he wished to drive the seer away, but the blessing of Jahveh flowed on from Balaam's mouth: "If Balak would give me his house full of silver and gold, I cannot go

---

[1] O. Kern, *AR.* 26, 1928, 3 f. E. Fascher, *ΠΡΟΦΗΤΗΣ*, 1927.
[2] *Allgemeine Psychopathologie*, 1923, 113.
[3] Codrington, *op. cit.*, 153.   [4] *Num.* xxiii–xxiv.

beyond the commandment of the Lord, to do either good or bad of mine own mind; but what the Lord saith, that will I speak."

We know that all the Old Testament prophets appeared with the word of Jahveh, whether their speech had more or fewer ecstatic features. Various excitant and intoxicating methods were employed for this; thus Elisha sent for a minstrel: "and when the minstrel played, the hand of the Lord came upon him".[1] Similarly, before declaring the oracle the Pythia of Delphi had to drink water from the sacred fountain Kassotis and eat laurel leaves as a kind of sacramental preparation for the divine speech.

With marvellous psychological penetration, Aeschylus has described the prophet's violent emotion and reluctant speech: a dreadful power forces the wretched Cassandra to speak in broken utterances:

> Otototoi . . . Dreams. Dreams.
> Apollo. O Apollo!

whereupon she perceives a horrid spectacle: the bloody children of the house of the Atreides, the axe of slaughter, the murder of Agamemnon in the bath, her own fate: and she asks the chorus:

> Be near me as I go,
> Tracking the evil things of long ago,
> And bear me witness.

Thereupon the ecstasy seizes her anew:

> Oh, oh! Agony, agony!
> Again the awful pains of prophecy
> Are on me, maddening as they fall;

and a terrifying vision follows.[2] In our own day, the grandeur of this description of depersonalized and objective speech is paralleled by the figure of Kundrie in Wagner's *Parsifal*, when with terrible outcries she is reluctantly conjured up by Klingsor.[3]

The relations between the prophetess and her lord were often interpreted sexually, as another mode of typifying the sacrament besides eating the sacred meal.[4] Thus Cassandra was beloved of Apollo, while

---

[1] 2 *Kings* iii. 15.   [2] Aeschylus, *Agamemnon*, 1072 *ff.*, 1184 *f.*, 1214 *ff.* (Murray).
[3] *cf.* further the affecting lament of Jeremiah: "My bowels, my bowels! I am pained at my very heart; my heart maketh a noise in me; I cannot hold my peace." (iv. 19).
[4] *cf.* the classical discussion of sacramental symbols by A. Dieterich, *Eine mithras-liturgie*², 1910, 92 *ff.*

the Pythia must be a virgin, and however old she might be, must be garbed like a girl; originally she prophesied only on the day of the god's epiphany.[1] The poet depicts the prophetess as a horse ridden by the god;[2] and a prayer from the world of syncretism is addressed to Hermes: "Enter into me, Lord Hermes, as babes into the bodies of women."[3] The prophetesses on the Indonesian Island of Buru, again, attribute their gift to intercourse in the forest with an earth-spirit;[4] and here we touch upon forms of communion with the god to which we shall return later.[5]

At present I shall refer merely to the utter elimination of the speaker's own personality. He has received the power of *objective speech*; and this utterance is essentially incomprehensible: objective speech cannot be understood. It must, therefore, be interpreted. At Delphi the *hosioi* translated the utterances of the enraptured prophetess into smooth hexameters; they themselves, as Farnell remarks, were "sane enough";[6] Plutarch calls these exegetes *theologians*. And it has indeed always been the theologian's task to transpose objective and unintelligible speech into subjective and comprehensible terms—and nevertheless preserve the potency of priest and prophet. We need not be surprised, therefore, that in Plutarch's opinion the theologians of Delphi seemed not to do justice to the truth![7]

2. But the speaker's objective utterance consists of no mere words. The *word*, the power-word, is equally a deed.[8] Faust's reflections on the commencement of the *Gospel of St. John*, therefore, do not hold good in view of the actual religious situation. For prophets are representatives of Power, and their pronunciations are at the same moment a celebration, and an exhibition, of Power. They can be soothsayers and doctors, exhorters, monitors, preachers and much else, their character being best observed in the Old Testament, where there are all kinds of prophets. The highest type is to be found in Isaiah and Jeremiah, Amos, Hosea, and Deutero-Isaiah, in whom the ecstatic and marvellous recedes almost completely in favour of the direct Word of God, frequently applicable to the prevailing conditions but often superior to these, or at least, as in *Isaiah* liii, soaring far above them. Less immediate and spontaneous, yet still claiming to be God's Word, is

---

[1] Plutarch, *Quaestiones graecae*, 292. E. E. Fehrle, *Die kultische Keuschheit im Altertum*, 1910, 7 ff., 75 ff. Farnell, *Cults*, IV, 186 ff.   [2] Virgil, *Aeneid*, VI, 98 ff.
[3] Dieterich, *Mithrasliturgie*, 97.   [4] Riedel, *Sluik- en kroesharige rassen*, 8 f.
[5] Chap. 67 ff.   [6] *Cults of the Greek States*, IV, 188 f.
[7] *On the Cessation of the Oracles*, XV, 417 f.   [8] Chap. 58.

the prophecy of Ezekiel and Zechariah.[1] But these names indicate the loftiest prime and the close of Israelitish prophetism, while its commencement and advance exhibit wholly different forms. Thus Samuel is the "seer" to whom Saul resorted when he sought his father's lost asses; but he is judge and priest also. The prophets wandering about the country, again, whom Saul unwillingly joined on returning from Samuel, were ecstatics raving like dervishes or members of the Dionysiac *thiasoi*, and even Elisha prophesied to the strains of the harp. The first prophet in the grand style was Elijah, while the acute psychological description of his appearance is, moreover, a fine example of the eternal struggle between objective utterance and the subjective striving and despair in the prophet's own personality; of this his "It is enough" is an absolutely classic example. Yet when the hand of Jahveh touched him he ran before Ahab's chariot to Jezreel,[2] and like Elisha he also performed miracles and cured diseases.

Plato, again, distinguished two types of mantic or "prophecy", the first the *mantike entheos*, the "inspired madness" or the ecstatic, *e.g.* that of the Pythia; the second the systematic interpretation of signs, such as augury from the flight of birds.[3] To the latter must be added the Babylonian inspection of the liver, Roman augury and the Chinese science of the water and wind sages (*fêng shui*), prophecy here very closely approaching sacred *science*,[4] with which it shares in common objective utterance. Similarly the soothsayers of primitive communities who smelt out the truth,[5] the wandering *sibyls* and *bakides* of Greek antiquity,[6] all held religious office by participating in divine wisdom, while the Scandinavian *völva*, too, was a female soothsayer and magician.

3. In the speaker's gift of healing, still further, an element of the character of the *saviour* plays a part. The "word" he speaks is a power-word; and hence a deed, a deed of salvation. The *logioi andres*, who wandered about the Grecian world from the sixth to the fourth centuries B.C., were conjurors, mountebanks, prophets, fortune-tellers, doctors, priests of purification, philosophers and *savants*, poets, divine men,

---

[1] Wundt (*Völkerpsychologie*, IV, 187 *ff.*) remarks that in genuine prophecy God and the prophet are one, while in the retrogressive and more reflective types God sends the prophet. The first is the dream, the second reflection upon the dream. But we find compulsory utterance, the almost spasmodic power of prophetic speech, in almost all the Israelitish prophets; *cf.* J. Pedersen, *Israel*, I, II, 1920, 116 *ff.*

[2] 1 *Kings* xviii. 46.   [3] *Phaedrus*, 244.   [4] Chap. 72.

[5] R. Thurnwald, *Lexikon der Vorgeschichte*, Art. *Orakel*.

[6] Rohde, *Psyche*, II, 63 *ff.*; English Translation, 292. Chantepie, *op. cit.*, II, 365.

gods. . . . The finest example of all this is Empedocles who, crowned as a god, permitted himself to be worshipped by the people, who came to him in thousands: "But now I walk before you no longer as mortal, but as an immortal god; everywhere I receive due honour as such a one, while garlands and fillets are twined about my head. As soon as I enter the flourishing cities, with these my followers, both men and women, I am worshipped, and thousands come after me, to discover *where the road leads to salvation*. Some desire oracles, others inquire about divers diseases, in order that they may hear some little word bringing salvation; for they have been writhing in harrowing torture for a long time."[1] Thus we perceive that the "mighty little word", εὐηκὴς βάξις, has many meanings: sin, sickness, and all sorts of life's emergencies are removed by it when they are confronted by "salvation". But Empedocles was also a great natural philosopher, and the sketch which he himself outlined in the passage quoted reminds us partly of the Gospel, and for the rest of a charlatan's consulting room. "Salvation", indeed, nearly always means healing also (as *e.g.* for Blumhardt), just as "healing", in its turn, always involves some sort of salvation; and if the doctor, even the modern practitioner, "cannot achieve magic, then the magnetopath or the quack takes his place".[2] Our artificial distinctions, then, between "spiritual", moral and bodily salvation *are* purely artificial, and cannot maintain themselves against the will to power and the human yearning for release.

To the poet too has been transmitted some part of the speaker's divine potency. For originally poet and prophet were one; Plato speaks of poets as being filled with God, and places them on the same footing as the oracular bards or soothsayers.[3]

H. ACHELIS, *Die Ekstase*, 1902.
J. VINCHON, VERGNES, P. SAINTYVES, M. GARÇON, *Les Guérisseurs* (*Revue Anthropologique*, 38, 1928).

[1] H. Diels, *Die Fragmente der Vorsokratiker*[3], 1912, I, 264 *f.*
[2] E. Kretschmer, *Medizinische Psychologie*[2], 1902, 255.
[3] *Apology*, 22; *cf.* on the Greek "man of words", Murray, *The Rise of the Greek Epic*, 118: "The ancient 'man of words' was not exactly a story-teller, not exactly a chronicler, not exactly a magician. He was all these, and something more also."

CHAPTER 28

REPRESENTATION. THE PREACHER

1. POWER, then, impels to speech, to utterance against one's will and with no intention of one's own. But it urges towards *preaching* also. Power sends someone forth with a message, either didactic or parabolic, that distinguishes him as *evangelist* from the prophet, while his ambassadorial status marks off the *apostle* from the priest. The priest *stands*, at the altar or in the pulpit: the evangelist and apostle *travel* on the highways, with neither pouch nor purse nor shoes, *per pedes apostolorum*. For something decisive has occurred, some marvel: the world has taken on quite a different aspect. Then there remains nothing else to do but set out and tell it to men, convey to them the joyful tidings, the warning, the admonition to conversion. It is no longer God Who speaks immediately by the mouth of the prophet: it is God Who *has* spoken and Who *has* acted; and His speech, His deed, have taken possession of certain men here and there, so that they can no longer endure their place of sojourn, but must set forth to relate what they have experienced. They can express this in widely different ways: in hearty admonition or ponderous theological lecture, in parable, anecdote or reprimand; but their utterance will always be preaching, *proclamation*: everything has changed, something great has happened. All else is now matter of utter indifference: let it be, then, and listen whilst ye are being told of this one thing: "Thus when I came to you, my brothers, I did not come to proclaim to you God's secret purpose with any elaborate words or wisdom. I determined among you to be ignorant of everything except Jesus Christ, and Jesus Christ the crucified."[1]

The word of Power cannot, indeed, be enclosed within the narrow limits of any single type. It grows, and often rankly increases; and thus the apostle and evangelist can become a prophet at any time. Since his word is potent, he heals as a matter of course; "he taught them as one having authority, and not as the scribes".[2] His own experience too,

[1] 1 *Cor.* ii. 1 *ff.* (Moffat); *cf.* Rud. Bultmann, *Die Bedeutung des geschichtlichen Jesus für die Theologie des Paulus*, Theol. Blätter, 8, 6, 1929 (in: *Glauben und Verstehen*, 1933, 188 *ff.*).
[2] *Matthew* vii. 29. Certainly this power can assume very various forms. It may imply the force of an outstanding moral personality, or even the revelation of some-

and also that of others with respect to himself, can expand to such a degree that he develops to the rank of saviour; and in the Gospel we possess the great example before whom we must all bow. Gerhart Hauptmann delicately describes the psychological detail of the experience. A man sets out to preach peace and love: "his ardent desire was to be able to speak with the voice of thunder"; and when he arrives at a place he must constantly repeat: "Thy king comes to thee". Ultimately the church bells do not exhort him to prayer: "He did not bow his head nor kneel down. He listened smiling as to the voice of an old friend, and yet it was God the Father Who was speaking to His son."[1]

2. The *teacher*, again, is to be distinguished from the preacher by the fading of the element of Power in the word. Of course potency is still presupposed, but the teacher's utterance is an application of this and not Power itself, nor even its proclamation. But after all no sharp distinctions can be drawn. For though teaching is not salvation itself, still it is its expression; and the teacher, like prophet and preacher, is an instrument of salvation. Nevertheless he is generally less important personally; for he neither imparts salvation nor announces it, but merely speaks *about* it, and in his teaching it must operate of itself. Thus could the Platonic Socrates tell his disciples: "I would ask you to be thinking of the truth and not of Socrates".[2] So too could Buddha speak to Ananda, even where it was a matter of first-hand religious discourse: "It may be, Ananda, that ye shall say: 'The Word has lost its master, we have a master no more'. Ye must not think thus, Ananda. The law, Ananda, and the ordinance, which I have taught and preached unto ye, these are your master when I am gone hence."[3] When however we place beside Buddha, the teacher, the Northern and Japanese Buddha, Amitabha, (Amida), who redeemed humanity by the vow that he would not accept eternal bliss for himself until all men had been saved, then the difference which makes the teacher becomes clear.[4] On the other hand the original potency, which is indeed the basis of the teacher's status also, continually compels the disciples to forget the absolute sufficiency of the doctrine in favour of their teacher. Thus the Hindu *guru* is very often revered as divine by even the most free-

thing "Wholly Other". But it may also be the direct inheritance of *shaman*-power, as F. C. Bartlett shows in the case of the negro preacher. *Psychology and Primitive Culture*, 122 f.   [1] *Der Apostel. Novellistische Studie.*
  [2] *Phaedo*, 91 (Jowett).   [3] Bertholet, *Lesebuch*, II, 24.
  [4] *cf. e.g.* J. Witte, *Die ostasiatischen Kulturreligionen*, 157.

thinking sects; or, as *dev-guru*, he becomes the actual object of worship.[1]

His *disciples* follow the teacher: their response is the result of a summons: "Follow me". Among them one or two special figures are particularly prominent as favourite, or principal, disciples:—Ananda, John, Peter, Elisha. *Women disciples* too are not lacking:—Mary Magdalene, St. Clare; and the imitation of the master consists not only in the adoption and propagation of his preaching, but also in the assimilation of life, to as high a degree as possible, to that of the hallowed teacher.

J. WACH, *Meister und Jünger*, 192.

[1] *cf.* H. von Glasenapp, *Religiöse Reformbewegungen im heutigen Indien*, 1928, 43.

CHAPTER 29

REPRESENTATION. THE CONSECRATED

1. LONG before Freud compelled them to admit it, wise men knew that human potency, which man directs upon his environment and its power, has its roots to no mean extent in sex life; and now many of them can give their attention to nothing else! In any case, the instincts of sex and hunger are the two great impelling factors whereby the will climbs to power and even rises to heaven; in face of these the consciousness of impotence collapses. Food and drink on the one hand, and on the other sex intercourse, are therefore not merely the two outstanding symbols of community with the god, but are also the means wherewith human potency sets to work.

That this powerfulness not only actually exists, but must also be modified by something being "celebrated", has been already sufficiently established.[1] Feminine sexual power, usually regarded as the most intense, is in many communities changed by the so-called *ruptura hymenis*, which is intended to remove the danger of initial intercourse as well as guarantee the efficiency of sex qualities. The operation is frequently performed by an old woman, but often also by a priest or stranger.[2] But the perforation may equally be a ritual defloration, for which likewise a priest or foreigner is engaged; for they are the potent ones. Here we are on the pathway to sacramental prostitution, which in the life of many peoples has played a prominent rôle.[3] Virginity then belongs to some powerful individual, not only because the husband relies on his own power too slightly to take it himself, but also because it falls essentially to the share of the greater. The offensive rite may however be replaced by a mere symbol such as intercourse with a youth, as on the isle of Naxos, or abstention during the so-called Tobias nights.[4]

But this "celebration" may also become a sacrifice to the divinity; and this again, in fact, with the purpose of enhancing power, either that

---

[1] Chap. 22.   [2] Crawley, *The Mystic Rose*, I, 168 *ff*.
[3] A. van Gennep, *Rites de Passage*, 48 *f*., 16.
[4] *cf*. M. P. Nilsson, *Griechische Feste*, 1906, 365 *ff*. F. Cumont, *Les religions orientales dans la paganisme romain*², 1909, 287. On obligatory prostitution among the Arabs, *ibid*.⁴. 1929, 258. Fehrle, *Die kultische Keuschheit im Altertum*, 40 *ff*. (The river god takes the virginity of the Trojan women.) K. Schmidt, *Jus primae noctis*, 1881.

of the individual making the sacrifice or of the community. The stranger or priest then becomes the representative of the deity, while the woman, as a *devoted person*, represents the group. In a celebrated passage in his *History*, Herodotus tells us of the Babylonian women who, in the name of Mylitta, the goddess of birth, once in their life had to surrender to a stranger in return for money.[1] In any case there were consecrated women in Babylon who, until their marriage, spent part of their life in seclusion, dedicated to the god. Their representation consisted either in the sacrifice of sex intercourse—that is in virginity, or else in its precise opposite, surrender to the god when he visited them in human form.[2] In both cases they were women of the god, his brides, *ḥarimtu*, "the segregated", *ḳadištu*, the consecrated; in ancient Sumeria also there were women of the god, who were probably put to death in the "gloomy room" which was their grave and their bridal chamber simultaneously.[3]

Whether virgins or prostitutes, the dedicated women administered their segregated status for the benefit of the whole community whose power they preserved. In Corinth, during the Persian wars, the *hiero-dules* prayed for the salvation of the city, and no less a poet than Pindar praises them in eloquent terms.[4] How firmly the system of dedication to the god by the sacrifice of virginity had taken root in the Greek-Oriental mind, until the imperial era, is shown by the story of Paulina, a lady of repute who was seduced in the temple of Isis by a freed-man wearing the mask of Anubis;[5] the seducer knew full well the situation in which he could take advantage of the religious hysteria of his victim.

The Hindu *bayaderes*, similarly, are regarded as women of the god.[6] Nevertheless the most remarkable feature, from our viewpoint, is the transition from virginity to unrestrained licentiousness; and this can be understood only in the light of the concept of Power. Abstinence, that is to say, is not chastity in our sense, but is "cultural chastity",[7]

[1] I, 199; *cf.* 93. Lucian, *de dea Syria*, 6: "The market is open to strangers only".

[2] D. G. Lyon, "The Consecrated Women of the Hammurabi Code", *Studies Presented to Toy*, 341 *ff. cf.* A. S. Hartland, "At the Temple of Mylitta", *Anthr. Essays Presented to E. B. Tylor*, 1907, 189.

[3] F. M. Th. Böhl, *Verslag van het Zesde Congres Oostersch Genootschap*, 1929, 21 *ff*. Traces of temple prostitution in the Old Testament: 1 *Sam.* ii. 22, *Ex*. xxxviii. 7; *Hos.* iv. 14. Jephthah's daughter was similarly dedicated—though in what sense will probably always remain debatable: *Judges* xi.   [4] *Fr.* 122.

[5] Dill, *Roman Society from Nero to Marcus Aurelius*, 566. In Nero's day there were girls in the Capitol who believed themselves to be loved by Jupiter. (Seneca, *Fr.* 37.) H. Usener, *Das Weihnachtsfest²*, 1911, 76 *f*.

[6] C. Clemen, *Die nicht-christlichen Kulturreligionen*, II, 1921, 15. *cf.* Crawley, *The Mystic Rose*, I, 235.   [7] Fehrle, *op. cit.*

or intercourse with divine power, celestial marriage. This can become realized in three ways; either by killing the bride, by virginity, or by unlimited surrender in the god's service. The mysticism centred upon death, upon the bride, and eroticism are therefore merely distinguishable but never separable; Aphrodite Pelagia, the goddess of harbour towns, was simultaneously prostitute and sacred.[1] The intoxication of love is a swooning and dying; turning towards the god, on the other hand, is the manifestation of erotic potency or of the will to power.

In bridal mysticism[2] the same schema subsists, not even always spiritualized. The brides of Christ have always devoted all their love, carnal or even hysterical as it often was, to the heavenly bridegroom. But for this they must not be despised. For I do not think that the purity of the relation to God depends on the eradication of the sex element. No one is able to remove completely the sexual from any relationship, even from that to Deity. There remains therefore only one method of differentiation:—to ascertain whether the devotion is an actual devotedness, that is to say a surrender of self, or is merely a manifestation of the will to power; in other terms, whether the dedicated woman desires to dominate the bridegroom more or less spiritually, but always erotically, or to love him genuinely.

2. Originally the Roman *vestals* were probably only the unmarried women of the household who carried water and maintained the fire.[3] They were the brides of fire[4] and wore bridal raiment all their lives. Associated with the state hearth by the state itself, they constituted a type of order, and their chastity guaranteed the power and well-being of the community.[5] A very ancient form of this idea is found in the test of chastity at Lanuvium, where a vestal had to bring food to a snake; if the animal ate it her chastity was established, and the farmers exclaimed, "the year will be fertile": (*clamantque agricolae: fertilis annus erit*).[6] Here cultural chastity is the exact parallel to intercourse on the ploughed field and other customs in which the development of

---

[1] H. Usener, *Vorträge und Aufsätze*[2], 1914, 189 *ff.*   [2] Chap. 75, 76.

[3] W. Warde Fowler, *The Religious Experience of the Roman People*, 135. On the duty of carrying water: Ovid, *Fasti*, III; *cf.* also R. Cagnat, *Les Vestales et leur couvent sur le forum romain* (*Conférences Faites au Musée Guimet*, 1906, 61 *ff.*).

[4] Chap. 6.   [5] Fehrle, *op. cit.*, 210 *ff.*

[6] J. Toutain, *RHR.* 89, 1924, 183 *ff.* Firmicus Maternus had an inkling of the polarity between cultural chastity and licence in asserting (contrary to the facts) of the vestals: "they are either forced into the sin of prostitution, or else they remain virgin, and so lose the honourable dignity of a glorious name"; *de errore profanarum religionum*, 14.

sex power promotes fertility, and in conformity with this its violation
is a damaging, or rendering impure, rather than a misdeed.[1]

This type of consecration has an obvious feminine touch. But, of
course, men dedicated themselves to the god also. It is, however, no
accident that in so doing they approximated to the feminine; and this
might happen in a horrible and perverted way, as was shown by the
self-mutilation of the priests in Asia Minor in the service of the
mountain mother. This was a sadistic self-laceration, as *The Book of
Kings*[2] depicts it for us, and as Apuleius still more clearly describes
it.[3] But it was also a direct sacrifice of virility, carried out in a state of
transport, and impressively described by Lucian: "they castrate
themselves in the service of Rhea"[4]; the castrated men received
women's clothing.[5] The Gospel also mentions "some which have made
themselves eunuchs for the kingdom of heaven's sake".[6]

In all this the sacredness of feminine life plays a prominent rôle.
In ancient Rome, for example, a criminal who met a vestal saved his
life;[7] similarly in the Middle Ages, when the veneration of women was
at its height, their protection ensured freedom: "should a wolf (a
fleeing criminal) take refuge with women, out of love to them he should
be permitted to live".[8] The knight too swore his oath "by all women";
to him the whole female sex was a sacred family, while as a protection
in battle Wolfram's Parzival sets woman above God; priests and women,
again, enjoyed the same sacredness and might not carry arms.[9] Here,
then, to dedicate oneself means to approximate to the feminine, to the
mother, for the salvation of the entire community; and thus the longing
to return to the mother's womb, and the will to sacrifice life, blend in a
curious way, while the Christian monk vacillates between a love of
Christ that exhibits feminine traits, and a reverence for the Virgin
that is typically masculine. For though the church extols virginity and
derives all evil from woman, still it well knows how to sublimate all
that is profoundly human in a unique way; as St. Bernard affirms:
"If a man fall not but through a woman, so he rises only through a
woman."

3. The life of those dedicated to the god is a new life, filled with
fresh power, and the rites leading to it are very similar to the rites of

---

[1] G. Wissowa, *AR.* 22, 1923–24, 201 *ff.*   [2] 1 *Kings* xviii. 28.
[3] Bertholet, *Lesebuch*, 5, 42 *f.*   [4] *de dea Syria*, 15.
[5] Bertholet, *Lesebuch*, 5, 43 *f.*   [6] *Matt.* xix. 12.   [7] Plutarch, *Numa*, 10, 3.
[8] San Marte, *Parzivalstudien*, III, 1862, 121.   [9] *ibid.*, 115 *f.*

transition already discussed.[1] They imply a death; in the ritual of admission to monastic orders, for instance, the liturgy of the obsequies is frequently incorporated.[2]

The vow,[3] taken by the person about to be dedicated, is of course not restricted to chastity, which is always merely the symbol of the surrender of the whole life.[4] It may however demand chastity, poverty and obedience, as with Christian orders. It operates in very different ways. In devoting his life to an uninterrupted cult, impossible in "the world", the monk represents the community. "Daily the monastic choir prays for all those who cannot pray, or who do not desire to pray; it renders to the infinite majesty of God that service and honour of which those standing without in the world, and working there, are incapable."[5] Monastic life, then, is perpetual adoration, like that of the angels (βios $\dot{\alpha}\gamma\gamma\epsilon\lambda\iota\kappa\acute{o}s$).[6] But representation is not merely that of the world as over against God; conversely, it is God's offensive against the world. Thus the Society of Jesus is a *militia Christi*, whose rules begin with the words: "Whosoever would fight under the standard of the Cross on behalf of God in our society, which we desire to seal with the name of Jesus."[7] And the calm submersion, the meditation *cum libello in angello*, the apparent unproductivity is representation: "It is not idleness to remain idle for God, but the business of all business."[8] Prayer, penance and the piety of the consecrated in fact augment the *thesaurus* on which the community can draw; the enfeebling of the individual's potency enhances the power of the whole.

4. The watchword of the consecrated, then, is the attainment of power by means of voluntary impotence. The sacrifice they offer effects greater fullness of power that may indeed be a form of magic, but which may also pertain to life after death, as well as the worship of the represented community. The *martyr* also, who surrenders his life, can generate power from complete impotence. "I must endure", the model child affirms, "more than any human being has ever had to suffer; for the crown of sorrow is the only crown to which I can attain";

---

[1] Chap. 22.   [2] A. van Gennep, *Rites*, 125, 140.   [3] Chap. 59.
[4] A peculiar form of dedication, sometimes even lifelong, prevailed among the Nazarenes of the Old Testament, who abstained from alcohol, did not cut their hair and avoided all contact with dead bodies. This type of avoidance (*cf*. Chap. 4) is to be found in the history of religion in endless variety.
[5] Heiler, *Katholizismus*, 452.
[6] *ibid.*, 438.   [7] *ibid.*, 313.   [8] *ibid.*, 474.

and the psychologist adds: "but this paragon will never realize that men can live without any sort of crown whatever".[1]

The entire situation, however, is transformed (and this holds good for *all* the consecrated) as soon as the surrendering personality accepts the power, to which he sacrifices himself, as supreme, and desires to understand his whole activity solely in its relation to this power. This constitutes the true concept of the martyr, μάρτυς, witness: even witness in blood. He who devotes himself is not, in the first place, one acting of his own accord, not one who "celebrates", but one who bears testimony[2] and has boldness, παρρησία, freedom of utterance[3] about his encounter with Power, about God's acts, and His word that has come to him. This boldness is a consecration: "It will end in your martyrdom".[4] Here, however, voluntary impotence is no longer attainment of power but simple obedience, unto death. But by his testimony God's witness wins for himself "boldness and access with confidence";[5] and thus feminine consecration has been exchanged for masculine *obedience*.

H. Delehaye, *Sanctus* (*Subsidia Hagiographica*, 17, 1927).
F. Dornseiff, *Der Märtyrer* (*AR*. 22, 1923–24).
E. Fehrle, *Die kultische Keuschheit im Altertum*, 1910.

[1] F. Künkel, *Einführung in die Characterkunde²*, 1929, 48.
[2] Dornseiff, *Der Märtyrer*, AR. 22, 1923–24.
[3] E. Peterson, *R. Seeberg-Festschrift*, 293.
[4] *cf. Luke* xxi. 13.   [5] *Eph.* iii. 12.

CHAPTER 30

SAINTS

1. SAINTS are no longer wholly representative; to a markedly high degree they are objects of veneration. Certainly, *orant pro nobis*—they are potent helpers of mankind as over against the great powers. But the principal feature is Power revealing itself in them. We fail however to imagine this potency sufficiently concretely; we speak, it is true, of the "odour of sanctity", and this fragrance is by no means merely metaphorical. For on approaching the human queen, the Egyptian god exhaled a scent,[1] and the dying Hippolytus sensed the nearness of Artemis by the "breath of heavenly fragrance" emitted by the goddess.[2] Thus too the medieval saints expired while glorious odours were disseminated.

In the first place, then, a saint is a person whose body possesses divinely potent attributes. Concealed in a sack, light emanates from it, while its little finger can set in motion a vehicle that is held fast.[3] These powers can be acquired, for example, by touch; in the famous El Hazar mosque at Cairo people touch a barred window with their hands: behind the lattice there is a saint's coffin. Still further, the personality of the holy one may retire completely behind his (physical) potency. Often it cannot be claimed even that it is he who performs miracles, since it is his power that effects them; thus the ashes of the mystic al-Hallaj, who was tortured to death and his body burned, caused a miraculous flood of the Tigris,[4] while kissing the saint's relics, preserved in glass cases, is still a prevailing custom in the Roman Catholic Church.[5] The saint is primarily a sacred, that is powerful, object—a relic.[6] Here also the cult of the dead exerts its influence;[7] but the desire to possess a portion of the powerful individual, a part of his body or even something that he has touched, begins even during his lifetime. On one occasion, in the fervour of his address, the American evangelist Billy Sunday

---

[1] Bertholet, *Lesebuch*, 10, 40.

[2] Euripides, *Hippolytus*, 1391 *ff.*; *cf.* E. Lohmeyer's brilliant "Study", *Vom göttlichen Wohlgeruch* (*Sitzber. der Heidelberger Ak. d. Wiss., Phil.-hist. Kl.* 1919, 9). H. Windisch (in *Meyers Kommentar*) on 2 *Cor.* ii. 15.

[3] Hertz, *Mélanges de sociologie religieuse et folklore*, 155 *f.*

[4] Louis Massignon, *Al Hallaj, martyr mystique de l'Islam*, I, 1922, 294.

[5] *cf.* Heiler, *Katholizismus*, 169.   [6] Chap. 3.   [7] Chap. 14, 24.

broke an ordinary chair; immediately the people in the front rows
fought for possession of a fragment of it, one carrying its leg and
another part of its back home with them.[1] From this attitude originate
both the cult of relics and the Anglo-American hunt for souvenirs;
it is always a matter of the power of something striking or extraordinary.
But the remarkable object must spring from someone who himself
remains in the background, and who may be a Catholic saint just as
much as a Napoleon or a film star.

The *grave*, which contains relics in the most literal sense, is therefore
the guarantee of sacred power; and in Christianity, just as much as in
Islam, it was considered important to have one's last resting place
inter sanctos, to be buried near the grave of the holy ones.[2] In ancient
Egypt, similarly, the nobles had themselves interred at Abydos, near
the grave of the divine and sacred Osiris. Conversely, the possession
of the holy grave is of high value, as power, to the community, and
the whole of Sophocles' *Oedipus at Colonus* is constructed on this idea.[3]
In Greece, again, the heroes were nothing but saints whose graves
occupied the best situations in or near the city.[4] Just like the medieval
ecclesiastical saints, the heroes too were the objects of the struggle for
power between different cities: Oedipus had four graves. Then the
grave and the relics became more important than the saint himself:
the thing prevailed over the person. Hence, still further, the so-called
translations. The Spartans brought Orestes from Tegea, just as the
Aeacids were lent to the Thebans by the Aegeans, and the Dioscuri
to the Locrians by the Spartans.[5] Similarly the bones of Theseus were
transported from Skyros to Athens,[6] and the oracle ordained that
Hector's bones should be taken to Thebes, while in order to ward off
plague the remains of St. Gennaros were brought to Naples.[7] People
were so far misled as even to steal a saint; in 1087 merchants from Bari
robbed the inhabitants of Myra of St. Nicholas, who on the first day
after his translation cured thirty sick persons.[8] When the dying St.
Francis was on his way to Assisi, Perugia had to be avoided lest the
people there might seize the saint; and on his arrival at Assisi there
were great rejoicings because it was hoped, with good reason, that he
would quickly die.[9]

[1] Chapman Cohen, *Religion and Sex*, 173.   [2] Söderblom, *Gottesglaube*, 87 f.
[3] cf. H. Usener, *Der Stoff des griechischen Epos, Kl. Schriften*, IV, 1913, 214.
[4] Rohde, *Psyche*, I, 159 f. E. T. 121, 166. cf. also Nilsson, *A History of Greek Religion*, 233 f.   [5] M. P. Nilsson, *AR.* 22, 1923–24, 372.
[6] Plutarch, *Theseus*, 36.   [7] Pausanias, IX, 18. Trede, *Heidentum*, II, 327 ff.
[8] Trede, II, 324 f.   [9] P. Sabatier, *Vie de Saint François d'Assise*[10], 1894, 362 ff.

Thus, in the first place, a saint is either a corpse, or a part of one. The world has no use for living saints: they are dead persons,[1] or still better: the potency of the dead. Even apparently secularized civilization continues to aspire towards this power. Alphonso the Great of Naples, for instance, obtained one of Livy's arm-bones from the Venetians only with great difficulty;[2] for the Renaissance sought its saints among the ancients. And whoever has seen Napoleon's tomb under the *Dôme des Invalides*, and the Unknown Soldier's grave under the *Arc de Triomphe de l'Étoile* on the same day in Paris, realizes that the nineteenth and the twentieth centuries, too, still discover a source of power in the translation and worship of sacred corpses and graves.[3]

2. If therefore the upward limit of the saints, as directed towards the gods, is a fluctuating one, so that they are the objects of worship rather than representatives, on the other hand the concrete and palpable potency in their structure predominates so intensely that it becomes a matter of indifference to what person this may be attached; and thus we find, in actual fact, all sorts of figures among saints. Nameless powers, kings and noble forbears became heroes in Greece;[4] among the saints of the Catholic calendar we find martyrs, teachers, prophets, national heroes, simple pious people, "*successeurs des dieux*", particularly of heathen deities, and very many "odd saints".

3. The empirical character of the fullness of power therefore, previously substantiated at the commencement of this volume, is dominant here also; he is sacred from whom power emanates. If he is still living, then this power can be manifested mainly in two ways: by miracles and by physical signs, among which *stigmata* take a leading place. But the church demands the attestation of *miracles*, performed after death, for the process of beatification or canonization, and thus remains wholly

---

[1] Chap. 14.
[2] J. Burckhardt, *Die Kultur der Renaissance in Italien* I[12], 1919, 194.
[3] *cf.* Chap. 37.
[4] Rohde, *Psyche*, I, 165 *ff.* E. T. 116 *f.* Nilsson, *A History of Greek Religion*, 233 *f.* The list of Islamite saints, who play an equally prominent part in popular piety to that of their Christian counterparts, and with whom also everything revolves around the grave and the miracles associated with it, is almost as variegated. A Greek hero was a "dead man who by death has attained to something like deity"; Rose, *Primitive Culture in Greece*, 32. Sophocles was honoured not because of his poetry but as a *dexion*—as the host—of Asclepius, *ibid.*, 93.—Sanctity is not a moral power. "The Sicilian peasant still reckons the *decollati*—decapitated persons of notoriety—as very much on a par with the saints": Marett, *Faith, Hope and Charity*, 86.

within the realm of power conceptions; and it scarcely escapes from this idea by insisting on heroic virtue. For according to old church language, virtue and miracle are closely related (*virtus*, ἀρετή). A quite different concept of sanctity arises, again, as soon as the latter is associated no longer with personal power, but with the idea of status or office; it is in this sense that the New Testament "saints" are to be understood, who owe their sanctity to the gift of grace bestowed on them. They were not saints, but were accounted saints or made into saints; this concept of the saint, also, has passed into the realm of ideas of the Christian church.

CHAPTER 31

DEMONIC HUMAN BEINGS

1. THE terrible figure, the evil will, which revealed themselves to man as Power,[1] take possession of him and thus form a very remarkable dual unity of subject and object, of representative and represented. To a certain extent, indeed, this is to be met with in all representatives; but it receives in the present instance a thoroughly specific character that is due to the manner in which man loves the object of his fear and represents his own awe. This is possible, however, only on the basis of that fusion of subject and object which has been already frequently discussed, and which must be described both here and later as possession.[2] The demon has thus gained such complete control of the man that he speaks through him and acts within him; yet nevertheless there persists the consciousness of a dual personality, of possession, indeed of a violation of the essentially human.

2. The *werewolves* in the first place, whose acquaintance we have previously made,[3] are demonic human beings; but above all women, as the "more powerful", become victims of possession. The *witch* is naked; but by this no natural, nor even Greek, nakedness is implied, in the sense of "emancipation of the flesh", but a rite,[4] a "celebration", which accentuates the witch's powerfulness. She unites herself with her demonic paramour, the counterpart of the heavenly bridegroom, this unity being sexual; *incubi* and *succubi*, too, exercise their activities; and Charles de Coster gives a magnificent and psychologically penetrating description both of the werewolf and of the witch living in a covenant with the devil.[5] It is of course to be presupposed that the witch herself believes in her sinister *liaison*, and in this respect many victims of the witch delusion cannot be regarded as "innocent". At the same time others exposed themselves to the suspicion of being witches solely because of some striking characteristic such as beauty, rapidly increasing wealth *etc*. Here again we discover the empiricism of the powerful: the extraordinary as such merits reverence, or suspicion,

---

[1] Chap. 15.   [2] Chap. 74.   [3] Chap. 8.
[4] Chap. 48.   [5] *Eulenspiegel und Lamme Goedzak.*

and in any case is "sacred". Owing to her union with the demon, again, the witch acquires all kinds of capabilities, although in most cases, like those of the demon himself, these only cause injury; she induces disease in man and beast, and all sorts of evil in general: the evil eye, transmutation and the whole medley of witchcraft.

B. THE SACRED COMMUNITY

CHAPTER 32

COMMUNITY

1. TO every human being *solitude* is familiar. "Every woman who bears a child, every man who risks his life, every human being who dies, must pass through the utmost extremity without the help of his fellow creatures who are willing to assist him."[1] But man cannot be solitary. Whoever is thoroughly isolated weeps like an abandoned child: or like Christ in Gethsemane. From the child to the God-Man, solitude excites dread in us all: for we possess power and life only in the community. It is in fact this primeval dread, and no mere trivial fear, that created gods. Dread leads to God, or to the devil: even with the devil there still is life, still a "Thou". But in solitude there is nothing whatever.

Loneliness is the culmination of the insecurity and *care* wherein we live. Hence its terror arises whenever we approach the boundaries of life and experience most intensely its powerfulness and uncertainty: in birth, death and sex intercourse. Then all terrors fuse into the one great dread:— that of our existence in itself, of death, and of life. But unless we were beings who possessed life only within the community, we should know neither dread nor loneliness. Solitude and fellowship condition each other reciprocally: to be alone is to stand before the Ultimate, before God. But we enter into solitariness only out of the community: and conversely every man (with the exception of the God-Man, Christ) repeatedly returns from solitude to the community, even though "with eyes still unused to it".[2]

2. "Community" is not "covenant". Since the age of enlightenment there has operated the tendency to depict a community as a society: the church as a religious society based on confession or creed, the state as a secular society resting on a *contrat social*.[3] But "community"

---

[1] Künkel, *Einführung in die Charakterologie*, 58 *f.*

[2] Schmalenbach, *Kat. des Bundes*, 62. *Einsamkeit*. Lohmeyer, *Vom Begriff der religiösen Gemeinschaft*, 45.

[3] *cf.* von Schlözer, who thought of the state "as analogous to a fire insurance company" (Schmalenbach, *ibid.*, 37).

is something not manufactured, but given; it depends not upon sentiment or feeling, but on the Unconscious.[1] It need be founded upon no conviction, since it is self-evident; we do not become members of it, but "belong to it". To-day the finest example is still the peasant, who has no "feelings" but simply belongs to his community, as contrasted with the *citoyen* invented in the eighteenth century! Even peasants who fight, or engage in law-suits, remain neighbours and brothers;[2] a peasant in the Eastern Netherlands who has a mortal enemy in the village nevertheless knows that on market-days he is obliged to greet his foe and walk up and down with him once, when the peasant community of the whole district is gathered in the county town, thus demonstrating to the eyes of "strangers" the fellowship of the village *ad oculos*.

Primitive man, again, thinks and acts collectively. Without his fellows the individual is nought; in him acts his family, his stock. To us mass conversion is repugnant, but to primitive man it is quite normal; when therefore the mass adopts a new religion one must act with them, otherwise one cannot exist at all.[3] Thus to the German tribes the murder of a relative was far more than a crime: it indicated madness, since it was really suicide.[4] In the eyes of the Greeks, similarly, the slaying of a relation was the deed that awakened the *Erinyes*. "The fact is that the individual cannot act unless everyone acts in and with him, nor can he suffer without the affliction extending over the entire community."[5] "Alone", man cannot live. That is the great dread. To be alone is to die.

Thus just as man is bound to the "world", being not opposed to it but having "community" with it, so he has this community, and lives in this "being in-common", with his fellow men.[6] And to-day we still become "primitive" as soon as we feel ourselves among the mass of living humanity; every revolution, every war, testifies to this. In times of crisis, then, man flees from his actually achieved, or pretended, independence, back to the original community that protects him from dread. But in religion, wherein his very existence is the issue, man is continually confronted by new crises; hence religion is, or becomes, communal. The rite is the deed of us all, and similarly the myth is a story, and the creed the belief, of everyone.

Thus whoever is severed from the community cannot live; home-

---

[1] Schmalenbach, *Kat. des Bundes*, 53 *ff.*
[2] *ibid.*, 57.
[3] Chantepie, *op. cit.*, II, 600.
[4] *ibid.*, 556.
[5] Grönbech, *op. cit.*, I, 28.
[6] *cf.* Chap. 8.

sickness gnaws at his soul. Even to-day we encounter the misery of
recruits and the arson of which maidservants from the country are
guilty; in such cases it is, however, not the "I" that has been damaged,
but the "we" which has been shattered. Ban and interdict, then, are
punishments synonymous with death, while prohibition of the sacrament by the church, and of intercourse with other members of the tribe
in primitive communities,[1] kills the person upon whom it falls.

3. Primitive man knows only *one* community: to him the distinction
between secular and spiritual communion is entirely foreign. Life
is essentially a single whole, and the communality of society is precisely
the powerful life. Life, however, can be communal in threefold form:
(*A*) as *blood*, which implies the soul.[2] (*B*) as *totem*, signifying the conjoint world,[3] both of which are "given"; and (*C*) as *property*, which
exhibits life's "possibility".[4] But these three forms by no means
subsist in any exclusive relationship.

G. LE BON, *The Crowd*.

E. LOHMEYER, *Vom Begriff der religiösen Gemeinschaft*, 1925.

G. MENSCHING, *Sociologie der Religion*, 1947.

H. SCHMALENBACH, *Die soziologische Kategorie des Bundes* (*Die Dioskuren*, I,
    1922).

   Die Genealogie der Einsamkeit (*Logos*, 8, 1920).

J. WACH, *Einführung in die Religionssoziologie*, 1930.

J. WACH, *Sociology of Religion*, 1940.

[1] *e.g.* Sophocles, *Oedipus rex*, 259.

[2] Chap. 39.   [3] Chap. 8.   Chap. 23.

MARRIAGE. FAMILY. TRIBE

1. *MARRIAGE* is "covenant" and "community" simultaneously: it is what is given *and* what is chosen. Its character as being something given becomes increasingly apparent to the degree that it expands into the family: choice, on the other hand, dominates it so far as it is a union of love. The common element that is sought, and at the same time discovered, is undifferentiated: it concerns the whole life. Differentiation thus relates not to the common factor but to the predominance of either the given, or the chosen, respectively. In every marriage, therefore, covenant struggles with community: in every individual, the spouse with the lover.

From the phenomenological standpoint, the old problem of primal marriage: was it monogamy or promiscuity? can be considered from this point of view—but only from this one! The older evolutionism set an absolute polygamy and polyandry at the beginning, together with polydemonism, while a more modern evolutionism enthusiastically attempts to assign a secure position to an original monogamy, side by side with an original monotheism. A circumspect ethnology, however, rejects every type of unilinear development, regards primal promiscuity as a figment of the imagination, and so-called group-marriage as a secondary formation;[1] but original monogamy is equally fantastic. Phenomenology is not concerned with any "primal conditions". It can apprehend only the element of promiscuity that is given potentially in every marriage, as well as the element of ultimate givenness involved in each relationship between man and woman. These are both expressed in the Biblical idea that the man leaves his father and mother for the sake of his wife—that is choice, but that God joins husband and wife together—that is givenness. Hence it is that the church regards marriage as a sacrament.

The communal element, in the first place, manifests itself particularly clearly in the widespread custom of so-called *couvade*, or male childbed. Rationalistic attempts at its explanation such as the man trying to secure the mother's privileges persisting from the matriarchal period, or the man submitting to the woman, are quite unsatisfactory; and

[1] F. Gräbner, *Das Weltbild der Primitiven*, 1924, 11.

this peculiar custom can be correctly understood only in the light of
the idea of community: where one member suffers, that is to say, the
other suffers also; *couvade* would then have arisen out of the same
intention as the simultaneous illness of the married pair, of which
Thurnwald gives a remarkable example.[1]

2. All this leads quite normally to the *family*; this is no joining
together of individuals, but a form of existence in its own right, from
which one cannot release oneself. Neither is it a covenant, but community in the truest sense, the common element of which embraces
the entire life, even in its physical aspects. Thus a Basuto girl who
ought to keep awake, but grows sleepy, can blame this on one of her
relatives who may be indulging in a nap in some corner.[2] The element
of covenant also, discerned in marriage, can in this way be completely
expelled therefrom by the family. In the Gaboon and Ogowe territory,
for example, a man has a certain right to his brother's wife; at least
adultery with a sister-in-law is not, as such, punished. In one typical
instance, an Ogowe man kills his brother's wife because she has rejected
his love; he denies the crime, but his brother, the murdered woman's
husband, says: "you are guilty; but because we are brothers, and not
two men but one, your crime is mine and I will acknowledge it in your
place"; the wife's family, however, is not content with this and demands
the surrender of the actual murderer.[3] Thus the family perceives one
thing only: one of its members has been stricken, and that must be
made good. But the husband too sees only one fact: he and his brother
are one, and he not merely feels no necessity for revenge, but even
acknowledges the crime which he should have punished. The murderer,
again, thinks of only a single point: his brother's wife naturally belongs
to him also; her refusal therefore deserves death. And this leads in
certain tribes even to a claim of the brother to his brother's wife, whom
he calls "my wife".[4] A similar over-growing of the marriage-character
by that of the family is to be found in so-called *levirate marriage*. In
the Old Testament, as well as among many primitive peoples, it is the
duty of the brother to marry his dead brother's wife,[5] and in the
Lampongs, in Sumatra, the offspring of a levirate marriage are regarded
as the children of the dead man. But if the levirate union remains

[1] G. van der Leeuw, *Structure*, 7.

[2] Lévy-Bruhl, *The "Soul" of the Primitive*, 88. He speaks of "physiological soli-
darity", which well describes the *couvade* also.   [3] *ibid.*, 90.

[4] *ibid.*, 91. The whole family has also paid the bride-price!   [5] *ibid.*, 92.

barren, the brother-in-law appoints one of his own sons to be the perpetuator of his brother's family. This son must then marry two wives: the son by the first wife becomes the successor of his own father, as though he were the son of the grandfather: the son by the second wife becomes his own successor.[1] Thus all life's power impulses are dominated by its common element: the family is all in all. In Israel the obligation to marry the widow was restricted by *Deuteronomy* to the brother, although originally it applied to the father of the dead man also. The first son who sprang from the renewed marriage counted as the son of the dead man, and perpetuated his name and inheritance.[2] Here then it is clear that the sacred that subsists in common need not be blood alone; and in this way what is given by Nature is modified, as so frequently elsewhere;[3] not however by a new union, but by an autocratic continuation of the impaired communal relations. Accordingly, marriage is in the first place the transition from one familial communality into another; the woman must become incorporated within the sacred subsisting in common with the husband. This train of ideas is presupposed by many marriage rites.[4] In ancient Rome, at the conclusion of the nuptials, the woman said "where you are Gaius I am Gaia", thereby adopting her husband's gentile name. The widow again, who by marrying has lost her old communality, would be completely solitary were not a position assigned to her in the husband's community. Thus Ruth attached herself to her mother-in-law although there was no longer the prospect of levirate marriage; Naomi dissuaded her, since she was too old to bear a new husband for her daughter-in-law (for this would have been the most desirable outcome!). But Ruth spoke the beautiful words, which should be interpreted in no merely sentimental mood: "thy people shall be my people, and thy God my God".[5] Here marriage has completely become community. Hence, too, its religious indissolubility: a covenant can be broken, but not marriage.

Blood is not the sole sacred common element; but it is probably the most important and, still further, it does not become severed from the other common factors. It is obviously the principal feature in the intense consciousness of unity ("belonging together" is far too feeble!). Of this blood vengeance is the best proof, since it is based directly on the common blood that has been shed; and in Greece "the heir could

---

[1] F. D. E. van Ossenbruggen, *Tydschr. Kon. Ned. Aardrykskundig Genootsch.*, 2. *Reeks*, 47, 1930, 223.   [2] *Deut.* xxv. 5 *ff.*; *Gen.* xxxviii, 26; *Ruth.*
[3] Chap. 23.   [4] Chap. 22.   [5] *Ruth* i. 12 *ff.*

evade the obligation of vengeance just as little as he could become the son of another father".[1] Hence the murder of relatives was accounted the most evil of all actions. Among the Greeks it awoke the *Erinyes*, the embodiment, as it were, of the spilt blood which, because it had turned against itself, resulted in madness. Thus in Aeschylus' *Eumenides* Apollo, as his protector, defends Orestes by opposing the infamous murder of Agamemnon by Clytemnestra to the matricide. But the *Erinyes* reject this justification:

"'Tis no murder to take the life of your own kin."[2]

Abel's blood, again, "crieth unto (God) from the ground" for vengeance upon Cain.[3] Among certain African tribes, likewise, community consciousness is so intense that fratricide is regarded not as murder but as suicide, as something abominable and insane. But it is not punished;[4] indeed, there is no one competent to punish it. For there is no "punishment" whatever in our sense: the power of the outraged blood reacts upon the murderer. In the case of the murder of relations, then, murderer and murdered are wholly and essentially one and the same person; and therefore nothing can happen unless the blood, in the guise of the *Erinyes*, turns against itself as madness.

The stranger by blood is outside the community. He is an "enemy" (*hostis*, foreigner or stranger and enemy); he participates in an alien power and we must therefore be on our guard. Such a measure of precaution is the greeting; when we say certain potent words and offer food, this results in a temporary blending of the two inimical powers.[5] The stranger or foreigner must therefore be met with either the utmost courtesy (hospitality) or unconcealed enmity. Both are directed against his power, before which we bow or which we assail, since he is already severed from his own community; but in both cases it is feared.[6] To the stranger also dangerous tasks are assigned, such as the defloration of girls or affairs connected with harvest *etc*.

That community of blood is not the sole common element constituting the family is shown by the possibility of its modification which we discerned in levirate marriage, while according to certain Mohammedan viewpoints, the Imam can accept someone into the family of Mohammed by pronouncing a benedictory formula.[7] In ancient Rome,

[1] U. von Wilamowitz-Möllendorff, *Griechische Tragödien*, II[8], 1919, 127 *f*.
[2] *Eumenides*, 212; *cf.* van der Leeuw, *Goden en Menschen*, 101 *ff*.
[3] *Gen.* iv. 10.   [4] Lévy-Bruhl, *The "Soul" of the Primitive*, 93 *ff*.
[5] Chap. 4; van Gennep, *op. cit.*, 46 *f*.
[6] van Gennep, *op. cit.*, 36.   [7] Massignon, *Al-Hallaj*, 507.

again, the law originally recognized only *agnatio*, that is relationship based on paternity, while *cognatio*, the sole assured blood relationship, occupied merely second place. But *agnatio* was founded wholly on *patria potestas*:[1] the married woman *in manu* was therefore agnate to her husband.[2] Thus the family in this instance depended on a power, *patria potestas*, which (as we have seen) was not necessarily connected with blood relationship at all.

Among many peoples, still further, *property* also plays a part as the common element of the family. For property is not just the object which the owner possesses. It is a power,[3] and indeed a common power. The Australian's property dies with its owner, and can therefore be employed by no one else,[4] while the Roman idea of *familia* signified a farmhouse with its fields and cattle.[5] Later these possessions were called *familia pecuniaque*, and afterwards *patrimonium*, this "property derived from the father" being originally inalienable, as contrasted with *possessio*, which implied only the use of a field or building and not these in themselves.[6] Thus we find the common element of the family bound up with blood and with property; but it is not confined to these, for it is sacred, and therefore cannot be derived without any remainder from the given.

3. Family limits are not finally fixed. It may thus be regarded as the narrower association of man, wife and children,[7] as well as the wider group conditioned by these; in this way the family gradually expands into the *wider family*. A special and highly important form of this is the *clan*, whose bounds are calculated according to either patriarchal or matriarchial derivation, and whose centre of power is usually a totem;[8] its perpetuation, as a rule, is dominated by an intricate marriage system which, in accordance with its two principal types, is described as either exogamous or endogamous. For us the crucial point, however, is not whether this mode of mutual life was the original type, but the fact that in this form of community the individual is never the mere individual but always only one particular instance of a class: there are

---

[1] Chap. 20.

[2] May, *Droit romain*, 139. Piganiol, *Origines*, 160. [3] Chap. 3.

[4] Joseph Wanninger, *Das Heilige in der Religion der Australier*, 1927, 87. cf. Julius Lips, *Die Anfänge des Rechts an Grund und Boden, Festschr. für W. Schmidt*, 1928, 485 *ff.* [5] Piganiol, *ibid.*, 172. [6] May, *ibid.*, 186, 197 *f.*, 203.

[7] This is intended to exclude neither polygamy nor polyandry. A unilinear development from the monogamous family is neither fact nor phenomenon, but dogma.

[8] Chap. 8.

women whom a man may marry, but also those whom he cannot marry because they pertain to the group of "mothers" or "sisters", even in cases where close blood relationship is not involved, and also where connection by blood is totally lacking and only totem community subsists.[1] Levirate marriage, as well as the frequently very far-reaching marriage prohibitions of Christian communities, appear to be survivals of this. One marries precisely not a personality, but rather the bearer of some specific power; and many primitive tribes do not recognize *the* father nor *the* uncle, but only fathers and uncles.[2]

But the inclusive family may also possess quite different bases, the most important of these being the patriarchal. The Roman *gens*, for example, was actually only the family in its widest conceivable extent. The "father" of this great family was *dux et princeps generis*, from whom the *gens* derived its *nomen gentilicium*, while the *sacra gentilicia* constituted the power centre of the *gens*. Whoever forsook the *gens* and entered another, as for instance through adoption, had to carry out the renunciatory ceremony, *detestatio sacrorum*, since he would otherwise pertain to two powers simultaneously; and the *pontifices* decided whether the *sacra* of the person adopted were not being damaged too seriously by those of the one adopting him, the *adrogans*.[3] The *gens*, too, had its common graves and sanctuaries,[4] and the cult of its own gods was secret. As in the family, community here also was always that of the cult: the sacred is the common element, and the common element the sacred. Thus in ancient Greece only the nobility originally formed tribes, because it carried on the cult; later, however, those who were not noble were received into the *phratry* as participants in the ritual, or *orgeones*; but frequently the cult practices, as at Eleusis, remained in the hands of specific noble tribes.[5]

4. The greater family, or clan, gradually expanded into the still more comprehensive community form of the *tribe*; the Germanic *Sippe* embraced everyone in the *Ting*. But actual community has its root in the presence of Power, so that what "elders" generally are in

[1] *cf.* Cassirer, *Symb. Formen*, II, 226: "The definition of Species is not based on empirical-causal principles of generation; the concept of 'genus' does not depend on the empirical connection between *gignere* and *gigni*, but the conviction of the ideality of the genus, as this develops from its basis in the reciprocal magical relations of humanity and animals, is the primary fact, with which the idea of common 'descent' becomes indirectly associated."

[2] Spencer and Gillen, *Northern Tribes*, 74; *cf.* 95: "The native names apply not to the individual, but to the group of which he is a member."

[3] May, *Droit romain*, 140, 148.   [4] Chantepie, *op. cit.*, II, 438.   [5] *ibid.*, 386.

the clan—that is potential fathers, and what the father is in the family, and similarly in the wider family the primal ancestor and his successors, that too is the status of the nobility, or the king, in the tribe. They were bearers of the power which the German peoples called "peace"—*Sippe*, from Old High German *sippa*, *sibba*, meaning peace;[1] and hence, in the *Ting*, persons had to appear unarmed before the king.[2] There was therefore no community without some centre of power which might be either a *sacrum*,[3] a certain specific god or a person, while the power subsisting in the tribal community was guaranteed by the lord, the king or the nobility.[4] Thus life is valid only when it is potent life; but it possesses power, again, only within the community; "mere separation from family and country sufficed to bring life into peril",[5] and he who was expelled from the Germanic community was as good as dead.[6]

Here again, therefore, blood is the common element only in so far as it is one of the most important manifestations of powerfulness and sacredness; but it may also be replaced by other forms of the sacred. The Toradja of Celebes, who live on the seashore and adopted Mohammedanism from the Bugis, afterwards called themselves "descendants of the Bugis",[7]—a reversal of *cujus regio ejus religio*. The foreigner, then, is one who is a stranger to the sacred. Membership of the tribe, and "religion", are wholly one: God is the "God of the fathers", of Abraham, Isaac and Jacob.

M. J. Bouwman, *La Couvade* (*Revue Anthropol.* 35, 1925, 49 *ff.*).
F. de Coulanges, *La cité antique* (Eng. tr., *The Ancient City*).
M. Weber, *Gesammèlte Aufsätze zur Religionssoziologie*, 1922 *ff.*

[1] J. M. N. Kapteyn, in: *Donum natalicium Schrynen*, 1929, 540.
[2] Chantepie, *op. cit.*, II, 577.   [3] *cf.* Chap. 3.   [4] Chap. 13.
[5] Grönbech, *Folkeaet*, II, 188.   [6] Chantepie, *ibid.*, 172 *ff.*
[7] N. Adriani, *Het animistisch Heidendom als godsdienst*, 54.

THE COVENANT

1. THE *community* is essentially one unified entity, and the life that is powerful within it is one and indivisible; compared with the community, then, the *covenant* is an additional organization of an essentially different type. Thus Abraham had two sons, Isaac and Ishmael: Isaac, however, was not only the child of his body but also the son of the promise. An order of salvation separates off from that of Nature, a divine possibility from the—likewise divine—givenness: the charism,[1] the power, becomes divided.

Whether one wishes it or not, he belongs to the community. But he enters into the covenant. Together with the givenness pertaining to destiny, then, there appears the possibility of the human will which, however, is immediately apprehended as vocation. But the principal feature is that the sacredness of what is given—of blood, property or totem—is here radically (as in the previous Chapter occasionally) intersected by another form of the sacred; and this holds true of the development of the primitive secret society from the original tribe equally as of His deed, Who said with reference to His disciples: "Behold my mother and my brethren".[2]

Of course the order of salvation, which here exists along with the "natural" order, is not always, and not from the outset, the spiritual bond which the modern world understands by the term. There is at first a large number of simpler distinctions:—

2. At the frontier between what is given, and choice, stands the so-called *age-class*, the principle of differentiation being inclusion in some definite phase of life:—children, young people, adults; and thus the age-grade has a powerfulness of its own incompatible with other powers, which presses for specific differentiation. To-day this is familiar to every village clergyman who has seen newly married persons immediately withdraw from the choral union that he has formed after so much effort, not because they have lost their voices or their need of sociability, but just because they now belong to another age-group;

---

[1] Weber, *Gesammelte Aufsätze zur Religionssoziologie.*
[2] *Mark* iii. 34. Schmalenbach, *Soz. Kat. des Bundes*, 44.

and that youth has its own feelings about life, and its peculiar potency,
is likewise quite obvious in our own day. Young country people, moreover, frequently form exclusive groups that play an important part in
popular customs and which in olden days, according as it was feminine
or masculine, had its *kora* or its *kouros* in Greece.[1] To-day, too, the group
system in a country village has a religious tinge: the youths in the
street in the evening, and the girls there also, or in earlier days in the
spinning-room, and the men in the tavern *etc.*; in the German division
of Transylvania the young men, from confirmation to marriage, form
a "brotherhood" with seven official servants.[2]

Of course age is something that is given, and can of itself constitute
no covenant. Yet it is here that the additional organization, to which I
have just referred, begins, because in the first place people leave the
age-grade voluntarily, usually by marriage, and in the next because this
grade gradually passes over into the covenant. In Mittenwald in Upper
Bavaria, for example, not every youth may belong to the "brotherhood",
the "rapscallions" being excluded.[3] Among primitive peoples, again,
the transition from the age-grade to the secret society is general, the
entire organization of the latter being already actually given together
with the age-group.[4]

3. The second division of powerfulness occurs with respect to
sex. Man and woman have different charismata: to woman, man is
sacred, and conversely. This is conditioned by the awe, or even the
reverence, with which they regard each other, just as by the mutual
disinclination subsisting between the sexes. Thus the youth's nervous-
ness in the girl's presence and his ecstatic reverence for her, and
similarly the coquetry with which woman both defends herself and
attracts, as well as the deeply rooted disesteem the sexes entertain for
each other, ultimately have a basis in religion. Power opposes power.
Children go to school: with haughty self-consciousness, the boys keep
apart from the girls walking about arm in arm and tittering while they
look mockingly towards the lads, who have their own pride mixed with
a disagreeable sense of insecurity, just as the girls too have their secrets;
later on, the men have their own clubs, and the women their afternoon
tea and gossip. *We* connect religious ideas with neither the profound
lack of understanding between man and woman, nor with the marvel

---

[1] Chap. 11.   [2] Schurtz, *Altersklassen und Männerbünde*, 112 *f.*
[3] Schurtz, *ibid. Bachbuben* is the German equivalent.
[4] On age-grades *cf.* further Merker, *Die Masai*, 71 *ff.* I leave to the reader the
application to modern conditions—*e.g.* student unions, *etc.*

of their mutual discovery; to us both avoidance and community are equally mundane conceptions. But wrongly so; and we should not sigh under the burden of complicated "sex problems" if only we could recognize both the repellent and the attractive factors in the contrasted sexes as powerfulness, instead of imagining that we can solve them by any arbitrary conventions.

In the Fiji Islands every village has at least two *men's houses*, since custom does not permit the husband to spend the night in his own home; he belongs to the "strangers' house", the hotel, and early in the morning he returns to his family.[1] In Doreh in Dutch New Guinea, the *rumslam* are men's houses in which the youths remain—the age limit being identical with the sex limit! These buildings are at the same moment sanctuaries and places for dancing;[2] there the young women resort and unrestrained love-making follows; the sacred flutes are kept there too, while sex symbols decorate the entrance.[3] Here then we perceive how from the one life the most widely different forms of our modern diversity of existence have developed: house, sanctuary, club, hotel, brothel—from the one community the most highly contrasted differentiations. Here also the given still remains the chief element— the specific power of sex. But the differentiation is plastic, and in secret societies the restriction of membership to men (seldom to women too) is essential.

4. The *secret societies* to be found among primitive peoples, above all in Africa, are indeed compacts rather than communities, although of course the prevalence of the covenant principle is restricted, since inclusion in the tribe is usually requisite for membership within the covenant; and we have already seen that its organization arises directly from that of the family or clan. "The magical-religious brotherhoods are based essentially on clan organization, that is on social relationship, but nevertheless they are something quite different".[4] In fact, differentiation according to membership with respect to the totem, within the clan, was a sort of "additional organization"; and the organization of age-classes passes over directly into that of the covenant.[5] The Papuans, again, exclude illegitimate children from the compact, and the Australians half-castes.[6] Rites of initiation for the secret society are approximately the same as those for puberty in connection with the tribe.[7]

[1] Webster, *Primitive Secret Societies*, 12.   [2] Chap. 29, 57.
[3] Webster, *ibid.*, 8.   [4] A. van Gennep, *op. cit.*, 109.
[5] Alviella, *RHR.* 81, 1920, 7.   [6] Webster, *ibid.*, 27.   [7] Chap. 22.

Although secret societies arise from the community, and are bound up with this to such a degree, indeed, that the age-grades and the men's groups, which themselves presuppose separation from the women and children of the tribe, are scarcely to be distinguished from the compact,[1] there still appears in the latter an element of extraordinary importance:— the covenant, that is to say, reposes upon a more or less free selection from the tribe. Thus community is no longer given as a matter of course, since the covenant is sought for: one not merely belongs to the community, but enters into the covenant also. Its purpose is originally no other than that of the community itself: preservation and strengthening of communal power, attainment of communal salvation. But the secrecy which, as has already been observed, also appeared spontaneously in the cult of the family, has in this instance had an unfavourable result, since secret societies usually exhibit a deterioration of community. Because the common element is, in principle, abrogated, so the common law no longer holds good; and under the protection of the peculiar and secret powerfulness, now grown independent of the communal essence, all sorts of crimes are committed: those not within the covenant are terrorized, debts forcibly collected, enemies robbed, maltreated and killed. In Loango, for instance, a state official is present, but after masks have been put on he is sent back to the village—a clear indication that community is now yielding place to covenant.[2]

The sacred common element of covenants is to a great extent the same as that of communities, sacred objects playing a prominent part, like the *churinga* already referred to;[3] to the initiates is explained the function of the "bull-roarer", which imitates thunder, while from others this remains concealed; or members are taught how to prepare the hats and masks used in the performances and processions *etc.*[4] The gods and spirits too, to whom homage is paid, are the same as those worshipped by the community, but their secrets, for example their names, are supposed to be known only to the members. The rites, again, are the same as those of the tribe: tests, feigning death *etc.*, grades of initiation taking the place of age-classes; in Calabar, for instance, there are seven to nine of these.[5]

In general, we conclude that while the secret society certainly inclines

---

[1] Webster, *ibid.*, 21, 135 *ff.*
[2] A. Bastian, *Die deutsche Expedition an der Loango-Küste*, I, 1874, 221.
[3] Chap. 3.   [4] Codrington, *The Melanesians*, 69 *ff.*
[5] M. H. Kingsley, *West African Studies*, 562.

the idea of community in the direction of that of covenant, still this transposition has not been successful: it is either a social excrescence or it sinks to the level of a popular custom, if not indeed to that of farce. Of the latter process the *Quimba* in Loango offers an example: the initiates appear out of the forest armed with sticks, with which they chastise unfaithful or quarrelsome women.[1] Moreover, the secret society has acquired no form of life of its own which is sufficiently distinctive from the organization of tribe or family.

5. The limits of the given are also transcended by *sacrificial* and *festival communities*, such as were familiar to the Greeks: *thiasos* and *eranos*.[2] These were usually dedicated to some secret cult or other, and held communal meals for which they demanded contributions from their members, being as a rule open to women, strangers and slaves. Members wore a badge, and if they had rendered noteworthy service to the society they received a eulogy that was recorded on a tablet. These societies occupied a position intermediate between our secular societies and the religious covenant, and frequently facilitated the introduction of foreign, oriental, divinities, in this way, as well as by their neglect of tribal limits, constituting a transition to the mystery communities.

In the case of societies in antiquity we are often unable to decide what their constitutive factor was, whether some religious purpose or communal labour;[3] but the medieval *guilds* found their sacred common element in the specific character of the work;[4] the powerfulness of the craft, incorporated in the patron saint, bound the members together. But here again the given factor was stronger than the possibility of choice, since the guilds formed closed corporations in which the occupation was not open to all, but on the contrary was often hereditary: the potency was actually already there and required no searching for. The ceremonial of their meals, again, was the same as was customary at the ancient cult festivals, while transitions to the dignity of journeyman and mastership bore the character of consecration; in the parish

---

[1] J. Réville, *Les peuples non-civilisés*, I, 1883, 103.

[2] P. Foucart, *Des associations religieuses chez les Grecs*. Ziebarth, *Das griechische Vereinswesen*.

[3] A remarkable instance:—The so-called Gallipoli Inscription, which refers to a fishermen's society, but in which its detailed grades receive varied interpretations from commentators, in some cases with regard to occupation, and in others to activities in the mysteries cult. *Mém. Ac. Inscr. et B. Lettr.* 35, 1896, 36. *Bull. Corr. Hell.* I, 1877. F. Poland, *Geschichte des griechischen Vereinswesens*, 1908, 86, 119 f., 405. Ziebarth, *Das griechische Vereinswesen*, 1896, 24.   [4] Chap. 2.

church, too, the guild had its own altar and its own saint; the entire community ritual was continued there, and inclined to the covenant only because of the arbitrariness—in itself very limited—of the vocation.[1]

6. In the *mystery communities*, as these were brought into existence above all by Hellenism, power ultimately became differentiated: from life in the world, which became correspondingly reduced in value, "salvation" was distinguished.[2] The origin of these mystery societies, however, still clearly shows community forms: the cult of Isis, from which the Isis mysteries of the imperial era arose, presents in the family of Osiris the primal type that is repeated in every family;[3] originally, too, the Eleusinian cult was the festal celebration of an agricultural village community and restricted to its inhabitants;[4] and until the cessation of these mysteries, indeed, the chief dignities remained in the hands of two ancient Eleusinian families. "Thus the conclusion is at least rendered probable that the form of the mysteries service may have developed by gradual expansion from the domestic cult",[5] while we have already seen that the rites of marriage and of the mysteries were closely related.[6]

But the mystery communities increasingly developed from communities to covenants; primarily this holds good of their purpose. For in the mysteries, life in general and powerfulness were no longer universally sought for, but a "salvation" sharply distinguished from them; and this tendency was connected with the urge towards the security of life which was more and more powerfully operative in the Greek world from the sixth century B.C. to the fifth A.D., and which manifested itself above all in the yearning for immortality.[7] The real purpose of the mysteries, then, was the attainment of eternal life; but even when salvation still concerned the whole of life, as in the case of Empedocles[8] it embraced both healing the body and the needs of the soul, it nevertheless became increasingly isolated from the community of the given and made into the aim of another community, that arose anew for the communal achievement of this deliverance. Thus individuals entered a mystery community: for this they sought, and for it a personal and voluntary decision was requisite. It is true that the

---

[1] Chantepie, *op. cit.*, II, 549. Huizinga, *Herfstty der Middeleeuwen*, 115, 131 *ff.*
[2] Chap. 11. [3] *cf.* A. Moret, *Mystères égyptiens*, 1913, 37.
[4] Farnell, *Outline History of Greek Religion*, 49.
[5] Anrich, *Das antike Mysterienwesen*, 7 *f.*; like the secret societies from tribal organization. [6] Chap. 22. [7] Chap. 46. [8] Chap. 27.

arbitrary element in this decision was again withdrawn immediately the *invocation* of the deity took the place of the given; and Lucius, seeking the consecration of Isis, attained this only after he had patiently awaited the nod of the goddess (*deae nutus*).[1] The covenant thus arising either from free choice, or from the god's summons, sets itself more and more harshly in opposition to other communities. The relationship to the god is no longer simply present: some possess it, and others do not, the latter being commiserated, the initiated extolled as blessed.[2] Thus the concept of "world", only neither as the conjoint world nor as the world in the background,[3] but as the mere lack of potency, is already clearly exhibited here.

According therefore as the limits of the covenant were left, in increasing measure, either to human decision or to the numinous decree of the god, and also according as the community was on the one hand restricted to those entering it, or those who had the vocation, so on the other hand the limits of the original tribal membership were extended or even suspended. In this way the Eleusinian mysteries, at first closed to all strangers, altered their character owing to the hegemony of Athens, which developed the mysteries of the capital out of those of the tribe; afterwards, indeed, from the second half of the fifth century, they were open to all Hellenes, and finally even to *hetaerae*, children and slaves.[4] The essential characteristic of the mystery covenant, then, was that in apportioning salvation, it made no distinction between foreigners and native born, between nationals and barbarians, between slaves and free; admission was by either unrestrained choice or vocation, but it remained always an individual and personal approach to salvation,[5] which spread itself freely over the world without any limits being imposed upon it. The saviour whom the mysteries celebrated, the sacrament that was offered in them, was for all. Only the specific bounds, given within the mystery itself, were valid: "For as many of you as have been baptized into Christ have put on Christ. There is neither Jew nor Greek, there is neither bond nor free, there is neither male nor female: for ye are all one in Christ Jesus."[6] Tribal rites, also, no longer had any essential significance: eating with heathen was

---

[1] Apuleius, *Metam.* XI, 21.
[2] *e.g.* Sophocles, *Fr.* 753: " . . . thrice blessed are those who, after having witnessed such initiations, wander to Hades; for them alone does life bloom there, others being doomed to misery"; (Campbell); *cf.* van der Leeuw, *Goden en menschen*, 59.
[3] Chap. 8, 18.
[4] Rohde, *Psyche*, I, 286 *f.* E. T. 221. Farnell, *Cults of the Greek States*, III, 153 *ff.*
[5] *cf.* J. de Zwaan, *Antiek syncretisme en hedendaagsche zendingsvragen, Mededeelingen Ned. Zendelinggenootschap*, 1929, 3.   [6] *Gal.* iii. 27, 28.

permitted and circumcision not unconditionally necessary;[1] there were Greeks and barbarians, Jews and heathen, no more, but only the faithful on the one hand and the "world" on the other. Of course the mystery communities also recognized limitations, usually as products of the ancient restrictions valid for sacrifice and cult: thus Eleusis excluded manslayers and barbarians, the latter being a vestige of the limitation imposed by givenness. The conditions of admission too—fasting, chastity *etc.*—were no different from those holding generally for performance of the god's service.[2]

The actual cult of the mystery society will be discussed in a later chapter. Here it need only be said that some sacred event was repeated as the "story of salvation" and spread among the members; and in the centre of this story stood the saviour's figure.[3]

7. Still more sharply does the covenant sever itself from the "world" in the form of the *monastic community*; in this the power of the devotees[4] must be guarded and nourished by the compact, although we must observe at the same time that it sustains the character of polarity. A monk is first of all an individual, one who is alone; and with his solitude his powerfulness is closely connected. But then one power seeks others: the anchorites' huts (*lauren*) form together a *monasterium, coenobium, claustrum*; in certain cases, also, the monasteries combine to form a sort of monastery town such as Athos. The monastery, then, is a community in the fullest sense, having its own church, agriculture and crafts, its own administration and churchyard, while initiation exhibits the features of tribal and mysteries initiation.

In all other respects, however, the covenantal character comes clearly into prominence; here powerfulness, not to be acquired in the "world", is realized. A common sanctity is attained in and through the uninterrupted cult, a common morality by observance of the *consilia* and not merely of the *praecepta evangelica*. Thereby even the church is estimated essentially as "world", and every community except the monastic designated as powerless; *patres, fratres, sorores*, are then merely spiritual titles.[5] The order of birth, similarly, is completely suppressed by that of consecration, and so the death is announced of Sister Teresa, "in the world" Miss A. B. The priest of the church, again, is accounted a "secular priest"; for salvation, in its truest sense, is to be found only in the *ecclesiola in ecclesia* called the monastic community; thence it extends itself over church and world.[6]

---

[1] Weber, *op. cit.*, II, 39.   [2] Chap. 49.   [3] Chap. 12, 61, 73.   [4] Chap. 29.
[5] Also an application of *Matt.* xii. 50, "Whosoever shall do the will of my Father . . ., the same is my brother . . ."   [6] Chap. 29.

In Buddhism, still further, the monastic covenant has attained world importance. Emanating, just as Christianity did also, from a loose connection between teacher and disciples,[1] community here develops into a gigantic monastic covenant. Buddhism, however, has cast off the form of the given, but has not discovered that of the church; for it, therefore, laymen are regarded only as "worshippers" and are not united by any kind of organizing bond. Thus far, Buddhism is merely the logical consequence of the Hindu practice according to which a man, after having completed the period of marriage and generating children, quits his home to live in solitude as a forest ascetic; and originally the Buddhist monks gathered together in the rainy season when it was impossible to wander about begging; subsequently, monasteries arose in thousands. Thus the "world" is rendered impotent finally and as a matter of principle: there can be community only apart from the world.[2] The house, the family home, the tribal hearth, the dwelling-place of power:—all have here become a stumbling-block and an offence. Whoever seeks genuine community, then, must "go forth", the latter being even the name for the lower grades of ordination (*pabbajja*).[3] Thus from the brahmin's command: "thus let him go forth from his house", Buddhism formed a community,[4] accession to this[5] being a "going forth from home into homelessness".[6] "Very straitened is life in the home, a state of impurity; freedom is in leaving the home".[7] Genuine community demands the surrender of the "given", which becomes depreciated to a false community.

W. ANRICH, *Das antike Mysterienwesen*, 1894.

F. CUMONT, *Les religions orientales dans le paganisme romain*[4], 1929 (Eng. tr., *Oriental Religions in Roman Paganism*).

P. FOUCART, *Des associations religieuses chez les Grecs*, 1873.

K. H. E. DE JONG, *Das antike Mysterienwesen*[2], 1919.

O. KERN, *Die griechischen Mysterien der klassischen Zeit*, 1927.

A. LOBECK, *Aglaophamus*, 1829.

A. D. NOCK, *Conversion, The Old and The New in Religion From Alexander the Great to Augustine of Hippo*, 1933.

R. REITZENSTEIN, *Die hellenistischen Mysterienreligionen*[2], 1920.

H. SCHURTZ, *Altersklassen und Männerbünde*, 1902.

N. TURCHI, *Le religioni misteriosofiche del mondo antico*, 1923.

H. WEBSTER, *Primitive secret societies*, 1908.

E. ZIEBARTH, *Das griechische Vereinswesen*, 1896.

---

[1] Chap. 28.   [2] Christianity had a narrow escape from this development!
[3] Oldenberg, *Buddha*, 347 ff.   [4] *ibid.*, 348.
[5] Which, in its own turn, does not recognize the "given" caste distinctions as a matter of principle; Oldenberg, *ibid.*, 152.   [6] *ibid.*, 355.   [7] *ibid.*

THE SECT

1. THE primitive world knew only of the sacred, and not specifically religious, communities; similarly, no specifically religious acts, but solely sacred. To it, therefore, any special cultivation of religious life, either individually or within the community, was quite foreign; and thus Scipio, who went before daybreak up to the Capitol to meditate in the *cella Jovis*, "apparently consulting Jupiter about matters of state", was a very rare exception that aroused a good deal of astonishment.[1] The first community devoted to specifically religious purposes, then, is the sect, which severs itself not only from the given community but from the "world" in general. Thus the sect does not repose on a covenant that breaks away from the church (this it does in only a secondary sense); primarily, it rests on one that releases itself from the community, and this in order to attain religious salvation in some quite distinctive way.

Thus the sect is not founded on a religious covenant that is severed from another religious community such as the church; it segregates itself, rather, from community in general, and constitutes religion a specific aim side by side with the usual purposes of life. The mysteries society also did something similar, and there were mixed forms of sects and mystery societies such as Orphism. But in general, mystery apprehends life more cosmically, more as a unity, than does the sect, which lets the world be in order tranquilly to be saved. The term "sect" is derived not from *secare* but from *sequi*; it is a religious party, a heresy, as the Greek word αἵρεσις puts it: that is, a choice or a tendency; it is the purest form of covenant that we know. As compared with the Judaic community, for instance, Nazarenes and Christians are sects;[2] but the pharisees and sadducees also, and in Islam the mutazilites. In principle these were all schismatics, belonging to the "separatist type";[3] but they severed themselves not from any particular community, but from every kind whether primitive-general, religious-national or ecclesiastical. The correlate of the sect is therefore not the church but the community; it is the most extreme outcome of the covenant.

---

[1] Gellius, *Attic Nights*, VI, 1, 6.
[2] *Acts* xxiv. 5; xxviii. 22.
[3] Wach, *Meister und Jünger*, 8.

2. The sect embraces a heterodox *doctrine*, another cultural *custom* than that of the community from which it cuts itself off: "false teachers will insinuate destructive heresies"[1] (αἱρέσεις). Phenomenologically, however, the divergent doctrinal or cultural element is not the determining feature; it is merely the manifestation of a conviction, of the sort of attitude that creates the sect. Thus Christianity as compared with Judaism and the Roman community, the Reformation as contrasted with the Roman church, Buddhism with the Hindu, and Islam with the Arabic community, were all sects which subsequently became churches, monastic societies or national unities. What constitutes the sect then, as such, is its sectionalizing and heretical disposition: adherents of the αἵρεσις are just heretics and a "factious person", αἱρετικὸς ἄνθρωπος, is a "perverted" man who should be avoided.[2] "Heresy" therefore concerns not simply opinion but life; it is sin, and schism on the heretic's part implies excommunication on that of the community; in the Middle Ages even moral aberrations, such as sadism, were accounted heresy.[3] No community, nevertheless, can be understood in its essence without some reference to the sects that have severed themselves from it,[4] since into these the community's own life has overflown. But whoever actually remains within the community cannot perceive this; to him, therefore, membership of the sect is just the proof of a different attitude and a foreign potency. In this respect, one can at best rise to the realization that "there must be also heresies among you, that they which are approved may be made manifest among you".[5]

3. The specific powerfulness of sects, then, is experienced as their special charism, and the choice as vocation; thus every trace of community can be eliminated in favour of some pure possibility, which must be realized by the *pneuma* or, again, by the pious will. Either vocation or performance attests membership: the one is *election*, the other *conversion*,[6] which may, however, accompany each other. But birth, once again, proves nothing: it was Sarah's son who triumphed; and by extreme sects sacrament and rite also are accounted impotent, or become modified as when adult baptism replaces that of children. In so far indeed—regarded phenomenologically—the sect precedes the church, which by contrast rather implies retrogression to the primitive community.

The impulse to the formation of a covenant arises from all kinds of

---

[1] 2 *Peter* ii. 1 (Moffat).   [2] *Titus* iii. 10.   [3] Huizinga, *Herfsty*, 414.
[4] Wach, *Religionswissenschaft*, 162, 53.   [5] 1 *Cor.* xi. 19.   [6] Chap. 79.

causes, among which the revival[1] assumes an important place; some intense shock to the feelings necessitates reflection on one's attitude towards the world and God, and compels the abandonment of the given and the search for new possibilities. Such were the Dionysiac outbursts in ancient Greece, the spiritual enthusiasm of the Reformation period, the Pentecostal movement *etc.*

The sect, however, can gradually lose its specific character again. But frequently it remains true to this and perfects it, this development taking the form of an increasingly thoroughgoing contraction. The demand for personal conversion, for the identification of faith and experience, for pure doctrine, becomes constantly sterner. In this connection the expansion of the views of Jean de la Badie (1610–1674) is remarkable: he attempted to form a community of those who had veritably been born again, and therefore could not be satisfied with any local congregation; so he formed a household congregation whose members were known to him as Christians who had been born anew. Thus by a wide *détour* he returned to the primitive "family": community-bond and family-bond in one. Subsequently, in the famous house congregation in Herford, spiritual jubilation and dancing became the characteristics of the communion of perfect love that, by this time, had been achieved. Marriages between members of the sect and non-members were declared invalid and new unions celebrated, the children of which would be free from original sin. After la Badie's death a further sharp distinction was made between those who had actually received God's grace and those in whom this assurance had not been manifested: the first group consisted of *frères et sœurs*, while the members of the second class were called *monsieur* or *seigneur*. Even the mode of addressing God was influenced by the degree of certainty of salvation: the brethren might call Him "Father", but not the others.[2]

Thus the world becomes ever larger: the community, the *Nova Sion*, the true Israel, the realm of the Spirit, constantly smaller, in accordance with the application of the "principle of the segregated and consecrated community which tolerates the state, but as far as possible avoids all contact with it, and austerely maintains the community apart from the world by means of clothing and customs, greetings, connubial relations and excommunication".[3] Actually, however, in this

[1] Chap. 94.

[2] H. Heppe, *Geschichte des Pietismus und der Mystik in der Reformierten Kirche namentlich der Niederlande*, 1879, 240 *ff.*

[3] As E. Troeltsch remarks about the baptists, but which is equally true of many other sects; *Kultur der Gegenwart*, I, IV, I², 510.

continually expanded purification, restriction and fixation of the sect's powerfulness, there is concealed a secret yearning for the dissolution of each and every community, for the return to solitude in the presence of God.[1] "He shall be the greatest who can be the most solitary";[2] and again to cite this writer, "Every community renders common". The dread of loneliness becomes a luxury, and the natural impotence arising from the sense of being abandoned by all given things is transformed into the unexpected, but all the more blissful, possibility of omnipotence.

J. LINDEBOOM, *Stiefkinderen van het Christendom*, 1929.
E. TROELTSCH, *The Social Teaching of the Christian Churches.*

[1] Lohmeyer, *Vom Begriff der religiösen Gemeinschaft*, 44 f.
[2] Nietzsche, *Beyond Good and Evil*, 155. (Foulis Edition.)

CHAPTER 36

THE CHURCH

1. THE Israelite קָהָל was at the same time the assembly of the people and the worshipping community,[1] the Greek word for this idea being *ecclesia*;[2] so that when Jesus chose His disciples and assigned to one of them a special status,[3] He not only called together men of like disposition, nor created a mere relationship of teacher and disciple, such as we have just observed in the case of Buddha. His founding of an *ecclèsia* must rather "be understood from His total attitude to His own people, from whom, for whom, and as contrasted with whom He gathered and commissioned the Twelve as a special congregation, פְּנִישְׁתָּא, in order to represent the congregation of Jahveh, קְהַל-יהוה".[4] The Twelve were certainly disciples, but above all they were the people, the true Israel,[5] while the events of Pentecost brought to the disciples, as the assembly of the people, the gift of the Holy Spirit. In this manner, then, the "pneumatic" and the given bonds were woven together into one, without either being absent: "Now if you are Christ's, then you are Abraham's offspring; in virtue of the Promise you are heirs."[6] The church is therefore the people of God in the spiritual sense, and the Body of Christ in the actual sense, which means that covenant and community are fused together and elevated to a higher unity. Neither the accession of man, nor the givenness of his position, is decisive, although each is not unessential; they find their foundation, as well as their ratification, in the act of God, Who stoops to meet man "*in Christo*",[7] and Himself desires to be the bond of their community.

From the moment of her origin, however, the church has been repeatedly in danger either of becoming irretrievably the "people", because the church's hierarchical organization implies nothing whatever more than the perpetuation of the idea of the people as this became transposed from Israel to the Roman empire: or again of being completely "pneumatized", most of the sects being influential in this direction. But at all times its essence remains as hitherto:—that is

---

[1] *Gen.* xlix. 6. 1 *Kings* xii. 3. 1 *Kings* viii. 14. *Lev.* iv. 13. *Num.* xvi. 3. *Ps.* xxii. 23. *Joel* ii. 16.

[2] Bultmann, *Glauben und Verstehen*, 162 *f.*   [3] *Matt.* xvi, 18.

[4] Schmidt, *Die Kirche des Urchristentums*, 291 *f.*   [5] Peterson, *Die Kirche.*

[6] *Gal.* iii. 29; Schmidt, *ibid.*, 314.   [7] Bultmann, *ibid.*, 170 *ff.*

neither the choice of man understood as vocation, nor his givenness in accord with fate, but both together and received as the fruits of God's own action, consummated in the Lord of the church.[1]

As a people, then, the church is certainly the continuation of the community, but now as the convened community, as the chosen people; while as resting on a covenant, it is the perpetuation of the mysteries covenant formed around the figure and the life of the "Lord", but also a covenant whose mystery participates in that of the world's givenness and each individual's life. To state all this in the language of the early Christian era: the church erected on a feeble man, Peter, cannot be overcome even by hell.[2]

2. A church actually exists solely in Christianity; for neither the Buddhist monastic community, nor that of Islam resting on the principle of mere agreement and conformity,[3] nor again the Judaic assembly of the people, merits the title of church. This historic fact, still further, is intimately connected with the church's essential nature, since it arose from the concrete historical situation which the Jews' rejection of Christ, and the subsequent turning towards the heathen, brought in their train.[4] In this concrete situation, then, there subsists on the one hand the transition from community to covenant, but on the other the concentration of the heathen religious consciousness, already manifested in various types of covenant, into a community given in a new manner. Thus the church is the church of the heathen, but "salvation is of the Jews".[5]

All this implies that in its essence the church, as it lives in the consciousness of the faithful, evades Phenomenology. For it is the Body of Christ, and as such escapes all comprehension, of which indeed it is itself the primary presupposition. Certainly it is both people and covenant, but always only as subject to the presupposition of the presence of Christ, of the "Lord", Who is the bond alike in the assembling together, wherein vocation and choice are involved, and in the given as the Mediator of creation. The church is therefore visible-invisible, at once humanly organized and mystically animated, spiritual and cosmic. It is not to be verified as a fact, but to be believed in: and

---

[1] cf. G. P. Wetter, La catholisation du Christianisme primitif (Revue d'Histoire et de Philosophie religieuse, 7, 1927).

[2] cf. Maritain's fine dictum: "the great glory of the Church is to be holy with sinful members". Religion and Culture, 40.   [3] Wach, Religionssoziologie, 51.

[4] Peterson, Die Kirche.   [5] John iv. 22.

it is no accident that it is precisely here that, for the first time, we encounter *faith* in our investigations.[1]

Therefore though it is erected upon the earthly given, the church is grounded in divine possibility. Until its elevation to *ecclesia triumphans*, or its dissolution in *communio sanctorum*, it is the salt of the earth, the actual ground of the world's continued existence; the Body of Christ sustains the body of earth. Hence the dignity of the church and of its adherents: "the saints shall judge the world".[2] Here the idea of community attains almost its highest culmination, since the community, thus given in the church, possesses metaphysical significance; its limits are world wide and its essence the nature of God Himself, the love of Christ. The primitive community between the family and the dead now persists in transfigured form: community with God includes that with the departed, the bond of the church binds even beyond the grave. The church is the virgin, the bride, the throne and the bosom of God; a virgin mother who continually gives birth to the faithful:[3] "Christ is the bridegroom and the church the bride, by whom are borne each day spiritual sons to the venerable Father."[4] Thus the mother's image[5] is again presented to our eyes, but a mother whose powerfulness rests upon the generative act of the Father.

3. In the consciousness of the faithful, finally, the church has the character of *catholicity*. The primary meaning of "catholic", however, is not that the church embraces the whole world but, in accordance with the term's original significance, that it is a whole, an organism, whose head is Christ. Its catholicity concerns therefore not so much the extension of the church as its all-sufficiency: "Where Christ is", asserted Ignatius, "there is the catholic church"; and as catholic, the church, the Body of Christ, is in its Head organically united to the universal omnipotence. It is from this, then, that the all-embracing nature of the church arises, not however as a fact, but as a task, a *mission*: for where two or three are gathered together in His name, there He is and there is the catholic church.

---

[1] Bultmann, *op. cit.*, 172.

[2] 1 *Cor.* vi. 2. "The church is an 'eschatological' fact; the worshipping community, that is to say, regards itself not as a worldly phenomenon, but as pertaining to the Beyond." Bultmann, *ibid.*, 154.

[3] *cf.* F. C. Conybeare, *Jungfräuliche Mutter und jungfräuliche Kirche, AR.* IX, 1906. Harnack, *History of Dogma*, III, 108, 109; *cf.* Luther's hymn "The holy Christian church":—"How dear to me is the faithful handmaiden", *etc.*

[4] Firmicus Maternus, *De errore profanarum religionum*, 19.   [5] Chap. 10.

The church's catholicity, again, implies its unity and its holiness. In it is completed what in other communities and covenants was merely outlined: the essence of community, the "sacred common element", is therefore not the mere being together, the fellowship to which one flees for refuge from dread. Far more is it something wholly different, something not given in the totality of the members, which creates a new organon. And this different factor is the first and the last, the essence and the primal ground of all things.

R. Bultmann, *Glauben und Verstehen*, 1933.
H. Frick, *Romantik und Realismus im Kirchenbegriff*, 1929.
E. Peterson, *Die Kirche*, 1929.
K. L. Schmidt, *Die Kirche des Urchristentums (Festgabe für A. Deissmann)*[2], 1927.

CHAPTER 37

NATION AND HUMANITY

1. FROM what has already been asserted about the sacred community there clearly follows the truth, as well as the one-sided exaggeration, of the so-called *sociological school*. That religion is no private affair, that in the realm of religion communality and collectivity assume an extraordinarily extensive status, in fact that the search for Power is essentially connected with the flight from solitude:—all these are facts. But all the less, therefore, have we any ground for allowing the religious to be merged in the social; for the sacred common element is not sacred because it is common but, on the contrary, common because it is sacred; and in worshipping God humanity does not worship itself, but worships God as it were in assembling itself together. Thus the sociological hypothesis is really only a new form of Feuerbach's which, as we observed,[1] ultimately originates from Xenophanes:—Man makes for himself a God after his own image: only here the image is that not of the individual but of the totality. Certainly all this is quite correct— "but the mischief is that the vital nerve of sacredness is lacking here. For it consists not in binding together in fellowship, nor in the audacious hypostatization of the spirit of common feeling, but persists obstinately in an irrationality. If that is taken away, then religion is powerless."[2]

2. Sacredness adheres to the community, however, even when it develops from tribe to *state* and *nation*, thereby gradually becoming secularized. Sacredness is thus preserved for a long time because the state is at first a city, *polis*,[3] and then the powerfulness of the locality coincides with that of the community. This city community, again, may become a world empire and yet remain essentially a city community, since the Roman empire, and in fact every empire, depended on the predominance of a town or a tribe until the development of nationality in its more modern sense; and in the course of this process power became concentrated in the figure of the ruler, who possessed an almost divine dignity.[4] The idea of the nation, then, arises very late as the coalescence of the concepts of tribe and empire. To it there

[1] Chap. 8.   [2] Söderblom, *Gottesglaube*[1], p. 210; *cf.* Wach, *Religionssoziologie*, X.
[3] Chap. 57.   [4] *ibid.*, 13.

pertain the common historical experience and the fact of having long lived together, associated with the now relatively unimportant blood relationship. The Jewish people is the first historic example of a nation, the other peoples of antiquity being either tribes or empires; and both types regarded themselves as being the actual world, while their rulers likewise had a cosmic significance. Egypt and Babylon were the world, but not nations, while Israel, oppressed among the peoples, experienced the potency of the people as something of its very own, as national. The same relationship subsists with respect to the Holy Roman empire and the European nations that have come into being since the Renaissance: Switzerland, the Netherlands, France *etc*. For long periods, however, the tribal power often combated the new idea of nation (Particularism), while it was frequently displaced by the concept of empire (Imperialism).

But in spite of all secularization the nation's potency still counts as sacred, as is perfectly obvious in times of great excitement; then a national altar is erected or, in the peril of war, the nation's God is invoked. From the standpoint of enlightened deistic belief in God, however, this is an absurdity, and considered in the light of the faith of the catholic church, even a sin. Phenomenologically, nonetheless, it possesses an intrinsic propriety, since it is precisely an attempt to bring one's own powerfulness into the closest possible relation to Power as such. *Nationalism* is always religious; and again the most grandiose example of such religious nationalism is to be discerned among the Jews. Israel is not the tribe nor empire whose limits are those of the world, or should be so: it is a people among peoples. But among all these it is the chosen: God is its God: the people is God's people. And the people's God is also the God of the history that has been experienced in common: the God of Abraham, Isaac and Jacob, who led the people out of Egypt, out of the house of bondage. But what we describe, phenomenologically, as a grand attempt to appropriate God's Power, appears to believers themselves as a glorious act of God who has chosen his people.

3. Social order also can be the expression of definite potencies, and thus *classes* and *castes* have their own religious value. Until modern enthusiasm for the working classes reminded us that these religious valuations do not belong wholly to the past, medieval knighthood offered the finest example of this principle. Frequently the caste is a tribe that has become merged within a foreign people either as rulers or as pariahs;[1] we know well,[2] for example, how profound is the separa-

[1] Weber, *op. cit.*, II, 14 *f*.   [2] *cf.* further Chap. 2.

tion between the potencies of the castes in British India. It precludes, for instance, communal eating: if an untouchable merely sees a brahmin's food it is defiled, while marriage between members of unequal castes is strictly forbidden. When the British authorities established public kitchens during a famine, the places assigned to the higher castes at the tables had to be separated from the others by chalked lines.

4. The equivalence of all potencies which the idea of *humanity* involves leads in the direction opposite from that of castes; this is however a comparatively recent development, and we can safely say that humanity, as such, was first discovered by the Stoics, and afterwards by the eighteenth century.[1] For in accordance with Schiller's dictum, from Christians Rousseau recruited men. That man as man has certain rights (*droits de l'homme!*), that humanity as such is the strongest bond that links men together, that all men are brothers so far as convention does not arbitrarily sever the connection—all this is the discovery of the age of enlightenment. Here mankind appears as itself worthy of adoration: and it is no matter of chance that the sociological theory, to which I have just referred, originated from the school of thought of the philosopher who in his later years founded a regular *culte de l'humanité*: Auguste Comte. *Humanité* is the *Grand-Être*, and the philosopher its high priest.

This "religion of humanity," however, has enjoyed scarcely any cult development in our secularized era; all the more powerfully, nonetheless, does the magic of humanity still operate: it is the sole entity worthy of worship that remained to thousands after the fierce conflagration of potencies in the nineteenth century. At one time virtuous, as for the age of enlightenment:

> He who delights not in such teachings
> Deserves not to be a man.[2]

At another time, realistically, as in Goethe's sense:

> For all human failings
> Pure humanity atones:

again, romantically: every mother a Virgin Mary: then as "reverence for life": it has persisted to our own time, especially in its woes. And

[1] To be human is in itself a value in the new Comedy; *cf.* the excellent history of the development of the idea in Mühl, *Die antike Menscheitsidee in ihrer geschichtlichen Entwicklung.*   [2] *The Magic Flute.*

there, at long last, it found cult forms also. Under the *Arc de triomphe de l'Étoile* burns the eternal flame from the grave of the *Unknown Soldier* who, in his anonymity, represents the whole of vast suffering humanity, and before whom the nations bow.[1]

Humanity then is the sole community that can vie with the church in catholicity. But it lacks the Head which constitutes the church a living organism;[2] nor has it any mission. And it is precisely in its mission that the paradoxical character of the church is revealed: the given people, which simultaneously is the spiritual community never existent in fact—the community that both is and is not—that is the church, and it embraces the world. On the other hand, humanity is far too existent: we all belong to it, and for us there remain no possibilities. This is the poverty of humanity as community.

E. Durkheim, *Les règles de la méthode sociologique*[7], 1919.

M. Mühl, *Die antike Menschheitsidee in ihrer geschichtlichen Entwicklung*, 1928.

[1] The so-called "Mother's Day" is a less significant expression of the same consciousness of humanity.

[2] On the contrast between humanity and the church *cf.* Mühl, *op. cit.*, 115: "the idea of universality prevalent in antiquity amalgamates with the church and is absorbed in the concept of *catholicity*"; *cf.* again Maritain, *Religion and Culture*, 10, 19, 21, 37. Humanity is the "naturizing" of the kingdom of God or the church.

CHAPTER 38

COMMUNIO SANCTORUM

1. *CREDO . . . communionem sanctorum*, of the *Apostles' Creed*, was added only at a later period to *credo . . . unam sanctam catholicam ecclesiam*. Perhaps its original meaning was: "I believe that there subsists a participation in the sacred elements (of the sacrament)", while in the Middle Ages the expression acquired the significance—community of all, both living and departed. The Reformation, however, opposed the community of saints to the visible hierarchy of the Roman church, and rejoiced that "it was no longer necessary to see it with our eyes nor feel it with our hands", because the essence of this community rests on election by God and the constancy of Christ.[1] In both interpretations, nonetheless, the departure from tangibility and visibility is important, although this does not distinguish essentially between *communio sanctorum* and the church, which after all also has its actual being in God's act unrestricted by the limits of life. The idea of *communio sanctorum*, then, as regarded from the phenomenological viewpoint, is independent of all other factors, and also of course extremely momentous, only in its ancient Christian form, according to which it is the community of angels and all "the elect".[2] Thus the congregation experiences a foretaste of this highest community in the sacrament, the *praefatio* of which proclaims God's holiness "with Angels and Archangels, with Thrones and Dominions, and with all the company of heaven";[3] here, in communion with the Lord Who became flesh, the celestial community is foretasted. But though its essence is "beyond", the church has firm roots on earth, in the people and the given: *communio sanctorum* can be understood only eschatologically. It is wholly possibility, that is the hope of man and the promise of God.

2. I think that the most remarkable feature of the supreme community that is the Christian church is that it represents the deed of Him Who in His life proceeded from solitude to solitude. When all had abandoned Him, in the anguish of death God abandoned Him

---

[1] Calvin, *Institutio christianae religionis*, IV, 1, 3.
[2] Harnack, *History of Dogma*, V, 243 *ff*.   [3] Chap. 16.

too: "My God, my God, why has Thou forsaken me?" From this utmost dread, however, from this most desolate solitude as we perceive it in Gethsamene and on Golgotha, there springs the most intense communion; and this is the paradox of Christian faith, which unites solitude and community in the "Body of Christ". The struggle against dread was decided once for all by the Head of that Body: in the agony of the Mount of Olives, in the forsakenness of the Cross, all dread and loneliness are overcome. The "Body", the church, experiences this victory; but she must repeatedly attain to it anew, since she is not *communio sanctorum*. She is the mother who cherishes and protects until the ultimate victory; for "there is no other means of entering into life unless she (the church) conceive us in the womb and give us birth, unless she nourish us at her breasts and, in short, keep us under her charge and government, until (*donec*), divested of mortal flesh, we become like the angels".[1] This *donec* is the great word of eschatology:[2] with it human community ends, and divine community begins, which was, however, always at the foundation of every human community, to be believed in as its sole powerfulness.

[1] Calvin, *Institutio*, IV, 1, 4.   [2] Chap. 87.

C. THE SACRED WITHIN MAN: THE SOUL

CHAPTER 39

THE SOUL AS A WHOLE

1. "THOU canst not discover the bounds of the soul albeit thou pacest its every road: so deep is its ground";[1] and the idea of the soul has never been a means merely of systematizing the functions of human consciousness. On the contrary it was always, and in all its most widely contrasted structures, numinous in its type and a means of indicating the sacred in man. Even the unconscious object can possess a soul, while it is the numinous that endows the living entity with consciousness, and not conversely. "There is life that is not also numinous. But the numinous quickens even the non-living; the stone that affects me numinously appears to me, at the same time, as a 'Something' which conceals within itself a mysterious and secret life."[2]

To the primitive mind then the soul it not a mere part of man, but the whole man in his sacredness; and we still speak to-day of a certain number of "souls" in the sense of men, not simply portions of men. Thus the experience of the mysterious and the remarkable, which gives rise to the idea of the soul, is here constituted by concrete reality, experienced as a unity.

Many years ago, following a suggestion advanced by Chantepie de la Saussaye, Kruyt coined the fine term "soul-stuff" for this soul structure.[3] Later, however, when in accordance with Dynamism he wished to assign to the idea of Power the first place in primitive thought, he withdrew the word; but it appears to me that in this he was somewhat precipitate. For it is the very characteristic of the concept of the soul that Power displays and reveals itself in stuff of any kind whatever. All souls have bearers: never and nowhere are they independent entities; correctly understood, therefore, the term "soul-stuff" includes the idea of Power,[4] and in the realm of primitive thought Power and stuff are never two distinct ideas. Thus we can speak of "soul-power"

---

[1] Heracleitus (Diels, *Fragmente der Vorsokratiker*, I, 86).

[2] Schmalenbach, *Die Entstehung des Seelenbegriffs, Logos*, 16, 1927, 330, 333 *et passim*. [3] *Animisme*, 2 ff.

[4] A. C. Kruyt, *Measa (Bydr. Taal-, Land- en Volkenkunde van N. I.* 74, 1918; 75, 1919; 76, 1920).

just as legitimately as of soul-stuff: in both cases it is a matter of certain powerful substances, or of a power attached to some substance.[1]

Current Greek popular belief, again, holds that widely spaced teeth make the retention of the "soul" difficult, so that whoever has these is short-lived, while at the same time they facilitate the inflow of soul-stuff: their possessor has erotic tendencies. As Hesseling remarks,[2] Homer knew long ago that "a hedge of teeth" is formed:—ἕρκος ὀδόντων: an example clearly exhibiting the connection between soul and power, "soul or *mana*", as Grönbech formulated it at the Congress at Leyden in 1912;[3] and in the interval, his thesis that soul and Power are essentially related has been brilliantly verified. Certainly this does not mean that every potency without exception is a soul entity, but that conversely the soul always implies powerfulness.[4]

This soul then, as one whole, is connected with some specific "stuff". It is not restricted to any single portion of the human body, but extends itself over all its parts according as these show themselves capable of some kind of powerfulness, just as blood is distributed throughout the whole body although certain organs are richer in blood than others. "As the sap oozes from the rubber plant whether it is notched on the trunk, a branch, or at the leaf edge: as the perfume of flowers arises from them and penetrates the surroundings: as blood flows through arteries and veins: and as perspiration runs from the pores and warmth emanates from the body: so the soul-stuff dwells in the body, proceeds from it and flows over everything that comes into contact with it."[5]

It is this powerfulness, thus conceived as "stuff", that the magician seeks to steal from his enemy or restore to his friend.[6] It is most carefully guarded, even in bodily excreta; strenuous effort is exerted to increase it and by every method prevent its disappearance. It is "stuff", matter, although in primitive modes of thought, which is aware of no dualism of body-spirit, this certainly implies no materialism. Stuff

---

[1] cf. also M. P. Nilsson, *Primitive Religion*, 1911, 16 f. Kruyt, *Animisme*, 1 ff.

[2] C. D. Hesseling, *Versl. & Meded. Kon. Akad. v. Wet. Afd. Lett.* 5. Reeks, 2, 1917.

[3] *Actes du IVᵉ Congrès d'Hist. des Religions*, 1913, 70. cf. Schmalenbach, *op. cit.* Söderblom, *Gottesglaube*, 66 f.

[4] But obviously not a specific potency such as *mana*. "Power" is something more than *mana*. In the sciences concerned with religion we should accustom ourselves to say in advance when a concept like *mana*, or *tabu*, is to be understood in the original and ethnologically specified sense, and when as a general or generic idea. This would obviate much misunderstanding; e.g. not every Melanesian soul has *mana*. But every soul, whether Melanesian or not, has *mana* in its sense of power.

[5] Ch. Kaysser, in Beth, *Religion und Magie*, 152; cf. N. Adriani, *Posso*, 1919, 87 f.

[6] Beth, *ibid.*, 137 ff.

is always and simultaneously power; but both the diminution and the enhancing of soul-stuff are conceived materially. Thus a soul can be eaten: to eat the enemy's heart implies augmenting one's own soul-stuff;[1] and the Egyptian *ka* was a soul-being which could eat and which eventually was also eaten; the term is even etymologically connected with the word for food.[2] According to a very ancient concept occurring in the *Pyramid Texts*, again, the dead king ascends to heaven as victor, and with his attendants catches the gods with a lasso. A dreadful terror then seizes upon the heavens; the earth's bones tremble; the king, "who lives on his fathers and consumes his mothers", who "eats men and lives upon the gods", strangles the celestial beings and disembowels them; then they are cooked in glowing pots. The great gods he eats for breakfast, the intermediate deities at midday and the lesser gods for supper; he lives "on the essence of each of the gods, when he eats the entrails of those who come, with their stomachs filled with *ḥkaw*, (a psychic power of a magical character)". He "eats their *ḥkaw*, he devours their *iakhw* (another psychic power)". "Him whom he encounters on his way he eats quite raw." "Behold the *ba* (yet another psychic being) of the gods is within the king's stomach."[3] This is cannibalism raised to the level of the myth, but not wholly deprived of a certain grandeur despite its crass horror; and it yields profound insight into the nature of the primitive soul as a whole. One can eat power, and food has a psychic quality.

2. Soul-power was definitely regarded as being present in almost every part of the body, even in what it extrudes; and the idea of power in the *breath*, or the so-called breath-soul, has had the weightiest influence upon the psychology of almost all peoples and times down to the present day. From this concept too were derived the most important terms for the essence of the soul: *ātman*, *spiritus*, *anima*, *Seele*, πνεῦμα, רוּחַ.[4] Certainly the powerfulness of breath was not only established negatively, as Animism supposed, by inferring its psychic quality from its disappearance at the moment of death; rather was an independent life discerned in it, a life not relaxed even in sleep; the pulse beat,

---

[1] F. D. E. van Ossenbruggen, *Het primitieve Denken* (*Bydr. Taal-Land-en Volkenk. v. N. I.*, 1915), 34.

[2] So in the first instance, W. B. Kristensen, *Aegypternes Forestillinger om Livet efter Döden*, 1896, 14 *f.*; later, several others; *cf.* Ad. Erman and H. Grapow, *Wörterbuch der Ägyptischen Sprache*, V, 1931, 86 *ff.*

[3] *Pyramidentexte* (Sethe), 393 *ff.*, 278, 444; *cf.* van der Leeuw, *Godsvoorstellingen in de oud-aegyptische Pyramidetexten*, 41 *f.*   [4] Jevons, *Introduction*, 44.

the rise and fall of the chest, appeared to be specific life and to possess specific powerfulness.[1] The kiss also, which so frequently has some ritual meaning, was probably intended as a reciprocal transference of the breath-soul and as an exact parallel of blood brotherhood. But equally when it is a question of the life of the Universe, of cosmology, breath is the mighty generator. God breathes into man the breath of life through his nostrils,[2] and still more generally:

> When thou recallest their breath, they die.
> Yet a breath from thee brings them into being.[3]

Together with breath, *blood* is a highly important soul-bearer; in the course of the sacrifice for blessing a house in the Dutch East Indies, for instance, the posts and pillars of the building are sprinkled with blood,[4] while in *Exodus* xii, the blood besprinkled on the Israelites' doors was intended to avert death. I may presuppose that the part played by blood in the sacrificial ritual of the Old Testament is quite familiar: the blood was the soul of the flesh,[5] and Christian thought about the redemptive value of the blood of Christ has, in essence, conserved this concrete conception of the soul. According to this idea, blood is not only "a quite peculiar sort of juice",[6] but the power of salvation in general:

> Unclean I am, but cleanse me in Thy Blood:
> Of which a single drop, for sinners spilt,
> Can purge the entire world from all its guilt.[7]

And we know that blood, regarded concretely and physically, has held and still holds, both in theology and in popular piety, *e.g.* in the Salvation Army, a very prominent rôle that is grounded on the sacrificial

---

[1] Schmalenbach, *loc. cit.*, 332; Wundt, *op. cit.*, IV, 135.   [2] *Gen.* ii. 7.
[3] *Ps.* civ. 29 f. (Moffat); *cf.* the remarkable cosmological speculation concerning breath among the Annamites, Saintyves, *Force*, 72 ff.
[4] Kruyt, *Animisme*, 23.   [5] *Lev.* xvii. 11.   [6] *Faust*, Part I, 1386.
[7] Thomas Aquinas' hymn, *Adoro te devote:*

> Me immundum munda
> Tuo sanguine,
> Cuius una stilla
> Salvum facere
> Totum mundum quit ab
> Omni scelere.

Huizinga compares the words from Marlowe's *Faustus*: "See, where Christ's blood streams in the firmament! One drop of blood will save me": *Herfsttty*, 368.

practice of the Old Testament and, like this, can be understood only in the light of the psychically powerful quality of blood.

Among bodily powers that are regarded as soul-stuff there emanate from the body, like blood and breath, *spittle, perspiration and urine*. *Corpse sweat* also pertains to this category, being used by the peoples of Madagascar, who believe that the newly incarnate soul arises from it.[1] Of a different type, again, are the souls called by Wundt *Organ-souls*, the potencies of separate parts of the body.[2] Here the *head* must be given special mention,[3] since as the receptacle of soul-stuff it became the keenly desired booty of head hunters in the Indian archipelago;[4] then the *heart*,[5] the *liver* and the *eye*.[6] The latter, painted on the bows of ships, has from ancient times protected the sailors of the Mediterranean, while in ancient Egypt the myth of the eye of Horus placed this part of the body in cosmic relations: it was brought to the dead, sometimes as the sun and again as a symbol for sacrifice as the fullness of life, "so that they may receive a soul from it".[7] Still further, the *larynx* and the *left side*,[8] the *great toes* and the *thumb*[9], must be mentioned.

In the case of all the above, further, it must be remembered that no bodily nor organ-soul embraces psychical powerfulness *entirely*, while excluding the remaining parts of the body. Soul-stuff actually exists in the whole body; but it is indicated only with reference to such place or places where it exhibits its power. Thus everything in man can be "soul", if only it is powerful; but in fact we cannot justifiably maintain this limitation to man alone. It has already been observed that in the primitive structure of the human mind, man is never opposed to his environment, but belongs to it; and in conformity with this, we discover no difference in principle between the soul of man and that of his environment, especially of the animal and the plant world. The Indonesians, for example, indicate both the human soul and that of the rice by the same word: *sumangat*,[10] while the Bahaus of Borneo call both souls *bruwa*;[11] and even so-called inorganic Nature possesses

[1] Wundt, *op. cit.*, IV, 148; Hertz, *Mort*, 77.

[2] Wundt, *ibid.*, 79; *cf.* Nilsson, *Primitive Religion*, 44. Kruyt, *Animisme*, 2 *ff.*

[3] Kruyt, *ibid.*, 17 *ff.*

[4] On the head as soul, *cf.* G. Weicker, *Der Seelenvogel*, 1902, 30 *f.*

[5] Schmalenbach, *loc. cit.*, 352.   [6] Wundt, *op. cit.*, IV, 105 *ff.*

[7] *Pyramidentexte* (Sethe), 578.   [8] By the Eskimo; Thalbitzer, *Actes*, 139.

[9] Fr. Pfister, *Blätter zur bayr. Volkskunde*, 11, 1927; *cf.* too the widespread fairy tales about Tom Thumb.

[10] Kruyt, *Animisme*, 136 *f.* W. W. Skeat, *Malay Magic*, 136 *ff.*

[11] A. W. Nieuwenhuis, *Zeitschr. f. Völkerkunde und Soziologie*, 1, 2, 1925, 1926.

soul-stuff. In all this there is certainly no "panpsychism" (a theoretical creation!), but at the same time no limits are imposed to the imparting of soul;[1] and the same absence of limitations prevails when man differentiates himself from other men. An individual therefore, in the nineteenth century sense of the term, was unknown to the primitive world: still less an "individual soul". According to our own phraseology two friends are "one heart and one soul", but to ancient German sentiment they were such without any metaphor at all. The tribe, which embraced all those who were united by "peace",[2] had a collective soul; its powerfulness, that is, was exhibited in its members, even if in varying degrees.[3]

No separation at all was possible, again, within the personality of man himself: potentially everything was soul, even if it did not manifest itself precisely as soul-power; and even what, according to our ideas, does not belong, or no longer pertains, to the person, could participate in the soul. Thus the bride in the fairy tale, who has lost the cloth with the three drops of her mother's blood, becomes "weak and powerless";[4] and the removal from the person concerned is in this instance twofold: in the first place, it is not her own soul-stuff whose loss renders her impotent but her mother's, which amounts to the same thing; and in the second, the soul-stuff has been separated from its bearer for a long time. The fairy tale *motif* of the protective, speaking, or otherwise influential drops of blood, actually belongs to another soul structure,[5] but here too it can exhibit that absence of limitations which is characteristic of soul-stuff structure. Similarly in the fairy story of *Beloved Roland*, the girl in her flight lets fall three drops of the slain man's blood, which delay the approaching witch.[6] In an Indian fairy tale, again, even moccasins play a warning part, and remind us that in the primitive structure of the human mind man was not a spirituality achieved by any artificial means but, just as he is, a totality in which everything might be "soul".[7]

For the "soul" designates not life and nothing more, and still less consciousness, but whatever is replete with power and effectiveness.

[1] Chap. 9.   [2] Chap. 33.   [3] Grönbech, *op. cit.*, II, 105, 111.
[4] Grimm's *Fairy Tales*, "The Goose Girl".
[5] Chap. 42; *cf.* further Arbmann, *Zur primitiven Seelenvorstellung* (*Le monde oriental*, I, XX, 1926; II, XXI, 1927); 366.
[6] Grimm, *ibid.* No. 56. In one variant, connected with Hänsel and Gretel, she spits thrice and the spittle gives the witch her answer—it is just another soul-stuff. J. Bolte und G. Polivka, *Anmerkungen zu den Kinder- und Hausmärchen der Brüder Grimm*, I, 1913, 498 f.
[7] W. Krickeberg, *Indianermärchen aus Nord-Amerika*, 1924, 164.

It implies that there is a "life" which is more than merely being alive;[1] the latter condition indeed is not observed by primitive man, who does not even appreciate the distinction between organic and inorganic; but the "numinous quickens even the non-living".[2]

Within this primary soul structure however, even that of soul-stuff, the soul is in one way a principle of separation; but it does not sever stuff from power, and still less body from soul; it only divides what is indifferent from what is full of the numinously effective.

For this type of soul, finally, *death* has but little meaning; the departed is no soul-being, but a complete, dead man.[3] In this primary form, then, the soul is not a being to be in principle differentiated from other religious forms, except in that it always requires a bearer. But even when regarded from this aspect the soul very closely resembles, for example, the power-object, the fetish. It is just one numinous formation together with others: fetishes, sacred trees, demons, spirits, gods[4]; the form of some numinous experience whose object is not even limited to man.[5]

ACTES du Ve Congrès intern. d'Hist. des Religions à Lund, 1929.

E. ARBMANN, *Zur primitiven Seelenvorstellung (Le monde oriental, I, XX*, 1926, *II, XXI*, 1927).

A. BERTHOLET, *Dynamismus und Personalismus in der Seelenauffassung*, 1930.

A. E. CRAWLEY, *The Idea of the Soul*, 1909.

G. VAN DER LEEUW, *Phénoménologie de l'âme (Revue d'histoire et de philosophie religieuses*, 1930).

L. LÉVY-BRUHL, *The Soul of the Primitive.*

H. SCHMALENBACH, *Die Entstehung des Seelenbegriffs (Logos*, 16, 1927).

[1] Schmalenbach, *loc. cit.*, 333.   [2] *ibid.*
[3] Chap. 14, 24; *Actes du Ve Congrès intern. d'Hist. des Religions à Lund*, 1929, 91; Nilsson.   [4] *cf.* Schmalenbach, *loc. cit.* 324.
[5] In ancient Egypt, the plural *baw* meant sometimes "souls", at other times "power", and again "divine beings" or "ancestors".

CHAPTER 40

SOULS IN THE PLURAL

1. THE second soul structure also, with which we are here concerned, includes not that differentiation between body and soul so familiar to ourselves, but merely that between soul and soul. Thus it can readily be understood how it has happened that we are able to represent the different potencies, experienced within man, as a number of more or less sharply outlined soul-beings; for the very character of soul-stuff, which is in no sense exclusive—in the heart for instance, but simultaneously in the head or elsewhere—itself leads to plurality.

Of course it is not here a matter of differentiating in accordance with our own categories—*e.g.* will, feeling, spirit *etc.* Soul-power is divided among various other powers which—and this as distinct from the previous structure—possess a certain consistency, but whose peculiar nature is determined by experiences that, to a great extent, are no longer available to us.[1] "The idea of a soul is not found among primitives. That which takes its place is the representation, usually a very emotional one, of one or more coexistent and intertwined participations, as yet not merged into the distinct consciousness of an individuality which is really one."[2] Certain influences upon definite vital activities, certain connections with specific experiences, are condensed into soul-beings—that is all that we can say. The distinction drawn by the Eskimo, for example, between body, soul and name, from which the soul then divides itself up according to its various potencies localized in different parts of the body, is quite clear to us.[3] Essentially, this is nothing more than a somewhat systematized view of soul-stuff. The division of soul-power in the *Brahmana Texts*, again, also seems fairly intelligible: spirit, breath, speech, food, the water pertaining to the body, bone, marrow, eyes and ears. These are partly body-, or organ-souls, and partly designations, like speech and spirit, which we appear to understand without difficulty, but which nevertheless we certainly do not completely apprehend in their original specific character.[4] But ancient Egypt offers us the most remarkable and most incomprehensible example. So long as bodily powers are

---

[1] Preuss, *Geistige Kultur,* 18.   [2] Lévy-Bruhl, *How Natives Think,* 89.
[3] Thalbitzer, in *Actes . . .,* 139.   [4] Oldenberg, *Lehre,* 18.

concerned we can grasp the differentiation here almost immediately, as for example: "air is in my nose, the seminal fluid in my sex organ".[1] But the precise meaning of *ka, ba, akh, šḥm etc.* is no longer apparent to us at all. Again and again well-meaning scholars attempt to force the Egyptian soul-beings into our current categories, but without our understanding them even slightly more clearly; and to-day it is no longer possible to say which human potency was really meant by the idea of *ka*, although we can certainly indicate a few characteristics. It is still more impossible, however, to establish the relationship between the various soul-potencies; but this is not at all remarkable, since even modern "faculty psychology" has been able to produce little in this respect. Only two points, then, are clear: in the first place, that the soul appears here *in plurali*; secondly, that each soul occupies the entire man and that it is not a matter of "the component parts of human personality". We should dispense finally with this mode of expression, derived from faculty psychology, since it accords with neither the soul of ancient nor of modern man.[2]

The dead person is addressed thus: "thy *ba* is in thee, thy *šḥm* is behind thee".[3] We know that the *ba* is a soul sometimes more of the soul-stuff type, and at other times more of the form type, appearing then in the guise of a bird. We know too that the *šḥm* was originally a staff, and that probably the soul-being was really the power of this staff. But we can gain no deeper insight into the mutual relationships of these two types; we can only be certain that the Egyptian, the higher he desired to elevate the power of the person whom he was addressing, the more soul-potencies he ascribed to him: "Thou art pure, thy *ka* is pure, thy *ba* is pure, thy *šḥm* is pure."[4] Further, it was possible to possess a plurality of some type of soul: already in the *Pyramid Texts*, the dead—but therefore all the more powerful—king had several *kas*;[5] subsequently, this plurality was systematized by the number fourteen, and thus each of the fourteen *kas* of the sun-god bears the name of some powerfulness such as abundance, riches, victory, splendour *etc.*[6]

---

[1] *Pyramidentexte* (Sethe), 1061.

[2] For Egypt *cf.* L. J. Cazemier, *Oud-egyptiese voorstellingen aangaande de ziel*, 1930, where a wide range of references may be found.

[3] *Pyramidentexte*, 2010, *cf.* 162, and further van der Leeuw, *Godsvoorstellingen in de oud-aegyptische Pyramidetexten, passim.*

[4] *Pyramidentexte*, 837; *cf.* 992 *ff.* K. Sethe, *Urkunden der 18. Dynastie*, I, 1906, 244.

[5] 396.

[6] A. H. Gardiner, *Proc. Soc. Bibl. Arch.* 38, 1916, 84. *cf.* F. W. von Bissing, *Versuch einer neuen Erklärung des kai, Ber. Münch. Akad.* 1911. J. H. Breasted, *Ancient Records of Egypt*, II, 210.

An even unlimited number could be assumed: "Ra's million *kas* were the protection of his subjects."[1] Thus on the one hand the plural expressed the quantitative character of the soul's power: one could possess more or less of it; on the other hand, the attempt was made to release this power from any mere plurality by differentiation. In this manner the specific soul-powers received a certain independence, which could further become the exact contrary of the stuff-like plurality of the soul. We can still observe the same process in the abnormal mind, in whose consciousness individual powers have become independent of each other: the sex organ is regarded as a child, hairs that have been torn out as snakes *etc.*[2]

In West Africa, for example, four souls are distinguished: that which survives the body: that dwelling within an animal in the wilderness, the so-called bush-soul: the shadow, and the dream-soul;[3] the Melanesians, again, distinguish a life-soul, *tarunga*, from the soul persisting after death, *tindalo*,[4] while the Bahaus, on the Island of Borneo, draw a distinction between a *bruwa* which can leave the body, and the *ton luwa*, the corporeal soul. At death the *bruwa* abandons the body for ever;[5] and many Malayan tribes enumerate seven souls.[6]

In this many-sided differentiation, still further, even the body itself may also be accounted a soul and included together with others; and to "modern"—that is to Greek—thought this must appear most surprising; to the Egyptians, however, the body, *d-t*, was a soul-power which is referred to together with *ka*, *ba etc.*[7] Dualism is here still remote: the body is one power among many others.

2. The plural soul thus approximates closely to the idea of undifferentiated power-stuff; quantity prevents clearly defined formation which, conversely, becomes more intelligible as differentiation is completed. To the Egyptian mind one might be "strong in *baw* (souls or soul-stuff), and manifold in being";[8] a person could have a "great *ka*"; and often we cannot tell whether the plural of *ka* and *ba* should be translated as

[1] P. Lacau, *Textes religieux égyptiens* I, 1910, Nr. 78.

[2] A. Storch, *Das archaisch-primitive Erleben und Denken der Schizophrenen*, 1922, 24.

[3] Mary Kingsley, *West African Studies*, 199 *ff.*; *cf.* C. G. Seligman, *Multiple Souls in Negro-Africa* (*Ancient Egypt*, 1915, 103 *ff.*).

[4] Codrington, *op. cit.*, 248 *f. cf.* Marett, *The Threshold of Religion*, 136.

[5] Nieuwenhuis, *Wurzeln des Anim.*, 36 *f.*

[6] Kruyt, *Animisme*, 6 *f.* Skeat, *Malay Magic*, 50.

[7] G. van der Leeuw, *Godsvoorstellingen*, 32 *f.*   [8] *Pyramidentexte*, 901.

plurals or as undifferentiated powerfulness.[1] The idea of the plural soul is therefore a genuinely transitional structure; and as such it constitutes the presupposition of every form of Dualism, whether body is separated from soul, or soul from spirit.

The differentiation arising here may then be compared to the formation of distinct divine forms; in both cases it is a matter of the division of power between different beings. Actual Dualism, however, is present just as little in Polypsychism as in Polytheism, although both are conditions of its coming into being.

[1] *Pyramidentexte*, 560. K. Hoffmann, *Die theophoren Personnamen des älteren Ägyptens*, 1915, 23: "Great are the *kas* of Ptah" (a proper name); *cf.* 24.

CHAPTER 41

THE FORM OF THE SOUL

1. SOUL-STUFF has no form other than that of the body or some part thereof, while this in itself is not thought of as soul. "Stuff" itself is formless; and a genuine form is first of all acquired by the soul when man sees his own image, when he perceives himself in a mirror. But this again we must not interpret—with Animism—as if the reflected image had become the cause or stimulus of any primitive psychology. Rather was the sight of oneself a numinous experience, and the mirror image a revelation of the power attached to the self which was yet foreign and superior to it. The awakening and slightly tremulous consciousness, which is at the same moment the dawning of a mysterious powerfulness, has been tenderly and movingly depicted in Wagner's *Siegfried* music:

> ˙I came to the limpid brook,
> > And the beasts and the trees
> > > I saw reflected;
> > > Sun and clouds too,
> > > Just as they are,
> > Were mirrored quite plain in the stream.
> > > I also could spy
> > > This face of mine.[1]

The Narcissus experience, then, is essentially numinous, the discovery of one's own powerfulness that is yet strangely foreign, uncontrollable, superior and mysterious. That man represents his soul by his own image implies, therefore, not that the soul is only one form of himself: on the contrary, it means that in the soul man seeks to fathom his own essence, which is concealed from him and yet superior to him.

Thus the image, the form of man and of things in general, is at the same time their power, their essence; and the replacing of attendants and of sacrifices by their images is very familiar, for example, in what we know of ancient Egypt. The representations of provisions, servants *etc.* in the *mastabas* or private tombs were frequently multiplied, "so

[1] *Siegfried*, Act I (Armour).

that if one of them was destroyed to such an extent that it seemed about
to lose its influence, then the substitutes stepped in and on their own
part brought to the dead man his revenues".[1] The image (to repeat)
is the essence; but the essence again is more than mere individuality:
it is power. Hence the danger of looking at one's own image; on the
Banks' Islands, for instance, there is a deep hole into which no one ever
ventures to look; for should the water in the cave reflect a man's face
he would die.[2]

Like the mirror image, the *name* also is the essence of the soul, and
even its form, in a stuff-like way that is very strange to ourselves; but
I have already given the name a detailed discussion.[3] Here therefore I
need add only that the rite of naming is equivalent to bestowing a soul;
and to the Germanic peoples the father's act in giving the child a
name counted as a birth just as much as did the *accouchement*.[4] In
Egypt, again, the names of gods were their limbs, created by the
sun-god;[5] one deity affirms: "I am this name, which the sole lord
created when as yet there were not two things on earth."[6]

2. A very striking human representation or image, and therefore
one of the most important forms of the soul, is the *shadow*;[7] this is
necessary to life, if indeed it is not life itself. Demonic beings belonging
to the nether world, have no shadows; thus in Java no shadows of spirit
animals, like black chickens and cats, can be seen.[8] The dead too lack
shadows, both for Dante and among Central African negroes, while
the Basutos believe that a crocodile can overcome a passer-by if it
seizes his shadow cast on the water.[9] Similarly at the erection of the main
pillar of a house, in Malacca, care must be taken not to allow the
workmen's shadows to fall on it, since that would cause all sorts of
misfortune;[10] and in Arcadia whoever entered the temple of Zeus
Lycaeus lost his shadow and died within a year.[11] But though the dead
man can have no shadow, he can be a shade, σκιά;[12] and here again the
element that is foreign, and yet is one's own, is stressed; the departed
is still *l'homme mort*, but he is at the same moment the "Other", the
stranger.

[1] G. Maspero, *Geschichte der Kunst in Ägypten*, 1913, 35.
[2] Codrington, *The Melanesians*, 186.   [3] Chap. 17.
[4] Grönbech, *op. cit.*, II, 128 *f*.   [5] *e.g. The Book of the Dead*, Chap. 17.
[6] Lacau, *Textes religieux*, No. 78; *cf*. A. H. Gardiner, *loc. cit.*, 37, 1915, 255.
[7] J. von Negelein, *Bild, Spiegel und Schatten im Volksglauben*, AR. 5.
[8] Kruyt, *Animisme*, 68 *ff*.   [9] Alviella, *op. cit.*, 33.   [10] Kruyt, *ibid.*, 70.
[11] Pausanias, VIII, 38, 6.   [12] Jevons, *Introduction*, 44.

Still more intensely do this attraction and repulsion live in the idea of the *wraith*.[1] The Egyptian *ka* was such a wraith, even if this did not exhaust its character;[2] meeting the *ka* implied life. In popular belief, however, the power to see one's wraith involves nothing good;[3] but in any case a power is revealed, and the romantics, above all E. Th. A. Hoffmann, have made us experience once more, at least at secondhand, all the horror of the foreign element that is yet one's own.

The soul has also been thought of as a little man, *homunculus*; in this the forms of certain body-souls may have played a part, as for example the pupil with its "little man inside the eye", and the phallus or (euphemistically) the thumb.[4] The Hindu *ātman* is *purusha*, the "Tom Thumb" soul,[5] and the Toradja of Celebes imagine the soul as a "mannikin", *tonoana*.[6] The same soul-figure is believed in in Malacca where, in the case of sickness or fainting, the soul is recalled with the words:

> Hither, Soul, come hither!
> Hither, Little One, come hither!
> Hither, Bird, come hither!
> Hither, Filmy One, come hither![7]

The form of the *homunculus*, still further, is the best proof that in the case of the image-soul it is a matter not only of outward resemblance, nor even of the dream figure, alone. We must therefore realize the awe of the Narcissus experience, and the grim horror of the encounter with the wraith, if we wish to understand the human form of the soul in its numinous essence.

E. MONSEUR, *L'âme pupilline, L'âme poucet* (*RHR.* 41, 1905, 1 ff., 361 ff.).
J. VON NEGELEIN, *Bild, Spiegel und Schatten im Volksglauben* (*AR.* 5, 1902).
O. WASER, *Über die äussere Erscheinung der Seele* (*AR.* 16, 1913, 336 ff.).

[1] J. von Negelein, *ibid.*   [2] Chap. 42.
[3] In Ireland, *e.g.*, the "fetch", H. Gaidoz, *Mélusine* II, 1912, 264.
[4] Monseur, *L'âme pupilline, L'âme poucet*, RHR. 41, 1905, 1 ff., 361 ff.
[5] Oldenberg, *Lehre*, 52 f.
[6] Ankermann, in Chantepie, *op. cit.*, I, 146.   [7] Skeat, *Malay Magic*, 47 ff.

CHAPTER 42

THE "EXTERNAL SOUL"

1. IN discussing the soul structures thus far referred to we have frequently met with the idea of a soul outside the body—an "external soul"; or as I should prefer to say: psychic powers existed apart from the bodily power of the soul: often the soul of a dead man, but not always. The "external soul", then, has its own structure: and quite a considerable time ago Frazer[1] made this the object of extensive investigations, but without succeeding in assigning to it its specific and relevant place among the many concepts of the soul. This can be done only if we bear in mind that originally the "external soul" was merely one of many souls.[2] Owing to special conditions, however, it received a distinct status; and these must now be considered.

Here also, in the first place, man discovers within himself a powerfulness that is superior to him; and the fact that this superiority is connected with his own person by no means prevents him experiencing it as such, since he reverences equally the powerful implements that he himself has made. But now power appears to man as intimately linked with the external world; and in this way a path has been opened towards modern concepts, since we too can conceive superiority outside ourselves more easily than within us. Nevertheless the essential unity of Inner and Outer, of personal and foreign elements, which meets us here as in the case of the wraith, is sufficiently non-modern. Man learns that his own being, or at least an essential part thereof, is to be found "without"; here again environment and ego are not yet separated; and our comprehension of this attitude will be somewhat less difficult if we realize that the exteriorizing of power refers not to the soul alone, but to every power alike. Thus certain human potencies can be interpreted as possession: some superior power has settled within man.[3] According to our modern standpoint this is demonology, not psychology at all; but if the human power is regarded as "external soul" we may speak of a kind of psychology, however strange this may be. For the primitive mental outlook, however, this distinction had no weight whatever.

[1] In *The Golden Bough*.
[2] *cf.* J. Böhme, *Die Seele und das Ich im homerischen Epos*, 1929, 91, 89.
[3] Chap. 31.

2. As an introduction to this situation, let us consider two typical folk-tales. The Frankish king Guntram is asleep under a tree with a single attendant; a small animal creeps out of his mouth, runs to the brook and acts as if it wants to cross. The servant, who has remained awake, lays his sword over the stream; on this the animal crosses, disappears into a hole, and some time later returns by the same route. Then the king wakens and says: "I have had a strange dream: I saw a great wide river, spanned by an iron bridge which I crossed and reached a cavern in the mountains, where there lay inestimable treasure." Then the servant tells him what he had seen while the king was sleeping, and the place being subsequently dug up much gold and silver was discovered.[1] Thus in this instance the soul leaves the body in animal form.

Of the second type of this idea there are endless variations, of which one example must here suffice.[2] The hero of the fairy tale has to release a maiden from the power of a wicked giant; and by a trick the girl learns from the stupid giant where his heart is (in variants, also "soul", "life", "death"): "far, far away in a lake, there is an island: on the island there stands a church: in the church there is a fountain: in the fountain a duck is swimming: in the duck is an egg, and in the egg— there is my heart". Thus the giant, as the fairy tale neatly puts it, did not have "his heart with him", keeping the soul at a distance in this way being of course intended to ensure the giant's invulnerability and complete security. But it turns out quite otherwise; for the hero, with the assistance of the famous "helpful animals" of the fairy story, sets out and secures possession of the heart and then has the giant completely in his power. In both cases the "external soul" is, as it were, man rising above himself, what is in man and yet is more than man; a power

---

[1] Grimm, *Deutsche Sagen*; in *Gesta Romanorum* also, and frequently elsewhere.

[2] In Asbjörnson. Further, Klara Stroebe, *Nordische Volksmärchen*, II, 1919, No. 23. To the same type belong the following: *Tausend und eine Nacht*, V, 283 ff. *Drei Zitronen* (E. Littmann's Edition); Stroebe, *Nordische Volksmärchen*, II, No. 4; *Meleager and the Log* (or *Natal Torch*), Ovid, *Fasti* V, 305 ff. *Metam.* VIII, 260 ff. Grimm, *Kinder- und Hausmärchen*, No. 9, 60; *Bidasari und der Goldfisch*, Wilken, *op. cit.*, III, 296 ff., together with the stories about Punchkin the Magician and *Koshchei and the Egg*; cf. Frazer, *GB*, XI (*Balder the Beautiful*, II), 108 ff. The Story of the Two Brothers in *Popular Stories of Ancient Egypt* (Maspero). G. Röder, *Altägyptische Erzählungen und Märchen*, 1927; M. Burchardt, *Zeitschr. f. äg. Sprache*, 50, 1913, 118 f. W. Aichele, *Zigeunermärchen*, 1926, No. 27; Pol de Mont and A. de Cock, *Wondervertelsels uit Vlaanderen*, 1924, No. 28; *Phrixus and the Golden Fleece*, cf. Wundt, *op. cit.*, V, 426; G. Jungbauer, *Märchen aus Turkestan und Tibet*, 1923, No. 10; A. Leskien, *Balkanmärchen*, 1919, No. 26; A. Dirr, *Kaukasische Märchen*, 1920, No. 27.

essential to him can move about freely and attain a measure of security denied to man himself.

3. Those soul-powers which are only loosely connected with the body and which, in order to remain within the metaphor, we may now call "semi-detached", constitute a transitional form between soul-stuff and the "external soul", the hair being in this respect very prominent as a seat of soul-stuff among many peoples. The story of Samson, for instance, shows how the hair is regarded as the hero's strength; but at the same time how, because hair is easily removed, this might can be lost with very serious consequences.[1] In the fairy tale, similarly, some helpful animal gives the hero a hair or a feather which he must rub whenever he is in danger; then the animal will immediately appear. The most frequent form of this semi-detached soul is the shadow, which has already been discussed. But the idea of the soul's immateriality, which attains its predominance in another structure,[2] is also connected with the shadow. Fear of losing one's shadow is widespread, being very intense for example in West Africa, where going out at midday is avoided because at that time the body casts no shadow; and the negro's reply to Miss Kingsley's question, why he did not hesitate to go about in the dark, when also no shadow was to be seen, is very fine: "that was all right, because at night all shadows lay down in the shadow of the Great God, and so got stronger".[3] Here a simple trust in God is expressed in very primitive form: the great shadow of the night nourishes that of the individual from its own plenteousness. It is related about Sankara, again, that when travelling in Nepaul he quarrelled with the Grand Lama, and rose up into the air; but the Lama struck his knife into Sankara's shadow; falling to the ground, he broke his neck.[4] In ancient Egypt too the shadow counted as one of the many soul-powers, which were frequently all enumerated together whenever the king's eternal life was to be affirmed.

In the next place, the *after-birth* is a soul-being that leaves the bearer at the moment of his birth; nevertheless it remains connected with his own existence, and is for that reason carefully stored away or buried *etc.* by most primitive peoples. Thus the Baganda of Uganda regard the placenta as a twin of the newly born infant; and after the death of their

---

[1] Wilken, *op. cit.*, III, 553 *ff.*   [2] Chap. 43.
[3] *West African Studies*, 207. On similar fears in the Indian Archipelago *cf.* Riedel, *Sluik- en kroesharige rassen*, 61; also Kruyt, *Animisme*, 68 *ff*; von Negelein, *Seele als Vogel*, 1 *ff.*; Maspero, *Études égyptiennes*, I, 300.
[4] Frazer, *The Golden Bough*, III (*Taboo and the Perils of the Soul*), 78.

king, his jawbone is united with his after-birth in the grave; in this way
he returns to his soul, which was external.[1]

4. In these "semi-detached" souls the idea of power-stuff predominated. But as soon as the separation of soul from body is completed
another element appears; the environment is as it were drawn into the
ego, or rather: is not yet delimited therefrom. From childhood we
moderns are committed to the popular view that the soul somehow
resides within the body; even to-day it is only at death that popular
belief imagines a freely hovering soul escaping from the body. But
except in this last instance we refuse to assume any closer connection
between the external world and the soul; for us then, in the first place,
soul is consciousness, and tree and animal cannot possess our consciousness; and thus we become immovably fixed in the egotistic attitude of
conscious subjects dominating the objective world. The idea of the
"external soul", however, draws the conjoint and the environing realms
into our own lives and, conversely, establishes our existence within a
wider environment. For the soul is here neither consciousness nor ego,
but a power superior to the ego even though it is also connected therewith. We can understand the dead person's soul residing near, or in,
the grave; it is much more difficult, however, for us to grasp the idea
that the tombstone itself is a soul (נֶפֶשׁ), as is the case with Jewish
popular belief.[2] That the soul is born with ourselves is again a familiar
concept, but we can scarcely comprehend the soul being simultaneously
born in a tree, the life-tree, simply because we habitually oppose ego to
world.[3] It is clear that the line of demarcation between environment
and ego is absent; but how has it happened that the limit was over-
stepped at exactly this point:—this tree, this stone or animal?

To obtain as deep an insight as possible into this mode of thought,
so foreign to ourselves, we must now consider the most important form
of the "external soul", that of the bird soul. This concept is extraordinarily widespread. In the ancient Semitic world the dead were a
kind of bird; they chirped, had wings,[4] and were "attired like a bird with

---

[1] cf. the later discussion of the ka; also Flinders Petrie, in *Ancient Egypt*, 1914, 161.
A. M. Blackman, "The Pharaoh's Placenta and the Moon-God Khons" (*Journal of
Egyptian Archæology*, 3, 1916, 235 ff.). G. van der Leeuw, "The Moon-God Khons
and the King's Placenta" (*ibid.*, 5, 1918.

[2] Nilsson, *Actes . . .*, 95.

[3] Frazer, *Golden Bough*, XI (*Balder*, II), 165 ff. Jevons, *op. cit.*, 207; Chap. 5.

[4] *Isaiah* viii. 19. M. Jastrow, *Die Religion Babyloniens und Assyriens*, II, 1912,
957 f.

a wing-kerchief".[1] The Egyptian *ba* too was a bird, probably a stork,
often depicted with a human head, while yet another soul, the *akh*, was
the bird-shadow.[2] The bird soul appears also in many Greek myths,
and on an amphora in the British Museum the soul, in the guise of a
bird, may be seen leaving the body of the dying Procris.[3] The Hyperboreans again, who were actually the people of the dead, had wings:
"there is a story of certain men in Hyperborean Pallene who gain a
covering of light feathers for their bodies".[4]

The sirens, birds with human heads, were souls of the dead like the
keres, *erinyes*, harpies, and *stymphalides*,[5] while the idea still persists
in popular belief, wherein there are all sorts of birds which are dead
people, together with persons clothed in feathers—valkyries, shield-
maidens, swan-maidens *etc*.[6]—the winged angels or the departed of
Christianity pertaining to the same category. I shall attempt to illustrate
the structural connection between soul and bird by two examples. One
is ancient: according to Dio Cassius "in 217 A.D., the people recovering
from the terror inspired by Caracalla, and assembled at the races in the
Roman circus to celebrate the beginning of Severus' reign, greeted a
cawing jackdaw, which had perched on the obelisk, with the name
of the executed murderer of the emperor, Martialis, as though by some
divine inspiration".[7] Here we obtain a glimpse into the experience of
the "external soul": the people, whose excited mood was most intensely
engaged with the murderer, spontaneously and without any proof
identified the bird, which had suddenly appeared, with the man's soul.

Still more illuminating is the second example, taken from modern
popular belief. Tobler relates the tale, taken from Strackerjan: "A
schoolboy learnt how to make mice—a typical magic trick; so the
pastor corrected the lad, who, however, died soon afterwards. But
before his death he had to promise the pastor that he would appear to
him and tell him whether he had been saved; so when the minister
was walking in his garden, a crow came flying and alighted on the lever
used to draw water. 'That you, Johnnie?' asked the pastor; whereupon
the crow replied: 'Yes. Whoever denies God and the saints once is
for ever lost'; then it flew away."[8] Here the minister's attitude is very
fine and characteristic, when with no hesitation he addresses the bird,

---

[1] *Ischtar's Höllenfahrt*, P. Jensen, *Assyrisch-babyl nische Mythen und Epen*, 1900, 81.
[2] Klebs, *Der ägyptische Seelenvogel*, (*Zeitschr. f. Äg. Sprache*, 61). W. Spiegelberg,
Or. Lit.-Zeit. 29, 1926.   [3] Weicker, *Der Seelenvogel*, 167.
[4] Ovid, *Metam.* XV, 356 *f*.   [5] Weicker, *ibid., passim*.
[6] Tobler, *Epiphanie der Seele in der deutschen Sage;* von Negelein, *Seele als Vogel*
(*Globus*, 79).   [7] Fr. von Duhn in *AR*. XII, 1909, 168.   [8] *op. cit.* 31.

as a matter of course, as "Johnnie". Again we encounter the experience of the "external soul"; and in general terms we can point to the speed of animals, or their sudden upward flight and strange cries, in order to understand the essential connection between man and bird. But we can advance still farther if we consider the original experience as it is depicted for us in these two examples. For emotion is far more impressive than the concept, and it is from emotion that form is born. The intensely moved people therefore, and the pastor concerned for the boy's salvation, effect the fusion of the soul with the bird suddenly appearing before their eyes.[1]

Then there naturally arises the endeavour to establish some structural connections between the soul-animal and man; and the smallness of many of these animals has certainly assisted in their being regarded as souls that can enter and leave the body. This is the case with the bee, butterfly and bat, where the power of flight must also have played its part, and with mouse and lizard, weasel and worm.[2] In the case of other soul-animals their uncanny or sinister characteristics may well have been influential; above all in the case of the snake, the mysterious creature crawling forth noiselessly out of the earth, the toad and crab.[3] The fish also, which acquired so important a place as a symbol in Christianity, pertains to this category.[4]

But all this is far from sufficient, since the unity between man and the soul-bearer is one that is directly experienced, not one that is understood. This is clear from the fact that there are also very big soul-animals that are not at all mysterious. Werewolves and bearskin folk have been dealt with already,[5] and similarly in the form of a stag, boar or ape the "external soul" kills men and eats their livers.[6] Ulf for example, a heroic figure in Icelandic sagas, became irritable and sleepy at dusk and then roamed about as a wolf, being therefore called *Kveldulf*, the evening wolf.[7] The human soul is here wolf- or bear-like, and there subsists an essential connection between man and animal.[8]

---

[1] The souls of two robber murderers, repentant of their misdeeds, fly away as white doves. St. Benedict saw the soul of his sister, St. Scolastica, fly to heaven as a dove, *op. cit.*, 29.

[2] Weicker, *ibid.*, 29 *ff*; Waser, *Über die äussere Erscheinung der Seele*, AR. 16, 1913, *passim.* Tobler, *op. cit.*, 13 *ff.*, 19 *f.*, 36 *ff.*

[3] Tobler, *op. cit.*, 20 *ff.*, 25 *ff.*; Gaidoz, *L'âme hors du corps*, *Mélusine*, XI, 26.

[4] I. Scheftelowitz, *AR.* 14, 1911, 1 *ff.* W. Spiegelberg, *AR.* 12, 1909, 574.

[5] Chap. 8.

[6] Adriani, *Posso*, 64; *cf.* Wilken, *op. cit.*, III, 25 *ff.* Nieuwenhuis, *Wurzeln*, 38.

[7] *Die Geschichte vom Skalden Egil* (F. Niedner), 1914, 29.

[8] Grönbech, *op. cit.*, II, 99 *f.*

But quite apart from lycanthropy, all sorts of larger soul-animals also occur—dogs, cats and horses.[1]

Here then we have once more regained, by other paths, the totemism and nagualism already discussed:[2] man's power is essentially connected with some exterior object and can therefore assume its form, and thus the "external soul" is actually merely an expression or form of this unity. Such symbols were also the favours which the gentlewomen of the Middle Ages gave, as those of the Toradja tribe still give, their lovers; on going into battle a Toradja youth requests his sweetheart to *moramè* for him; she then gives him her loincloth, head-kerchief or a coral necklet, and two pinches of *sirih*. The youth may not accept these love tokens from two girls simultaneously, for that would turn out ill for him.[3] "Soul endowed" too was the knight's blood-stained shirt which the gentlewoman of the Middle Ages wore next to her body: it was supposed to guarantee the community of their essential nature.[4]

5. The removal of the soul from the body, still further, assures man of life, if it does not result in insecurity as in the fairy tales. In any case the remoteness connected with the idea of the "external soul" is regarded as safety; and this holds good also beyond earthly life, since the external soul cannot be affected by death. On the contrary: death often counts as a union between man, or his soul, with the other, "external", soul, as it did especially in ancient Egyptian thought: "to die" was "to go with one's *ka*";[5] and of the departed it was said, "each goes with his *ka*," which was a good thing; while whoever did as the king desired would have a peaceful end, "as one who goes to his *ka*".[6] It was the destiny of the gods, again, who always accompanied their *kas*, to bear with them always their complete power of life,[7] the finest expression of this idea being afforded by the passage: "when I die my *ka* is powerful".[8] Man's essence is assured, and shows its power fully, only when that of life is

[1] Tobler, *op. cit.*, 44 f.   [2] Chap. 8.   [3] Kruyt, *Bydr.* 75, 121.

[4] As soul-bearers, besides those already considered, must be mentioned: the amulet called "houses of the soul", *Isaiah* iii. 20, A.V. Margin, lights and will-o'-the-wisps; Tobler, *op. cit.*, 82 ff.

[5] G. van der Leeuw, *External Soul. Pyramidentexte* (Sethe), 17, 826, 1431. "Go to his *ka*", as well as "go with", which is immaterial in this connection; occasionally "go to his *akh*", *Pyramidentexte*, 472; cf. Sethe, *Urkunden*, I, 34; van der Leeuw, *Godsvoorstellingen*, 13 f.

[6] B. Gunn and A. H. Gardiner, *Jour. Eg. Arch.* IV, 1917, 248.

[7] *Pyramidentexte*, 829, 1165.

[8] *ibid.*, 1055; van der Leeuw, *External Soul*, 62.

disappearing. Thus Persian thought about the reunion of the soul with the *fravashi* after death,[1] and the reunification of the body-soul (*liau krahang*) with the "soul-marrow" (*salumpok liau*) after the final burial among the Oloh Ngadju of Borneo, are parallels.[2] Here we perceive the distant dawn of the idea of the soul's immortality. "Distant", however: for the "immortal" component is merely safe: it is not as yet contrasted with the body or the corporeal soul as being eternal, divine, since psychological dualism has not yet arisen. The soul that continues to live, the so-called soul of the dead, is a special case of the "external soul". It is not a matter of belief in immortality, but of the experience of power in its direct relation to man;[3] and security, even in death, is only a conclusion drawn from this.

6. The dream-soul, similárly, is not a theoretical construction; dream, sickness and death are only particular instances of the soul's externality, the dream journey being one of the most frequent dream experiences, whose classical example was discerned in the story already told about Guntram. In case of sickness, fainting or sleep, again, the Indonesian peoples believe that the soul is absent, the *sumangat* being called back by name or in the same way as poultry are called,[4] while the priestess of the Bahaus of Borneo brings the soul of a sick person back along the "soul road", fastened to a cord after she has enticed it to her; then she blows the soul back into the body through the skull.[5] The Toradja of Celebes likewise believe that during sleep the soul is on a journey:

> I slept so fast and deeply
> That my soul left me.
> Sleeping and dreaming,
> I came to the realm of the dead.[6]

In Rarotonga, one of the Cook Islands, when anyone sneezes somebody calls out: "Ha! you have come back!" and the medicine-men often set a trap for a sick person's soul.[7] From all this, therefore, it is clear that it was not merely the absence and interruption of power which evoked

[1] N. Söderblom, *Les Fravashis,* 1899, 51.
[2] Hertz, *op. cit.* 57 *f.* Wilken, *op. cit.,* III, 59 *f.*
[3] *cf.* W. F. Otto, *Die Manen,* 1923.   [4] Kruyt, *op. cit.,* 82 *ff.*
[5] Nieuwenhuis, *Wurzeln,* 43; *cf.* his *Quer durch Borneo,* I, 103.
[6] Adriani, *Animistisch Heidendom,* 24.
[7] Frazer, *The Belief in Immortality,* II, 229 *f.*

the idea of the soul, as was maintained by Animism, but equally the obvious and striking presence of power. Thus the novelty in this structure is only the freedom of movement, the soul's capacity to leave man or to seek him out, and powerful human beings, such as magicians and witches, possess this liberty of movement to a special degree.[1] In Betzingen two maids were sleeping in the same bed in the mill when two lovers visited them; one of the girls could not be wakened, but towards morning a beetle came crawling into her mouth while she slept; and this is a proof of witchcraft:[2] the witch had sent out her soul; similarly a magician sends forth his soul to deliver a letter and bring him the answer.[3] Ecstatics also can do the same as witches and magicians: as the apocalyptic writer says: "and immediately I was in the spirit"; that is, he leaves his body.[4]

7. Finally, the structure of the ' external soul" is closely related to, and indeed sometimes identical with, the idea of the angel, particularly the *guardian angel*.[5] The "dual experience of form", which we discerned in discussing angels, has here an application to human personality itself. Its structural basis consists in the community of essence accompanying "being a soul", and once again the finest example is the Egyptian *ka*, "thou art the *ka* of all the gods" being asserted of one very powerful deity,[6] which means: thou art their powerfulness, they must obey thee. Or yet more clearly: to the god Osiris it was said: "Thou art the *ka* of all the gods; Horus protected thee when thou becamest his *ka*."[7] The community of soul conditions the protective relationship, and thus it can be understood not only how the *ka* can simultaneously be soul-stuff, an external soul and a protective spirit,[8] but (further) the whole conception of guardian angel or spirit, as this occurs quite early in Christianity[9] among other instances, can be readily interpreted by means of the idea of the soul. I need not recall the *fylgja* and similar concepts,[10] and only wish to add that the "external soul", in accordance with its character as I have already stressed this, can also have an obstructive and inimical effect. Of this the *erinys*, the soul, really the blood, of a murdered relative provides a good example,

---

[1] Chap. 31.   [2] Tobler, *op. cit.*, 38 *ff.*
[3] Bin Gorion, *Der Born Judas*, VI, 103 *f.*   [4] *Rev.* iv, 2.
[5] Chap. 16.   [6] *Pyramidentexte* (Sethe), 1623, 1831.
[7] *ibid.*, 1690; *cf.* 136, 610, 647, 1653. Hoffmann, *Theophore Personsnamen*, 53, 60.
[8] G. van der Leeuw, *External Soul.*
[9] Harnack, *History of Dogma*, II, 362, Note 3; *cf.* 361, Note 3.
[10] Chap. 16.

the *erinys* being hostile to the murderer not however as an alien power, but as a personal soul related to him by blood.[1] The *keres* also are avenging soul-beings of a similar nature:

> like sleuth-hounds too
> the fates pursue.[2]

Finally, the connection existing between the idea of the "external soul" and that of personal fate must be considered.[3] The *aklama* of the Ewe natives, for example, is an "invisible thing that the god has given to man, so that it may always be around him and accompany him everywhere"; thus it is at the same time a sort of protective spirit, soul, and fate, and if something has succeeded they say: "my *aklama* was gracious to me, *aklama* was around me, or my *aklama* has given me some good advice".[4] Parallels are the Nordic *hamingja*, and the later Greek *Mira* (*moira*) which appears in fairy stories as adviser and protective spirit[5]; here the soul once again appears as a form of what man has experienced in himself as superior.

H. Gaidoz, *L'âme hors du corps* (*Mélusine*, XI, 1912).

L. Klebs, *Der ägyptische Seelenvogel* (*Zeitschr. f. Äg. Sprache*, 61, 1926).

G. van der Leeuw, *External Soul, Schutzgeist und der ägyptische ka* (*Zeitschr. f. Äg. Sprache*, 54, 1918)

J. von Negelein, *Seele als Vogel* (*Globus*, 79, 1901).

E. Rohde, *Psyche* [9-10], 1925.

O. Tobler, *Epiphanie der Seele in der deutschen Sage*, 1911.

G. Weicker, *Der Seelenvogel*, 1902.

[1] E. Samter, *Die Religion der Griechen*, 1914, 52. The *erinyes* were regarded as souls of the underworld also in the magical tablets of "defixion"; Weicker, *op. cit.*, 5.

[2] Sophocles, *Oedipus rex*, 470.   [3] Chap. 21.

[4] D. Westermann, *Über die Begriffe Seele, Geist, Schicksal bei dem Ewe- und Tschivolk* (*AR*. 8, 1905).   [5] P. Kretschmer, *Neugriechische Märchen*, 1910, Nr. 36, 48.

THE UNIQUELY POWERFUL AND DIVINE SOUL

1. IN the structure of soul-stuff, as in that of the plural and the "external soul", we discerned superior power as being always the basic experience; and the differentiation of the second of these structures, and in the third the separation between ego and environment, alter nothing whatever in this situation. But as soon as a portion of the environment, or of the ego, is *deprived* of its power, thereby becoming incapable of being a soul bearer, everything is changed. In the three preceding structures we know of "no corporeality which was nothing more than mere stuff";[1] but now *Dualism* arises, for which the soul's power, living, potent and divine, can exist only in association with soulless, impotent and godless stuff.

The natural condition for this is the freedom of movement of the third structure just referred to; the persistence, for example, of the Egyptian *ba* depends simply on the possibility of its "going forth to the day". It left the grave in order to breathe and nourish itself; air and food were powerful and necessary, and the *ba* was merely an "external soul" that had attained a higher degree of security. But when all power-fulness is denied to the material world, and when the whole environment, including the body itself, is reduced to the level of mere "matter" or "thing", then this freedom of the soul appears entirely different;[2] and the Greek mind effected this revolution. For Heracleitus, whose dictum on the depth of the soul harmonizes with every soul structure, as for the pre-Socratics in general, the soul was one power among other powers; there was no condition whatever of complete impotence: everything was conceived in terms of stuff, and the entire life process was a sort of metabolic process, while stuff itself was divine.[3] But Plato, starting from Orphic-Dionysiac ideas, removed the soul out of the material world and changed the latter from being a divine whole to the realm of evil;[4] while in the course of the succeeding centuries this Greek concept of the soul proved itself so highly influential that even

---

[1] Otto, *Die Götter Griechenlands*, 87.   [2] Chap. 3.
[3] Rohde, *op. cit.*, II, 148 *f.*; *cf.* K. Joël, *Der Ursprung der Naturphilosophie*, 1906.
[4] The Dionysiac excitement in Greece was not, as Klages' school has recently maintained, a reversion from spirituality to the "primitive ground of life", but just the converse.

the last generation regarded the dualism of body and soul as being almost self-evident.

2. This conception of the soul, then, found the schema of the "external soul" existing ready for it; and the *transmigration of souls* is nothing more than an extreme conclusion drawn from the soul's liberty of movement. It is to be found in many regions quite apart from India and Greece, where the doctrine of soul migration attained its highest development. Originally, again, transmigration involved no disparagement whatever of matter: life was a cycle in which death marked only a stage and not a conclusion: indeed, there was no conclusion.[1] In the popular beliefs of primitive peoples reincarnation is accepted without further ado, and the newly born are identified according to definite distinguishing marks:—among others resemblance,[2] while in folk-tales the persecuted hero can adopt constantly fresh forms, like Proteus and Loki.[3] Similarly, in order to escape the dangers of the realm of the dead the Egyptian *ba* had the ability to adopt many guises; and metamorphosis yields no more than enhanced security, as so many of Ovid's stories prove. This, however, was not a static idea but continued to expand; and we can understand that, in this development, the soul becomes more and more the single stable entity in the flight of the merely apparent. Thus the world and the body were subjected to many changes, but the soul remained the same; the bearer changed, but what he bore continued unaltered. As one example: "Torsten initiates his boy into life with these words: this boy shall be called Ingemund, and I expect a *hamingja* (soul destiny) for him because of the name"; Ingemund being the mother's father.[4] Yet one step more, and the soul not only persists during change, but subsists *eternally in the transient, and powerful in the impotent.*

The expression "transmigration of souls" is, therefore, a most serious misconception: for while everything changes its place and all is transformed, the soul alone persists. It endures and will continue to endure, even when the body dies—whether we rejoice, or lament this inability to die as in Orphism and Buddhism; while in Mazda

---

[1] Chap. 22.

[2] K. Th. Preuss, *Tod und Unsterblichkeit im Glauben der Naturvölker*, 1930, 23. Wilken, *op. cit.*, 111, 72.

[3] Nilsson justly observes that the gift of metamorphosis in Greece was preferably accorded to maritime creatures: *A History of Greek Religion*, 57.

[4] Grönbech, *op. cit.*, II, 124.

theology the soul was thought of as even pre-existent: as in being
before the world and persisting after the world has ceased to be.[1]
The soul, thus rendered eternal, more and more receives its form
from the semi-material world; the concrete soul-stuffs are allotted to a
world-stuff which is reduced to impotence; and as forms, breath and
wind *etc.*, are preferred. The degree of power corresponds to the grade
of insubstantiality; and to the world of things the eternal and divine
soul is hostile. In a universe of dead materiality, of substantiality
replete with destruction, the soul is the heavenly spark, the divine
shoot; and the Orphics deplored calamitous reincarnation, the "sorrow-
ful weary wheel" which rolls on into eternity and heaps sin on sin.
The soul that has escaped from this cycle returns to the world of the
gods: but on its entrance into heaven its watchword is the appeal to its
origin: it may approach the gods because it is akin to them. "I am indeed
a 'dual being', half heavenly, half earthly", as a gold tablet discovered
in a grave at Petelia represents the dead Orphic saying:

> Say: "I am a child of Earth and of Starry Heaven;
> But my race is of Heaven (alone)";[2]

and an inscription of a later period gives the soul ascending to heaven
the formula:

> I am your fellow wanderer, your fellow Star.[3]

3. The simplest form of this dualism is separation at the moment of
death, when the two parts, the powerful and the impotent, betake them
each to its own place: "earth to earth, the *pneuma* upwards", γᾶ μὲν ἐς
γᾶν, πνεῦμ' ἄνω; or, "the ether receives the souls, but the earth the
bodies".[4] It is true that where this duality prevails, the spirituality of
the soul is not always stressed; and the primitive breath-soul retains
its validity always as to its name, *pneuma*, and very often also as to its
essence. Many primitive peoples, again, are familiar with an ascent to
heaven on a ladder of arrows,[5] while the ancient Egyptian *Pyramid
Texts* depict the dead king as a bird, a falcon or goose, flying up to
heaven, or climbing thither with ropes or on an animal's skin, or a
ladder (Jacob's ladder!). In the oldest formulas, still further, a latent

---

[1] Söderblom, *Les fravashis*, 62 *ff.*
[2] A. Olivieri, *Lamellae aureae orphicae*, 1915, 12. O. Kern, *Orphicorum Fragmenta*,
1922, *Fr.* 32a, 105.   [3] A. Dieterich, *Eine Mithrasliturgie*[2], 1910, 8.
[4] Rohde, *op. cit.*, II, 389, 257 *ff.*, where additional instances are cited; E. T. 170,
541. *cf.* Dieterich, *Mithrasliturgie*, 200 *ff.*   [5] *e.g.* Wundt, *op. cit.*, V, 264 *ff.*, 272.

dualism is already manifest: "the soul (*akh*) to the heavens, the body to the earth", or "the soul (*ba*) to heaven, the body (*d-t*, originally the body-soul) to the earth".[1] A Chinese parallel from the *Li-ki*: "When someone died people climbed immediately on to the house roof and called out his name: 'So-and-so, come back!' "—the external soul!— "afterwards his mouth was filled with uncooked rice. . . . While he was being buried in the earth, they looked up to heaven; for while the body with the animal-soul sinks downward, the spirit soars upward."[2] Here there still subsists the idea of the plurality of souls, but the body is separated from the "spirit"; the latter goes upward, the body downward!

"To primitive thought such a contrast was foreign; and behind our concept of the soul lies a prolonged spiritual process of development. Homer and Plato, St. Paul and Christian thought have contributed towards spiritualizing, individualizing and expanding the purified idea of the soul in modern terminology, in a way that finds its counterpart only in India."[3] Here then originate all speculations leading theoretically to the manifold hypotheses of psycho-physical dualism and parallelism,[4] and mythically to the magnificent idea of the "heavenward journey of the soul".[5]

4. In these forms, too, Dualism still continues to employ the primitive mode of expression. For the soul is no pure spirit, but only a subtle stuff; its form not immaterial, but merely "similar to light winds and fleeting dream":—*par levibus ventis volucrique simillima somno*. Thus Dualism attains its truest form only when the body loses its value completely, and even becomes an object of aversion; it is the soul's prison, its grave: *soma sema* ("the body is a tomb");[6] and man's salvation is bound up indissolubly with liberation from the embrace of matter.[7] The soul is imprisoned in matter, which repeatedly pulls it down into the slime, and the many forms of this immortal myth of the soul, from Plato to the Romantics, are well known: "The soul flies away into the pure blue heaven of truth and innocence like a bird that has been set free, to hover in the clear light. And with the wretched

---

[1] *Pyramidentexte* (Sethe), 474. *Urkunden*, IV, 481; *cf*. 484.

[2] Lehmann, *Textbuch*[1], 11 *f*.   [3] Söderblom, *Gottesglaube*, 65.

[4] *cf*. the striking characterization of humanity as Descartes regarded this: "an angel driving a machine"; Maritain, *Religion and Culture*, 24.   [5] Chap. 44.

[6] Plato, *Gorgias*, 493a; *cf*. *Cratylus*, 400c. The expression was previously employed by Philolaus: Diels, *Vorsokratiker*, I, Fr. 14.

[7] *cf*. Rohde, *op. cit.*, II, 35; E. T. 342, 345.

net, with lime, the immortal is again drawn down and held fast in the mire".[1]

In this connection the so-called *Song of the Pearl*, from the Gnostic *Acts of St Thomas*, is typical. As a very little child the prince is sent from the East, his home, to Egypt to seek the one pearl (soul) which is in the sea (matter). At first he forgets the treasure which he ought to discover, and also that he is a king's son; then he finds the pearl and, returning to his home, at the frontier he receives his royal raiment so that he may make his entry garbed in splendour. Old fairy tale *motifs* again—a snake guarding the pearl: the hero forgetting his task while he eats the Egyptians' food, *etc.*—acquire the new content: the soul's salvation.[2] Similarly, and no less impressively, in Islam, as influenced by Neo-Platonism: "The soul descended upon thee from the lofty station; a dove rare and uncaptured. . . . It came to thee unwillingly. . . . It resisted at first . . . it grew accustomed to the desert place (the world). Methinks it then forgot the recollections of the protected park (heaven), and of those abodes which it left with regret . . . it was united to the infirmity of the material body. . . . It now remembers the protected park and weepeth with tears which flow and cease not till the time for setting out towards the protected park approacheth. . . . It then cooeth on the top of a lofty pinnacle . . . and it has come to the knowledge of every mystery in the universe, while yet its tattered vest hath not been mended.

"Its descent was predestined so that it might hear what it had not heard, else why did it descend from the high and lofty heaven to the depth of the low and humble earth?"[3]

From this stage man's most urgent problem is *asceticism*.[4] So far as the flesh is concerned he must die, in order to be able to live in the spirit: only thus can he be adequate to his destiny, his divine essence. We find this idea, in fact, in Plato, in connection with the σῶμα σῆμα metaphor: "And indeed I think that Euripides may have been right in saying,

'Who knows if life be not death and death life';

and that we are very likely dead; I have heard a philosopher say that at this moment we *are* dead, and that the body is a tomb."[5]

[1] Ludwig Tieck, XIV, 358. In Indian speculation a parallel idea is found in the relationship between *prakriti* (matter) and *purusha* (spirit).
[2] Lehmann-Haas, *Textbuch*, 218 *ff.*
[3] C. Field, *Mystics and Saints of Islam*, 101 *f.* (Avicenna's Poem).
[4] Chap. 66. [5] *Gorgias*, 493 (Jowett).

5. In this purification however, which is equivalent to dying, man cannot remain halfway. For as soon as his corporeality has attained either moral and religious value, or disvalue, it can no longer be restricted to the body proper. The condemnation of the body does not suffice to ensure the spirituality of the soul, since this soul contains ideas and thoughts, impulses and desires, of a wholly material kind. Thus the soul must now be released not only from the body, but also from the corporeality residing within itself; within the soul itself the lower elements must sever themselves from the higher. Among the Greeks, indeed, it was the asceticism of the soul that first created *spirit*: it is only the suppression of the instincts, the rendering impotent not merely of the body but of fleshly lust, of appetite and stress, that render the spirit potent.[1] Here again we immediately encounter Plato: he depreciated not only the body but the soul also; the latter pertains to the lower "world of becoming". It certainly participates in the higher realm of the Ideas, and is immortal; but it is not absolute: it assumes an intermediate position and shares the nature of both these worlds. Thus arises the so-called *trichotomy*: above corporeality subsist soul qualities, and superior to these again pure spirituality. Spirit is elevated above soul. Psychologically, this implies a stratification of human nature in accordance with lower and higher impulses and instincts, while theologically it is the attempt to seek out the superior and the divine in man, despite all else: body and soul both manifest their inadequacy, and spirit now becomes the symbol of the soul's unfathomable depth.[2] The irony of history, however, has decided that the principal term for this spiritualizing, this ultimate elevation to a completely immaterial power, should be no other than precisely the old word from the soul-stuff-structure: *pneuma* (*Geist*, *esprit*, spirit, *etc.*). We have already observed that "soul" is not a comprehensive name for the phenomena of consciousness; and this holds good to a far greater degree of "spirit", which is in no sense a psychological concept: "for spirit may be abstract, unreal, powerless, more so than the soul. But the spirit has a clearer

---

[1] Scheler, *Die Stellung des Menschen im Kosmos* (1928), 74 *ff*. "The reciprocal penetration of the originally impotent spirit, and the originally demonic impulse blind to all spiritual ideas and values, by means of the developing idealization and spiritualizing of the misery subsisting behind the symbols of things, and the simultaneous enhancing and vitalizing of the spirit, are the aim and end of finite being and history"; *ibid.*, 83.

[2] Rohde, *op. cit.*, I, 4. E. T. 5. On the separation between spirit and soul in Plutarch *cf.* W. Bousset, *Die Himmelsreise der Seele*, *AR*. IV, 1901, 252; in Origen, *cf.* Harnack, *History of Dogma*, II, 362; for a good survey, W. Windelband, *History of Philosophy*, 301 *ff*.

recollection that it was never mere life in the purely biological, and above all never mere consciousness in the purely psychological, sense."[1] On the contrary: the concept of consciousness could arise only on the basis of some experience of superiority.[2]

6. Mysticism, in conclusion, follows the path of the enfeebling of stuff and the spiritualizing of soul to its ultimate end. "Thou canst not discover the bounds of the soul albeit thou pacest its every road: so deep is its ground. Dig as deeply as thou canst: then wilt thou come to the ground that is unfathomable; deprive thine own self of all power, then wilt thou find God"; thus the "ground of the soul", *fundus animae*, implies man's ultimate impotence, but simultaneously God's primal and true powerfulness; everything material, all desires and impulses, all thoughts and concepts, must disappear. Heavy sleep or intense rapture must deprive man of his self: "I mean by the chalice the wine of Eternity; and for me the meaning of this wine is the surrender of the self, the suppression of selfhood", asserts Hafiz.[3] Or a modern woman mystic: "The understanding sees with eyes without sight, hears with ears without hearing: the emotions, the will and its changing moods, have ceased. By this process spirit escapes from itself and from all selfhood; it also evades every activity and becomes devoid of working and of spirit."[4] Again: "Clothe thyself with this nought, this misery, and strive so that this misery and this nought may become thy daily nourishment and place of sojourn, so that thou mayest become completely merged with them; I assure thee that when thou art thus nought, God will become the All within thy soul".[5] The expressions that German mysticism in particular has coined for this ultimate deprivation of power and of value are manifold: "to deprive of being" (*entwerden*), "to renounce" (*entsagen*), "to deprive of form" (*entbilden*), "to empty oneself" (*entledigen*), "to be utterly naked", "to remove one's clothing", *etc.*[6] The spirit must become as thoroughly vanquished as the body and soul:

---

[1] Schmalenbach, *op. cit.*, 344.   [2] *ibid.*, 351.
[3] A. Merx, *Idee und Grundlinien einer allgemeinen Geschichte der Mystik*[1], 1893. For what follows *cf.* the entire Chap. 75.
[4] L. de Hartog-Meyes, *Mystiek* (*Nieuwe Banen*, IX, 1916, 220 *f.*).
[5] Miguel de Molinos, *Der geistliche Führer, Buch III, Kap.* 20.
[6] G. Siedel, *Die Mystik Taulers*, 1911, 99; on this, and also on what follows, *cf.* Grete Lüers, *Die Sprache der deutschen Mystik des Mittelalters im Werke der Mechtild von Magdeburg*, 1926.

> Would ye know how I came forth from Spirit?
> When in myself I perceived nought whatsover.
> Nought but sheer unplumbed Deity;
> Then no longer could I keep silent; I must proclaim it:
>   I ceased to be.[1]

There then remains only the tiny spark, the *scintilla animae*, the ground of the soul, which cannot be described because it contains nothing but the All: God:

> Since thus I have been lost in the Abyss,
> I would fain speak no more. I am dumb.
>   Thus hath Deity
> Manifestly absorbed me within Itself . . .
>   I have been annihilated.[2]

"The *fundus animae* is the place where God and the soul are one and the same".[3] Thus the soul's ground is the most ultimate idea of the soul possible, which is indeed no longer even an idea, and which proves that he who seeks the soul is in the end seeking not for this, but always for something that exists beyond, *epekeina*.[4] Quite close and yet eternally sublime, God subsists in man at the place where His ineffableness coincides with that of the Ultimate in humanity:

> Why is all so well with the soul
> When it finds its long sought Good
> So near its heart?
> Now has it all, whate'er it will.
> Embraced, beloved, it lies still,
> With its God, in the ground.[5]

Never and nowhere, therefore, is the soul a rational explanation of life's activities, but always and everywhere an experience on the borderland; and the human spirit has found no rest until it has banned from the soul all that was impotent within it. Bodily asceticism, then, is quite insufficient: asceticism of the soul, and indeed of the spirit, must be added to it; and this leads to a blessed nothingness which—paradox of mysticism!—is experienced as powerfulness *par excellence*.

---

[1] Merx, *op. cit.*, 13.   [2] *ibid.*
[3] F. Delekat, *Zeitschr. f. Theol. u. Kirche*, N. F. IV, 1923, 280 *ff.*
[4] It is true that Southern Buddhism goes still farther by simply denying the soul.
[5] G. Tersteegen.

The vacuum is the richest fullness, the negative the highest degree of positivity:

> Thirty spokes meet together in a single hub.
> The waggon's usefulness depends on their nothingness; (on the empty space);
> Clay is moulded into vessels;
> The vessels' utility depends on their nothingness.
> To build a house, holes are made in the walls for doors and windows;
> On their nothingness depends the usefulness of the house.
> Hence:—Being yields possession, but Non-being utility.[1]

[1] *Tao-teh King*, 11.

CHAPTER 44

THE IMMORTAL SOUL

1. WE have already observed that ecstasy is a particular case of the "external soul";[1] and it is not difficult to understand that the evaporation of the weight of life, and the cessation of the vital functions as this occurs in ecstasy, have powerfully reinforced the idea of the ultimate duality of body and soul. The soul's destiny is to become free from the body, and to survive in another world untrammelled by all the heaviness of earth; so that what in ecstasy is a momentary liberation must after death manifest itself as eternal reality. The Tupi Guaranis of South America, for instance, attain by dancing to the "land without evil", to eternal youth and freedom from toil and hardships: "they believed that they would become light enough to cross over the sea dryshod, or straight from the dance be taken up into heaven, together with their huts, by incessant dancing combined with strict fasting";[2] while even for a less primitive culture, which no longer seeks the "land free from evil" on earth, ecstasy nevertheless means a glimpse of the other world. Thus it is related of certain rabbis that they "entered Paradise" in ecstasy;[3] and St. Paul tells us: "I knew a man in Christ caught up to the third heaven; (whether in the body, or out of the body, I cannot tell: God knoweth)", he adds significantly.[4] Greek antiquity too was familiar with a series of such ecstatic experiences in which the mysteries of the other world were perceived;[5] it was reported of Aristeas that he could leave behind his body like a corpse, but that his soul, after abandoning the body, mounted into the aether.[6] Thus the body became increasingly a garment that could be put on or off at will.

But where the element of power in humanity becomes more and more exclusively sought in soul and spirit, the idea is not far off that death, which finally separates body and soul, is genuine liberation and admission into powerful life: the soul—no longer the man!—is regarded as immortal. As regards Greece, Rohde has clearly explained in a masterly exposition this connection between immortality and the powerfulness (divinity) provisionally attained in ecstasy. In Greece

---

[1] Chap. 42.   [2] Preuss, *Tod und Unsterblichkeit im Glauben der Naturvölker*, 5.
[3] Bousset, *Die Himmelsreise der Seele* (*AR*. IV, 1901, 136 *ff*.).   [4] 2 *Cor*. xii. 2.
[5] Bousset, *ibid*., 253 *f*.; *cf*. Rohde, *op. cit*., II, 28 *ff*., 91 *ff*. E. T. 30, 255, 293.
[6] Rohde, *ibid*., 92. E. T. 281.

the ecstasy of Dionysiac religion led to the belief in an immortal soul;[1] but for this intoxicating liquors were also useful; and by many peoples these were sublimated into the beverage of the gods, so that the *soma* of the Hindus, the Persian *haoma* and the nectar of the Greeks, ensure eternal life.[2] They facilitate and contribute to the enfeebling of the body and of the daily activities of the soul. It is for the same reason that the Persian mystics drink:

> Knowest thou the cup-bearer who gives drink to spirits?
> Knowest thou the beverage which the cup-bearer pours forth?
> The cup-bearer is the beloved, who pours out for thee annihilation,
> The drink is fire, wherein thou drinkest illumination.
> Drink the draught of ecstasy, burn in the glow of love!
> Gladly the droplet seeks extinction in its mighty flood.
> The whole Universe is a wine lodge: every thing a goblet;
> It is our friend who holds the chalice, and we are the drinkers.
> Even wisdom is drunken and completely sunk in rapture.
> Heaven and earth are drunken: every angel is drunken.[3]

2. Rapture, deprivation of being (*das Entwerden*) and collapse assume various forms, one of the most remarkable being the flight towards heaven or the "heavenward journey of the soul". We have already observed that the soul has wings;[4] but even without these it pursues its upward way to heaven, which implies purification; and the final goal is union with the godhead. Probably of Iranian origin, this idea found its classical expression in the Gnostic, Hellenistic and Judaistic tendencies of the centuries at about the commencement of our chronological era. The universe consists of seven planetary spheres, each having a guardian, a star-god, whom the soul must pass in its ascension. Stage by stage it mounts to highest heaven, usually regarded as the eighth sphere, the empyrean. The *Hebdomad* or *Ogdoad*, again, is a purifying by degrees, the soul leaving the earthly level farther and farther behind.[5] Mithraism also recognized this seven grade ascent: a

---

[1] Rohde, *op. cit.*, II, *passim*. E. T. 264 f. But *cf.* Nilsson, *History of Greek Religion*, 210.   [2] *cf.* G. Dumézil, *Le festin d'immortalité*, 1924.

[3] Mahmud's *Gulshan I Raz*; in Lehmann-Haas, *op. cit.*, 376.

[4] Negelein, *op. cit.*, 59. Holland, *Zur Typik der Himmelfahrt*, *AR*. XXIII, 1925, 215. The soul may also descend to the underworld; thus the Babylonian Ishtar seeks life below, and is compelled to leave behind portions of her clothing at each of the seven subterranean gates—an exact parallel to the ascent through the seven gates of heaven. Jensen, *Assyrisch-babylonische Mythen und Epen*, 81 ff. On the journey to heaven *cf.* also Dieterich, *Mithrasliturgie*, 90 ff., 179 ff., 200 ff.

[5] Bousset, *loc. cit.*, 148 f. On the Persians *cf.* Edv. Lehmann, *Zarathustra, en bog om Persernes gamle tro*, II, 1902, 250 ff.

ladder composed of eight gates, "of which the first seven consisted of seven different sorts of metals, served in the temples as a symbolic reminder of the path that must be traversed to attain the highest region of the fixed stars"; each gate was guarded by an angel, and "the farther the soul . . . advanced the more it discarded, like clothing, the passions and capacities it had received when it first came hovering down to earth", until naked, freed from all sensuality, it reached the eighth heaven where it found bliss.[1] There it was made part of a magnificent vision of the universe, and psychology transformed into cosmology; the angels of the stars indicated the way to the soul.[2]

In Judaistic versions of the soul myth, also, clothing symbolism is very vivid. Enoch for instance is carried off by two angels; he mounts through the seven heavens and in the seventh he sees God, who commands the archangel to remove his earthly clothes and garb him in raiment of "glory". Thus he becomes "one of the glorious".[3] The soul must become unclothed: this is the proper meaning of the myth: nakedness alone can qualify for donning the celestial garments.

And since it is not only cosmically, but at the same time psychologically apprehended, ascension can be translated wholly into the inward. Thus mysticism finds heaven within the soul itself, in the "ground"; the stations on the heavenward journey are then stages of inner purification. Mohammed's ascent to heaven, which represents an extension of the prophet's so-called "night journey" from Mecca to Jerusalem referred to in the *Koran*,[4] is by the Sufis related to the mystic union: Mohammed, conducted by Gabriel and Michael, mounts through the seven heavens; he arrives before the throne of Allah, where angels must remain behind:

> When, solitary, he communes with his God,
> Suddenly he is transformed into his God.
> Behold! Mohammed straightway disappears,
> And at the covenanting place God stands alone.[5]

In St. Paul also we find the schema of the journey to heaven interpreted ecstatically as well as cosmically.[6]

---

[1] F. Cumont, *Die Mysterien des Mithra*[3], 1923, 129 *f.*; *cf.* Bousset, *loc. cit.*, 165 *ff.*

[2] Chap. 7, 16.

[3] Bousset, *ibid.*, 138 *ff.*; *cf.* further 140 (*Leviticus*), 141 (*Isaiah*), 151 *ff.*, 268 *ff.*

[4] *Sura* 17 (Mecca). Lehmann-Haas, *op. cit.*, 350.

[5] Fariduddin Attar, in F. A. G. Tholuck, *Blütensammlung aus der morgenländischen Mystik*, 1825, 265; *cf.* Bousset, *ibid.*, 249 and Note 1.

[6] *Romans* viii. 38 *ff.* Bousset, *ibid.*, 136.

In all this there is expressed a yearning for the completely subtle, the unformed, the indescribable and unutterable. Riding, flying and soaring appear as the proper motions for which man is fitted; relinquishing the world and the body is the sole demand:

> Jerusalem! Thou city built on high,
> Would God I were in thee;
> My yearning heart so longs for thee,
> It *is with me no more*;
> Far over hill and dale,
> Far over open fields,
> It *soars* above them all
> And *hastens from this world*.

The soul, again:

> In a moment it will *mount*
> *Up to the firmament*,
> As it *forsakes*, so softly and marvellously,
> The *Elements' abode*;
> It *rides in* Elijah's chariot
> With the *angelic host*,
> Who bear it in their hands
> Encompassing it around.[1]

This longing is Christian, but also Platonic and even pre-Platonic, for Euripides' marvellous Chorus depicts precisely the same images and the same craving:

> Could I take me to some cavern for mine hiding,
>   In the hill-tops where the Sun scarce hath trod;
> Or a cloud make the home of mine abiding,
>   As a bird among the bird-droves of God!
>
> Where a voice of living waters never ceaseth
>   In God's quiet garden by the sea,
> And Earth, the ancient life-giver, increaseth
>   Joy among the meadows, like a tree.[2]

3. "Thus the so-called belief in immortality is not generated by the previously discovered idea of a soul, but conversely":[3] the soul concept is modified in accord with the type of experience of the beyond; here again the search for the soul reveals itself as a seeking for God. To the

---

[1] Johann Mathäus Meyfart. Italics indicate the old images.
[2] Euripides, *Hippolytus*, 732 *ff*. (Murray).
[3] Preuss, *op. cit.*, 17.

Semite the beyond was unattainable, and eternal life was reserved for the gods;[1] the soul therefore could never become the bridge to the beyond, and an "immortality of the soul" was inconceivable.

For the Greeks, however, conditions were different:[2] in his soul man finds the *arche*, the primal substance, of immortality. The Platonic soul, which in its intermediate status has the capacity of being able to remember the eternal Ideas and to raise itself up to these (*anamnesis* and *Eros*) *must* be immortal: but to attain eternal life it must pursue the path of purification. The Euripidean question, whether "life be not death, and death be not life," dominates all these ultimate thoughts concerning the soul; the experience of death leads to eternal life: the abandonment of this world conquers another. "Thither" always means in the first place "hence"; and Goethe too has expressed this in his unfinished drama, *Prometheus*, in which life is apprehended as profoundly as is death:

Prometheus. When from the innermost and profoundest depth,
　　　　　　Completely shattered, thou feelest all
　　　　　　Of joy and grief that ever surged within thee,
　　　　　　When, in this storm, thy swelling heart
　　　　　　Would find relief in tears,
　　　　　　Heightening its own passion,
　　　　　　And all within thee resounds and thrill and shakes,
　　　　　　When all thy senses fade,
　　　　　　And thou seemest to sink
　　　　　　Into dissolution,
　　　　　　While all around thee is swallowed up in night,
　　　　　　When, in thine inmost self,
　　　　　　Thou embracest a world—
　　　　　　Then it is that man dies.
Pandora.　O Father, let us die.

W. Bousset, *Die Himmelsreise der Seele* (*AR.* IV, 1901, 136 *ff.*).
J. G. Frazer, *The Belief in Immortality and the Worship of the Dead*, 1913 *ff.*
R. Holland, *Zur Typik der Himmelfahrt* (*AR.* XXIII, 1925, 207 *ff.*).
W. B. Kristensen, *Livet fra döden*, 1925.
K. Th. Preuss, *Tod und Unsterblichkeit im Glauben der Naturvölker*, 1930.

---

[1] *Gen.* iii. 22. Kristensen, *Livet fra döden*, 10.
[2] That is as regards the Orphic-Platonic Greeks; for the Homeric Greeks, as with the monistic mysticism of the pre-Socratics, everything was different; *cf.* Rohde, *op. cit.*, II, 149, 253; E. T. 24. W. F. Otto, *Die Götter Griechenlands*, and my Article, *SM.* 7, 1931.

CHAPTER 45

THE CREATURE

1. THE Greek idea of the soul seeks the superior power within man, even if it previously releases him from all the ponderousness of earth. What remains is divine and immortal. Both these expressions have the same meaning: the Greek spirit participated first of all in the Semitic fear of *hubris* that placed man equal to the gods (but in this respect racial distinctions will not suffice!), until the religions of Dionysus and Orpheus brought immortality and identity with the god, as *one* reality, within the human sphere.[1] The seed present in man needs only to be developed, the spark only to be blown into flame; although many hindrances must undoubtedly be overcome. But however difficult this may be, it is not impossible; and for the soul, confined within the cycle of births and fallen into bondage to matter, there is the hope of liberation:—

> To stop the wheel and breathe once more from ill.[2]

This classical version of the idea of the soul is harshly opposed to those others, according to which there is nothing whatever in man which might be in itself divine, nothing that could ascend, nothing which, however purified, implied any genuine powerfulness. The phrase in the Anglican church's *General Confession*, "and there is no health in us", expresses with magnificent curtness equally the most primitive conviction that there subsists no powerfulness, and the essentially Christian principle that nothing could endure before God. Man is a unity, a complete whole, consisting not of two parts, one powerful and the other impotent; rather is everything in him powerless, while all is placed in the world by the Creator's sole Power. Man therefore is a *creature*, which as such came from God's hand, and which perhaps God does not permit to leave His hand. If then an eternal life awaits him, this can never be *attained*, but merely *granted* to him: to man, that is to say, life, and eternal life, are both given. In him, then, there is nothing whatever that may approach nearer than

---

[1] Rohde, *op. cit.*, II, 2 *ff*. E. T. 263 *f*.
[2] Olivieri, *Lamellae aureae*, 4. Kern, *Orph. Fragm.*, Fr. 229, p. 244.

anything else to Deity; rather all that is within him is equally remote
from each and every power, unless Power condescends to raise him
from death. Christian belief, therefore, recognizes not immortality but
resurrection, that is, a new creation; man at no time nor place becomes
God, but remains first and last a creature, his blessedness consisting
precisely in his being a creature.

The Old Testament, further, knows nothing of a soul to be saved:
the soul is man himself in his essential nature, in his powerfulness,
exactly as in the primitive structure of the soul;[1] God saves man, or
rather the people. It is just as little a matter of a divine soul as of
immortality; nor is it otherwise in the Gospel. For Jesus, too, man's
soul is his essential nature.[2] For St. Paul, however, the situation is
certainly altered, and a definite dualism predominates; nevertheless the
soul in itself is not immortal. Undeniably the "flesh" is depreciated in
value, but it is not the soul that is contrasted with it as the powerful
element, but the *spirit*. And this *pneuma* is not the highest stage in a
trichotomous psychology, but the gift of God, the imparting from
God to man, indeed the Lord Himself.[3]

He who has received the Spirit, therefore, is a "new creation": the
first man, Adam, was a "living soul', but the last Adam a "quickening
spirit".[4] The "pneumatized" man is therefore not man in accord with
his own highest potency, but he who has received the *pneuma* from God
and thereby has become a new creature. He *is* not spirit, but *has* spirit
or is "in the spirit".

But it is one of the most remarkable facts in the whole of the history
of religion that this concept of man as a creature, as a unity of body
and soul from the hand of God, was in later times almost lost owing
to the omnipotent influence of Greek thought. Even to-day the ideas of
the "immortal soul" and of the valuelessness of the body are still
widely supposed to be essentially Christian. This negates, however,
not only the Israelite origin, but also the New Testament foundation,
of Christianity.[5] Nevertheless the church has always been able to preserve in its essentials the genuinely Christian view of man as a totality,
and by the emphatic stressing of the "resurrection of the body"
has erected a dam against its own Platonism and asceticism. Still
further, hardly any idea remained so confused within the Christian

---

[1] For an important and fundamental discussion of the primitive basis of the
Israelitish idea of the soul *cf.* J. Pedersen, *Israel*, I, II, 1920, 68 *ff*. "The body is the soul
in outward form", 125.

[2] *cf.* R. Bultmann, *Jesus*, 51.   [3] "The Lord is that Spirit"; 2 *Cor*. iii. 17.

[4] 1 *Cor*. xv. 45.   [5] W. Stählin, *Vom Sinn des Leibes*, 1930.

church as did that of the soul;[1] and its members were unanimous only in rejecting the principle of *pre-existence* maintained by Plato and Origen. But whether soul and body originate together at conception (*Traducianism*), or whether God implants the soul in the embryo on each occasion by a new creation (*Creationism*), Augustine was unable to decide, and the church remained hesitant;[2] for in Traducianism it was probably desired not to forfeit the unity of body and soul, and in Creationism the special creation, the immediate derivation from God. Certainly in the second instance, however, the unchristian dualism has had to be accepted in addition.

2. It is indisputable, then, that the Israelite-Christian conception of the soul is much closer to the primitive structure of soul-stuff than to the Platonic. Man is not a soul in a body, but a body-soul; he *has* no body, but *is* a body;[3] and his soul is not an ultimate power, but is he in himself, either powerful or impotent. This soul structure, again, has certainly not been entirely lacking in its philosophic and psychological expansion, even though the latter occupies an unimportant place in the scheme of popular belief. And like Plato as regards Dualism, so Aristotle discovered the philosophical and psychological schema for the concept of totality. The soul is an *entelechy*—that is, completeness with the subsidiary significance of activity or energy; it is the form that realizes itself in the functions of the organized body.[4] This presupposes an organic unity between body and soul: the soul is no longer a foreign element within the body, but an inner form. To-day also this Aristotelian conception, which regards Dualism as untenable and unchristian, repeatedly asserts itself. The soul is the "concealed unity of the body", and the body "the total expression of the psychical".[5] To a marked degree, indeed, in this retrogression Christian theology allowed itself to be led by its own most pronounced opponents, Nietzsche and his present-day adherents, Ludwig Klages and his school.[6] For the spirit, that "invention of the Greeks", is there proscribed as being a power hostile to life, the "unsouling of the body" is controverted and life's centre transferred to the "instincts". And that

---

[1] Schmalenbach, *op. cit.* 312. The so-called Christian Materialism in England forms an exception, since it denies immortality and believes in both the death and the resuscitation of the *whole* man; Denis Samat, *Milton et le matérialisme chrétien en Angleterre*, 1928.

[2] Harnack, *History of Dogma*, III, 259.   [3] Stählin, *ibid*.

[4] Aristotle, *De Anima*, 2, 1.   [5] E. Brunner, *Gott und Mensch*, 1930, 75.

[6] H. Prinzhorn, *Leib-Seele-Einheit*, 1927.

this reorientation is no theoretical fiction of the philosopher and the psychologist is attested by the cult of the body as this prominently appears to-day in the swimming-bath, on the sports field and in the dance.

Until quite recent times, still further, the dispute between the Platonic-Christian and the Jewish-Christian concepts of the soul has prevented any logical development of psychology. For the assertion of the soul's divinity and immortality, and the manifold difficulties of psycho-physical parallelism, have long hindered science from seeking therein for man as a totality, and have led the psychologist astray into assigning it the status of mere consciousness; only to-day is science gradually discovering the way back to the soul—and therewith to its bounds!

But in the rejection of Dualism Christianity has a still weightier interest than the scientific and psychological;[1] for it recognizes an antithesis far surpassing in depth that between flesh and spirit; with all primitive thought, with Nietzsche and Klages indeed, it replaces this in the first instance by the contrast between Power and impotence. But then, when the Christian says "there is no health in us", he knows at the same time that he has not merely told himself this, but has said it to Someone else, and that it has thus become a confession. Then Will[2] takes the place of Power, both within him and apart from him: an unholy, sinful will opposes itself to a holy Will. And at that moment when this confession becomes prayer: "O God, have mercy!", then man, who sought the utmost depth in the soul, has found it in God.

[1] *cf.* Wach, *Typen rel. Anthropol.,* 23.   [2] Chap. 9.

A. Gehlen, *Der Mensch, seine Natur und seine Stellung in der Welt,* 1940.
Romano Guardini, *Welt und Person,* 1940.
G. van der Leeuw, *Der Mensch und die Religion,* 1940.
H. Pringhorn, *Leib-Seele-Einheit,* 1927.
W. Sombart, *Vom Menschen,* 1938.

CHAPTER 46

THE COUNTRY OF THE SOUL

1. THE superiority sought by man in the soul is not only of another type than the ordinary life of every day, but also, as we have already observed, is localized elsewhere. For it is precisely a life "beyond"; and the most ancient Egyptian *Texts*, in fact, speak of "that land" whither the dead go and where "to eternity they neither hunger nor thirst".[1]

To begin with, then, the country of the soul exists in the world: it is wholly an earthly Paradise. Somewhere or other there is a sinister region, an infamous heath, a dark forest, a mysterious cavern: there is a *descensus Averni*, an entrance to the underworld, a *Plutonion*. Alternatively, the entire domain is regarded as "beyond", *chthonic*, as the Greeks expressed this; in Greece and Southern Italy they could point to many of these "birdless lakes".[2] The whole area around Cumae, for example, was such a realm of the dead, a country of the soul.

Thus to the consciousness of man in primitive times and in antiquity there was nothing absurd in the idea that such a "beyond" was solitary and untrodden, and yet at the same time quite close to human dwellings, and indeed within reach in case of need. This is wholly in accordance with the "catathymia", or subjectively oriented attitude, of primitive mentality, which experiences values in its environment that can transform this either into the infernal regions or into Paradise.[3] Whatever lies outside the tilled land of the village, the enclosed home possessions, is "uncanny", the abode of demons, the sojourn of the dead. To Northern peoples moors, bogs and mountains, and to the inhabitants of the South steppes and deserts, pre-eminently appeared as such localities: the dwelling-place is *Midgard*, around this is *Utgard*, and there begins the realm of the dead. Its frontier may be removed very far away, even below the horizon; nonetheless it can be reached; the hero of the fairy tale goes into the other world as a matter of course. Further, this is regarded not merely spatially, but temporally also: as

[1] *Pyramidentexte* (Sethe), 382; *cf.* further the Antef stela, *Urkunden*, IV, 965; the "fear of the other country".
[2] ἄορνοι λίμναι; Rohde, *op. cit.*, I, 213; Ninck, *Wasser*, 76 *ff.*
[3] "Catathymia" is Kretschmer's term describing the mental state in which everything is perceived in accord with one's own subjective mood.

soon as night spreads its dark shadows, the world belongs completely
to the "beyond" where everything is uncanny.[1]

The dreadful feature in "that land", however, is not always its chief
characteristic; it may equally be a beautiful, marvellous country, a
Paradise—that is, a lovely garden. Thus the Paradise of *Genesis* is an
oasis as contrasted with the steppes which Adam had to till after the
Fall.[2] The garden is far removed in space, and also by time as with the
Golden Age; there the gods reside and the blessed dead.[3] It is the
"garden of the gods" of Euripides, "the ancient garden of Phoibos" of
Sophocles,[4] the Elysium whither the heroes are carried away, the
"islands of the blessed": "the Elysian plain and the world's end,
where is Rhadamanthus of the fair hair, where life is easiest for men.
No snow is there, nor yet great storm, nor any rain; but always ocean
sendeth forth the breeze of the shrill West to blow cool on men".[5]
Greece knew several soul-realms of this type, whither one journeyed
"neither by ships nor by land", and where neither disease nor destroying
age ruled, where a sacred people lived released from all misery and
strife.[6] Israel too recognized the realm of the future and of remoteness:

> And there instead of broad streams circling round
>   we have the glorious Eternal as our river,
>   a river never raided by a galley,
>   sailed by no ships of war;
>   the Eternal himself rules us,
>   the Eternal is our captain,
>   the Eternal is our king,
>   he, he alone, defends us.[7]

All the magnificence of the world exists in the soul's country, and
the familiar "fools' Paradise" is the comically sounding echo of a much
sublimer language;[8] all the dubious features of terrestrial existence are
completely absent from the land of the soul. There Pindar finds the

---

[1] Grönbech, *op. cit.*, II, 7 *f.*
[2] *cf.* Edv. Lehmann, *La pensée du Jahviste, SM.* 3, 1927.
[3] Lietzmann, *Weltheiland*, 44; Preuss, *Tod und Unsterblichkeit*, 30.
[4] *cf.* Otto, *Götter Griechenlands*, 81.
[5] *Odyssey*, IV, 564 *ff.* (Butcher); *cf.* P. Capelle, *Elysium und die Inseln der Seligen,*
AR. 26, 1928.
[6] Pindar, *Pyth.*, 10, 38, with reference to the country of the Hyperboreans; *cf.* O.
Schröder, *AR.* 8, 1905, 69. G. van der Leeuw, *Goden en Menschen*, 92 *ff.*
[7] *Isaiah* xxxiii. 21 *ff.*; *cf.* H. Gunkel, *Das Märchen im Alten Testament*, 1921, 47.
[8] H. Thimme, *Das Märchen*, 1909, 91 *f.*

Muses' domain, the virgins' dance, the voice of the flutes, and the
sound of the lyre.[1] Nor does food lack there; the goodness of "that
country" is manifested first of all in its abundant viands. The Egyptians,
for instance, believed in a "field of food", and also a "field of rushes"
into which the departed, who could recite his magical formulas, entered
with joy: "I know Ra's field of rushes: the surrounding wall is of
bronze; the height of its Lower Egyptian barley is four ells, one ell its
ear and three ells the stalk; the height of its spelt is seven ells, two ells
the ear, and five ells its stalk."[2] From time immemorial, still further, the
West has been regarded as the region of the world in which these
splendours are to be found, whether they are localized in heaven or,
as probably was originally the case, on earth. For in the West the sun
sets; and there man built the great cities of the dead, there the "beauteous West", in the guise of a woman with lovely hair, makes its friendly
advance to meet the dead.[3] But frequently all the emphasis falls on the
decline that the sun, and also man, experience in the West. In that
case the East of the world receives precedence: in the Eastern heaven
stands the tree of the gods, "that high sycamore on which the gods sit,
the tree of life on which they live";[4] its fruits nourish the dead. In the
case of Egypt, indeed, it is often difficult to decide definitely whether
the land of the soul is earthly or heavenly; it is the destiny of the
blessed king to travel to and fro in heaven with the same ease as on
earth.[5] But this at least is certain: the country of the dead lies always
in the beyond, even when it is on earth: however near it may be, it is
nevertheless always far away. The Egyptian king flies away from man:
"He flies, he flies away from you men like the geese; he frees his hands
from you like a falcon, he tears his body away from you like a hawk."[6]
Hence the land of the dead is sought on some distant island or lofty
mountain, behind the Northern mists, in heaven or the depths of the
earth, and everywhere else where man feels he is not at home, and
where on that account an eternal home might be supposed to be.[7]
That in this way different localities often arose simultaneously troubled
neither primitive mentality nor the thought of antiquity, as has already
been observed in the case of Egypt; and the inhabitants of Eddystone

[1] *Pyth.* 10, 38.
[2] *The Book of the Dead*, Chap. 109, in Bertholet, *Lesebuch*, 10 [Kees], 52.
[3] *Pyramidentexte* (Sethe), 276 *ff*.   [4] *ibid.*, 916.
[5] *ibid.*, 186, 363, 1249.   [6] *ibid.*, 1484.
[7] Thus Pylos, on the Western sea-coast, was regarded by the most ancient inhabitants of the Peloponnesus as the sojourn of the dead: "in Pylos amid the dead", *Iliad*,
5, 397; *cf.* U. von Wilamowitz-Möllendorf, *Der Glaube der Hellenen*, I, 1931, 337 *f*.

Island (Solomon Islands) also seek the beyond in a distant country, but at the same time in a cave on their own island.[1]

2. Much the most preferable place, however, for this near-and-far, sought by the soul, is the underworld, or rather in the earth: there is the home of the mother and of all life.[2] Of course burial customs, wherever these prevailed, contributed to this subterranean idea of the beyond: the dead man is in the grave, that is beneath the earth. But so long as the grave remains a mere grave, as at a certain phase of the Egyptian viewpoint for which the dead man's whole life is spent in the grave, and his bliss consists just in being able to "go forth by day", the concept of the underworld is not yet really present. The "beyond", therefore, in the case of Egypt, was much rather the life of "day" which was bestowed on the dead than their subterranean sojourn;[3] and of a beyond in the earth we can speak only when the near-and-far is stressed in one way or another, whether *in malam* or *in bonam partem*. Such ideas of the underworld are to be found, as is well known, in Greece, the Old Testament and often elsewhere.[4]

Besides the concepts of the earth and the grave, the observation of the heavens by night has contributed to the view that was taken of the underworld, and thus in ancient Egypt the *Duat* or *Da-t* was simultaneously the heavens by night, and the underworld;[5] the latter was a kind of counter-heaven, the contrasted image of the dark earth,[6] while from the nightly heavens the sun rises like vegetation from the earth.[7] In this way there arose in Egypt the remarkable idea of the sun nightly traversing the underworld (or the night heaven), and of the dead greeting it on its entrance into the realm of the shades. The hue of the underworld, however, was generally gloomy: it was indeed the realm of shadow, as well as of shades, into which the soul descended. None the less the conviction never completely disappeared that this gloomy underworld was at the same time the mother's fruitful womb.

---

[1] W. H. R. Rivers, "The Primitive Conception of Death", *Hibbert Journal*, X, 1912, 393 *ff.*; *cf.* some remarkable examples in Wilken, *op. cit.*, III, 49 *ff.*
[2] Chap. 10.   [3] [*cf.* Maspero, *Popular Stories of Ancient Egypt*, lxi.]
[4] C. Clemen, *Das Leben nach dem Tode im Glauben der Menschheit* (1920), 42 *ff.*
[5] W. B. Kristensen, *Livet efter döden*, 1896, 57 *ff.* J. Lieblein, *Gammel-aegyptisk Religion*, III, 1885, 29.
[6] *Pyramidentexte* (Sethe), 820, 1275. In Egypt heaven, as the land of the soul, was more and more displaced by the West and the underworld; *cf.* H. Kees, *Totenglaube und Jenseitsvorstellungen der alten Ägypter*, 1926, 80, 220 *f.*
[7] Preuss, *Geistige Kultur*, 42 *f.* K. Th. Preuss, *Die Nayarit-Expedition*, I, 1912, XXV *ff.*

3. The Egyptian king who flies away from men "is no longer on earth, he attains heaven".[1] Indeed, as we have just seen, the heavens were not separated from the underworld, which originally was no other than the night heaven; but in course of time, in Egypt and elsewhere, heaven became increasingly the exclusive abode of the gods, as of the dead;[2] and this, in fact, precisely in the sense of that psychological dualism[3] which assigns the body to the earth, but the soul to the ether.

Thus almost from the beginning the heavens were "Heaven", that is the fullness of pleasure and well-being. Certainly, in the case of many peoples there still remained celestial dangers; but the good preponderated, and heaven was never the sombre desert such as the underworld was frequently depicted to be. For there is the home of the sun, although it is true too that the abundant fertility, enjoyed by the earth, is never to be found. However dismal its habitations may be, still the earth is always the bestower of new life, while the heavens are unfruitful, a brilliant culmination, but not a rebirth.

4. Exactly in the same way therefore as, in the dualistic structure, the soul becomes ever emptier and more contentless until finally its purity is equivalent to sheer nullity, so the soul's country can become divested of every visible and palpable concreteness. For from the beginning it was remote and pathless; and in being completely spiritualized it became the place that had no position whatever, the immeasurable and unlocalizable point. To this, indeed, the Platonic vision was an approximation—the relation to the "beyond" consists in man remembering not what he has experienced but what he has actually seen. "They might have seen beauty shining in brightness, when, with the happy band following in the train of Zeus, as we philosophers, or of other gods as others did, they saw a vision and were initiated into mysteries which may be truly called most blessed, and which we celebrated in our state of innocence; having no experience of evils as yet to come; admitted to the sight of apparitions innocent and simple and calm and happy, shining in pure light, pure ourselves and not yet enshrined in that living tomb which we carry about, now that we are imprisoned in the body, like an oyster in his shell."[4] And Buddhism goes very much farther in prohibiting for itself every type of "something". *Nirvana*, the "extinction" of every one of life's activities, the

---

[1] *Pyramidentexte*, 890.　　　　　　　　[2] Clemen, *op. cit.*, 55 *ff.*
[3] Chap. 43.　　　　　　　　　　　　　[4] Plato, *Phaedrus*, 250 (Jowett).

cessation of detested rebirth, still shows the outlines of the blessed isles, but dissolved into complete nullity: "where there is no something, no permanence, the island, the unique, is named Nirvana, freed from age and death".[1]

This consistent spiritualizing of the country of the soul, simultaneously with an ever advancing enfeebling of "this side", as also of "this side" in the beyond, is opposed to the other tendency which seeks the soul's true home on "this side" itself. Man then finds his beyond in himself: not in a height dimension far above life, but in a depth dimension within himself.[2] Thus speaks modern Immanentism in many keys: but still more concrete and still less Platonic is Nietzsche, because he appeals not from the beyond to the innermost ground of the soul, but from the beyond directly to "this side": "I conjure you, my brethren, *remain true to the earth*, and believe not those who speak unto you of superearthly hopes! Poisoners are they, whether they know it or not."[3]

[1] Oldenberg, *Lehre der Upanishaden*, 311.
[2] Joh. Wendland, *Die neue Diesseitsreligion*, 1914, 8.
[3] *Thus Spake Zarathustra*, 7. (Foulis' Edition.)

CHAPTER 47

THE DESTINY OF THE SOUL

1. PRIMARILY life is a cycle, uninterrupted by death if only the correct rites are observed:[1] "I live after I am dead, like Ra," the sun-god,[2] if only the requisite celebrations have been executed. As has already been observed, *burial* is the most important of these celebrations; and similarly *mourning*, which in the entire primitive world had a ritual character. Man laments not merely to relieve his grief, but above all because he thereby assists the life of the departed over the critical point; as one Egyptian *Text* says: "I am one of the mourners for Osiris, who make him victorious over his enemies."[3] This victory over death is, of course, very differently described in accordance with the predominating idea of the soul. The simplest concept is that of resurrection in its literal sense, so that to the Egyptian dead it was said: "Arise: thou hast shaken off the earth from thy flesh."[4]

More complicated, however, is the idea according to which a *passport* is given to the dead man, guaranteeing his entry into the beyond; and the incantations placed in the grave with the departed, the most remarkable collection of which constitutes the so-called Egyptian *Book of the Dead*, served this purpose. They were *Guides* for the dead man, like the little golden tablets of the Orphics,[5] but not in any rationalistic sense; they were not only a kind of celestial *Baedeker* (although of course they were that as well!), but above all a key to the gate of the beyond; in Iran sacred formulas were whispered into the dying person's ear, while at the same time some of the holy beverage of the gods (*haoma*) was poured into his mouth. The passport to heaven and the *viaticum* are associated: Lehmann gives the text of a Chinese Buddhist passport to heaven which in official language prepares the way for a dead person: "Instructions for the woman Shan: as soon as thou receivest this passport, thou must prepare to set out for the place of the blessed, where thou mayest expect great bliss and peace."[6]

In still another way the *sacrificial cult* guarantees the destiny of the

---

[1] Here, and also on what follows, *cf.* Chap. 22.
[2] *Totenbuch* (Naville), *Kap.* 38, Note 8.
[3] *ibid.*, *Kap.* 1, 11 *f.*
[4] *Pyramidentexte* (Sethe), 654; *cf.* 1067 *f.*
[5] Olivieri, *Lamellae aureae*. Kern, *Orph. Fragm.*
[6] *Textbuch*[1], 23 *f.*

dead, although this term is perhaps somewhat magniloquent. For this cult it was sufficient that the life of the departed should be nourished by his relatives or their representatives, either in the grave or wherever he appeared; and in ancient Egypt it was "the son, who loves him", who sustained his father's life by sacrifices to the dead. Afterwards, however, when this sacred filial duty was left more and more to the professional priesthood, the expression became the settled name for the priest of the dead: "thine heir is on thy throne; he cultivates the grain crop for thee", they exclaimed to the dead king to pacify him.[1]

To the same category pertain masses for the dead and *oratio pro defunctis*. Here no longer the mere existence, but the salvation of the dead person (although it is difficult to separate these two ideas completely!), is assured by sacrifice and prayer; and this custom is "transposed"[2] to quite different connections when prayer for the dead expresses the persisting union of the members of the congregation before God, and the desire only to appear when together. Then the idea may even arise that the dead never release the living and that their own bliss is perturbed by the absence of those yet alive, so that they intercede for them:

> "I wish that he were come to me,
>   For he will come", she said.
> "Have I not pray'd in solemn Heaven?
>   On earth, has he not pray'd?"[3]

2. The nature of this life, thus gained, is very varied. Among primitive peoples eternity is usually not attached to it; the idea is altogether too abstract, and hence only very long life is spoken of,[4] which may be simply a continuation of earthly existence in so far as the departed experience just the same needs, pursue the same aims and are exposed to similar perils as are the living (and also, together with these, the possibility of again dying—the "second death"). But very often, when compared with terrestrial life, it represents an advance either for good or conversely; and an almost endless series of examples can be cited. Instead of this, however, I shall select a few that are characteristic: the African Yoruba, in the first place, have no high estimation of the beyond: "a place in this world is better than in that of the spirits."[5] And similarly Achilles: "Nay, speak not com-

---

[1] *Pyramidentexte*, 1388.   [2] [On "transposition" *cf.* pp. 31, Note, and 610.]
[3] Rossetti, *The Blessed Damozel*.   [4] Preuss, *Tod und Unsterblichkeit*, 24.
[5] Alviella, *Idée de Dieu*, 205.

fortably to me of death, O great Odysseus. Rather would I live on
ground as the hireling of another, with a landless man who had no
great livelihood, than bear sway among all the dead that be departed."[1]
The life beyond is a shadow existence, not a complete life, as in the
case, too, of the Israelite *Sheol*; even praising God, the highest activity
of the living, was denied to the dead in the underworld.[2]

An advance to the good, however, is implied by the lot of the dead
in the many ideas of the Paradise type, and as a simple example I select
the Egyptian concept of the tree in the West to which the dead person
attains, and under which he seats himself in the form of the *ba* bird
(but frequently also as a "complete" man). A goddess, originally
probably only the power of the tree, the goddess of the oasis, then
Nut the goddess of heaven (for here the earthly and the celestial
Paradise are already confused) bends down towards him from the tree,
hands him food and pours water for him from a pitcher;[3] and thus the
dead man receives divine life—"food of eternal life".

3. The soul's destiny, then, when differentiated in this way, depends
on various circumstances. Since continued existence in itself, and also
the enhancement of life's capacities, are both alike potencies, they are
at first conditioned by the power possessed by the living person himself. Among primitive peoples, therefore, the souls of the dead often
receive powerful life only when they have already had this during their
lifetime;[4] whoever possesses much *mana* enjoys a better fate after
death too,[5] and thus warriors, hunters and child-bearers, who were
manifesting their potency at the moment of death, are more fortunate
than other dead people.[6] The Tongans of Polynesia, again, assume
immortality only for their nobles,[7] and the Greeks also allotted a particularly happy destiny to those who were already in possession of some
extraordinary family *mana*: "But thou, Menelaus, son of Zeus, art not
ordained to die and meet thy fate in Argos, the pasture-land of horses,
but the deathless gods will convey thee to the Elysian plain and the
world's end"—whereupon there follows the description of Elysium—
"for thou hast Helen to wife, and thereby they deem thee to be son of
Zeus."[8]

[1] *Odyssey*, XI, 488 *ff.* (Butcher).   [2] *Ps.* vi. 6; cxv. 7; *Isaiah* xxxviii. 18.
[3] *Totenbuch* (Naville), *Kap.* 59–63.   [4] Preuss, *Glauben und Mystik*, 30.
[5] Tiele-Söderblom, *op. cit.* GENERAL LITERATURE, p. 19 *ante.*
[6] Söderblom, *Gottesglaube*, 57 *ff.*; Grönbech, *op. cit.*, II, 166.
[7] Frazer, *The Belief in Immortality*, II, 146.
[8] *Odyssey*, IV, 561 *ff.*; *cf.* Capelle, *AR.* XXV, 1927, 258 *ff.*

To a great extent, too, the type of death decides the *post mortem* power; and in Egypt it was believed that death from drowning or by snake bite made man divine, or a kind of hero.[1] To the manner of dying, however, man can make his own contribution, and Egyptian burial was a magnificent attempt to make the dead person, in his type of death, and consequently of his resurrection, equal to the god Osiris; for whoever had died like Osiris (originally, had been drowned!), been dismembered and buried, shared also in the "justification", in the blessed destiny of the god, while another "celebration" assimilated the lot of the departed to that of the sun-god. Among other peoples different ideas predominated, but the rites after death almost always mean an endowing of the dead person with power; thus burning the corpse implies hastening the severance of soul from body—recalling the dualistic structure!—bringing about the ultimate death and therewith rendering possible a new life.[2] Interment, again, signifies a renewed entrance into the mother-womb of the earth, upon which a rebirth can follow.[3]

4. The gradation of powerfulness after death then proceeds according to the standard of good or evil conduct during life: sin[4] decreases the power of the dead, while righteous behaviour strengthens it; and the earliest appearance of immortality, morally and religiously conditioned in this manner, is to be found in Egypt. In the celebrated Chapter 125 of *The Book of the Dead* the departed enters the hall of the two truths. There Osiris is enthroned, with forty-two assessors, as the judge of the dead. The departed commences with the assurance that he knows full well the names of the god and the assessors; thus he casts a spell on them. Then he continues: "Behold, I come unto thee and bring thee the truth, and have avoided sin against thee: I have not sinned against man, I have made no man miserable, I have not slaughtered the god's cattle. . . . I have committed no murder. . . . I have not shortened the ell measure. . . . I have not stolen milk from the mouth of little children. . . ." *etc.*; a "negative confession of sins", as the whole utterance has been aptly called. But now there again follows a second assurance of powerfulness in the purely magical sense: "I am pure", thrice repeated, and the renewed avowal that the person before the

[1] The drowned were called *hsiw*—"the exalted"; Osiris is the type. F. Ll. Griffith, *Zeitschr. f. ägypt. Sprache,* 46, 1909, 132 *ff.* W. A. Murray, *ibid.,* 51, 1914, 127 *ff,* G. van der Leeuw, *Godsvoorstellingen,* 67.

[2] Rohde, *op. cit.,* I, 27 *ff.* English Translation, 21.

[3] Chap. 10; *cf.* further Otto, *Götter Griechenlands,* 33.   [4] Chap. 66, 78.

court knows the accurate names of the assessors—and they are terrifying demons! Again a negative confession follows: "I have not stolen the god's property, I have not lied . . ." *etc.*, whereon the adjuration once more occurs with the aid of the names.[1] After this speech of the deceased comes the actual judgment of the dead. This we learn not from the *Texts*, but even better from the drawings accompanying them: a monster, a sort of Cerberus, sits before the throne of Osiris, in front a crocodile, behind, a rhinoceros and in the middle a lion: this will devour the departed if the gods' assembly condemns him. In the centre of the Hall of Truth there is a balance on which the dead man's heart is weighed against the symbol of truth; the god Anubis is "master of the scales", and Thoth the clerk of the court, while the judges are at the same time the executioners, holding knives in their hands.[2] The dead person who has been acquitted is "justified", that is, originally, his "voice has prevailed": he has recited the incantations in the correct manner; but the expression (*makhrw*) also means victorious, and ultimately blessed. The departed receives the "crown of justification" from the god's hand.[3]

It is scarcely necessary to discuss the many and extremely various ideas depicting the bliss or the damnation of the deceased. They are known universally. The dead are admitted to heaven and hell in accord with their powerfulness which on its part, again, may be either magical-religious or morally-religious, or both combined; and the very widespread *motif* of the *Two Ways* open to man after death clearly expresses this view of the soul's destiny. Heaven and hell, again, have been depicted by the most varied peoples with the utmost detail, and a very fine description of simple Christian belief in heaven and hell is given by the fifteenth-century poet François Villon, when he introduces his old mother as saying:

> *Femme je suis, pauvrette et ancienne,*
> *Qui rien ne sais; oncques lettre ne lus;*
> *Au moûtier vois, dont suis paroissienne,*
> *Paradis peint, où sont harpes et lus,*
> *Et un enfer, où damnés sont boullus:*
> *L'un me fait peur, l'aultre, joie et liesse.*[4]

---

[1] For the most important Sections of the *Text cf.* Lehmann-Haas, *Textbuch*, 272 *ff.*
[2] Haas, *Bilderatlas, Ägypt. Religion*, Fig. 138.   [3] Haas, *ibid.*, Fig. 140.
[4] *Ballade que Villon fit à la requête de sa mère pour prier Notre-Dame*: "I am a poor old woman, too ignorant to read a single letter. In the parish church I see Paradise painted, with its harps and lutes, and Hell, where the damned are being boiled. The one terrifies me, but the other gladdens and rejoices me."

If the ultimate endowment with power was thus sought in heaven, the idea of hell was also something more than merely voluptuous indulgence in the consciousness of one's own impotence. On the contrary man always retained the feeling, even when infernal punishment was regarded as eternal, that he could attain to power again through hell itself or, at all events, escape from his own impotence; and a modern mind, whose egotism has become abnormal, confirms this in strikingly profound terms: "I have learnt to know hell, and I surmise something about God. Now I also know what the medieval painters meant by their pictures of the torments of hell. These are no sadistic fancies, but genuine representations of the first stage of the way of salvation. . . ." "For this reason our earth, as the unavowed hell, is a double hell; and if we fall into the genuine, honest hell, then we are already half in heaven."[1]

It would therefore be quite wrong to attempt to derive the whole cycle of ideas about heaven and hell, and their thousand parallels, from the hope of reward or fear of punishment. For in the first place it is no affair whatever of recompense or penalty, but of power; and this power has accumulated during our earthly life: "Blessed are the dead which die in the Lord from henceforth: Yea, saith the Spirit, that they may rest from their labours; and their works do follow them."[2] Thus "works" can enhance or diminish power, deify us or deprive us of divinity.[3] But power is never taken as purely moral and never as purely eudemonistic; it is always primarily religious. And the most vivid descriptions of infernal torments are only the foil against which human longing for deliverance and trust in salvation arise:

> While the wicked are confounded,
> Doom'd to flames of woe unbounded,
> Call me with Thy Saints surrounded.

Here the oppressive power of the *tremenda majestas* and the *fascinans* of unconditioned redemption fuse into one:

> King of Majesty tremendous,
> Who dost free salvation send us,
> Fount of pity, then befriend us!

---

[1] Künkel, *Einführung in die Charakterkunde*, 180 f.
[2] *Rev.* xiv. 13; *cf.* E. Maass, *Orpheus*, 1895, 217 *ff.* C. Clemen, *Religionsgeschichtliche Erklärung des Neuen Testaments²*, 1924, 152, 317.
[3] Steinmann, *Der religiöse Unsterblichkeitsglaube*, 50.

5. An Indian soothsayer possesses the "death's head formula". He drums on a skull and then communicates the dead man's place of rebirth. He also approaches Gotama Buddha, who lays the skulls of three beings before him; and the soothsayer asserts correctly that they have been reborn respectively in hell, in man's world, and in heaven. But when the Buddha shows him the skull of a man who has passed into extinction (*Nirvana*) the seer can find no answer at all; "he saw neither limit nor end", and with perspiring brow and shamed expression he had to confess that his knowledge failed.[1] For here human yearning is directed to neither the cyclic continuation of life, nor its advance to either good or evil, but against life itself. Power is striven for in complete impotence, in extinction: the life cycle must be reversed, the wheel of births stayed. Thus no curiosity as to the soul's destiny ever agitates Buddhism; it finds its bliss in release from every lot: "From the negation of Being and Non-Being . . . the presage of Nirvana meets the gaze of the pious man, who strove not to solve its riddle but to lose himself within it. The way in which thought silently turned away from this enigma may seem feeble and faint-hearted to the Faustian yearning to know 'the force that binds creation's inmost energies'. But how completely had Buddhism rejected such a longing! An intrinsic greatness, and indeed a unique poetry, subsist within, as man stands here before the veiled image of the Beyond, free from the desire to unveil the glory unseen by any eye, while in the depths of his own being, silently and blissfully, he experiences this glory itself."[2] In a Buddhist fairy tale, again, a king sees two mango trees, one standing tranquil but barren while the other, which had been richly laden with fruit, is completely plundered and its branches broken into small fragments. Then the king realizes that "life in the home"[3] is similar to that of the fruitful tree, rich but quickly poor, and he resolves henceforth to be like the sterile tree: "for me," he confesses, "the miserable hut of the maternal womb has been destroyed; torn asunder is the bond of rebirth in the three forms of being; the dunghill of the cycle of births has been cleaned; the sea of tears has been dried, the wall of bones thrown down. For me there is no longer rebirth."[4] Here life's power has turned against itself.

[1] W. Caland, *Boeddhistische Verhalen*, 1923, 33 *f.*
[2] Oldenberg, *Lehre der Upanishaden*, 332.
[3] Chap. 34.
[4] E. and H. Lüders, *Buddhistische Märchen*, 1921, No. 36; *cf.* the similar, but less passionate ideas in Orphism in Rohde, *Psyche*; van der Leeuw, *Goden en Menschen*.

6. Human thought which, in doubt or sullenness, thus withdraws from the enhancing of power as from self-destruction, often finds consolation in the return to the maternal womb of the life of the Universe. In this respect primeval and modern viewpoints encounter each other: I quote both an Egyptian *Pyramid Text* and a poem of to-day. The conflict between the two gods, Horus and Set, is adjusted by the god *Atmu* (here his name means "all the gods"), and their wounds are healed. The dead man implores the god to have pity on him also, as he has shown mercy to the two combatants, and receives the answer: "there is no divine seed that I could allow to fall into ruin; thou also shalt not be destroyed".[1] Nothing will come to destruction: everything is securely preserved by the god of the Universe. Here death and life both lose their true meaning: in their eternal change, whose perpetuation was originally also the aim of Egyptian belief in immortality, they are now only two transitional points which the all dominating divine life traverses in its measured rhythm. Similarly Heracleitus, for whom too death signified only a turning-point, so that death and life meet in the eternal flux: "it is death to souls to become water, and death to water to become earth; but from earth comes water, and from water soul";[2] "mortals are immortals, and immortals are mortals, the one living the other's death and dying the other's life".[3]

But even after two or three thousand years this attitude to life has remained precisely the same: all that lives, lives eternally in God; there is no death, just as there is no life; there is but life or death, whichever one will: the term is a matter of indifference. All this means that there is only Power, whatever form the destiny of soul and body may take; and the most impressive presentation of this belief I have always found in the poet's magnificent *Song of the Sower*:

> Make your stride rhythmic! Likewise your swing!
> Yet awhile will Earth stay young.
> There falls a grain of corn. It dies. It rests.
> Sweet is its rest, and good.

[1] *Pyramidentexte* (Sethe), 140 *ff.*; *cf.* van der Leeuw, *Godsvoorstellingen*, 53 *ff.*; *cf.* also the very fine and appropriate version of the Egyptian belief in immortality given in his own day by P. Pierret, although this has received slight notice from Egyptologists: "There is no death in the world, but merely transformations; bodies are incessantly metamorphosed owing to molecular interchanges, but without the loss of a single atom, and with no annihilation ever occurring"; *Le Dogme de la Résurrection chez les anciens Égyptiens*, 17. By replacing here the modernizing expressions "atom" and "molecule" by the "seed" of our *Text*, which was unknown to Pierret, we should obtain the genuine Egyptian standpoint.   [2] Diels, *Fr.* 36 (Cornford).
[3] Diels, *Fr.* 62 (Burnet); *cf.* Rohde, *op. cit.*, II, 149, 253. E. T. 368 *f.*

> Here thrusts another upward through the soil.
> Again good: for sweet is the light.
> And nought is lost from the World,
> While to all there comes what pleases God.[1]

In strange and yet scarcely surprising manner the firm foundation of this primal, and yet eternally young, faith in the securely fixed and enduring earth is expressed here also.

7. Continuation, enhancing, denial and also pacification of Powerfulness: all this is repudiated by that weary scepticism which, at all times and in all quarters, in the country of the soul imagines the land that knows no return and places its destiny on just the same footing as that of the leaves on the trees. Rather than cite many examples of this, a few expressions of Egyptian lassitude of power will amply suffice which, in that land of passionate faith in resurrection, speak all the more eloquently. In *The Songs of the Harpist*, then, some ancient Egyptian table songs have been transmitted to us which struck that characteristic, half melancholy and half frivolous, note in the midst of the joyousness of the funeral banquet, which we discern also in *Ecclesiastes* and *Omar Khayyám*. Everything that, according to Egyptian faith, was invigorating in the struggle against death, is here derided as powerless, while on the other hand fleeting life is praised. Correct burial, knowledge of the formulas, the "beloved son's" sacrifices for the dead: it all avails nothing:

> How well have things gone for that good prince (the dead man).
> It is most providential
> That these disappear
> And depart, while others remain.
> Thus was it since the time of our forefathers,
> And of the gods, that were of old:
> In their pyramids they rest,
> The nobles and the great together,
> Buried in their pyramids;
> And they have built for themselves funerary temples.
> But their places no longer exist.
> What has become of them?
> I knew the sayings of Imhotep and Hordedef (famous sages),
> Wise ones and celebrated.
> Observe their places:

[1] Conrad Ferdinand Meyer, *Gedichte*, 1922, 78.

The walls are destroyed,
Their places exist no longer.
It is as though they had never been.
None returns thence,
To tell us how they fare,
Or to report their fate to us,
So as to calm our hearts . . .
Until we also go
Thither where they have gone.

Then the mood apparently changes, though like a heavy death-knell, like a *basso ostinato*, despair repeatedly rings through all the joyfulness:

Let thy heart take courage and forget!
Be of good cheer and take thy pleasure,
So long as thou livest.
Sprinkle myrrh on thy head,
Garb thyself in fine linen
Steeped in costly perfumes,
In the pure frankincense of the gods!
Increase thy pleasure!
Let not thy heart grow weary!
Follow thy wishes and thy desires;
Direct thy earthly fate
According to the dictates of thine own heart . . .
Until the day of lamentation comes to thee—
But he whose heart is stilled (the dead man) will not hear it,
And he who lies in the grave will not feel the affliction.
Celebrate the joyful day!
Sleep it not away!
For lo! none can take with him his possessions.
Lo! none returns who has gone·hence.[1]

Or in one variant:

Celebrate the joyful day!
Enjoy the scent of the finest frankincense,
Wreathe lotus flowers about thy shoulders and thy neck,
And about those of the beloved who resides in thy heart,
And who sits by thy side.
Let music and song resound!
Cast the evil things behind thee.
Think only of joy,

[1] Another translation in Ad. Erman, *The Literature of the Ancient Egyptians*, 133.

Until the day of death arrives
When man goes to that land which loveth silence;
Then shall thy heart be at rest.
For life is not prolonged,
Neither for him who possessed granaries,
And bread for sacrifices and gifts,
Nor for him who had nought:
It is not prolonged, not for one single hour.

Or again:

Those who built in red granite,
Who built for themselves a burial chamber,
Who desired to be noble by erecting splendid buildings,
Who are pictured as gods:
Their sacrificial tables are empty,
As are those of the weary to death, who died by the river bank,
Without leaving behind them even one person to honour them . . .[1]

A weary mood, weary to death, prevails, which expressed itself in ancient Egypt in the fine *Dialogue of him who is weary of life with his soul*:[2] death he greets as a friend. In Israel, again, it was the writers of *Ecclesiastes* and *Job* who experienced this weariness. The cycle of natural life, that basic ground of all primitive hope, avails nothing here:

There is hope for a tree that is felled;
  it may flourish again,
  the shoots of it need not fail;
though its root decays in the soil,
  though its stump is dead in the ground,
it may bud at the scent of water,
  and put out boughs like a plant.
But man dies and departs,
  man breathes his last—and where is he?
Like the water of a vanished lake,
  like a dry, drained river,
man lies down, never to arise,
  never to waken, though the skies wear out,
  never to stir out of his slumber.[3]

The domain of darkness and of deepest gloom permits of no return.[4] Compared with this despair, Greek and Roman scepticism appears

---

[1] cf. the parallel, *Job* iii. 11 ff.   [2] cf. Erman, *ibid.*, 86 ff.
: *Job* xiv. 7 ff. (Moffat).   [4] *Job* x. 20 ff.

colder and less tragic; "for though altogether to disown a divine nature in human virtue were impious and base, so again to mix heaven with earth is ridiculous."[1] And the sober spirit of Rome found in the course of the stars, which granted hope to the Egyptian, the most forcible refutation of any expectation of the beyond: "it is a double evil and a twofold madness to denounce destruction to the heaven and the stars, which we leave just as we find them, and to promise eternity to ourselves, who are dead and extinct—who, as we are born, so also perish."[2]

But deep and heavy as the death-knell, there rings out in religion again and again the tragic lament: could we only escape from the struggle for power! could we only have peace before the Power of God as before our own! Only peace!

> Why didst thou ever take me from the womb?
> Why could I not have died there in the dark?
> Then I would be as though I had not been,
> borne from the womb straight to the tomb.
> My days are few! let me alone awhile,
> that I may have life bright with a brief smile,
> before I leave it to return no more.[3]

8. Finally, there is a human destiny, though not of the soul, for body and soul are equally transient and, what is more, equally under the wrath of God, that is bestowed on man, a deed of God towards him, a new creation. His own life has no powerfulness: no celebration whatever can create nor perpetuate potency; but "Omnipotence" imparts to him the gift of eternal life, which is neither continuation nor increase of earthly life but absolutely new and original; a life that intrinsically implies powerfulness no longer, but is grace alone: a life knowing reward and punishment no more, but only God's love.[4]

Despite many contrary views within Christianity itself, this is in fact the truly Christian apprehension of man's destiny: "the gift of God is eternal life through Jesus Christ."[5] And: "this is life eternal, that they might know thee the only true God, and Jesus Christ, whom thou hast sent."[6] This means that the soul is no immortal goddess, but only a turning towards God: that neither celebrations nor moral actions have any ultimate influence on man's lot, but God alone: that while eternal

---

[1] Plutarch, *Romulus*, XXVIII, 6 (Clough).
[2] The heathen Caecilius, in Minucius Felix, XI, 3.   [3] *Job* x. 18 *ff.* (Moffat).
[4] Steimann, *Der religiöse Unsterblichkeitsglaube*, 78 *ff.*
[5] *Romans* vi. 23.   [6] *John* xvii. 3.

life is indeed bestowed on man, it comes not from himself but solely from God; so that whatever man's destiny may be, it rests ever in the love of God. Thus arose the magnificent idea which Dante expresses— that this very love created even hell:

> Justice the founder of my fabric moved:
> To rear me was the task of Power divine,
> Supremest Wisdom, and primeval Love.[1]

H. SCHOLZ, *Der Unsterblichkeitsgedanke als philosophisches Problem*, 1920.
TH. STEINMANN, *Der religiöse Unsterblichkeitsglaube*[2], 1912.

[1] *Inferno*, III, 4 *ff.* (Cary); *cf.* H. Scholz, *Eros und Caritas*, 1929, 53.

APPENDIX TO THE TORCHBOOK EDITION

(NOTE: This appendix represents in condensed form the new
material found in the revised German edition)

PART I

THE OBJECT OF RELIGION

CHAPTER 1—Power
Section 3: *Mana* is also a substance which lets itself become defined in various ways; *mana* is honour, authority, wealth: a rich man has *mana*; he has *auctoritas*! For further references see, M. Mauss, "Essai sur le Don, Forme Archaique de l'échange" (*Année Sociolog.*, *nouv. série*, I, 1925, 97). *Mana* may also signify the prestige and success of the warrior as well as his weapon. (*cf.* R. Thurnwald, *AR.* 27, 1929, 101 *ff.*) The *dema* of the Marind-Anin (New Guinea) is even more comprehensive. Everything can become *dema* as soon as it stands as extraordinary or, if the thing is seen from a purely external viewpoint, thus taking on a distinctive form because of its individuality. Furthermore, ancestors are also *dema*; they have, that is to say, become concrete *dema*. (For further description of this see L. Lévy-Bruhl, *La Mythologie Primitive*, 1935, 56 *ff.*)

Section 4: The concept of power can also be translated into truth, in a way, however, which has more of a practical, rather than ethical meaning. Thus in this context *mana* among the primitive peoples often means the power of truth, effective truth, over against which the lie corresponds to bad luck. Whoever predicts a good catch of fish has *mana* if the prediction becomes true. If it does not the man has lied. (*cf.* R. Thurnwald, "Die Lüge in der primitiven Kultur", in O. Lippman and P. Plaut, *Die Lüge*, 1927, 402.)

Section 5: For a specific reference indicating a religion where power is not explicitly assigned a name see M. P. Nilsson, *Geschichte der griechischen Religion*, I, 1941, 60.

Section 6: The concept of power is also a "vox media" between a sacred substance and God. This is the meaning of the Hebraic *el* which is power as well as God. It is said that, "*el* is suspended from off my hand", that is to say, from the power of my hand (on the other hand, *elim* are personal deities). *cf.* O. Eisfeldt, "Der Gott Bethel", in *AR.* 28, 1930, 26.

CHAPTER 2—Theorizing About Power
Section 1: For further indications of what has already been cited

under the first footnote see H. Oldenberg, *Die Religion des Veda*, 1917, 478 *ff.*; E. Cassirer, *Philosophy of Symbolic Forms*, Vol. II, 1955.

Section 4: Further examples of power as inherent in man, yet superior, or distinguished from him as impersonal power, can be seen in H. Oldenberg, *Religion des Veda*, 478 *ff.* The idea is also expressed in K. Zeininger, *Die magische Geisteshaltung im Kindesalter*, 1929, 60. In this later work we have reference to a sister warning her younger brother that certain death follows when anyone touches the mouth with certain picked flowers. Her little brother then asks her, "Is death in them?"

CHAPTER 3—Things and Power

Section 2: On the use of the word "fetishism", as coined by de Brosses, see his famous monograph, *Du Culte des Dieux Fétiches*, 1760. He was not the first, however, to use this word, since it appears in a study by Godofridus Carolinus, in 1661. (*cf.* R. F. Merkel, in *Forschung und Fortschritte*, II, 1935, 36, 451). It is certain that de Brosses used the word for the first time as a scientific and phenomenological expression. He used fetishism as a general term for the religion of the Negroes. He was also the first to write on the psychological origin of fetishism.

For an example of the development of fetishism into a higher form, *cf.* M. P. Nilsson, *The Minoan-Mycenean Religion and Its Survival in Greek Religion*, 1950, 407.

Section 3: For the significance of tools as potent, see E. Cassirer, Vol. II; L. Noire, *Das Werkzeug und seine Bedeutung für die Entwicklungsgeschichte der Menscheit*, 1880, also, E. Kapp, *Grundlinien einer Philosophie der Technik*, 1887.

Section 4: Potency as the hoard of a community is also found among the Zuni Indians in the form of a "medicine bundle" which is sacred. Only certain people (priests, *etc.*) can enter the room where it is located. For a description see Ruth Benedict, *Patterns of Culture* (Mentor Books, 1949) 60.

Power as manifested in family *pusaka* is also known in Goa (Southern Island of Celebes). Here it takes the form of a chain which is worn by the individual. The chain is weighed every year, if it weighs less at the end of twelve months it signifies bad luck. Again, only priests and kings have the right to view these *pusaka*. In times of crises they are known to be carried about in a procession. (*cf.* J. Ph. Duyvendak, *Inleiding tot de Ethnologie van de Indische Archipel*, 1935, 132 *ff*., also L. Lévy-Bruhl, *Le Surnaturel et la Nature dans la Mentalité Primitive*, 1931, 5.

CHAPTER 5—Sacred Stones and Trees

Section 2: The presence of power in stones can be seen in villages where one finds a rock pile on the side of the street and upon which stones are thrown by those passing by. This ritual is still observed by the Amanebele in South Africa. (*cf.* Fourie, *Amanebele*, 99). These power-filled stones are able to guarantee the welfare of the community. Similarly, in Indonesia, the "village stones" give health and power. In many cases there is a differentiation made between male (phallic) and female (concave) stones. The accession of the king is also celebrated on these stones and in some cases they are believed to have fallen from heaven. See: A. C. Kruyt, "De West-Toradja's op Midden-Celebes" (in *Verh. K. Ned. Akad. V. Wetensch. Afd. Litt., N. R.* 40) I, 355 *ff*., 401, 427 *ff*., and 443, also J. C. van Eerde, "Investituursteenen in Zuid-Celebes (in *Tijdschr. K. Ned. Aardr. Gen.* 2, R., 47, 1930), 820.

There are also specific instances of power in metals; metals are born, not made, and they are also capable of marriage. Minerals are embryos which have prematurely glanced at the light of the world. Metallurgists and alchemists have the duty to ripen them until in the end they become gold. For further references, *cf.* Mircea Eliade, "Metallurgy" (*Cahiers de Zalmoxis*, I), 1938.

CHAPTER 6—Sacred Water and Fire

Section 1: Water in its essence corresponds to womanhood and the mother. It is the bounty of life and renews the life of all being. The water of chaos, out of which the world springs forth, and the water which surrounds the embryo in the mother are parallels. We can understand therefore the great difference between water and fire; the latter is in the sphere of anthropology, the former is essentially theological. In a communication from W. F. van Lier (1938), the following conversation took place with a Negro from Surinam: "A man cannot live without water." When the native was asked, "But what about fire?", he answered "Oh no, Sir, we cannot compare fire with water. Man can make fire, but water, only God alone can do this. Water is everything that lives, it is essential for man, animals and plants. It is only man who cannot live without fire."

CHAPTER 7—The Sacred World Above

Section 5: Rain is also related to the Sacred World Above; it is the heavenly powers that divide and impart the rain. Rain is a power which makes the earth fruitful. Thus in ancient Greece we find the origin of Zeus in pre-Homeric times as a magician and rainmaker. Dew is nothing but his own sperm with which he fertilizes the earth. For further references see A. B. Cook, *Zeus*, III, 31, 180; also, Nilsson, *Greek Popular Religions*; also R. Dussaud, *Les Découvertes de Ras Shamra et L'Ancien Testament*, 1937. Notice also that in the Old Testament it is claimed that Jaweh is as good as, if not better than, Baal in bringing rain.

CHAPTER 8—The Sacred "Conjoined World" Animals

Section 2: For another illustration of Nagualism in the Osage tribe of the Southern Plains see R. Benedict, *Patterns of Culture*, 36 *ff*. In this example of the "Mussel", individual totemism proceeds toward a social totemism. But the essential unity between the animal (here a mussel) and he who "finds" it is a very clear one.

On the meaning and role of dreams in totemism see L. Lévy-Bruhl, *Expérience Mystique et les Symboles chez les Primitifs*, 1938, 107, 122, *etc.*; also R. Thurnwals, under "Totem", in *Lexikon der Vorgeschichte*, for an Australian comparison.

CHAPTER 10—The Form of the Mother

Section 2: The form of the mother as gruesome and terrible is best seen in the goddess Kali of India. For a description of her ritual and sacrifice see H. Zimmer's article in *Eranos Jahrbuch*, 1938, 180 *ff.*, also S. Cave, *Hinduism or Christianity*, 1939, 152 *ff.*

CHAPTER 13—Power and Will in Man. The King

Section 2: That cosmic events are subject to kingly power can be documented from the Natchez tribe where the chief is called the Great Sun. He has the power of setting the sun on its course, he has the power over the growth of grain, the rain, *etc. cf.* R. R. Marett, *Sacraments of Simple Folk*, 1933, 129. Among the tribesmen of the Ba-Ronga in Africa, the king is called the "prince of the earth". He is the cock who is master of the yard, he is the bull without whom the cows cannot calve. Without him the earth is like a woman who has left her mate in the lurch. *cf.* R. Thurnwal's article under "Mana", in *Lexikon der Vorgeschichte*.

CHAPTER 14—The Mighty Dead

Section 5: All Souls Day is celebrated almost everywhere. For an example of its celebration among the Trobriands see B. Malinowski, *Myth in Primitive Psychology*, 1926, 97. In this example the dead live with the living, they visit once a year.

G. Meiners, in his work *Allgemeine Krit. Geschichte der Religionen*, 1806–1807, Vol. I, 290 *ff.*, had noticed quite accurately that the cult of the dead is a repetition of the funeral rituals. It is a "memoria" for the early Christians, *cf.* H. Lietzmann, *Geschichte der Alten Kirche*, Vol. II, 1936, 133, also J. Quasten, *Musik und Gesang in den Kulten der heidnischen Antike und christlichen Frühzeit*, 1930, 230 *ff.*

CHAPTER 17—Power and Will Given Form in the Name

Section 1: From the study of the names of God, it would be possible, as well as desirable, to write the typology of religions on the answer to the question: "Does God have a name?" The variations are vast; either God does not have a name or one names him with a generic name in plural form, or his name becomes specific because of characteristic actions, or, finally, he has a specific name in an essential way.

The Israelites did not find rest until they had given their God a truly particular name. This means that one could now know this God and that this God could now also reveal himself. On the other hand, the God of Goethe, who is without a name, cannot reveal himself. This had to be the case, since the name is not just a reference or a technique; the name is "the soul" of an essence. We do not need a name to differentiate one essence from another; we need it, however, to give form to the being which is expressed. This is the reason why name giving is man's privilege. Man finds specific names for specific things and thus creates his own world in a familiar way.

Section 3: For an example of special gods, *cf.* L. R. Farnell, "The Place of the Sondergötter in Greek Polytheism," in *Anthrop. Essays Presented to E. B. Tylor*, 1907, 81 *ff.*

CHAPTER 18—The Sacred World in the Background

Section 1: The extensive reading and enormous work of P. Wilhelm Schmidt finds its culmination in the Synthesis where he formulates his inferences (provisionally?) from the material; *cf.* "Endsynthese der Religionen der Urvolker Amerikas, Asiens, Australiens, Afrikas", in his *Der Ursprung der Gottesidee*, Vol. VI, 1935. The above mentioned section, though it is very diffuse, has the merit of presenting to us Schmidt's opinions. These opinions are typical of rationalism and are, unfortunately, far too Roman Catholic. The entire synthesis is concerned with the idea of God (which is, in any case, not theological) and not about God, faith or revelation. What we find is a system which attempts to pull together all religious innovations; thus we find God and his revelation, as well as other effective powers, inserted into history and thereby degraded in that very moment; God is only a very great man and revelation only a spiritual current. This approach, rich in material, can only become the occasion for discontentment for both historical and theological studies.

The thesis throughout his work is quite simple and finds its culmination in the phrase, "God is the origin of the oldest religion" (cf. 491). But one cannot, as Schmidt does, have history beginning before creation. By virtue of the above thesis, that "God is the origin of the oldest religion", he knows the complete chronology of our first relatives and can therefore quite naturally assert that it is only much later that "Naturism", "Mana-ism", in fact all "isms" come to have any share in primitive religions. In any case Naturism is only a "personification of nature" (379). Magic is also placed in a secondary position because, "anyone who was on guard against much of the jumble and disorder of magical thinking, through the light of a higher religion, as well as through the human spirit, illuminated positively, was able to think rationally and causally in a higher degree" (386).

The naïveté of this way of thinking, which is neither theological nor historical, could lead us to the loss of self-composure. P. Schmidt, however, is a scholar, who in the usual manner is thoroughly convinced about the infallibility and reasonableness of his system. Thus he can speak bluntly, for example, about "the oldest common religion", about an "isochronous whole, which as such stands before us from archaic times until now" (447, 469 ff.). A few years ago we could have countered this opinion with a description of primitive culture as composed of numerous cultures from various times and places. "This distinction no longer remains, for the investigations of the present volumes on 'The Origin of the Idea of God' have amply removed it" (471). This is indeed a conclusion which is amazing in its certainty, approximating a fifth gospel!

Sections 2 & 3: For further examples as given in these sections see also the following: N. Soederblom, *Werden des Gottesglaubens*, 176; Tor Andrae, *Mohammed, The Man and His Faith*, Chapter I; R. Otto, *Das Gefühl des Überweltlichen*, 200 ff.; and K. Th. Preuz, in *Zeitschr. f. Missionsk. und rel. Wissensch.*, 47, 1932, 236 ff.

CHAPTER 19—Powers

Section 1: The development of polydemonism and polytheism is certainly not a compulsory one. The *elohim* of Judaic religion are a typical polydemonistic phenomenon. *El*, however, is only a manifestation of power; opposed to this, Baal and Melek are men. Baal is the lord of the earth, Melek is the lord who leads through the wilderness, and *El* is power alone. Out of these specific powers arose a monotheism, not a polytheism; the plural *elohim*, an original polytheistic name, became quite simply a name for Jaweh. *cf*. M. Buber, *Königtum Gottes*, 63, and also A. J. Wensinck, *Semietische Studien*, 1941, 31.

Section 4: Christianity alone can advocate an anthropomorphism which is an essential and theological motif; God has become man. The central point of the incarnation gives us the right to represent God in human form. Thus anthropomorphism is not a last resort in the Christian religion, it is natural and is absolutely essential. For further literature on this see: H. Kraemer, *The Christian Message in a Non-Christian World*, 131; G. van der Leeuw, "L'Anthropomorphisme Comme Forme d'Anthropologie", in *Le Monde Non-Chretien*, N.S., 2, 1947, 170. For the opposite of the above in religious phenomenon *cf*. Fr. Altheim, *Rom. Rel. Gesch.*, II, 187, and M. P. Nilsson, "Mycenaean and Homeric Rel", in *AR*. 33, 1936, 87. *cf*. also Pearl S. Buck, *House of Earth, The Good Earth*, 67, 127 *ff*., for a Chinese example of the divine and human conflict of power in polytheism.

PART II

THE SUBJECT OF RELIGION

CHAPTER 27—The Speaker
Section 2: There is a relationship which we shall call "displacement" between prophetism in the strict sense and shamanism. That is to say, the forms remain practically the same, while the content changes. There is, for example, a conformity between the prophet Jeremiah on the one hand, and the dancing, unruly prophets on the other. There is also, however, an essential difference. The shaman and prophet have a common trait; they are only a mouthpiece. cf. A. C. Kruyt, *De West-Toradja's op Midden-Celebes*, II, 506 ff.; H. S. Nyberg, *Rel. Iran*, 176, 187, 202, 215 and 224, where we see that Zarathustra was in the first place a prophet not a reformer. cf. also F. M. Th. de Laigre Bohl, "Priester und Prophet" (*N. Theol. Stud.* 22, 1940); S. Mowinckel, "Ecstatic Experience and Rational Elaboration in Old Testament Prophecy" (*Acta Orient.*, 13, 1935); H. Th. Obbink, "The Forms of Prophetism" (*Hebrew Union College Annual*, Cincinnati, 14, 1939, 23 ff.).

CHAPTER 29—The Consecrated
Section 2: There is a polarity between ritualistic licentiousness and temperance. In the first instance power is mobilized and, so to speak, squandered. In the second instance power is unified and, as it were, hoarded. From this arises the amazing fact that in religion the sacred prostitutes have almost the same function as the sacred virgins. cf. G. van der Leeuw, "Virginibus Puerisque, A Study on the Service of Children in Worship", in *Deus et Homo*, 1953.

CHAPTER 30—Saints
Section 1: The classical religion of relics is Buddhism. The cult of Buddha is to a great extent a relic cult. One carries a tooth of the Buddha in a procession; worships the impression of his feet, *etc.* The Pagoda is nothing else but a relic shrine. cf. H. Von Glasenapp, *Der Buddhismus*, 47, 132, 139.

CHAPTER 31—Demonic Human Beings
Section 2: For a more archaic example of the relationship of women

to demons see B. Malinowski, *Argonauts of the Western Pacific*, 239 *ff.*
cf. also H. Th. Fischer, *Inleiding tot de Volkenkunde von Ned. Indie*,
1940, 194 *ff.*, for a description where women only can become united
with demons. For an example of Shamans who change their sex, *cf.*
Nyberg, *Rel. des alten Iran*, 255, where men possessed by a demon
become, *ipso facto*, women,

CHAPTER 37—Nation and Humanity
    Section 2: Both nationality and authority construct the selfsame
object: the state, which thus takes on a religious character of its own.
It does not just possess its own gods, it becomes god itself. Carl Schmidt
has shown in a convincing way that the ideology of states is nothing
but secularized theology. (See his *Politische Theologie*, 1934, 51.)
    Christianity has caused the great break between the Kingdom of
God and the state. The early Christians broke up the world and so
vindicated the words of their Lord, "My Kingdom is not of this world."
The archaic communities do not know of this kind of dualism; religion
is collective-social and the political power has a religious and divine
character. For examples of the identification and conflict between
Church and State, see St. Augustine, *City of God*, 14.4; Jose Ortega y
Gasset, *Über das Romische Imperium*, 1943; R. Pettazoni, *Religione e
Politica Religiosa nel Giappone Moderno*, 1934; W. Gundert, *Japanische
Religionsgeschichte*, 1935, 13 *ff.* and 127 *ff.*; H. Kraemer, *The Christian
Message in a Non-Christian World*, 1938, esp 259 *ff.*, 395 *ff.*, 243-45;
and C. Eschweiler, in *Religiöse Besinnung*, 4, 1931, 32, 72 *ff.*

CHAPTER 40—Souls In the Plural
    Section 1: Pater Trilles, in an article in the *XVI Congrès Intern.
d'Anthropologie et d'Archéologie Préhistorique*, 1935, 803 *ff.*, gives the
following account of the plurality of souls in an African tribe. "The soul
is very complicated and comprehensive: 1. 'Eba' is the creative principle,
situated in the head . . . it disappears at death. 2. 'Nlem', the knowing
heart which administrates daily activity and also disappears at death.
3. 'Edzii', the individual name, which after death continues a certain
mode of individuality. 4. 'Ki' and 'Ndem', power and sign (or mark) of
the individual; they remain eternally connected to the 'stuff of the soul'.
5. 'Ngel' or 'Ngwel', the working principle of the individual soul as
long as it lives in the human body. 6. 'Nsissim', the shadow, it is also
the same as the essential soul. 7. 'Khun', the ghost, the spirit or that
which is the 'soul-stuff'."

CHAPTER 45—The Creature

Section 1: N. Berdyaev was certainly correct when he wrote, "One could say that knowledge is founded on the rupture of man from himself because the knowing subject finds itself outside of being and likewise being as external to man." (*cf.* his *The Destiny of Man*, 1955, 1960.) The human being becomes human by the fact of consciousness, that is to say, by the fact that man is capable of standing at a distance from himself; that he knows himself and grasps his own point of selfhood from outside himself. The phenomenon "Man" can only be understood with the help of a dimension which is external to man, be it biological or theological. On this point what has been presented by modern anthropology harmonizes with archaic man. For an illustration of the above point see the conversation between Leenhardt and a New Caledonian native in M. Leenhardt's book, *Gens de la Grande Terre*, 1937, 194 *ff*.

In the awakening consciousness, which makes man human, man finally uncovers the inner life which is neither bodily, or, a life of the soul, nor spiritual life. We must never forget that religion begins of itself with this removal of man from himself. For the archaic cultures this religious externalization has its oldest form of manifestation in clothing and ornamentation. Man attempts to become distant from himself, thus he paints, mutilates and clothes himself.

This externalizing can lead of itself to a dualism of body and soul. It can also, however, lead to the comprehension of the "man-creature", the soul which comes from the hand of God. (*cf.* W. Sombart, *Vom Menschen*, 1938, 27, 61, *etc.*).

INDEX TO VOLUME I

The figures in italics indicate the Chapters; those in ordinary type the Sections.